FANNY TROLLOPE

The Life and Adventures
of a Clever Woman

PAMELA NEVILLE-SINGTON

VIKING

VIKING
Published by the Penguin Group
Penguin Putnam Inc., 375 Hudson Street,
New York, New York 10014, U.S.A.
Penguin Books Ltd, 27 Wrights Lane,
London W8 5TZ, England
Penguin Books Australia Ltd, Ringwood,
Victoria, Australia
Penguin Books Canada Ltd, 10 Alcorn Avenue,
Toronto, Ontario, Canada M4V 3B2
Penguin Books (N.Z.) Ltd, 182-190 Wairau Road,
Auckland 10, New Zealand
Penguin India, 210 Chiranjiv Tower, 43 Nehru Place,
New Delhi, 11009 India

Penguin Books Ltd, Registered Offices:
Harmondsworth, Middlesex, England

First American edition
Published in 1998 by Viking Penguin,
a member of Penguin Putnam Inc.

1 3 5 7 9 10 8 6 4 2

LIBRARY OF CONGRESS CATALOGING IN PUBLICATION DATA
Neville–Sington, Pamela.
Fanny Trollope : the life and adventures of a clever woman / Pamela Neville-Sington.
p. cm.
Includes index.
ISBN 0-670-85905-2
1. Trollope, Frances Milton, 1780-1863—Biography.
2. Women authors, English—19th century—Biography. I. Title
PR5699.T3Z77 1998
823'.7—dc21
[b]   98-21629

This book is printed on acid-free paper.

Printed in the United States of America
Set in Monotype Bell

For David
and
in loving memory of
Sasha

But I suppose that, as real pictures of life, novels show us more truth than works of higher pretension ... I record this fact distinctly, because I flatter myself that these pages may be of use to my fellow creatures long after I have ceased to exist.

An excerpt from the heroine Charlotte Morris's diary,
in *The Life and Adventures of a Clever Woman* by Fanny Trollope

CONTENTS

LIST OF ILLUSTRATIONS

ACKNOWLEDGEMENTS

There are many libraries and archives, both in Britain and America, to whom I owe much gratitude for assisting me in my research and kindly allowing me to quote from the letters and papers in their collections. First and foremost, I would like to thank Leslie Morris, curator of manuscripts at Houghton Library, Harvard University; Alexander Wainwright, curator of the Morris L. Parrish Collection, and Mark Farrell, curator of the Robert H. Taylor Collection, both at Princeton University Library; Saundra Taylor, curator of manuscripts at the Lilly Library, Indiana University; Robert Parks, curator of manuscripts at the Pierpont Morgan Library, New York; and Alfred Kleine-Kreutzmann, curator of rare books at the Public Library of Cincinnati and Hamilton County; as well as the staffs of the manuscript collections at UCLA Library, Boston Public Library, University of Illinois Library at Urbana-Champaign, the Historical Society of Pennsylvania, the Beinecke Library at Yale University, the New York Historical Society, the Joseph Regenstein Library at the University of Chicago, the University of Michigan Library, the Library of Congress in Washington, DC and the New York Public Library, including the Berg Collection.

In Britain, I would like to thank John Thackeray, archivist of the Geological Society, R. Custance, archivist of Winchester College, T. C. Barnard, archivist of Hertford College, Oxford, Julia Walworth at the Senate House Library, University of London, Joanna Corden, archivist of Hendon Library, Barnet, Alisdair Hawkyard, former archivist of Harrow School, and Ben Wyne at the London School of Economics Library, as well as the staffs of the John Murray Archives, the Bristol Record Office, the Devon Record Office, Reading Public Library, Woburn Abbey, Gloucestershire Record Office, the Public Record Office, the Greater London Record Office, the London Library and the British Library.

I would also like to acknowledge the much appreciated assistance of Carron Greig and his son Geordie, who allowed me into their wonderful collection of Trollopiana and provided me with much information, Deirdre Le Faye and Laurie Guilfoyle, who helped me to establish the links between Jane Austen and Fanny Trollope, Lady Zuzanna Shonfield for Poggio al Sole in Tuscany, Brody and Nadine Neuenschwander LeBaq for their detective work in Bruges, Mary James at Bernard Quaritch for bibliographic detail, Mr and Mrs Phillip Hulme for inviting the Trollope Society into their Monken Hadley home, John Letts and other members of the Trollope Society for their ideas and enthusiasm, Jane Pepper for her French translations, Elizabeth and Bailey Bishop for their hospitality in Boston, Rupert Maas, Henry Ford and Sandra Altman for their efforts to trace various paintings, and Clare Alexander, formerly of Viking, for her support, as well as my present editor Antonia Till, my agent Rachel Calder, Giles Mandelbrote, David Alexander, Tom Freeman, Simon Lamb, Gerald Laing, Daniel Johnson, Susanne McDadd, Teresa Ransom and Victoria Glendinning for all their help and suggestions. Many thanks, too, to my friends and family, especially my mother, Joanne Neville, who have sent me clippings, books and other interesting tidbits.

I most especially want to thank my husband and 'in-house' editor, David Sington, who somehow in his busy life as a film-maker found time to follow in Fanny Trollope's footsteps with me from Florence to Cincinnati and to spend many an hour discussing the Trollopes. I could not have written this book without his friendship, love and patience.

PREFACE

In 1875, on board the *Bothnia* bound for London out of New York,
Anthony Trollope, aged sixty, sat down to write his autobiography.
During his entire literary career there had been two well-known
novelists with the name of Trollope whose works were before the
public. One was Anthony himself. The other was his mother, Fanny,
who had been a celebrated author long before her son was first
published and whose books continued to be reprinted after her death
in 1863. Anthony devotes a chapter of *An Autobiography* to his famous
parent. In it every word of praise is tempered with criticism. Anthony
claims that in the early days of his mother's marriage 'she had loved
society, affecting a somewhat liberal *rôle*, and professing an emotional
dislike to tyrants, which sprung from the wrongs of would-be regicides and the poverty of patriot exiles'. 'In after years, when marquises
of another caste had been gracious to her, she became a strong Tory,
and thought that archduchesses were sweet. But with her politics
were always an affair of the heart, – as indeed were all her convictions.
Of reasoning from causes, I think that she knew nothing.' At the end
of the chapter Anthony sums up his mother's life and works: 'She
was an unselfish, affectionate, and most industrious woman, with great
capacity for enjoyment and high physical gifts. She was endowed, too,
with much creative power, with considerable humour, and a genuine
feeling for romance. But she was neither clear-sighted nor accurate;
and in her attempts to describe morals, manners and even facts, was
unable to avoid the pitfalls of exaggeration.' This condescending

portrait of Fanny Trollope has quite naturally been accepted as painted from life, and if Fanny is remembered at all today, it is as an admittedly courageous and hard-working woman who nevertheless neglected her talented son, and was herself a second-rate writer, a political dilettante and a bit of a snob.

Yet, to her other surviving son Tom, 'there is hardly a word of this in which Anthony is not more or less mistaken'. Tom wrote that this 'passage in my brother's *Autobiography* . . . grates upon my mind, and, I think, very signally fails to hit the mark'. In his own memoirs Tom painted his mother's portrait in very different colours: this woman was completely free from affectation, cared deeply about the pressing political issues of her day, was often brutally honest but never unkind, and above all, though her life was marred by appalling tragedy, was 'the happiest natured person I ever knew – happy in the intense power of enjoyment, happier still in the conscious exercise of the power of making others happy'.

Who was Fanny Trollope? Writing a book which I hope answers this question has been difficult only in the wealth of material. Throughout a life packed with enough adventure, triumph and disaster to fill several novels, Fanny was an indefatigable correspondent; she was also a person who excited comment wherever she went, much of which survives in letters and memoirs. Beyond this is the evidence of her own work. Fanny began her literary career as a travel writer, and her novels too draw heavily on her own experiences, as she herself admitted. The same is true of Anthony.

A marble plaque outside the English Cemetery in Florence notes the many well-known writers who lie within, among them Elizabeth Barrett Browning, Walter Savage Landor and 'Frances Trollope Mother of Anthony'. Anthony was Fanny's crowning achievement, yet his reputation has eclipsed her memory. She herself was far more than the mother of a famous novelist, and her own story is well worth telling.

CHAPTER ONE

Days of the Regency

'The concert went off extremely well, and the house quite full. We had no vacancy in either of our boxes, as Mrs Terry (her sister not coming as she expected) applied to me on Thursday morning, and I was happy in giving her the only vacant place. For fear of consequences, I durst not put Monck and her in the same box . . .

'Mr and Mrs Lefevre were on the opposite side of the house, so that we had no conversation till the concert was finished, when Mr L. came to pay his compliments to me and my friends, and old dad went round to chat with Mrs L. When the house was sufficiently cleared to afford me an easy passage, I joined her also, and was agreeably surprised to find that, during the time we were waiting for their coach to get up, Mr L. had desired your friend Monck to put his night-cap in his pocket, and accompany them and us back to Heckfield. The night was dry, though cold, and, being moonlight, our drive was a very pleasant one; and we reached their truly hospitable mansion before twelve. Sandwiches, negus, etc., were immediately brought in, and after half an hour's pleasant chat, we separated for the night.

'I cannot attempt to detail what an agreeable day we had on Friday. The gentlemen dedicated the morning to field sports; the ladies accompanied me round the grounds, and afterwards we took a ride round Lord Rivers' park before we dressed for dinner, when there was an addition to our numbers of a Mr Milton, his wife, and two daughters; the youngest of whom, Miss Fanny Milton, is a very

1

lively, pleasant young woman. I do not mean to infer that Miss
Milton may not be equally agreeable, but the other took a far greater
share in the conversation, and, playing casino great part of the evening
with Mr S. Lefevre, Mr Monck, and your old Mumpsa, it gave me
an opportunity of seeing her in a more favourable light than her
sister.'[1]

One could be forgiven for thinking that this passage, composed in
1802, is a scene from a Jane Austen novel: tea before the concert in
a provincial English town, a hint of *frisson* (perhaps an old lovers'
quarrel) between two of the concert-goers, and then a moonlit drive
to a Hampshire country house; the next day filled with field sports,
long walks, rides in the local lord's park, and ending with an evening
of cards and conversation. The *dramatis personae* even include a
suitable heroine not unlike Elizabeth Bennet: the 'lively, pleasant'
Miss Fanny Milton. In fact, this is a letter from Mrs George Mitford
to her fifteen-year-old daughter, Mary Russell Mitford. But the
resemblance to Jane Austen's fictional world is not merely coinciden-
tal, for many of the people mentioned were known to her and formed
part of the small world in which she lived and about which she
wrote.* As for the vivacious Miss Fanny Milton, she is indeed the
heroine, not of an Austen novel, but of our story.

To imagine the world in which Fanny Trollope, née Milton, grew
up, one need go no further than Jane Austen's fiction. Jane was only
four years Fanny's senior; their fathers, George Austen and William
Milton, were the rectors of Steventon and Heckfield, respectively,
both situated in the same Hampshire deanery of Basingstoke. The
Revd Milton, however, installed a curate and moved to the Bristol

---

* Charles Shaw-Lefevre, Lord Rivers and Mrs Terry are all names mentioned in
Jane Austen's correspondence. The author of the letter, Mrs Mitford, was the
daughter of Dr Richard Russell, who immediately preceded the Revd George Lefroy
and his family, Jane Austen's close friends, in the vicarage at Ashe. Her daughter,
the writer Mary Russell Mitford, later wrote of Jane Austen that 'mamma knew
all her family very intimately' and that Jane was 'then the prettiest, silliest, most
affected, husband-hunting butterfly she ever remembers' (Vera Watson, *Mary Russell
Mitford*, London, 1949, pp. 119–20). See Deirdre Le Faye, ed., *Jane Austen's Letters*,
3rd edn, Oxford, 1995.

area before Fanny was born, only returning to Heckfield with his family in 1801, a few months before the Austens moved to Bath. Although we cannot place them in the same room at the same time, Jane and Fanny would, nevertheless, have admired the same red coats of the local militia, visited the same milliners' shops, worn the same fashions, subscribed to the same circulating libraries and danced in the same assembly rooms above Basingstoke's town hall. They enjoyed the same pastimes: dancing, country walks, amateur theatricals and reading. They would both have discussed Napoleon's advance across Europe before turning to the local gossip, that 'epidemic of a country town', as Fanny called it in her first novel, *The Refugee in America.*

There was, however, one important if subtle distinction between Jane Austen and Fanny Trollope. Both women had an impeccable pedigree on their mothers' side; but, whereas Jane's paternal grandfather was a surgeon whose family belonged to the landed gentry, Fanny's grandfather, John Milton, was in trade, variously described as a 'distiller' and 'saddler' in the city of Bristol. John Milton had been able to ensure that his son William would rise above the status of tradesman, and thus 'considerably [assist] the gentility of his family' (*Jessie Phillips*), by sending him to Winchester, then Oxford, in preparation for the Church. None the less, the stigma was ever present, and when Mary Gresley* married the young clergyman William Milton, her family evidently thought it 'a *mésalliance* for the lady'.[2] They were directly descended from Sir Thomas Gresley (1552–1610) and could boast Norman ancestry. The 'illustrious Norman blood that flows in our veins', as Henry Milton wrote to his sister Fanny, became something of a family joke which later surfaced in her novel *The Three Cousins.*[3]

The Bristol Gresleys were not aristocrats, but they were professional men: clergymen, apothecaries and, when merchants, very prosperous ones. The family firm was located in the elegant Queen Square, at that time the largest square in Europe, near the docks in the heart of Bristol and around the corner from the famous Bristol

---

* Anthony Trollope gave the name Mary Gresley to the heroine of one of his short stories.

Theatre. The Gresleys' cousin, the well-to-do merchant Ames Helli-car, also carried on business from Queen Square. Mary Gresley's father no doubt hoped that she would marry someone with a better pedigree than the son of a small-time saddler for, as her grandson Anthony Trollope remarked of Dean Lovelace, a character in *Is He Popenjoy?* whose father had been a stable-keeper and tallow-chandler, 'The man looked like a gentleman, but still there was the smell of a stable.' Gresley may have feared that 'a host of aunts and cousins of the same breed, might come down upon [him] in the event of this ill-sorted marriage' – a thought which crossed the mind of one potential in-law of Fanny's creation, the vulgar Widow Barnaby, granddaughter of a tallow-chandler (*The Widow Barnaby*). But Mary Gresley, like another 'woman of good birth' in Fanny's novel *One Fault,* the beautiful Mrs Worthington, defied her family's wishes and 'persisted in her determination of becoming a poor country clergyman's wife'.

William Milton's children were no doubt made to feel inferior in rank to those around them in Bristol and Hampshire: 'I have heard,' writes Fanny Trollope in 1836, 'that it requires three generations to make a gentleman' (*Paris and the Parisians*). This was the received wisdom of the age: in Jane Austen's *Pride and Prejudice* Lady de Bourgh remarks to Elizabeth Bennet, whose maternal uncle lives in London's Cheapside: 'True. You are a gentleman's daughter. But . . . who are your uncles and aunts?' Perhaps Fanny had in mind a Heckfield neighbour when she describes in her novel *Town and Country** a good and friendly lady who never once 'permitted us to forget for a moment, that, although all men are equal before God – and women too – yet nevertheless, there would be something rather impious in supposing that this state of things was to begin while we remain on earth; and therefore that, at present, her place is in the manor pew, and mine is in the Vicarage ditto'. Although she may have come up against such attitudes, Fanny chose to believe, not without some foundation, that 'the clergy of England, their matronly wives and highly-educated daughters, form a distinct caste' which

---

* *Town and Country,* first published in 1848, was reissued in 1857 as *Days of the Regency.*

'has a dignity and aristocracy of its own': they 'mingle freely in society
... and bring with them the females who form their families' (*Paris
and the Parisians*). After all, as she wryly remarks in *Town and Country*,
'a beneficed clergyman *may* become a *bishop*'.

William Milton's marriage with Mary Gresley took place at
St Thomas's Church in Bristol on 23 June 1774, a month after he
had taken up the living of Heckfield, aged thirty-one. But the couple
remained in Heckfield for only a year before installing a curate in
the country parish and returning to Bristol. The living of Heckfield
was worth a mere £120 per annum, and as his wife was expecting
her first child, William would naturally have been concerned about
money. They may also have wanted to be nearer to their parents,
especially as Mr Gresley was an apothecary – in modern parlance a
general practitioner. Besides the necessity of finding a second post
to supplement his income, the young clergyman probably thought
the small Hampshire village rather dull compared to the ancient port
of Bristol: its economic and strategic importance made the city a
bustling place. The first English ships to explore and colonize the
New World had belonged to Bristol merchants and departed from
the city's docks, situated as they were on the west coast, facing out
on to the Atlantic. In 1668 Samuel Pepys considered Bristol 'in every
respect like another London', and it soon became second only to the
capital in size and wealth. By the middle of the eighteenth century
it led the infamous Atlantic trade in rum, sugar and slaves as well as
other commodities.

The young couple apparently lived first with Mary's parents, close
by the family firm in Queen Square, then with William's in nearby
Trinity Street: a narrow lane which passed between St Augustine's
Church and Bristol Cathedral down to the river – a less fashionable
if equally central address. Although exciting, Bristol was also dirty,
smelly and generally unhealthy. No doubt for this reason William
and Mary took a house in Stapleton, a village then about two and a
half miles north-east of the centre of the city. At some point William's
father, who was to reach the age of ninety-nine, came to live with
them. Stapleton is now a suburb of Bristol, but Lower Grove Road
where the Miltons lived still retains a country feel to it: the narrow
lane, lined with the remnants of an old stone wall, looks out over

green fields down to the River Frome. The clergyman took up a number of posts to supplement his income, including Clerk of Holy Orders at St Michael's in central Bristol, where all but two of the Milton children were baptized, and curate of Almondsbury, Gloucestershire, five miles north of Stapleton.

The story of William and Mary's life together was an all too familiar one to their contemporaries. They experienced the joy of having three healthy children: Mary (1776), Fanny (10 March 1779) and Henry (1784). But they also felt the great sadness of losing three others in infancy: Cecilia, born the year before Fanny, and John and Emily, who came between Fanny and Henry. Mary Milton died soon after the birth of Henry, leaving William to bring up the three children on his own as well as care for his ageing father.* In *One Fault* the description of Colonel Seaton, who lives with his son's family, seems more reminiscent than imaginative: the old man had 'a sweet and kindly temper, which neither age nor misfortune had spoiled'. He would sit for hours with his eyes half closed, but from time to time 'there would burst from those withered lips a flow of anecdote that richly repaid the attention with which it was listened to, for it always transported the hearers, as by the wand of a magician, into the middle of the last century. Names that have long borne the permanent value which history gives to renown, were familiar in his mouth as household words; and traits of character, *bons mots*, and epigrams were poured forth as from a storehouse.'

Fanny would have been only five or six when her mother died. Her older sister Mary was, according to Fanny Trollope's first biographer, Frances Eleanor Trollope, 'a kind, excellent creature, sufficiently sensible, but not of shining parts'. One gathers as much from Mrs Mitford's letter to her daughter quoted above. Henry was, like his older sister Fanny, vivacious and quick-witted: 'a peculiarly delightful companion in society and quick to appreciate all that was best and brightest in the conversation of others', but he was very much the younger brother. In later years Fanny and her brother were very close, and she came to depend upon Henry's help and advice. However, one can easily imagine that while growing up in Stapleton their relationship consisted entirely of his 'attempts to quiz and plague his sister', while she 'treated him much as a large and powerful dog does a little one – enduring his gambols and annoying tricks with imperturbable patience for a while, and then suddenly putting forth a heavy paw and driving him off in an instant' (*The Vicar of Wrexhill*).

At this time a girl's education was a very haphazard affair, which usually depended upon the talents and inclinations of her parents. The Miltons were never affluent, and if Fanny had had a mother she would certainly have been well taught in the domestic sciences, including the ability to alter old clothes so as always to appear well dressed. But this was not the case: Fanny, according to both her sons Tom and Anthony, tended towards extravagance (usually manifested in entertaining and generosity towards friends); and both she and her children had the reputation of being badly turned out. Her daughter-in-law, Rose Trollope, wrote that 'she was somewhat indifferent as to her own personal get up'. A friend turned critic in America, Timothy Flint, remarked on 'her want of taste and female intelligence in regard to dress', also ascribing it to 'her holding herself utterly above such considerations'.[5] Perhaps she was guilty of the same 'country town indifference to decorum' exhibited by Elizabeth Bennet when the latter arrived at Netherfield with her ankles covered in dirt. Fanny almost certainly agreed with the Widow Barnaby's genteel niece Agnes that 'it was a great happiness . . . that satin-stitch had never ranked as a necessary branch of female education at Empton Rectory; had she been able to embroider muslin, her existence would have been dreadful' (*The Widow Barnaby*). Martha (the 'Widow') Barnaby, on the other hand, had been a young lady endowed with brilliant talents: she could make pasteboard card-boxes and screens and, of course, work satin-stitch. Satin-stitch was something that Jane Austen was particularly good at.

Fanny Milton, like Jane, was a child of the Georgian era, when both men and women enjoyed a relatively unrestricted choice of reading material and topics of conversation. Thus, while other young ladies were employed with their needle, Fanny preferred, and was permitted, to indulge in 'the solitary reading that makes so immensely important a part of female education' (*A Visit to Italy*): Shakespeare, Milton, Spenser, Gray, Racine, Corneille, La Fontaine, Boileau, Dante, Tasso and Petrarch. Fanny would also have known the works of

Alexander Pope, James Thomson, William Sherlock, Richard Sheridan, Oliver Goldsmith, William Cowper, Henry Fielding, Samuel Richardson, Laurence Sterne, Ann Radcliffe, Fanny Burney and Maria Edgeworth. Jane Austen declared that her family were 'great novel-readers and not ashamed of being so'; and Fanny Trollope thought that 'it is good for us to read trash occasionally' (*Paris and the Parisians*), though French romances were apt to give a young girl, like the scheming Lucy Dalton in *The Attractive Man*, the wrong moral guidance. All Fanny's heroines are voracious readers, like Mary King, whose father's 'old-fashioned library had wherewithal to supply her with enough, and more than enough, to occupy every leisure moment which her necessary needlework and her long walks left her' (*Mrs Mathews*).

Fanny was probably educated at home, perhaps because William Milton, like Mr Marshall in *Town and Country*, could not bear to part with his daughter so soon after the death of his wife. While her brother was away at a good boarding-school, Susan Marshall was taught by a family friend, Mrs Hartwell. 'This sort of intercourse drew the two families very closely together', and when Susan reached fifteen, she helped with the lessons of Mrs Hartwell's young children. This was very much the relationship between the Miltons and the family of John Garnett, a Bristol merchant and William's closest friend, who helped tutor Fanny in mathematics and science. Her great passion, however, was Italian literature, especially Dante: 'Going through life without a tolerably intimate knowledge of the *Divina Commedia*' practically constituted a sin in Fanny's eyes (*A Visit to Italy*). She 'contrived, with a little help from her father, to teach herself to read very fluently both French and Italian. But,' Fanny writes in *Town and Country*, 'this help from the learned vicar was only such as a good Latin scholar can always give, and went solely to construction, and in no degree to pronunciation.' Both Fanny and her father seem to have been natural linguists. Probably like Mary King in *Mrs Mathews*, she could not, like public school boys, compose nonsense verse in Latin, but 'she could read the language with perfect facility'.

William Milton was a devoted father. His grandson Tom remembered the Revd Mr Milton as 'an excellent parish priest after the fashion of his day', that is charming, kind, liberal, and gentlemanlike, 'with a sort of Horatian easy-going geniality about him'. One of William's contemporaries at New College, Oxford, was James Woodforde, author of *The Diary of a Country Parson*. In a typical entry dated 14 January 1774 we get a glimpse of the young Milton and the sort of world he lived in:

> Had a new Wigg brought home this morning, which I put on before I went to dinner, it is a more fashionable one than my old ones are, a one curled wigg with two curls of the sides. I like it, and it was liked by most People at dinner. I gave the Barber's man, Jonathan 0.1.0. At Back-Gammon this evening with Milton only one gammon, and I lost to him by bad luck 0.16.6.

The diary also records that on at least one occasion, when Woodforde was a candidate for the living of Weston Longeville, Milton 'talked nothing but nonsense' (he had voted against Woodforde).

The college records note that Milton was a 'person of considerable mechanical genius'. In fact, he preferred inventing gadgets to saving souls, and he instilled in Fanny a keen interest in mathematics. On a winter's evening the candlelit parlour table in Stapleton may have resembled that described by a contemporary country vicar's wife with four daughters: 'We have French, Italian, History, Divinity, Biography, Arithmetic, Penmanship, Needlework, and to crown all Mathematics.'[6] But William Milton was also, according to his grandson, 'crotchety and full of schemes'. Like one of the characters in his daughter's novel *Tremordyn Cliff,* he 'had an excellent understanding, a shrewd wit, and a most warm and generous heart – nevertheless, he had his defects. The most prominent of these, perhaps, was . . . the pertinacity that worked out any purpose once taken, though the doing so might involve an expense of time and trouble, greatly disproportioned to the apparent value of the object.' William himself had a name for it, according to Tom Trollope: ' "*au-mieux-ing*" – i.e. never being satisfied of anything when it seemed practicable to improve it'. One can imagine the crotchety side of the clergyman coming out at the family dinner table when he decided that he had had enough of the dreadful sound of knives scraping porcelain. His tenacity drove him to design and commission special plates, doubtless at great expense, with small circular pieces of silver set into the centre, to ensure a greater measure of peace and quiet at mealtimes.

William Milton was an eccentric character, so much his daughter and grandchildren testify to. But, although he always spent and never made money on his various schemes, some of these, and in particular his plans for Bristol harbour, were far from ridiculous. As we have seen, Fanny's father had grown up in Bristol, the son of a tradesman who lived on one of the many busy commercial streets leading down to the all-important River Avon which meanders through Bristol. Alexander Pope described the Bristol of William's childhood:

in the middle of the street, as far as you can see, [are] hundreds of ships, their masts as thick as they can stand by one another, which is the oddest and most surprising sight imaginable. This street is fuller of them than the Thames from London Bridge to Deptford, and at certain times only, the water rises to carry them out; so that, at other times, a long street, full of ships in the middle and houses on both sides, looks like a dream.

But the extreme tidal range of the river, although making for a dramatic picture, was the port city's biggest drawback: ships – and their cargoes – were at the mercy of the tides. As Milton wrote, 'Our ships lay, with much mischief, dry at their wharfs, eight hours in every twelve, and without possibility of going up or down the river during the continuation of neap tides.' It was clear to everyone that Bristol could not maintain its importance as a port unless a solution to the problem was found.

In 1791, when Fanny was twelve, the clergyman presented to the ancient Society of Merchant Venturers a scheme to convert the port of Bristol into a floating harbour: 'The author of the present mode is as anxious as anyone can be, that the Port of Bristol should avail itself of every advantage which art can give to nature; and sees, though little interested in ships, the great importance to the town in general (whose essence is its commerce) of keeping them constantly afloat.' In fact, since 1765 numerous proposals for the improvement of the harbour had been put forward, but William Milton was the first to come up with the idea of a tidal bypass; that is a channel, or 'cut', built to the south of the city to accommodate the Avon's tidal flow. The old winding path of the river along the docks would then, in effect, become a canal where water levels could be controlled.

The committee considered the scheme, involving as it did major excavations, too expensive. Nevertheless, the merchant Ames Hellicar, William's relation by marriage, took an interest in the matter. In December 1792 he proposed to finance the work by subscription and shortly afterwards published a pamphlet warning of the adverse effects of building a dam across the Avon – a step which Milton's plan had rendered unnecessary. However, the city councillors vetoed Hellicar's private enterprise, declaring that 'all such works should be for the sole benefit of the public' and no individual or private body should profit from it. Within a year Britain had been forced to intervene in the War of the First Coalition against France, bringing all new and costly projects to a halt.

Ten years on, during the brief respite from the war with France following the Peace of Amiens, the city engineer Mr Jessop submitted his own proposal for a floating harbour in Bristol – the key element in it being William's idea of a tidal bypass. However, no credit or remuneration was given to the clergyman. The Bristol Dock Company was established by an Act of Parliament and the floating harbour was built between 1804 and 1809 at a cost three times that of Milton's original estimate. The clergyman fought for recognition. In order to prove his case and 'to assume only what is mine', he printed, at his own expense, three separate pamphlets setting forth the correspondence he had had since 1791 with the Merchant Venturers and other prominent townsmen. The grudging recognition which he eventually received only added insult to injury: a silver plate, with the arms of the corporation engraved upon it, 'not exceeding the value of 100 guineas ... in testimony of the high sense they entertain of his ORIGINAL SUGGESTION for the improvement of the Harbour of Bristol' (Milton's emphasis). In his last letter on the matter, dated December 1812 and addressed to his friend, Richard Bright, he wrote of his contribution with bitter resignation:

Time, the Tell-Tale, seems already to lisp its praising Sanction of the Work. In 50 years hence, all Variance between Estimate

11

and Loss will be forgotten – The Frome will be rendered as sweet as her Sister – and Bristol will have learned to look with as confident an Eye on Liverpool as ever she did 100 years ago.

I will not sign *Cassandra* – but

Yours very sincerely,

W. Milton

Milton must have felt doubly betrayed as many of the Merchant Venturers were well known to him and to his father, including the secretary of the corporation, Jeremy Osborne, who had witnessed John Milton's will.[7]

The young Fanny would have shared in the clergyman's frustration as well as his triumphs. Of all his children, Fanny resembled her father most; certainly she was a compulsive *au-mieux*-er, incapable of sitting still and doing nothing if there was a problem to be solved or a situation to be improved. Without the guidance of a mother, Fanny had also learned to be self-reliant. Together these traits, initiative, tenacity and independence of mind, were to give her the courage, strength and ability to overcome the many crises which she would have to face in her lifetime; but, they also made her sometimes act rashly, without thinking, and thus court disaster. Fanny came to realize through experience the disadvantages of growing up without a mother's restraining influence, and her novels (like her son Anthony's) abound with motherless young women. In *Mrs Mathews* the heroine considers that 'she would probably have been a very different person' had she known her mother, for 'decidedly the chief defects in Mary King's character arose from her having been too much accustomed, almost from infancy indeed, to depend upon herself and her own resources upon all occasions which require judgement and decision, either for the regulation of her conduct or her opinions'.

Some time after the death of Fanny's grandfather in 1788, William Milton had decided to move to Clifton in Gloucestershire, then a popular and fast-growing spa town situated on the steep hill west of Bristol – high above the stench and noise of the city but still within easy walking distance of Bristol Cathedral. As the distiller and saddler had, according to his will, 'sustained sundry losses' in the last ten years of his life, William Milton would not have inherited very much from his father, and he could probably only have afforded to move to fashionable Clifton after 1793, when the war with France caused all building to cease and house prices to slump.* Milton would have had good reason to leave Stapleton around this time, for two thousand French prisoners of war were kept just outside the village in a notoriously badly run camp, where the inmates lived in wretched conditions. In any case, Stapleton must have seemed like a cultural wilderness to the clergyman; in Clifton he was at the heart of Bristol's intellectual community. And it was the perfect location from which to pursue his harbour project: his scientific friends and the more influential merchants resided there, and from Clifton's Brandon Hill he had a perfect view of the Bristol docks below. Another reason for the move was that his daughters, Mary and Fanny, aged seventeen and fourteen in 1793, were ready to enjoy the benefits of good society which Clifton had to offer.

Clifton was then, and is now, a beautiful spot.[8] Neat Georgian terraces, 'like so many palaces in fairy-land', border on the verdant downs and the dramatic precipice of the Avon Gorge. 'Looking down upon the course of the Avon, winding its snake-like path at their feet, with the woods of Leigh, rich in their midsummer foliage, feathering down on one side, and rocks of limestone, bright in their veins of red and grey, freshly opened by the quarrying, rising beautifully bold on the other, Agnes stood rapt in ecstasy.' Fanny was no doubt recalling her own life in Clifton when, in *The Widow Barnaby*, she pictures Agnes and her friends amusing themselves at a spot near the Gorge, 'sometimes with idle talk, sometimes with listening to the reverberating thunder that arose from the blasting of the rocks below them, and sometimes by sitting silent for a whole minute together, pulling up handfuls of the fragrant thyme'.

Jane Austen too had happy memories of the spa town. After she left the detested Bath in 1806, she spent the summer in nearby Clifton: 'it is two years tomorrow since we left Bath for Clifton,' she later reminded her sister Cassandra, 'with what happy feelings of escape!'

---

* In 1807 Robert Southey wrote that in Clifton 'as well as at Bath is the dismal sight of streets and crescents which have never been finished, the most dolorous of ruins'.

13

Many of the characters in her novels, when not taking the waters at Bath, do so in Bristol: either at Hotwells, the old spa on the river just below Clifton, which boasted three taverns, two ballrooms and a promenade, or at the newer and more fashionable amenities above. In *Northanger Abbey* Isabella Thorpe and her party 'walked down to the Pump room [of Hotwells], tasted the water, and laid out some shillings in purses and spars' (crystalline mineral fragments from the Avon Gorge). In *Emma* Jane Austen reveals the subtle distinction between tradesmen living amid the noise and smell of the Bristol docks and well-to-do merchants who can afford to live in the terraces of Clifton. Miss Hawkins lived in 'the very heart of Bristol'; she claims her father was 'a Bristol merchant', though Emma suspects him of a lowly trade. Her sister Selina had escaped the nastiness of the city and married the successful Mr Suckling, a resident of the sought-after Maple Grove, clearly intended to be Clifton.

Fanny Milton lived in Clifton during an extraordinary time, when the spa town hosted such literary and scientific figures as Maria Edgeworth, Robert Southey (whose father was a Bristol merchant), Wordsworth, Coleridge, Joseph Priestley, Humphry Davy and Thomas Beddoes. The Miltons may have met many of these local celebrities through the clergyman's friend in the floating-harbour affair, Richard Bright. Bright, the son of a wealthy merchant (the family firm was next door to the Gresleys' in Queen Square), had been taught chemistry by Priestley and was a friend and collaborator of Beddoes. It was Bright who helped Priestley flee to America in 1794 after Bristol citizens rioted in protest against his support of the French Revolution.[9] Bright's spacious house in Abbots Leigh, a village across the Avon where the Hellicars also had a mansion, was a gathering place for scientists, chemists and enthusiasts. Like Richard Bright, Sir Herbert Monson in *Tremordyn Cliff* was a 'man of science', and his interest 'amounted almost to a passion'. 'His ample fortune gave him leisure and power to indulge this without restraint.' At one of the Monsons' soirées, besides musical instruments, chessboards, playing-cards, engravings, albums, annuals, sculptures and pretty miniatures, there was a large round table 'covered with a soft, rich, crimson carpet, on which were spread various delicate models in brass, of newly invented, or newly improved instruments. A miniature steam engine, a small galvanic apparatus, and such curious specimens of newly ground lenses, as might make an astronomer's eyes water to look through them.'

But direct connections are hardly necessary in order to imagine Fanny Milton, as she went about her daily life in Clifton and Bristol, encountering such colourful characters as Southey and Coleridge when they had rooms in College Street, at the bottom of Clifton Hill. She may well have been a frequent visitor to the Bristol bookshop of Thomas Cottle, the friend and publisher of Coleridge and Southey. Perhaps she overheard the two poets spreading the gospel of Pantisocracy, their proposed utopian settlement on the banks of the Susquehanna in Pennsylvania. Walking down the hill from her house in Clifton Place (now Clifton Road) to Bristol Cathedral, Fanny might have seen, as did Richard Bright, Southey and Wordsworth dancing in the street, leaping over dogs and giggling hysterically, having just inhaled Beddoes's and Davy's new discovery, nitrous oxide, otherwise known as laughing gas. 'Davy,' remarked Southey, 'has invented a pleasure for which the language had no name.' The young Fanny certainly would have been surprised, if not shocked, to see Maria Edgeworth in the same state. The author of *Moral Tales* described it as a 'gas which inebriates in a most delightful manner, having the same obvious effect of Lethe and at the same time giving the rapturous sensations of the nectar of the Gods'.

The Widow Barnaby, much of which takes place in the 1810s, gives a vivid picture of the Clifton of Fanny's girlhood. The widow takes lodgings in Sion Row, the most fashionable area, on the very edge of the town; today it still overlooks Observatory Hill towards the downs and the Gorge, the site of Brunel's suspension bridge (built between 1831 and 1864). Martha Barnaby's relations by marriage, the prosperous merchant Mr Peters and his family, have a house in one of the most beautiful terraces in Clifton, Rodney Place, where Davy and Beddoes lived in 1798. Martha Barnaby is at first disappointed that her brother-in-law is a mere clothier, but she soon discovers that he 'held a much higher station in society than she had anticipated'. Mr Peters, perhaps based on Ames Hellicar, was 'an active and prosperous manufacturer, neither above his business, nor below enjoying the ample fortune acquired by it'. Mr Peters's handsome establishment includes a carriage, footman, boy and coach-man. The elder son had already joined the family firm; the younger son, intended for the Church, was soon to go up to Oxford; the Peters's daughters, 'from appearance, education, and manners, were perfectly well qualified to fill the situation of first-rate belles in the Clifton ballroom'.

After taking lodgings, the widow sets about initiating herself into the mysteries of Clifton society. The first task is to put her name down at the assembly rooms, where dances were held on a regular basis, and at the 'library', which was at one and the same time a bookshop, newsagent, stationers and circulating library. At the assembly rooms, when she inquires, 'what is it the fashion to do? To subscribe for the season, or pay at the door?', she receives the knowing answer: 'You may do either ... but if you wish your arrival to be known, I believe you had better put your name in the book.' Martha Barnaby soon learns that the library is the gathering place of the smart set. She exclaims to her niece Agnes, 'and as for the library, it's perfectly like going into public! What an advantage it is every morning of one's life to be able to go to such a place as that!' Elsewhere Fanny Trollope describes another Gloucestershire library in loving detail. On market day Mr Stephens's library

was thronged. Many very well dressed ladies, seated on chairs and benches between two counters, and a still greater number of gentlemen, wedged in every nook and corner that could furnish standing room, were engaged in discussing provincial politics, or metropolitan *bon ton* ... Nearly the whole of the party seemed more or less known to each other, as was made manifest by an occasional nod, or smile, or a hand raised to the hat, or a chin lowered to the breast, or a little dip from an unfortunate lady who had not obtained a seat, or a shrug of the shoulders from a gentleman more unfortunate still, who found himself jammed into a corner. The conversation, meanwhile, if carefully listened to, would have resembled the cross-readings from a newspaper, for it was going on in at least a dozen groups at the same time.

Yet, 'Notwithstanding the well-dressed crowd in his shop, Stephens knew that it was not likely he should sell much to any of them' (*Tremordyn Cliff*).

In Clifton the fashionable crowd was also drawn to the pastry shop, where they could sit down at the counter and indulge in cakes, ices and gossip. Church-going on Sundays was also 'of great importance to strangers about to be initiated into the society of the place' (*The Widow Barnaby*). And, of course, in a spa town one subscribes to pump rooms at one's own peril. Fanny Trollope does not record if Mrs Barnaby visited Hotwells or the Clifton facilities, but the experience would have been similar to that at Cheltenham, which she later patronizes:

> Her spirits rose as she approached the fount on perceiving the throng of laughing, gay, and gossiping invalids that *bon ton* and bile had brought together; and when she held out her hand to receive the glass, she had more the air of a full-grown Bacchante, celebrating the rites of Bacchus, than a votary at the shrine of Hygeia. But no sooner had the health-restoring but nauseous beverage touched her lips, or rather her palate, than, making a horrible grimace, she set down the glass on the marble slate, and pushed it from her with very visible symptoms of disgust. A moment's reflection made her turn her head to see if Agnes were looking at her, 'I think it might do you a vast deal of good, Agnes' (*The Widow Barnaby*).

But the focal point of the social life in any town, certainly for a young woman, was the assembly-room balls. Both Jane Austen and Fanny Milton were especially fond of dancing, as were many of their heroines. Jane wrote to her sister Cassandra of one particular ball: 'There were twenty dances, and I danced them all, and without any fatigue . . . I fancy I could just as well dance for a week together as for half an hour.' One of Martha Barnaby's accomplishments was that she 'could dance every night, and very nearly all night long' (*The Widow Barnaby*), and Fanny herself wished to make dancing 'more general and of more frequent occurrence than it is' (*Paris and the Parisians*). However, as a visitor in a provincial town one's first ball could be a tricky affair. There was a real horror of walking into the assembly room and not recognizing a soul. However, as is made clear in *The Widow Barnaby*, if a newcomer to Clifton had not already made an acquaintance at the library or the pump rooms, then a master of ceremonies was at hand to make the appropriate introductions, often inviting the older guests to join one of the whist tables while the dancing continued apace near by. Then, at some point later in the evening, the two groups reconvened in another room for tea and refreshments before the orchestra started up again.

The Clifton assembly balls would have been especially colourful affairs when the Miltons were living in Clifton Place, for members of the Bristol regiment and militia (one of the Gresleys had joined the Light Infantry) would have been seen parading about in their handsome red uniforms and flirting with the native beauties – until, that is, they were called away to face the French. (In fact, the only duty they saw was patrolling the Stapleton prisoner-of-war camp.) 'Volunteering was the order of the day,' wrote Mary Russell Mitford of this period;[10] the very name of the barrack was 'redolent to all provincial female hearts as much of terror as of joy' (*The Widow Barnaby*).

Rather surprisingly, in 1800, after fifteen years of being a widower, the Revd Milton decided to remarry. His bride was a Clifton resident, Sarah Partington. Perhaps he realized that, without a mother's guidance and advice, his daughters, by now aged twenty-one and twenty-four, were like sheep among the Clifton wolves. Fanny, rather petite in stature, with small hands and feet, full lips, a pleasant smile and blue-grey eyes set rather far apart, certainly seems to have made an impression on the ballroom floor. Many years later a certain peer of the realm spoke to Anthony Trollope of his mother, 'I danced with her when she was Fanny Milton, and I remember she had the neatest foot and ankle I ever saw!'[11] Perhaps the young Fanny fell in love with a handsome young man in a red uniform, and wrote her name together with his all over the margins of her French exercise book, as did Caroline Hartley in *The Blue Belles of England*.

More likely, William Milton may have seen that Mary and Fanny were not able to show themselves to full advantage in the assembly rooms without money for the new dresses, gloves, shoes and hats necessary to keep up with the fashionable set. 'I know', wrote Fanny later, 'that a young lady's ball dress is considered . . . as something sacred to the Graces, and that the whole fabric should consist of materials lighter and brighter than any clothing that ordinary mortals can presume to wear' (*Vienna and the Austrians*). Clothes were a perpetual problem for a woman of limited income: a young Jane Austen wrote to her sister that she was 'tired and ashamed' of her wardrobe. The Milton girls needed a woman who, like Martha Barnaby's mother, had the ingenuity to convert 'the relics of her own maiden finery into fashionable dancing-dresses for her girls'. Fanny Trollope goes on to describe almost wistfully – yet not without a touch of characteristic sarcasm – something which she herself never had, that is the

> unwearied industry of a proud, poor, tender mother, when labouring to dress her daughters for a ball . . . the dyings, the ironings, the darnings, that have gone to make misses of ten pounds a-year pin-money look as smart as the squanderer of five hundred . . . the light of morning never steals into the eyes of mortals to spur them on again to deeds of greatness after nightly rest, without awaking many hundred mothers whose principal business in life is to stitch, flounce, pucker, and embroider for their daughters! . . . All this is very beautiful! . . . I speak not of the stitching, flouncing, puckering, and embroidering . . . but of the devotion of the maternal hearts dedicated to it (*The Widow Barnaby*).

However, if this were the case, things apparently did not quite work out according to plan. Rather than help the girls gain a firmer foothold in Clifton society, within a year of his marriage the Revd Milton had moved his family back to the country vicarage in Heckfield after an absence of twenty-five years. It is not hard to imagine – or to sympathize with – the new Mrs Milton attempting to stifle her husband's obsession with the floating harbour by moving well away from Bristol. (This was, in fact, to have little effect: the clergyman's most bitter correspondence in the matter was written from Heckfield vicarage between 1803 and 1812.) Mrs Milton may also have been anxious for their safety since coastal towns, and especially major ports like Bristol, would be prime targets if Napoleon were to invade Britain – a real fear at the time.

As she grew older, and especially after her father's death, Fanny came to look back on her life in the village of Heckfield with nostalgia. Thus, in *One Fault* she describes the parsonage of the kind-hearted, good and beloved Henry Worthington, modelled in part on her father William Milton, in terms of a country idyll: 'In one of the richest valleys of Somersetshire [read Hampshire], where hedgerows green, abounding herbage, and unshorn elm trees, make every separate field look like a separate paradise, nestles the white-washed village of Abbot's Preston.' The Worthington's parsonage, which closely resembles the vicarage in Heckfield, was beautiful: 'Though large enough to be a commodious dwelling for a numerous family, it was a cottage in aspect, the roof thatched, and the windows opening in the fashion of casements, though their leaded lozenge-shaped panes had been exchanged for others, giving a fairer proportion of light.' Anthony Trollope set *Ralph the Heir* in just this spot: 'there is no prettier district' with 'a sweeter air, or a more thorough seeming of English wealth and English beauty and English comfort. Those who know Eversley and Bramshill and Heckfield and Strathfieldsaye will acknowledge that it is so.' In middle age Fanny wrote to Mary Russell Mitford, by this time the author of a popular series of stories set in rural Hampshire entitled *Our Village*, concerning her description of Bramshill: 'That part was the favourite, and in summer often the daily haunt of my youthful days. There was one particular spot under a high oak, where I have sat alone for hours. It was within hearing of the great clock, and but for that I should often have been benighted there.'[12] Nevertheless, the young Fanny must also have been bored and frustrated on many occasions in the quiet Hampshire village, agreeing with Henry Tilney in *Northanger Abbey* that 'one day in the country is exactly like another'.

There were the drives in Lord Rivers's park near by and parties at the Lefevres' spacious mansion, where we caught our first glimpse of the Milton sisters that November evening in 1802, but Fanny was not over-fond of her wealthy neighbours. It was a commonly held belief that Lord Rivers was 'a model of a modern fine Gentleman', that is, 'well-bred, accomplished, and debauched'. Apparently, he ill-treated his wife, 'the most charming in the world', until 'he deserved to be hated'.[13] Sir Charles Otterborne in *Mrs Mathews* was just such a 'county worthy', though 'it would be difficult to find any individual less deserving honour or distinction of any kind', 'for he was silly, selfish, and unprincipled'. 'But there was a Lady Otterborne, who was as deserving of all admiration and esteem as he was the reverse.'* Lord Otterborne's neighbour, Mr Steyton, had acquired his great wealth in the same way as Heckfield's local MP, Charles Shaw-Lefevre, through trade. Perhaps, like the Mathews, the Miltons wondered that 'Steyton does not contrive to get a little air manufactured on purpose for his own private use, for that he always looks as if he thought what he was breathing was not good enough for him'.†

From her later letters it also appears that Fanny was not particularly fond of her stepmother, who evidently held the purse-strings. (Again one can sympathize, knowing how much William Milton must have spent on his various schemes.) Fanny had always had things too much her own way, and she no doubt found it very difficult to adjust to another woman having authority over her. Anthony may have been remembering his mother's practice when he observed in *Cousin Henry* that the strong-willed Isabel Broderick never referred to her stepmother as 'Mother' but always 'Mrs Broderick'. Apparently, Fanny's children shared their mother's indifference to Mrs Milton: in later years Mary Russell Mitford had to remind Fanny's eldest son Tom of his duty to visit his widowed step-grandmother.

But perhaps the most serious objection to life in Heckfield was that at age twenty-five Mary Milton had, according to Lydia Bennet's calculations in *Pride and Prejudice*, already reached old-maid status and Fanny, aged twenty-two in 1801, was only a year short of it. True, these were the 'palmy days' when the militia's 'country quarters still existed, and many may still remember the tender sensibilities

---

* Otterbourne is the name of a Hampshire village south of Winchester.
† In 1810, while staying with her father at Heckfield, Fanny wrote to her husband of just over a year that the Lefevres 'have a young man called Gauntlett staying with them, whom I am quite in love with – he called here one day, and took great notice of Tom', her new-born son (F T to TAnT, 12 August 1810: Taylor Collection). The Gauntlett family was known to Jane Austen.

excited by a departing regiment, and the gay hopes generated by an arriving one' – all calculated to relieve the 'unbroken routine of ordinary existence' (*The Widow Barnaby*). Both Fanny Milton and Jane Austen had had experience of regimental towns in Hampshire: Martha Barnaby's native West Country village, Silverton, is remarkably like Meriton in *Pride and Prejudice*, where military galas are held and redcoats are to be found everywhere, eating ices at the pastry-cook's, posing in the library and lounging in the shade of the village green. However, the experience of a young woman without a fortune was all too often like that of the young Martha Barnaby in Silverton, who 'had seen so many colonels, majors, captains . . . ay, and lieutenants too, march into the town, and then march out again, without whispering anything more profitable in her ear than an assurance of her being an angel' (*The Widow Barnaby*). The Milton girls had fallen into that category of young provincial girls looking for husbands which Jane Austen studied so closely.

'If adventures will not befall a young lady in her own village, she must seek them abroad,' wrote Jane Austen in *Northanger Abbey*. Within two years of arriving, Fanny and her sister Mary had decided to leave Heckfield for London. Their younger brother Henry had started work as a clerk in the War Office and needed someone to keep house for him. Perhaps the Milton girls set out on such an April day as the Hartley ladies in *The Blue Belles*: 'A heavy shower had fallen', 'the dust was laid, the sun was shining, the birds singing, the primroses sleeping, the violets breathing vigorously and the post-horses pricking their ears, and looking as spruce as if they had nothing to do but trot out a little for their own amusement'.

CHAPTER TWO

The Lottery of Marriage

In 1803 Henry and his two sisters took up residence at no. 27 Keppel Street. The street (demolished in the 1930s to make way for the University of London) was part of the Duke of Bedford's estate. Since the mid eighteenth century London had resembled nothing so much as one large building site, as the illustrations to James Elmes's *Metropolitan Improvements* (1827–30) testify. This was the period when the architects John Nash and Sir John Soane were busy remodelling the city: Regent's Park, Regent Street, the Nash terraces on The Mall, Buckingham Palace and the Bank of England are all their designs. In the face of this development fever, the conservative Bedfords were determined to maintain the quiet, dignified feel of their estate. To this end, they put in place their own building regulations, restricted the number of shops, banned taverns altogether and eventually set gates at the entrances. This residential oasis was particularly popular with members of the legal profession, owing to its close proximity to the Inns of Court and Chancery. Henry Milton would not have had much further to walk to the War Office in Whitehall.

However, the Bedfords could not stop construction on their doorstep, and around 1800 the area which includes Brunswick, Mecklenburgh and Russell Squares was developed with the remit 'rather to raise than depress the Character' of the Foundling Hospital, owner of the land. As with the Bedford estate, the houses were solid rather than fashionable.[1] Many years later, in 1835, when writing about a fast-developing district of Paris where handsome dwellings were

23

springing up 'as white and bright as new-born mushrooms', Fanny Trollope was reminded of 'the early days of Russell Square and all the region about it' (*Paris and the Parisians*). Jane Austen also knew this area well: she visited her brother Charles when he was staying with his in-laws at no. 22 Keppel Street. 'Our part of London is very superior to most others!' remarks Isabella Knightley in *Emma*. 'You must not confound us with London in general, my dear sir. The neighbourhood of Brunswick Square is very different from almost all the rest. We are so very airy!'

All in all London was a relatively comfortable place to live at the beginning of the nineteenth century, with many of those small but important conveniences which cities on the Continent lacked, for example, sewers and drains, well-lit streets, spacious pavements and running water on the second and even third floors. In *Paris and the Parisians* Fanny notes that at a building site in London the first thing to be done is to surround the premises with a high paling and arrange a footpath; in Paris all is constant chaos and mayhem when a building is going up, as though there had just been an accident or a fire.

Possibly news of the Milton girls' arrival in London is buried somewhere in the pages of the *Morning Post*, for, as Fanny points out in *The Blue Belles of England*, if a young woman did not already have friends in the city, it was deemed necessary to 'advertise' one's arrival in order to gain an entrée into London society – otherwise morning calls and invitations would not be forthcoming. In any case, the outgoing Henry would have introduced Mary and Fanny to the acquaintances which he had made through the War Office and about town. Bristol and Heckfield neighbours would also have armed the Miltons with letters of introduction to friends and acquaintances in London. The twenty-four-year-old Fanny's first year in the capital may have resembled Mary Ringold's London 'season' in *A Romance of Vienna*: 'almost a surfeit of waltzing without room to turn, visiting menageries where nothing could be distinctly seen but human curiosities, and parading at horticultural meetings where the only flowers she could get near enough to see, were those that bloomed in ladies' bonnets'. Other leisure pursuits included walks in the parks around the city. During his first summer in London, Vauxhall appeared to Fanny's young hero Charles Chesterfield 'the realization of the most brilliant fables of the Arabian Tales, Kensington Gardens a royal Paradise, Richmond a courtly arcadia, and the river Thames an unceasing regatta, on which the barge of Cleopatra seemed ever before him when the Lord Mayor or any of his golden compeers "disported on its azure wave" ' (*Charles Chesterfield*).

As for the more cultural pursuits, Fanny attended operas at Covent Garden and Her Majesty's Theatre, Haymarket, and, after it opened in 1831, choral concerts at Exeter Hall in the Strand. She was familiar with the music of Mozart, Beethoven, Handel and Haydn, and had heard the great violinist Paganini play. She had a discerning ear: when in Vienna Fanny claimed that the singers at the opera house had 'murdered' the airs of Mozart's *Don Giovanni* and threatened never to return 'unless they get some vocal recruits' (*Vienna and the Austrians*). Fanny was critical of the more flippant side of the music scene. In *A Romance of Vienna* she describes the moment when the overture has ended and the curtain is drawn up: 'every pretty little hand raised a glass, needful or needless, to discover who was in presence and who was not; who and who were together, and which of these unions must be respected, and which broken by an invitation from the eye, the fan, or the finger'. And one gets the distinct feeling that Fanny had suffered through many an evening of amateur music:

> that dear resource of young ladies, whether they can play or not play, whether they can sing or not sing, – that pretty occasion of display for faces and graces, – that concealer of yawns, – that relaxer of aching limbs, – in one word, the piano-forte, formed a centre about which the three Misses Wilkyns . . . continued to walk and talk, for a considerable time; till at length, after a great deal of coaxing and pressing, refusing and coquetting, Miss Elruda Wilkyns sat down to play, and the Misses Elfreda and Winifred strode up to sing . . . much in the style that might have been expected from ladies who had been 'rather particular' by having a master once a week from Swansea (*The Ward of Thorpe-Combe*).

Fanny Milton had never learned to play the piano, owing perhaps to her love of music, or more probably to her love of dancing, for as the eldest Miss Wilkyns points out: 'the moment girls are known to play waltzes, they are never left in peace to dance them'.

Art was a particular passion of Fanny's brother Henry, and the publisher Longman commissioned the young War Office clerk to compose, as Fanny later described it in *Paris and the Parisians*, an 'elegant and curious little volume on the Fine Arts, written at Paris just before the breaking up of Napoleon's collection', entitled *Letters on the Fine Arts, Written from Paris in the Year 1815*. In later years he became a patron of the painter John Lucas, whose father had worked in the War Office with Henry. Through him, Lucas was to paint several portraits of Fanny's girlhood friend, the author Mary Russell Mitford. She wrote that Henry Milton was 'one of the best judges of art in England' and goes on to give us a further glimpse of his personality, describing him as 'a lively, agreeable, enthusiastic person, who always carries things his own way'.[2] It must have been a diverting, if exhausting, experience to tour the galleries, such as the British Gallery on Pall Mall and Somerset House on the Strand, in company with Fanny and her brother. Perhaps, like Judith Maitland in *Petticoat Government*, 'when once a picture had got possession of her, it was like being torn away from a half-read volume of the deepest interest to make her move on to another'. Fanny preferred the contemporary English painters, for example Sir Thomas Lawrence, to their French counterparts, such as David, despite the fact that 'one of our spring fashions in London is to declare unanimously, every year, that "the Exhibition at Somerset-house is very so, so;" – "very little worth looking at;" and the like' (*Belgium and Western Germany*). One can imagine Fanny and Henry examining and discussing every picture in detail, with their poor, tired sister Mary trailing behind, endeavouring to find a nearby bench on which to rest.

Fanny shared her brother's enthusiasm for art, but her great love was the theatre. Her first exposure to it would have been at the famous Bristol Theatre, where many of the great actors played. London was, of course, a theatre-goer's paradise, and over the years Fanny went to Covent Garden, Drury Lane and Her Majesty's Theatre to see Edmund Kean, Mrs Sarah Siddons and her brothers Charles and John Philip Kemble perform – all legends in their own time. Perhaps, as with Constance Ridley in *The Blue Belles of England*,

' "The School for Scandal," excellently well played' at the Queen's Theatre, was the first performance which Fanny attended in London. So devoted was Fanny to the theatre that, on at least one occasion, she queued at two o'clock in the afternoon for the privilege of sitting in the pit, which was cheaper and closer to the stage, to see Mrs Siddons play Lady Macbeth that evening. 'Sundry women were carried out from the crowd at the theatre door fainting.'[3] She remembered 'in the days of Argyle-street luxury', 'coming home from one of Mrs Siddons's readings with a passionate desire to see her act the part of Hamlet; and from another, quite persuaded that by some means the witch-scene in Macbeth should be so arranged that she should speak every word of it' (*Paris and the Parisians*).

We know almost nothing of the first five years of Fanny's personal life in London except that she grew older and remained single. By 1808, a spinster of twenty-nine, she must have spent many an evening at a ball like 'the fair Miss Brandenberry' who, 'notwithstanding she had the advantage of knowing nearly every gentleman in the room, was not so fortunate as the young *débutantes*, for she got no partner at all. The circumstance, however, was not new to her, so, like the eels of natural-historical celebrity, she did not much mind it, but amused herself, as she had often done before, by distinguishing dresses that were her old acquaintance, from dresses that were not, and by watching whether young Mr This danced with young Miss The other, as often this ball as the last' (*The Ward of Thorpe Combe*). Fanny was 'no longer the creature she was' and her style of dress would have changed accordingly: 'Instead of pale pink ribbons, and variegated wreaths of roses and geraniums, she now wholly confined herself to white muslin, and the dark, but gracious decoration of *la fleur des veuves*,* producing together a sort of transition state' (*The Widow Married*).

During her first years in London Fanny may have had some flirtations; possibly she thought that one or two men might propose; she may even have suffered from a broken heart like the heroine in *Mrs Mathews*, when her lover goes off to India and marries a girl in Madras. Or perhaps she met too many men like Lord Broughton

* 'widows' flower'.

in *The Ward of Thorpe Combe*, whose 'manners, and perhaps in some degree his conversation too, were those of a class. He was easy, gentlemanlike, and neither particularly animated nor particularly dull, but requiring stimulants, considerably stronger than either of the ladies then present could offer, to make him give out any symptoms of individual character.' The most likely explanation for her single status, however, is that Fanny appeared too 'blue', that is too intellectual, for most men's taste. Again and again in her writing she describes women's 'terror of being called learned', which 'is in general more powerful than that of being classed as ignorant'. In *Paris and the Parisians* she remarks that among Englishwomen, unlike the French, 'the dread of imputed bluism weighs down many a bright spirit, and sallies of wit and fancy are withheld from the fear of betraying either the reading or the genius with which many a fair girl is endued who would rather be thought an idiot than a BLUE'. Thus, the very 'blue' Miss Maitland in *The Old World and the New* is still single at thirty-three 'less owing, perhaps, to the blindness or indifference of the male sex to her numerous attractions, than to her inveterate love of conversation, in preference to flirting'. A woman, 'if she have the misfortune of knowing any thing, should conceal it as well as she can', advised Jane Austen in *Northanger Abbey*. But perhaps it had never been Fanny's ambition to marry. She may have felt, like Lady Mary Mortlake in *Tremordyn Cliff*, that to live with her brother, 'and if he married to dote upon his wife and children, had been her favourite day-dream through all the happy years of her young life, and no other attachment, of a more exclusive nature, had as yet arisen to make it fade upon her fancy'.

However, in 1808 the inhabitants of no. 27 Keppel Street began to receive regular calls from a young barrister in his early thirties, Thomas Anthony Trollope. He did not have far to walk for he lived a few doors down, at no. 16 in the same street. The Miltons may have got to know him as a neighbour; or perhaps their stepmother, Mrs Milton, arranged the meeting, for Thomas Partington, a close relation of hers – possibly her brother – had married Thomas Anthony's sister Penelope. The young lawyer and Henry Milton had much in common. Thomas Anthony, too, was the son of a country parson, the Revd Anthony Trollope; he also had grown up without a mother (she had died when her son was in his early teens); and he could commiserate with Henry on having no brother, only sisters – he had three of them, Penelope, Diana and Isabella. Like William Milton, Thomas Anthony had gone to Winchester followed by New College (via St John's, Cambridge); but, instead of entering the Church, he studied law at the Middle Temple and was called to the bar in May 1804. He is described in the *Law Lists* as a 'conveyancer and equity draftsman'; as a Chancery lawyer he would have been well-versed in laws dealing with land, estates and inheritance. Law was something of a family tradition: his grandfather, Sir Thomas Trollope, the fourth baronet of Casewick, Lincolnshire, had also been a 'notable Middle Templar' and, curiously, his father, Anthony, although ordained since 1761, was admitted at the Middle Temple in 1784.

We do not know much about Thomas Anthony's father, the Revd Anthony Trollope, except that, as the youngest son of a baronet, he had to earn his keep. After leaving Pembroke College, Cambridge, he became the rector of Cottered, Hertfordshire, and in 1770 the vicar of nearby Rushden, where his wife Penelope Meetkerke's father was the local squire. The Meetkerkes, descendants of the Flemish ambassador to the court of Elizabeth I, lived in the beautiful seventeenth-century manor, Julians, where as children Thomas Anthony and his sisters spent much time. The Revd Anthony Trollope also served as chaplain to Charlotte, Duchess of Somerset, until his death in 1806. He would seem to have been a quiet, reserved person, for in his will the dying man requested that he 'be buried in as private a manner as may be consistent with decorum'. His father's death had left Thomas Anthony with a small income, which meant that the barrister could begin to think of marrying.[4]

There is no portrait or even verbal description of Thomas Anthony Trollope. His son Tom, who had fair skin and blond or light brown hair, is supposed to have taken after him. His three sons, Tom, Anthony and Henry were rather stocky in build, probably like their father, who, according to his oldest son, had a 'remarkably powerful frame' (he had once leapt from his carriage to stop a runaway horse from going over a precipice). Perhaps like Tom, Thomas Anthony did not go bald but had a rather distinguished receding hairline. He was almost certainly clean-shaven, as were most men in England up until the late 1830s. The fashion for beards and moustaches began on the Continent, as Fanny documents in her two travel books *Belgium and Western Germany in 1833* and *Paris and the Parisians* in 1835, and she makes it very clear that she did not like it. In Germany she describes a 'most hideous' sight, a man whose face was 'literally covered with hair' except for about one square inch below the eyes: 'In dancing he waved his beard, his favoris, and his moustaches, as if to fan his partner: and what made this profusion of hair the more comic, was the fact that, spite of careful combing, he was very nearly bald.'

Fanny's young heroes are, predictably, slight of frame with big expressive eyes and rich brown curls. Her more mature male protagonists usually have, like Colonel Hubert in *The Widow Barnaby*, fine teeth, a solid athletic build, clean-shaven skin, of course, and a 'noble expression of his forehead, from which, however, the hair had already somewhat retired, though it still clustered in close brown curls round his well-turned head'. If this is a fondly remembered portrait of Thomas Anthony in his prime, perhaps we can pick out his face from among the lawyers in George Hayter's painting, 'The Trial of William Lord Russell', for which he sat in 1824.

No doubt, when Thomas Anthony first entered the Milton's drawing-room, after greeting the ladies, he and Henry 'conversed together for a few minutes on the ordinary topics of Russia, the harvest, the slave-trade, and reform' (*The Vicar of Wrexhill*). However, it was probably not long before Fanny joined in the discussion, and the rather serious-minded Trollope found himself attracted to Henry's lively and intelligent sister. By July 1808 Thomas Anthony was sending Fanny a copy of Crowe's verses and a few Latin odes for Henry to translate. 'Now it almost invariably happens, that when a young gentleman begins lending books to a young lady, something more or less approaching to a flirtation between them is the consequence' (*Fashionable Life*). For the next six months servants were constantly going back and forth between nos. 16 and 27 Keppel Street with Miss Edgeworth's novels and the latest issue of *The Edinburgh Review*. Umbrellas also drifted between the two residences and their ownership became a matter of friendly contention. In September

Thomas Anthony wrote to Fanny from his chambers in Lincoln's Inn:

My dear Madam,

As your brother will probably have left Keppel Street before my servant is able to get there with the umbrella he was so good as to lend me last night, I take the liberty of addressing this note to you expressing my best thanks for the loan of it. At the same time I really hope you will indulge one in the request that it may henceforth be safely deposited in your house, since experience has shown that they are very apt to ramble from mine – I shall have left town before this reaches you, & if you should inhospitably persist in setting your doors against this poor unoffending supplicant, it will not be in my power to afford him any further shelter, altho' so much gratitude is due from me for his protection from the pitiless storm last night; but he will fall into some more charitable hands, where some snug corner no doubt will spontaneously be allotted for his reception – Altho' the stern unrelenting heart of your brother may be inexorable, permit me on the behalf of my trembling client now at your doors, to indulge better hopes from the clemency of the female disposition – In full expectation of this my humble request being complied with I shall consider myself as ever bound to pray &c &c I am my dear Madam with my best respects to your sister whom I hope to enlist as an advocate in my cause, your most true & very humble ser. *Tho: Anth: Trollope*

Fanny scribbled at the bottom of the same piece of paper:

My Dear Sir,

I am afraid you have applied to a very bad pleader for *all my eloquence* has proved vain – Henry still feels it *impossible* to accept your umbrella, and therefore like an honest counsel I really advise you to give up the cause. To *you* I will confess that I think he sees this matter in a right point of view, for whenever said umbrella met his sight I think it would give him a disagreeable sort of sensation – But as I was engaged on the other side, you may be sure I did not trust this to *him*. – He desires me to say that he wishes you would prove you forgive him so pertinaciously insisting on having his own way, by giving him the pleasure of your company at Dinner on Friday.[5]

'There is nothing more difficult to trace with a skilful hand than the process by which a young man and maiden often *creep* into love, without either of them being at all aware at what moment they were first seized with the symptoms' (*The Vicar of Wrexhill*), and so it was with Fanny and Thomas Anthony. But their courtship progressed apace, and in a letter dated 1 November 1808 the barrister, in his rather stiff yet charming manner, proposed to Fanny: 'In the course of the last Spring I was not little delighted with the subject a certain debating society had chosen for their weekly discussion, which to the best recollection was in the words, or the effect following. "Is it most expedient for a man to make an avowal of his attachment to a lady viva voce . . . in a tête-à-tête, or by epistolary correspondence?" ' Fanny had apparently in some previous conversation stated her preference for the latter, and so he pleads with his pen that 'my future happiness on earth is at your disposal . . . If indeed, as I trust is the case you are not entirely unaware that my chief delight has long since had its source in your society & conversation; and if, permit my vanity to indulge the hope, there has been the slightest degree of mutuality in this delight, then perhaps – I confess I scarcely know what I was going to say, but perhaps you would not require *three* weeks for passing a sentence on which I must so anxiously depend.'

Thomas Anthony thought that they should enter into 'that most important of all human transactions, matrimony' (*The Blue Belles*) with their eyes open, and in this same letter he set forth his financial position: 'There is no one perhaps that has a greater contempt for those who are induced to contract alliances upon motives of a pecuniary nature than I have; but at the same time I have had experience enough to teach me that happiness is not to be expected where the parties are no longer capable of enjoying those necessaries & comforts of life to which they have been accustomed, and which are commonly incident to the rank & situation they hold in society.' He then goes on to explain that his annual income is about £900 per annum, including his Oxford fellowship, worth £200; this, however, would cease 'should I no longer be deemed a fit member of that society', that is, if he were to get married.

Fanny had probably guessed the contents of the letter. Perhaps, as with Martha Maxwell in *Jessie Phillips*, on the occasion of their last meeting 'the final shake of the hand concluded with so gentle yet so firm a pressure, that it was quite impossible the young lady could have gone to sleep that night without confessing, in strict confidence, to her own heart that she *did* think' the serious young lawyer 'Henry Mortimer was a little in love with her'. When it first arrived Fanny no doubt 'fell into that most remarkable practice, equally general and incomprehensible, of studying the outside of the epistle in order to guess vaguely concerning what [she] had both the right and the power to learn perfectly, if [she] would only have been pleased to break the seal' (*Charles Chesterfield*). In any case, Fanny did not need three weeks to think over the proposal; she replied to Thomas Anthony the very next day with equal frankness: 'The letter you left with me last night was most flattering and gratifying to me. – I value your good opinion too highly not to feel that the generous proof you have given me of it must, for ever and in any event, be remembered with pride and gratitude. – But I fear you are not sufficiently aware that your choice, so flattering to me, is for yourself a very imprudent one – You have every right in an alliance of this kind to expect a fortune greatly superior to any I shall ever possess.' She explains that she has only £50 yearly allowance from her father and £1,300 in stock, probably from the Gresley family. (She later learned from Mrs Milton, who 'settled all these things', that she was to receive no more than £1,200 stock and another £100 for clothes.) 'I have to thank you for choosing that manner of addressing me, which I once so vaguely said I thought the best, but I have more than once since I began writing this, wished I had not said so. – I have not, nor can I, express myself quite as I wish. – There is something of cold formality in what I have written, which is very foreign to what I feel, – but I know not how to mend it.'

It may be that, as they were both 'gently-born', 'many were the warnings and the scornings, the jokes, and the gibes, which the wedding called forth from the better-off-in-the-world relatives on both sides'. 'But at thirty, when people are really in earnest, they generally do what they like in such matters' (*The Blue Belles*). Thomas Anthony probably allowed himself to calculate that by the time their household had grown too large for his modest income of £700 per annum he would have inherited the Hertfordshire estate of Julians belonging to his uncle Adolphus Meetkerke, an elderly gentleman with no children. Presumably, as in 'the natural course of London love-making', 'the "Morning Post" and the "Court Journal" announced the approaching happiness of both pair; young ladies tittered as they saw them pass, and young gentlemen raised their lorgnettes, whether near-sighted or not, in order to pronounce judgement on the choosers and the chosen' (*The Blue Belles*). The forth-coming marriage, planned for May of the following year, 1809, meant that the Milton family circle at 27 Keppel Street was to be broken up and the house sold. Henry found new bachelor lodgings and Fanny and her sister returned to the Heckfield vicarage to prepare for the wedding. It was early December 'when the lovers parted, to live in the interval upon hope, and upon the sweet relief afforded by the general post' (*The Refugee*).

Fanny found life at the vicarage, compared to 'London gaiety', fairly dull. She writes to her betrothed that, besides country walks in Lord Rivers's park, she occupies herself chiefly by reading Dante and hemming sheets alternately. In response to Thomas Anthony's protest that she should not strain her eyes, she comments: 'What else would you have me do? I must read and hem.' Nevertheless, she seems to have found it difficult to find a quiet moment in which to write.

> The most disagreeable of created beings (by name, Col. Addin-brook) . . . is while I am writing talking in an animated strain of eloquence to Mrs Milton, frequently seasoning his discourse with the polished phrase of 'blood and thunder ma'am' – for a time, I *genteelly* laid aside my pen, but his horrible staring eyes, and his polite speeches so insufferably annoyed me, that I have resumed it on purpose to be rude; so if I happen to *swear* a little,

before I conclude, be so good as to believe that I am accidentally writing down what he is saying.

In *Jessie Phillips* Fanny has Mr Dalton chiding his daughters that, if they persist in chattering in the same room while he is composing an important letter, 'I shall be sure to write, "Caroline says this," and "Charlotte says that." ' On another occasion, Fanny remarks: 'Pardon me if my style seems somewhat incoherent, and know, for my excuse that Mrs Milton is giving a French lesson to the little Miss Jacksons', the local doctor's children, 'and my ears are ringing with "Je suis, tu es" etc.'

No doubt, Fanny eagerly looked out for the postman, who might have 'stopped at the gate, and held up a letter, in token that the person whose face he saw peeping out of the window above the porch, should come down and take it, without his having the trouble of descending from his donkey' (*Charles Chesterfield*). Otherwise, the bride-to-be passed the time by indulging each morning in 'a little of the *Grosvenor* discipline', that is a thorough massage by Mrs Milton's housemaid, who handled Fanny's rheumatic shoulders 'as she would a piece of furniture that greatly wanted polishing'. She probably did not get out very much, since most of the neighbours were away and even her walks were curtailed at one point when a performing bear escaped from its owner and terrorized the area. On one occasion, however, she left Heckfield to see the prisoners of war at Odiham (near Reading) perform a Molière play. This was still the period of the Napoleonic Wars.

There was, however, plenty of local gossip to occupy her mind when she was not reading Dante or writing letters. In the same year that Fanny and Thomas Anthony were engaged, Sir Arthur Paget ran away with Lord Boringdon's wife, and the infamous pair took a house in Heckfield. Lady Boringdon obtained a divorce and she and Paget were married in February 1809, six weeks before their child was born. To her great amusement, Fanny discovered that their neighbour at Heckfield Place, the MP, Mr Shaw-Lefevre, had tried to wrangle an introduction to the 'great' Sir Arthur Paget through the 'blood and thunder' colonel, a friend of the Paget family; he offered to conduct some parliamentary business on the adulterer's behalf.

Referring to the seemingly 'moral family man' Shaw-Lefevre, Fanny comments that this anecdote 'shows exactly what he is'. Her evident dislike of the MP may have stemmed from the fact that, with the money inherited from his wife's tradesman father, Shaw-Lefevre was determined to become the biggest landowner in the area. Fanny perhaps had him in mind when she observed in her novel *Jessie Phillips* that Mr Baxter the brewer, 'though daily becoming a more important personage, from various purchases of lands recently made in the neighbourhood, was as yet only in a sort of transition state between the tradesman and the country gentleman'. (Fanny reports with great glee that the escaped bear devoured three of Shaw-Lefevre's dogs.)

Back in London Thomas Anthony was left to oversee the refurbishing of his Keppel Street house to make it a fit residence for his bride. It is easy to imagine Trollope's house resembling that of the forty-year-old bachelor Mr Knowles in Fanny's early novel *Tremordyn Cliff*. The interior was in

no way womanlike. The curtains of rich and heavy damask, with serviceable blinds beneath them, were mixed with no transparent drapery, contrasting its snow-white delicacy with their massy crimson. The carpet showed no pale pigeon-wing tints, but sunk deep and soft beneath the feet, in all the dark-eyed splendour of an eastern loom; chairs formed for every possible variety of lounge, stood temptingly in all directions. There were, however, neither footstools nor mirrors – but over the chimney piece, and the doors, and, in short, wherever books were not, hung some precious gem of art, guarded with a miser's care, by curtains that went and came again by the touch of a spring (*Tremordyn Cliff*).

Thomas Anthony moved into his chambers in Lincoln's Inn and walked to and from Keppel Street in order to oversee everything: moving furniture, arranging for grates to be put in the fireplaces, ordering new carpets, shopping for mirrors in the Strand and, of course, selecting new blinds and curtains (this last task proved too much for the barrister and he left it entirely to the discretion of the draper). Most of his time, however, was spent chasing up the agent,

Mr Melville, who was supposed to be supervising the work. Thomas Anthony even had charge of the wedding cake: pieces of cake were to be distributed among friends in London and elsewhere who did not attend the wedding. The barrister insisted on ordering a second cake, which Fanny thought unnecessary, and she pleaded, '*Pray* order no more cakes.' The prospective groom was clearly overwhelmed by the business. He writes that, even after nine separate visits to the baker's in two days, 'there is yet some difficulty in respect to distributing this important cake'.

Thomas Anthony sorely missed Fanny's company – and her advice on practical matters. However, he saw quite a lot of Henry Milton – except on Sunday, which, he informs Fanny, was Henry's 'courting day'. Fanny's brother was apparently quite a flirt. In February the barrister reported that Henry had received two valentines

from *different quarters* (mark how extensive his gallantry must be) . . . but he nevertheless tells me that every thing is regular & in due form. So I submit to his greater experience & consequently better judgement in these weighty affairs, never myself having had the good fortune of receiving one before; no, not even from Betty Chapyre. In fact till I was informed by you I was so totally ignorant of subjects of this kind that I did not even know that a valentine was *a letter upon business* till I was informed so by you – The promise however every valentine virtually carries within itself I certainly shall not forget – viz – *three kisses at the first subsequent meeting of the parties* – and any attempt to evade this promise, as I am told upon the best authority, always operates to double the effect of it. – & so *toties quoties* – I know you like a little Latin.

Thomas Anthony describes an evening the two bachelors spent at the Putney home of 'the fair Miss Hutchinsons. If [Henry's] heart should be wandering he must take care of it. They are very lively, very sensible, & well informed, but I believe you have seen them or some of them, being 7 in number.' By all accounts, Henry was charming; he was also somewhat impetuous. In early April he writes to Fanny that he 'has *entirely* given up flirting'. Within a month

Thomas Anthony writes that 'Harry is heartily tired of Putney . . . but this is a *great secret.*' Perhaps Henry had found himself in danger of being ensnared by a young woman not unlike Isabella Thorpe, the heartless flirt in Jane Austen's *Northanger Abbey*, who also lives in Putney. No doubt wary of Henry's bad influence, Fanny appeals to her fiancé apropos a forthcoming London ball: 'Do not, *if you can help it*, fall in love with Miss Foote.'*

Besides reports of her brother, Thomas Anthony writes to Fanny on more esoteric matters, such as the latest issue of *The Edinburgh Review*, containing articles on Burns's poetry, Watt's steam engine, the emancipation of slaves in South America and the dilemma facing the West Indian planters since the official abolition of the slave trade the previous year. He is clearly opposed to slavery, but takes the practical view that all proposed remedies 'tend in fact to increase the evil'. 'The truth is the evil can only cure itself, & if left to itself it will effectually do it tho' undoubtedly many must fall.' Thomas Anthony also mentions the new periodical lately proposed, *The Quarterly Review* – the result, he has heard, of a quarrel among the editors of *The Edinburgh Review*. The barrister is 'sorry to see these talents divided & to give 10d. for what we have given only 5d. for'. The engaged couple come down on opposite sides on the authenticity of the poems supposedly written by a fifteenth-century poet, Thomas Rowley. Thomas Anthony is convinced that they are the work of the young Bristol poet, Thomas Chatterton: Fanny, on the other hand, replies that 'your powers of believing must greatly exceed mine if you can subscribe to the doctrine of those who assert that the ballad of Charity was written by an uneducated boy under seventeen years of age'. The barrister struggles with an Italian sonnet which Fanny has sent him, assuming that a good knowledge of Latin is enough to be able to read Italian. When he pleads that he can make neither head nor tail of it, she acknowledges temporary defeat but adds '*you positively must read Dante*'. (Fanny's letters to Thomas Anthony are dotted with Italian terms of endearment, *amico mio* and the like.)

There were the usual discussions between the prospective groom

---

* This Miss Foote may be one of the London banker John Foote's five daughters, mentioned by Jane Austen in her correspondence.

and father-in-law about money before drawing up the marriage settlement, wherein the barrister settled £6,000, which amount was at that time invested in property in and around the Bloomsbury area, on Fanny and any children.[6] After one of these meetings, Thomas Anthony writes to Fanny that he has discovered from her father that 'you are entitled to a property which you have hitherto omitted to mention to me – Indeed I apprehend that you meant to reserve it snugly for a little secret pin-money – I mean 1/8 of the patent coach, which Mr Milton tells me he has made over to you. Pray are you to bear the same proportion in the expenses of it?' 'And so you have found me out!' Fanny replies in her next letter. 'I did hope that *my share* of the patent coach would have supplied all my little private extravagances and you have been never the wiser.' Fanny, who had endured an 'eight miles jumble in the *patent cart*' *en route* to Heckfield in preparation for the wedding, confessed that she was looking forward to the time when she shall 'drive a few patent coaches of my own'. The 'patent coach' was the indefatigable William Milton's latest invention, intended to make road travel safer. Shortly after his return to Heckfield the clergyman had begun to be alarmed at the number of road accidents he witnessed: 'I know of 9 accidents that happened, in the course of a fortnight . . . within 20 miles of my own house.'*

William realized that coaches overturned so easily for two reasons. Firstly, they were top-heavy, with the luggage rack invariably at the top or high on the back of the vehicle. Secondly, a coach had no way of keeping its balance if a wheel came off while travelling at speed. His remedies were, as always, ingenious. He proposed placing the luggage box below the axle to lower the coach's centre of gravity and fitting small 'idle wheels' below to 'catch' the falling vehicle in the event of losing one of the primary wheels. With his usual thoroughness, William states that he first built a small model indoors, and then fitted up a small cart 'and repeatedly took off the wheel, while a horse was drawing it at a pretty good rate, and two or three persons in the carriage': 'Gentlemen in the neighbourhood . . . and even ladies trusted themselves and their children' to take part in the

---

* William Milton, *The Danger of Travelling in Stage-coaches; and a Remedy Proposed to the Consideration of the Public*, London, 1810.

tests. One wonders if Fanny and her sister were obliged to act as early guinea-pigs. In 1805 William obtained a patent and the next year a commercial coach was built for Messrs Edwards and Moody in Reading. William organized several trials in London in early 1807 to advertise his coach.

However, there was one objection to the 'patent coach' which its inventor had to admit could not 'possibly be avoided or palliated. It is, in short, that the look of the Coach is so very clumsy and so very ugly' – and, more seriously, the low centre of gravity made it more difficult for the horses to pull. Nevertheless, William tirelessly promoted his invention. A month before his daughter's wedding, the clergyman was busy gathering signatures for a petition to submit to Parliament, asking that his designs be made mandatory on all coaches (the government was at that time drafting legislation concerning road safety). A model of the 'patent coach' was displayed in one of the committee rooms in the House of Commons for six weeks, and in 1810 William Milton published a pamphlet entitled *The Danger of Travelling in Stage-coaches; and a Remedy Proposed to the Consideration of the Public.* Although Milton's coach had its supporters, from coachmen in Reading to bookkeepers at the Gloucester Coffee-House in Piccadilly, the invention never really took off and Fanny did not receive her pin money.

'Every body who knows any thing about young ladies who are in love must be aware that at all times when the dear object of the passions is not to be got at, the next best thing is to get hold of his sister. Oh! there are so many nice little words and phrases, which may be dropped, that if the sister *should* repeat, might make him hit upon so many amiable inferences about them, in so many different ways!' (*Jessie Phillips*). When Fanny and Thomas Anthony became engaged she duly began to correspond with his sisters, Penelope and Diana. 'Die' had married the Revd Henry Trollope, her first cousin and brother of the fifth and sixth baronets of Casewick; Penelope's husband, Thomas Partington of Offham, Sussex, was, if not a brother, then certainly a close relation of Fanny's stepmother. The fact that there was already a strong connection between the two families through Mrs Milton had no doubt helped to break the ice. Thomas Anthony wrote to Fanny that Penelope's little girls, Catherine and

Anne, 'were much pleased with their aunt Milton's letters, but that the one to Catherine was the most admired, as it contained the great news of my intended marriage with one of the Miss Miltons, & that they all expressed their happiness at the hopes of having another aunt'.

Indeed, one gets the impression that Trollope's sisters were delighted, and not a little relieved, that their sober, somewhat shy brother was finally getting married, and to such an affable and suitable woman. Certainly, Die knew her brother's good and bad points. Fanny informs her fiance that she has received another letter from Die: 'You would approve this perhaps better than the last, for this time she *abuses* you – She speaks of *flattering*, and says, "My brother always contends against it, in any garb & I always tell him he can use it in a neat style as well as others, & perhaps he renders it still more forcible by the half concealment." I shall certainly endeavour to profit by this hint, and do all I can to be on my guard against your *sly ways.*' Fanny had already been made aware of Thomas Anthony's views on this matter in, of all places, his letter of proposal, when he declared that compliments 'were always my detestation – fit tools only for knaves, & to be employed against fools'.

Fanny clearly believed that this uncompromising attitude was a sign of integrity; a more objective observer might see it as a mark of intolerance. Thomas Anthony's letters display a certain awkward but endearing charm and wit; however, they also reveal a dark side to the man. Fanny's daughter-in-law and biographer, Frances Eleanor Trollope, observed that the barrister often misplaced and even omitted words: 'It is as if the stream of his mind, though clear in itself, were constantly fretted by little rocks and boulders in the course.' Besides his refusal to pay a compliment, he is solicitous of Fanny's health to the point of being overbearing (he himself was given to incapacitating headaches, probably chronic migraine); he insists that she send him frequent health bulletins and is angry when she does not. 'This sort of petty persecution was greatly more tormenting in action than it is possible any description can make intelligible,' Fanny later observed in *Town and Country*. When Fanny tries to fend off his accusation of neglecting to write by explaining that she did not want to trouble him with her letters, Thomas Anthony twists her argument as if he were cross-examining a witness for the defence: 'Now my dear Fanny, I think *you* will *confess* that my accusation, if that indeed which was merely a conjecture can be called an accusation, was not unjust, & that you yourself have already admitted it to be true.' Fanny's next letter begins, with no other introduction,

> I know you lawyers with ease
> Twist words and meaning as you please.

'None but a lawyer could have twisted my words so much against me'; 'you and your logic are too hard for me – but I must keep it till we meet for like the rest of my sex my *tongue* is more agile than my *pen*'.

In answer to Fanny's insistence that her fiancé had shown real anger with her for not writing, he replies: 'I trust my dear Fanny will soon learn that I cannot either write or speak to her in anger, & that any impressions of the nature of those quoted by her in her last letter must be used by me in irony.' However, irony can be a hidden, and thus more hurtful and damaging, form of anger. Fanny wanted to believe Thomas Anthony, and promised that 'I will not in future so easily *take fright* and fancy you are angry with me. – In truth the idea did not make me feel particularly comfortable and therefore it will be very contrary to my usual *mental politics* to encourage it again.' Nevertheless, there were still doubts – prompted by glimpses of her fiancé's intractable manner or perhaps simply pre-nuptial jitters – which caused Fanny to write: 'It is a solemn business my dear friend – does not the near approach of it almost frighten you? I tremble lest you should love me less a twelvemonth hence than you do now – I sometimes fear that you may be disappointed in me, that you will find me less informed, less capable of being a companion to you, than you expect, and then – but I am growing very dismal – this will never do – I must go and sun myself upon the heath.' Thomas Anthony wonders where these doubts have come from:

> Perhaps they have arisen from the cold & phlegmatic manner
> of telling you how anxious I always am of knowing you are well

& particularly of receiving that intelligence from yourself, but my dearest love, are you still to learn my character & sentiments? Still to be made acquainted with my lifeless manners, my stone-like disposition? Are you still to be informed in what detestation I hold all ardent professions & in what admiration actions that want not the aid of declamation but boldly speak for themselves?

Perhaps another woman would have taken fright (or flight) when her fiancé expressed such sentiments, but one feels that Fanny appreciated the fact that Thomas Anthony, rather than blandly reassuring her with pretty words, was prepared to take her doubts seriously. She replies with her characteristic feeling and candour:

What you say of professions is very just, nay I think it is great and noble – but yet one cannot help being pleased, (at least women I believe cannot) with *expressions*, as well as *proofs*, of tenderness from those they love – vehement professions I think I detest as much as you can – indeed vehemence tho' it may express passion can never express tenderness, which is the only affection I could ever wish to inspire – but I own my heart welcomes a look or a word of fondness from those who are dear to me as cordially as it does more unequivocal proofs of attachment. – Do not mistake me however, I entreat you, and fancy I wish to have 'Soft nothings whispered in my ear'. I think I never could have loved a man who gave me reason to suppose he thought me a fool – As to your honor, you may call yourself by what names you please, but were I in a humour to abuse you, I would say that you were a deep politician and that you knew how to make words of value – You are certainly right – the quietest expression of *good will* as you manage, goes deeper than whole volumes of love from other people.

The personalities which peer through these letters might put one in mind of Elizabeth Bennet and Mr Darcy in *Pride and Prejudice.* Elizabeth and Fanny both had grandfathers who had been in trade, a social disadvantage. Like Fanny, Elizabeth 'had a lively, playful disposition, which delighted in any thing ridiculous'. She also had

Fanny's exuberance and strength: 'Elizabeth was not formed for ill-humour; and though every prospect of her own was destroyed for the evening, it could not dwell long on her spirits.' Darcy and Thomas Anthony came from aristocratic families; both were men of few words, rather shy and prone to intolerance. One feels that, like Darcy, the earnest barrister 'had yet to learn to be laughed at'. Nevertheless, opposites attract, and Thomas Anthony clearly loved Fanny for the same reason Darcy admired Elizabeth, the 'liveliness' of her mind. These parallels between the real and fictional characters are not so surprising. There were, no doubt, many men and women like Fanny and Thomas Anthony in this period, with the same attitudes, preoccupations and expectations. Jane Austen was drawing on the small world which she and Fanny inhabited.*

A more direct connection can be made between the Trollopes and another famous literary couple. In 1869, sixty years after they were written, Fanny's son Anthony read his parents' love letters for the first time. 'In no novel of Richardson's or Miss Burney's have I seen a correspondence at the same time so sweet, so graceful, and so well expressed.' In his autobiography Anthony marvels at how unlike they are to the love-letters of his day: the language 'beautifully chosen, and fit, without change of a syllable, for the most critical eye'. Nevertheless, he adds, Fanny indulges in a little slang and writes to the young barrister in, what seemed to him, bold familiarity. There is certainly something of his mother in Glencora Palliser, whom Anthony first introduces in *The Small House at Allington*, published 1862–4, around the time of Fanny's death. Although Glencora has the advantage over Fanny in being rich and well-born, in every other way they are very alike: both women are candid, sometimes sarcastic, always witty, with a touch of romanticism.

And Plantagenet Palliser, Glencora's husband, has much in common with Thomas Anthony Trollope. Palliser, like Fanny's husband, is gravely earnest, often unmoveable in his convictions, and always hard-working. When a Member of Parliament, wrote

---

* Two of the signatories supporting Milton's 'patent coach', Mr Henry Marsh and Thomas Powys of Hardwick House, Oxon., appear in Jane Austen's letters, showing once again how much their worlds intersected.

Anthony, Palliser 'devoted himself to work with the grinding energy of a young penniless barrister labouring for a penniless wife'. Both men particularly dislike rhetoric: Palliser 'was very careful in his language, labouring night and day to learn to express himself with accuracy, with no needless repetition of words'. Like Thomas Anthony, Palliser loved Glencora 'with all his heart, but with a heart that was never demonstrative'. Yet, despite their differences, Glencora and Plantagenet enjoy a relatively happy marriage. Fanny and Thomas Anthony's life together was to be very different.

As the day of the wedding drew near, the couple's good humour seemed to return, although their maladies increased. Thomas Anthony, who endured a long spell of migraine, followed by an eye infection, hoped that Fanny 'may not have a blind husband – unless indeed you were to prefer it'. Fanny had been suffering from terrible toothache, and just a few days before the nuptials her gum had to be lanced to make room for a new tooth: 'If I go on at this rate,' she warns her fiancé, 'I shall be a perfect *shark* – I would seriously advise you to take the opinion of the learned before you proceed any further – imagine the extreme unpleasantness of finding you unexpectedly bitten in two!' But the couple recovered from their respective illnesses and the wedding took place on 23 May 1809, Thomas Anthony's thirty-fifth birthday, in the early Tudor church of Heckfield, a stone's throw from the vicarage. The pathway leading to the church door would have been strewn with flowers, as was the tradition. William Milton preferred to act as father rather than clergyman, and he gave the bride away. We can only hope that there was enough cake to distribute among those friends and family who did not attend the ceremony.

In *The Life and Adventures of a Clever Woman* Fanny's thirty-year-old heroine Charlotte Morris writes in her diary on the eve of her marriage, 'unless my life be prematurely cut short, my history does not end here, although the event which usually concludes the history of a woman may be said to be reached'.

CHAPTER THREE

The Mother's Manual

'I wonder whether you ever think of the old days when we used to be so happy in Keppel Street?' muses the middle-aged Mrs Furnival, feeling neglected by her husband, a successful barrister in *Orley Farm*. Anthony Trollope's depiction of the Furnivals' first poverty-stricken, but contented, years in Keppel Street closely mirrors his parents' early life together: the hopes and dreams expressed by the young couple while strolling arm in arm around Russell, Bedford and Bloomsbury Squares; Mr Furnival's 'dingy' chambers in the Old Square of Lincoln's Inn; the greatcoats, thick shawls and double gloves deposited in the hallway when the barrister came back 'cold and weary from the circuits'. Fanny had also thought her husband's chambers 'dingy': in *Uncle Walter* she describes a 'small dingy room' in Middle Temple, 'reached by hard climbing up three flights of dark, steep, dirty stairs', with a view of 'the preciously quiet, but very dingy garden'. Thomas Anthony, like Thomas Furnival, was attached to the home circuit in Hertfordshire and was often on the road for up to nine weeks at a time. It might have been from her husband that Fanny heard the story concerning the open and shut case of a husband who had murdered his erring wife. To the judge's dismay, 'the foreman and jury returned with the verdict "Guilty – but sarved her right, my lord" ' (*Paris and the Parisians*).

During Thomas Anthony's long absences, Fanny paid visits to the Meetkerkes at Julians and her father in Heckfield, from where she wrote loving letters to her '*Antonio mio*' and '*sposo mio*'.* She invariably gives a description of all her little aches and pains: 'You see how implicitly I believe that all the little details respecting my health are interesting to you', but adds that his reply will be 'the best medicine I can take'. Within a year of her marriage she had a second set of health bulletins to include, those of little Thomas Adolphus, born in April 1810. 'A baby in such a household is apt to make things go sweetly,' Anthony Trollope says of the Trevelyans in *He Knew He Was Right*, and so it was in the Trollope household. Thomas Anthony was devoted to young Tom and grieved to be away from him: 'give him a kiss for me every morning & tell him his papa sends it to him', he bade Fanny.

The young mother was besotted with the baby:

I complied with your *hard* command, and delivered your kiss to the boy, and then told him to kiss your letter in return, and the dear creature held it to his ruby lips, as if he understood me. I do not seriously mean to say he was *quite* equal to this but it is really wonderful, how greatly his intelligence increases from day to day – My father is perfectly delighted with him, and every day after dinner plays some new trick to try his sagacity. Yesterday he put two glasses, the one empty, and the other full, before him – The latter the young tippler eyed with perfect indifference, the former he tried all his little powers to get possession of, and at last drew it to his mouth – the experiment was frequently repeated. – Were I not *too wise* to be vain, I should certainly become so here – every body exclaims that my darling is the loveliest creature they ever beheld, and most add (now pray endeavor to be as wise as I) that he is very like his father – I screw my features into all possible forms, that I may not look as delighted as I feel.

No doubt like Juliet's companions in *The Abbess*, Fanny's friends and

---

* Jane Austen disliked Italianate terms of endearment. In *Emma* the heroine derides Mrs Elton, formerly Miss Hawkins, daughter of a rich Bristol merchant, as 'a little upstart, vulgar being, with her Mr E., and her *caro sposo*'.

family 'wearied not' – or tried to appear to weary not – 'of listening to her discoveries of [her baby's] talents, and most cordially agreed in opinion, that her little Ferdinand promised to be quite as lovely' as any other infant.

Fanny was utterly happy and fulfilled as a mother. No woman who has just given birth, wrote Fanny in *One Fault,* ever 'awakens from her first sleep, after such an event, without feeling for the moment almost astounded at the change that has come over her'. 'In these first hours of maternity everything,' if the mother and child are both in good health, 'appears *couleur de rose.*' Over the next eight years Fanny gave birth to six children, Henry (1811), Arthur (1812), Anthony (1815), Cecilia (1816) and Emily (1818). However, these early years were not without sadness: Thomas Anthony recorded in the family Bible that another child, their first daughter, Emily, only survived long enough to be privately baptized before she died that same day in 1813. However, Fanny was able to take consolation from the love and sympathy of her husband, who had sent her a present, perhaps a poem, while away at the assizes: 'Dearest, dearest Trollope,' she wrote soon after the sad event, 'how shall I thank you for the enclosure in your last letter? I know you sent it to soothe and solace me under all I have been suffering – and it was indeed a most healing balsam – God send you safe home to us and I shall feel nothing but gratitude for my fate.'[1]

In his autobiography, written at the age of seventy-seven, Tom Trollope records happy memories of the Keppel Street nursery. 'My mother's disposition,' he remarks, 'was of the most genial, cheerful, happy, *enjoué** nature imaginable. All our happiest hours were spent with her; and to any one of us a *tête-à-tête* with her was preferable to any other disposal of a holiday hour.' What probably most delighted the children was their mother's 'comic power of description or recitation. There was, moreover, a fund of fanciful invention . . . which seemed to defy the possibility of her ever being at a loss, when seeking the means of amusement, either for herself or for others' (*The Young Countess*). London amusements to which Fanny would have treated the children included Punch and Judy shows in Russell Square, a

---

* 'sprightly'.

visit to Mr Pidding, Confectioner, in nearby Store Street and, of course, the pantomime at Christmas. Fanny was an indulgent mother. From a very early age Tom and his younger brother Henry were allowed to roam the London streets on their own, from the coach house at the White Horse Cellar in Piccadilly, where they watched the Telegraphs, High Flyers, Magnets and Independents, to the docks in the East End 'with the outgoing ships bearing, tied to the shrouds, boards indicating their destinations'. Both Tom and Henry showed early signs of wanderlust.

Back at no. 16 Keppel Street, a 'highly trustworthy and responsible middle-aged woman', called simply Farmer, ruled the nursery. She was 'an austere and somewhat grim sort of body', and an Anabaptist to boot.

> Old Farmer is an Anabapt*ist*!
> When she is gone, she will not be missed![2]

If Fanny had ever heard Tom and the others recite this rhyme, she would certainly have scolded them. Yet one senses that, like the Stephenson children in *The Widow Married*, 'it was not part of the family discipline to deny the younger branches their fair share and participation in all the enjoyments of quizzing', that is of teasing or making fun. In fact, Fanny does not appear to have been much of a disciplinarian at all, and on a visit to Paris she is mystified as to how the French are able to keep their little ones from screaming (*Paris and the Parisians*).

Fanny certainly does not seem to have taken to heart the old English proverb that 'children should be seen and not heard'. When Dr George Frederick Nott, an old family friend and tutor to Princess Charlotte, asked the children, assembled in the drawing-room for inspection, whether they were good boys, Tom, as chief spokesman, answered in the negative and attributed this 'to the painful fact that our nurse was an Anabaptist'. The anecdote ascribed to the young Willoughby in *The Widow Barnaby* seems very like one of Tom's outbursts, fondly remembered by Fanny: 'It is a very, *very* shocking thing, mamma, that everything that is nice is called wrong, and everything that is nasty is called right.' One can easily imagine Fanny

allowing Tom and Henry into the drawing-room when her husband
– or Farmer – was not around, 'and for about half an hour the children
were as happy as their mother . . . could contrive to make them in a
fine drawing room, where every article was "TOUCH ME NOT" '
(*The Ward of Thorpe Combe*). Most shocking of all to Tom, writing
at the very end of Victoria's reign, was the memory of his mother
singing to them in the nursery an 'old world ditty' about an 'unfortunate Miss Bayly' and her seducer, 'a Captain bold of Halifax, who
dwelt in country quarters'.*

Fanny had the knack of making almost anything fun – even
learning. Tom recounts that, when he and a neighbour's daughter
were at a very young age, his mother tossed bone counters bearing
letters of the alphabet over the floor and held crawling races, awarding
prizes to whichever child brought the letter demanded first. She no
doubt made sure that the nursery, 'that receptacle of all litter' (*The
Widow Married*), was 'full of globes, slates, guitars, dumb bells,
dictionaries, embroidering-frames, and sundry other miscellanies
connected with an enlarged system of education' (*Michael Armstrong*).
She even enlisted her friends in the children's education. The young
Cecilia and Emily were later taught algebra by Captain Kater, also
known as 'Pendulum' Kater (he employed the pendulum in mapping
India), when they visited him and his wife in their Regent's Park
house.

However, to their father, whose great ambition was that his sons
should follow in his footsteps at Winchester and New College, education was a much more serious business. From the tender age of
six, Tom lay in front of the drawing-room sofa every morning before
breakfast, head in hands, his eyes fixed on the *Eton Latin Grammar*
given to him by his father. An account of the morning's studies would
be rendered every evening at five o'clock when Tom and Henry
trotted alongside their father on his way back to Keppel Street from
his chambers at Lincoln's Inn. During Latin lessons at home, Thomas
Anthony sat 'with his arm over the back of the pupil's chair, so that
his hand might be ready to inflict an instantaneous pull of the hair'

---

* Tom's brother Anthony also remembered this 'ditty', and refers to it in his novel
He Knew He Was Right.

at every blunder; 'the result being to the scholar a nervous state of expectancy, not judiciously calculated to increase intellectual receptivity'. Anthony Trollope remembers taking his place beside his father as he shaved at six o'clock each morning and repeating the rules from the *Latin Grammar* or the Greek alphabet. Anthony was 'obliged at these early lessons to hold my head inclined towards him, so that in the event of guilty fault, he might be able to pull my hair without stopping his razor or dropping his shaving brush. No father was ever more anxious for the education of his children, though I think none ever knew less how to go about the work' (*An Autobiography*).

Tom remarks that there was 'a strange sort of asceticism' about his father, which made 'enjoyment or any employment of the hours save work, distasteful and offensive to him'. Thus, if his students were seen to be 'idling', Thomas Anthony immediately set them to work, whether or not they had already completed that day's homework. Nor were lessons abandoned during the holidays. One Christmas William Milton sent them 'a strange folio Greek Grammar, printed in 1580', with 'a Caution given, to the two Lads there', Tom and Henry, 'not to think of going [home], for their next Holidays, in any Expectation of Pastime; as their sedulous Father would hold them close to this old Book'.[3] One wonders if the good-natured grandfather fully realized the misery his gift might have caused. On another occasion, when setting off for a tour of the West Country, with nine-year-old Tom on the carriage floor between his mother and father, the latter pulled out a copy of Virgil and intimated that the journey need not interrupt his son's studies. Tom conjures up another painful memory of his father: his reading aloud to the assembled family in the evening. 'There was not one individual of those who heard him who would not have escaped from doing so, at almost any cost. Of course it was our duty to conceal this extreme reluctance to endure what was to him a pleasure – a duty which I much fear was very imperfectly performed.' Even Richardson's *Sir Charles Grandison*, one of Jane Austen's favourite books, became loathsome to Tom when read aloud by his father over the course of one long winter.

We do not know whether Fanny enjoyed listening to her husband reading aloud – she once remarked that *Sir Charles Grandison* was a woman's book – but it must have been painful for her to see his harshness towards, and subsequent unpopularity with, the children. Fanny probably drew on the painful memories of watching her husband with their four sons, especially during their lessons, when she wrote of Sir Joseph Lexington's erratic behaviour towards his son in *The Three Cousins*. Sometimes he treated him with tyrannical harshness 'of so wanton a nature, as to suggest the idea of an absolute aversion'. Yet, at other times the young man's 'existence and his health' had seemed especially 'precious to his capricious father'. 'Never, however, at any time did he seem to wish for any demonstration of either gratitude or affection in return'. Fanny might also have been recalling her own sons' sufferings when she describes the childhood of Lady Augusta Arundel in *Tremordyn Cliff*, a 'childhood passed in one continuous series of irksome discipline' – 'Words of caution, forbiddance, and restraint, were the only ones addressed to her.' On one – and probably not the only – occasion, Fanny interceded on her children's behalf: that copy of Virgil did not appear on the second day's journey to the West Country. 'It was reserved for the days when we were stationary,' Tom adds wryly in his memoirs.

Thankfully, not every evening was filled with the sound of Thomas Anthony's droning voice, reading aloud *Sir Charles Grandison* or some other volume. Fanny was devoted to her family, but family life was never enough for her. She continued to thrive on the society of other people. At the beginning of the nineteenth century, a woman's social life usually centred on the ritual of morning calls. However, Fanny found these 'incessant, time-consuming' and generally stifling (*Vienna and the Austrians*). For the whole of the 'morning', which lasted until the 'three o'clock *sortie* for shopping' (*The Widow Married*), a woman was kept prisoner in her own drawing-room 'in that pretty state of busy idleness which betokens readiness to be interrupted' (*The Blue Belles*). There are few things more tedious, Fanny writes, than 'a morning visit from a lady who sends her carriage to fetch her boys from school at Wimbledon, and comes to entertain you with friendly talk about her servants till it comes back' (*Paris and the Parisians*). She had better things to do with her time, and bemoaned the fact that a woman cannot 'devote her mornings to the study of Greek, Hebrew, Arabic, or algebra, – or even sedulously superintend the education of her children, – without necessarily sacrificing . . . fashionable engagements for it' (*Vienna and the Austrians*). And in any case, Fanny observed, 'morning visits rarely produce a meeting between the parties, as everybody goes out at the same time' (*The Life and Adventures of a Clever Woman*).

What Fanny liked best was to assemble friends and acquaintances together in the evenings: 'At Homes', she called them. To provide conversation and entertainment, morocco-bound volumes of albums and annuals, as well as engravings, were invariably scattered about on tables; a pianoforte or perhaps a harp may have stood in an adjoining room. Light refreshments would be provided, including ices and cakes. Although, as one wise friend told her, 'a large party kills such a prodigious number of birds, that it is the most extravagant thing in the world to have a small one', Fanny preferred the intimacy of smaller gatherings (*Paris and the Parisians*). She calls 'unfriendly' any hostess who, to gratify her own vanity as well as her ideas of economy, likes to see her friends densely packed together, struggling for standing room and half fainting in the process. As for dinner parties, 'the number must neither be less than the graces, nor more than the muses' (*The Blue Belles*). This form of entertainment, however, was deemed an extravagance in Keppel Street; and it was only on these rare occasions that Thomas Anthony, maintaining 'a nicely-regulated balance between generosity and economy' (*Charles Chesterfield*), placed a magnum of vintage port on the table after the ladies had retired to the drawing-room and the cloth had been removed. This was then followed, when the men had rejoined the ladies upstairs, by yet another luxury, coffee: 'the perfect coffee, as black and as dear as the Eastern eyes that best love to look upon it, but which even our colder natures welcome now' (*The Blue Belles*). Fanny's guests would have been invited to dine at five o'clock, 'allowing more time in the drawing-room, than at the eventually more fashionable hour, 8 o'clock, by which time people were starved' (*Paris and the Parisians*).

Certainly in later years, if not in this earlier period, Fanny grew to hate the formality thrust upon her by fashion. She ridicules the English custom in which 'every one who enters among a circle of friends' must hear 'his or her name pronounced from menial to menial with elaborate distinctness, as if to put all the world upon their guard, and protect them from a disagreeable surprise' (*Vienna and the Austrians*). Even more absurd was the 'pang' which an Englishwoman felt 'at her heart because she saw more footmen in her neighbour's hall than in her own' (*Paris and the Parisians*). In Fanny's novel *Charles Chesterfield* the heroine's aunt states that she will institute certain domestic economies, especially 'about our table', to 'enable us to keep a smart-looking footman, which I must own, I think in justice to myself, I ought never to be without'. This, indeed, was the attitude taken by the genteel folk of Fanny and Thomas Anthony's generation. Tom recounts that, although wax candles were deemed too expensive and only 'two tallow candles with their snuffer dish supplied the whole illumination of the evening', 'it would never have occurred to [my father] or to my mother that they could get on without a man-servant in livery'.

The guests who frequented the Trollopes' at-homes were a motley assortment. Fanny liked to refer to these gatherings, where one might come across poets, painters, philosophers, tragic actors, even a peer of the realm and 'that peer's elegant, eloquent, and much more illustrious banker', as '*soirées antithèstiques*'* (*Paris and the Parisians*). 'A great part of the enjoyment she found in society, arose from her taking considerably more than a common degree of interest in the characters and peculiarities of those with whom she associated' (*Fashionable Life*). Anthony remarks that, in this early period, his mother affected 'a somewhat liberal *rôle*', and welcomed 'would-be regicides' and 'patriot exiles' to the 'modest hospitality of her house'. 'With her,' he adds disapprovingly, 'politics were always an affair of the heart' (*An Autobiography*). Anthony, writing at the height of the Victorian era, makes it sound as though Fanny was a political dilettante who collected exiles as a child would stray puppies. But in Regency England the French Revolution was still a recent event, and the engine of democratic reform in England was being set in motion, fuelled by popular riots such as that at Peterloo. Whether the topic of conversation was slavery in the West Indies or Napoleon's march across Europe, every English person had his or her political opinion.

The Bristol in which Fanny grew up was home to many a radical

* 'antithetical soirées'.

amongst its merchants and intellectuals, and many of William Milton's friends and acquaintances espoused liberal – often radical – ideas. Even the sober-minded Thomas Anthony Trollope was considered a 'Liberal' in his day; Fanny pretends to be 'shocked at the seditious tone' of certain writings which the barrister commends in an early letter.[4] Perhaps Fanny was assigning her husband's opinions to Sir James Ridley in *The Blue Belles* when he exclaims to a female acquaintance, 'if you had ever been at Oxford, you would know what Tories were made of. D—d strait-laced, pragmatic puppies, who scruple not to interfere with the liberty of the subject, and the rights of a free-born Englishman, whenever their confounded discipline happens to be interfered with.'

Thus it was that the Trollopes welcomed the Italian exile General Guglielmo Pepe when he was introduced to them by Fanny's girlhood friend, Lady Dyer and her husband, Sir Thomas Dyer, a champion of Italian independence from Austrian rule. Pepe's fellow patriot, the fiery-tempered poet Ugo Foscolo, was also to be seen at no. 16 Keppel Street. Pepe states in his memoirs that he chose to limit his circle of friends to those who had similar political views: 'even the society of the radicals was often irksome to me from the perpetual necessity I found of justifying my unfortunate countrymen for having lost their freedom'. Pepe seems to have been genuinely fond of the Trollopes' society, and he remained a life-long friend. Fanny translated Italian verses into English for the general; he, in turn, presented the Trollope children with dried Neapolitan figs and mandarin oranges. Tom remembers that Pepe had a 'kind of simple, dignified, placid manner of enunciating the most astounding platitudes'. Fanny, Lady Dyer and another good friend, Mary Gabell, daughter of Winchester's headmaster, conspired to give the handsome general the sobriquet '*Gâteau de Plomb*'.* Mary Russell Mitford clearly had him in mind

---

* Fanny may also have known Sir Thomas Dyer from her Bristol days. An Ann Dyer had witnessed her grandfather John Milton's will in 1777; she was a neighbour of Mary Milton's family, the Gresleys, in Queen Square, Bristol. The Gabells were known to Jane Austen, whose nephews were Wykehamists. When Jane Austen moved to Winchester to be near her doctor in 1817, she wrote that she had a 'neat Drawing-room with a Bow-window over looking Dr Gabell's garden' (JA to James Edward Austen, 27 May 1817, in Deirdre Le Faye, ed., *Jane Austen's Letters*).

when she recalled forty years on that Fanny 'used to be such a Radical that her house in London was a perfect emporium of escaped criminals. I remember asking her at one of her parties how many of her guests would have been shot or guillotined if they had remained in their own country.'[5]

The eclectic guest list for these at-homes also included, besides the Italian exiles and the playwright Miss Mitford, the actors Mr and Mrs George Bartley, Edmund Kean and William Charles Macready, the painter George Hayter, Thomas James Mathias, author of the satirical *Pursuits of Literature* and an Italian scholar, his two nieces Henrietta and Marianne Skerrett (Marianne was to enter Queen Victoria's household), the poets Letitia Elizabeth Landon and Thomas Campbell, and, of course, 'Pendulum' Kater and Dr Nott. Nott, who was an Italian scholar and prebendary of Winchester as well as royal tutor, must have cut a rather dashing, if old-fashioned, figure with his perpetual 'black gaiters to the knee, and his elaborate white neckcloth'. Fanny's son Anthony had this clergyman in mind when he created the elegant-looking but 'plethoric' Revd Dr Vesey Stanhope in *Barchester Towers*.* Probably owing to her irrepressible enthusiasm as much as to her intellect, Fanny could not shake off the stigma of being 'blue', even amongst such distinguished company. During one evening party at which the Trollopes, Foscolo and Kean were gathered, a fellow guest recalls that 'Mrs Trollope came in her deepest blue stockings . . . the "Siddonian glances" which Kean detected the other night in Mrs Trollope were entirely thrown away on Foscolo, who shrugged up his shoulders and observed that she was *very blue*.'[6]

As much as Fanny undoubtedly enjoyed London society, Keppel Street was not an ideal place for the Trollopes' growing family. For one thing, the house was not big enough. For another, London itself was 'going on, stretching and spreading herself out, without let or hindrance, over fields, and groves, parks, till every idea of end or limit to her brick and mortar seem[ed] out of the question' (*Vienna and the Austrians*). By 1820 the Regent's Canal had been built just to the north of Bloomsbury, bringing with it unsightly coal wharfs,

---

* Tom also clearly based one of his fictional characters, Cyril Henningtree in *Artingale Castle* (1867), on Dr Nott.

builders' yards and gas works. The city was taking on a 'smoke-grimed complexion' (*Uncle Walter*). In *Our Village* Mary Russell Mitford describes a London fog of the period as 'a sad thing': 'dingy, dusky, dirty, damp; an atmosphere black as smoke and wet as steam, that wraps round you like a blanket'. 'Silks lose their gloss, cravats their stiffness, hackney-coaches their way; young ladies fall out of curl, and mammas out of temper; masters scold; servants grumble . . . Of all detestable things, a London fog is the most detestable.' Bloomsbury, in particular, was becoming decidedly shabby. In *Orley Farm*, as soon as they can afford to, the Furnivals move west of Keppel Street, to the more exclusive Harley Street; in two of Fanny's novels professional men, both bankers, decide to remove their families from Bloomsbury Square to the more fashionable parts of town (*The Robertses on their Travels; The Life and Adventures of a Clever Woman*).

The Trollopes could not afford a large house in the West End; in any case, Thomas Anthony had for some time dreamed of becoming a gentleman farmer. In August 1810, only a few months after Tom's birth, he put a bid of £3,600 on a property which he had seen while on circuit not far from his uncle's house in Hertfordshire – even though the land was 'not nearly so good' as he expected and the house only 'tolerable'. This was more than anyone else was willing to pay for it, but not as much as the owner wanted. Fanny was relieved. 'If the place you went to see is *only* pretty, I am not very sorry you have not got it – the profit of such a purchase must I should think be precarious.'[7] Two years – and two more boys – later, Thomas Anthony took out a twenty-one-year lease (with an option to renew) on close to 160 acres in and around Illots Farm, just south of Harrow-on-the-Hill in Middlesex, from John, Lord Northwick of Harrow Park. The annual rent was £660, calculated at £4 an acre. This was not a bargain, but nor was it excessively high in a wartime economy when corn and hay were fetching good prices. Until the farm began to pay for itself, the barrister would be able to keep up his law practice, as Harrow was within commuting distance – a sixteen-mile drive in his gig – of Lincoln's Inn. And, in preparation for Winchester, the Trollopes would be able to send their three (soon four) sons to the local parish school, Harrow, as 'day boys' with no fees to pay.[8]

The Trollopes did not make the transition from city to country immediately. Thomas Anthony evidently did not think the original farmhouse suitable for his family as a permanent residence. The temporary solution was to keep their London home, and divide their time between Keppel Street and, in the summer months, Illots Farm. However, moving back and forth between two households is always trying and not very economical. Fanny writes to her husband from Keppel Street of 'the extreme confusion of our affairs at Harrow just before we left it'.[9] It was during this period that the newborn Emily died. The situation would have seemed more and more untenable as each year passed, especially as the two oldest boys would soon be old enough to enter Harrow School. Following the birth of their fourth son, Anthony, in the spring of 1815, the Trollopes took over the Harrow farmhouse and found a tenant for Keppel Street. A much-wanted daughter, Cecilia, followed in 1816, and by the middle of 1817 Fanny was pregnant with the second Emily, her sixth living child. It was at this point that Thomas Anthony took the fateful decision to build a spacious new house on a corner of the farm. Still standing, it is a handsome red brick mansion, with an elegant two-storey bowed window at one end, commanding an impressive view of London in the distance. Along with the rest of the property, the house would revert to Lord Northwick at the end of the lease period. In view of the trouble – and the £3,000 construction mortgage which the barrister had taken out – Northwick reduced the annual rent by £240. To build a house on land which one does not own does not seem a very sensible decision. One can only imagine that, under the agreement with Northwick, Thomas Anthony considered the house to be, in effect, rent free. He must also have been confident that he could pay off the mortgage one way or another.

The family christened the new house 'Julians' – marking the happy coincidence and, more significantly, the expectations which went along with it, that one of the fields belonging to the property had the same name as his uncle's Hertfordshire estate. In July 1817 Adolphus Meetkerke's wife had died. The widower was in his sixties and had no children: his sister Penelope's son, Thomas Anthony Trollope, was the heir to the Meetkerke property and its income. His father, Tom Trollope later remarked, had undertaken to build the house in the firm belief that 'come what might of the Harrow farm and the new house, I was to be the future owner of Julians [Herts.], and live on my own acres'. Indeed, on visits to his great-uncle's estate in Hertfordshire, the young Tom was 'shown to the tenantry as their future landlord, and all that sort of thing'. Fanny remembered these walkabouts. In *The Abbess* the Earl of Arlborough takes the infant Ferdinand around his estate, and declares to the miller's young son: 'When you are miller of Fullford, as your father, grandfather and great grandfather, have been before you, this young sir shall be your landlord – at any rate, he shall be your son's landlord, my boy – so drink his health in a bumper.'

In his memoirs Tom Trollope paints a vivid picture of the household at Julians which loomed so large in his childhood. Adolphus Meet-kerke was a Tory of the old school, a good landlord, sportsman, magistrate and husband. 'But there was a sort of flavour of roughness about the old squire', an 'almost clownish rusticity'. He never missed a church service, and did not hesitate to shout in the middle of a disagreeable or over-long hymn 'That's enough!' or to bellow 'Come up to dinner' as the clergyman descended the pulpit after the sermon and before the blessing. In 1812, the year in which Fanny sets her novel *Town and Country*, the fear 'of the horrible pestilence of treason and blasphemy which has overrun France' was still very much alive, and old Adolphus Meetkerke might well have declared to his nephew over the port that he considered 'liberal' a 'hateful and dangerous word, and there are few crimes, sir, that I would not rather be accused of than that of being liberal'. Mrs Anne, an old maiden sister of the squire, took charge of the housekeeping and always carried a little basket in her hand, with the keys and a copy of *Pride and Prejudice*, which she read over and over. Tom drew on his memories of his great-aunt for Miss Immy in his novel *Lindisfarn Chase* (1864). Miss Immy 'never appeared without a little basket full of keys in her hand, and the perpetual and never-changing volume of "Clarissa Harlowe" '.

Tom also trawled his childhood memories for his depiction of the Earl of Linacre and his nephew and heir, Bentham Linacre, in the *Garstangs of Garstang Grange*. The Earl is, like Meetkerke, an old-fashioned Tory who talks a lot of nonsense very loudly. Bentham is a barrister with liberal leanings who is upright, honourable, industrious and intelligent, but intolerant and logical to a fault. He treats his uncle 'with no whit greater consideration or courtesy than he treated the attorneys, and, indeed, every other person with whom he came in contact'. One of many points of disagreement concerns hunting. Whereas the earl is a keen sportsman, Bentham 'had never taken a gun in his hand in his life, and considered the game-laws a remnant of feudal barbarism'. This might well have been the topic of a heated conversation which Tom overheard between his great-uncle and father at Julians. Bentham, like Thomas Anthony, was not popular with his rich relation, but 'this was the case between so many venerable gentlemen and their expectant heirs, that [one] attached very little importance to it' (*The Three Cousins*).

Nevertheless, it was a matter of the greatest importance. Tom speculates that had his father made an effort to get along with his uncle, or at least humour him, the old man 'might have sought affection and companionship elsewhere than from a young wife. But . . .' In October 1818, the very year that the Trollopes bestowed the name 'Julians' on the new house and walked across its threshold for the first time, Adolphus Meetkerke married the young Matilda Jane Wilkinson of Portman Square, London. After all, 'a bachelor was a bachelor, and a baronet was a baronet, let him be as old or as sour as he would' (*The Three Cousins*). The Trollopes remained strangely optimistic, hoping against hope that an heir would not appear. Perhaps they felt compelled to finish what they had started: '*to carry on the war*', as Fanny remarks of the heir apparent, Edward Lexington, in *The Three Cousins*, 'as he and his class denominate the mystery of spending more money than ever belonged to them, with extraordinary courage and spirits'. The Trollopes enlarged the property still further (thereby bringing the annual rent up to nearly £450) and set about landscaping the grounds, which entailed draining a pond and planting a shrubbery. In *Ralph the Heir* Anthony Trollope wrote of his eponymous hero: 'He had been hard at work during the last four months doing all those wonderfully attractive things with his new property which a man can do when he has money in his pocket, – knocking down hedges, planting young trees or preparing for the planting of them, buying stock, building or preparing to build sheds, – and the rest of it. There is hardly a pleasure in life equal to that of laying out money with a conviction that it will come back again. The conviction, alas, is so often ill founded, – but the pleasure is the same.' In February 1819 Fanny and her husband wrote to Lord Northwick nearly every day asking for a new road to be built which would make 'the approach worthy the situation of the house'. In fact, Thomas Anthony had already begun the work and, not surprisingly, had managed to antagonize several neighbours as well as his landlord. It seems that a Mr Earle had agreed to the 'improvements' to Trollope's land without first consulting 'the ladies of his family', who heartily objected. However, by midsummer the second Mrs Meetkerke knew she was pregnant. On 22 December 1819 a healthy baby boy, young Adolphus, was born to the Meetkerkes; by an awful irony, this was the same day that Thomas Anthony signed a revised lease agreement, with strict and binding terms and conditions, for the whole of the Harrow property.

It could not have been a happy Christmas for the Trollopes. His inheritance had disappeared in what must have seemed to Thomas Anthony the blink of an eye: 'To be the promised future owner of the acres on which he had lived, of the coverts through which he had ridden, of every tree and bank which he had known from his boyhood, had been to him a source of gratified pride not the less strong because he had concealed it . . . He now found that they were to be no more than dreams, – but with this additional sorrow, that all around him knew that they had been dreamed' (*Ralph the Heir*). Thomas Anthony had now only his law practice and the farm – which had yet to show a profit – to pay the rent and mortgage payments, maintain his family, and educate his children. Not to own the property where he and his family lived must have grated on Thomas Anthony's nerves, for 'the consequence was that he had no vote in the county, – a circumstance which he often very deeply lamented in secret'. And as he eventually came to realize with bitter regret, 'every shilling you lay out upon it is just so much money spent, instead of so much money saved' (*Mrs Mathews*). When an old man, reflecting on his family's sudden change in fortunes, Anthony set part of *Mr Scarborough's Family* near the Meetkerke property around Rushden, Hertfordshire. A nephew's inheritance is threatened when his rich uncle, Peter Prosper, courts a spinster whose name, like the second Mrs Meetkerke's, is Matilda.

As with Tom's Bentham Linacre, Harry Annesley has managed to offend his elderly uncle by displaying 'his own intellectual superiority'. Both writers, Tom and Anthony, provide their stories with happy endings. Mr Prosper remains single and no little Prospers blight Annesley's fortunes. Bentham Linacre, who had at one point thought of marrying the earl's daughter to secure the inheritance, decides that bachelorhood and hard work suit him best.

What were Fanny's own feelings? It was not in Fanny's nature to harbour a grievance. The loss of the Meetkerke inheritance was only the first of many instances in which she displayed that remarkable ability, as Tom put it, 'to throw sorrow off when the cause of it had passed'. Perhaps, like Mrs Chesterfield, she had warned her husband concerning the inheritance, 'Don't let us believe it till we have got more certainty, Thomas! Pray don't' (*Charles Chesterfield*). Nevertheless, she was not unmindful of the cruel effect of Adolphus Meetkerke's behaviour on her husband. In *The Ward of Thorpe Combe*, a friend reassures old Mr Thorpe that he had acted for the best in never letting on to the rest of the family that he feared his son and sole heir dead. 'Perhaps you have done more good than harm in not letting them all live for years in a state of doubt and expectation.' Most galling of all, Fanny might have heard the whispers behind her husband's back when concerned friends and neighbours saw that he was looking a little pale or haggard: 'I rather think [he] frets about the birth of the little boy, for [he] would have had the whole property, if there had been no son' (*Tremordyn Cliff*). Fanny later wrote that 'it matters little what the projects of man may be; the great and leading features of his destiny will ever be found to depend upon accidents with which his wishes, his will, his intentions, and his resolutions, have little or nothing to do' (*Jessie Phillips*).

Misfortune and financial pressures had begun to take their toll on Thomas Anthony's already weak constitution. His headaches were becoming more frequent and debilitating, and he seemed unable to decide on a course of action. In February 1820 he advised Lord Northwick: 'The continued ill state of my health has induced me with the advice of my medical friends to return to my residence in town. I have it in contemplation therefore to let my house at Harrow, and to fit up the farm-house for the summer vacation and other occasional visits to my farm', as before.[10] One can imagine a chorus of objections to this plan, not only from Fanny but also from the children. In any case, Tom and Henry had already spent a year at Harrow School, and there were still Arthur and Anthony to consider.

In the end, the Trollopes decided that the best course of action was to keep a tenant in Keppel Street and to find another for Julians, the house they had built at such expense. They themselves would move back to the original farmhouse on their leased estate. To this end they spent a further £500 to enlarge and improve it, making it 'irregular and straggling, but at the same time roomy and picturesque', as Anthony, with his childhood home in mind, describes the residence of Lady Mason in *Orley Farm*. The Trollopes, who strove to hide their disappointment from the children, bravely named the farmhouse 'Julian Hill'. It was this 'pretty cottage', as Fanny called it, which both she and her children would always think of as home. The house was not as grand as Julians, but from its vantage point the Trollopes could see 'all the undulations of the landscape between Harrow and London', as far as the spires of Westminster Abbey.[11] Although the Harrow farm had been up to now a loss-making operation, Thomas Anthony must have believed that, if he continued to supplement its income through his law practice, he could in time turn his finances around. He had set himself a difficult task, as the price of corn and hay had been steadily dropping since the end of the Napoleonic Wars in 1815. Perhaps there is a little of Anthony's father in Lady Mason's son Lucius. 'Well grounded in Greek, Latin, and Euclid', Lucius is determined to apply scientific methods to farming. In his conceit – or perhaps one should say naïvety – he tells his mother that 'capital is a bugbear . . . The capital that is really wanting is thought, mind, combination, knowledge' (*Orley Farm*).

For her part, Fanny set about making Julian Hill a pleasant and cheerful home for her family. 'We all like a play,' remarks Charles Musgrove in Jane Austen's *Persuasion*, and Fanny, like Jane, loved to gather friends and family for an evening of amateur dramatics. In Fanny's novel *Michael Armstrong*, set in Manchester and its environs, Lady Clarissa proposes to put on a play. 'We will all act it . . . and all the neighbourhood shall be assembled to enjoy the fête.' 'Is it not the duty of neighbours, residing within reach of each other,' she extols, 'to exert every facility with which nature has endowed them', in order to ease 'the privations to which their distance from the metropolis obliges them to submit?' Sir Matthew Dowling offers to have one of the rooms in his mansion 'fitted up as a theatre' and volunteers most of his family members as thespians. The performance which follows is close to farce – ill-fitting costumes, forgotten lines, floods of tears – probably not unlike one or two performances at Julian Hill.

Fanny's mind, 'which was active to excess, and ever eager for fresh materials to work upon, became, to all intents and purposes, a spiritual knight-errant, roaming through the intellectual world in search of adventure' (*The Three Cousins*). Besides 'the mighty project of private theatricals', other entertainments included 'drawing-room characters on Twelfth Night', 'gradations of speaking charades and dumb charades, tableaux vivans, fancy fairs, and costume quadrilles' (*The Young Countess*). A speaking charade, made up of three dramatic scenes, sometimes in full costume, was a very complicated affair. The first scene was meant to suggest the first syllable, the second scene the second syllable, and the third scene the word in its entirety. But, as Fanny would explain in her comic poem, *The Mother's Manual*:

> Les tableaux vivans, are perhaps surer yet,
> And 'tis so easy, you need only get
> An ample frame, and strain some dark red gauze –
> Italian pictures gain the most applause.

As a painless method of teaching the children French, Fanny staged Molière's plays. For *Les Femmes savantes* she 'fitted up the stage with every kind of thing you can imagine fit to fill the drawing-room of a *blue lady*, – books, maps, plans of the moon, telescopes, rolls of paper, MSS., etc.'. No one was left out of the festivities; even Thomas Anthony took part in these private theatricals.[12]

Fanny's other great passion, if one can call it that, was for a picnic. 'I have heard,' she remarks in *Paris and the Parisians*, 'a great many very sensible remarks, and some of them really very hard to answer, upon the extreme absurdity of leaving every accommodation which is considered needful for the comfort of a Christian-like dinner, for the sole purpose of devouring this needful repast without one of them. What can be said in defence of such an act?' The fact is no other method of dining produces 'one half so much light-hearted enjoyment as the cold repast round which the guests crouch like so many gypsies'. 'As long as men and women,' she concludes, 'continue to experience this singular accession of good spirits and good humour from circumstances which might be reasonably expected to destroy both, nothing better can be done than to let them go on performing the same extraordinary feat.' Like the Dowager Countess of Setterton in *Father Eustace*, Fanny 'always proposed a pic-nic, let the season be what it might', even a winter picnic in an old farmhouse with a roaring fire. Years later, when Fanny spent a long winter in Vienna, she could not wait for spring to arrive and organized a picnic in April, less than a month after a great snowstorm.

Anthony, no doubt as a result of being dragged out in all sorts of weather, had an aversion to picnics and expressed his views on the subject in his novels. ' "I am very fond of a picnic," said Sir Lionel, as, seated on a corner of a tombstone [in the Holy Land], he stretched out his glass towards Miss Todd, who had insisted on being his cupbearer for the occasion; "excessively fond. I mean the eating and drinking part, of course. There is only one thing I like better; and that is having my dinner under a roof, upon a table, and with a chair to sit on" ' (*The Bertrams*). Like Fanny's Dowager Countess, Anthony's Arabella Greenow has a penchant for unorthodox outings and organizes a 'marine picnic' on the sands of Yarmouth, to the narrator's disapproval: 'Yarmouth is not a happy place for a picnic' (*Can You Forgive Her?*).

In addition to picnics and theatricals, Fanny also occasionally rode to hounds – without her husband. In a letter she describes to Tom, away at Winchester, how she rode the family pony, Jack, in 'a very delightful hunt in Wembley Park'. ('Jack' is the name of the hunter which Lord Rufford offers to Arabella Trefoil in Anthony's *The American Senator*.) 'The little girls amused me exceedingly,' she continues.

They had been talking and wondering a good deal about Mama's going hunting; and when they saw me equipped and ready to mount, Cecilia said, 'But Mama, you have not got a gun! You must have a gun!' I laughed heartily at this, and told her I was not going shooting but coursing; upon which, with a great air of contempt, and to show off her superior knowledge, Emily said 'No; Mama ought not to take a gun, but she ought to take Neptune.'[13]

Neptune, the Trollope's Newfoundland dog, finds his way into both Anthony's *Dr Wortle's School* and Fanny's *One Fault*. Some evenings there were whist parties, a pastime which, unlike hunting, Thomas Anthony also enjoyed.

Perhaps what Fanny appreciated most about her life at Harrow – and her happiest years were undoubtedly those spent at Julian Hill – were her neighbours. Just on the other side of the garden hedge lived Colonel James Grant, his wife Penelope, their son Owen and three daughters, Anna, Mary and Kate. Years later, soon after Anthony's death, Tom wrote to Mary Grant (then Mrs Christie): 'I have never forgotten and never can forget the days when – as you say, – Trollopes and Grants seemed to be one large family. They were happy days; and that intimacy made for me the happiest part of them . . . How is Anna? How is Kate? . . . And you are a grandmother!! Heaven and Earth! Will you come out and swing under the old elm tree? Or will you let me wheel you down the hill in a barrow?' Tom had been in love with Kate, he wrote, 'in those old boy and girl days, something more than half a century ago! Not that she ever knew it, dear innocent hearted child that she was!'[14]

Another neighbour, Sir Francis Milman, physician to Queen Charlotte, lived at Pinner, near Harrow, with his wife and daughter. He died soon after the Trollopes arrived at Illots Farm, but Lady Milman was to be a close friend and ally of the Trollopes for many years. Her sons, William and Henry, were no longer living at home but were, of course, frequent visitors to Harrow. The Revd Henry Milman was a poet, historian and later Dean of St Paul's, London. Tom thought Henry's wife was very beautiful, but preferred Sir William, whom he thought a perfect gentleman, to his brother, who was a little too worldly, cynical and probably pompous, although he does not use the word. The Milman family joke was that 'Henry reads a book, not as other mortals do, line after line, but obliquely, from the left hand upper corner of a page to the right hand lower corner of the same!' Fanny no doubt liked the fact that Lady Milman was a touch eccentric. Tom recounts that she always carried a volume of South's sermons with her to church to read in full view of priest and congregation if that morning's homily was not to her taste.

And, finally, there was the Drury and, by association, the Merivale clan, which both Fanny and Thomas Anthony had almost certainly come across before their marriage. Both the Merivales and Drurys had lived at some point in or near Exeter (John Merivale lived in a house in the cathedral close), a city which Fanny knew well. She often visited her cousin on her father's side, Fanny Bent, in Devonshire: first at Sanford, near Crediton, then in Exeter and at nearby Dawlish in the summer. John Merivale's son, John Herman, was an exact contemporary of Thomas Anthony, and they were at St John's, Cambridge, together before the latter migrated to New College, Oxford. They were both called to the bar in the same year, 1804; and they had chambers within a few yards of each other in Old Square, Lincoln's Inn. Perhaps it was John Herman Merivale who first introduced Thomas Anthony to the Miltons in Keppel Street. The Revd Joseph Drury, formerly headmaster of Harrow School (1785), had retired to Dawlish. His daughter Louisa was at school in Exeter with the Merivale girls and his son Harry became great friends with John Herman Merivale at Cambridge. John Herman and Louisa married in 1805 and set up house in Red Lion Square, near the Miltons (they moved to Woburn Place, Russell Square, in 1817, just as the Trollopes were leaving the area).

It may have been John Herman's advice which made the Trollopes decide on Harrow to settle in. Merivale had recently sent two sons, Herman and Charles (he was later to send a third, John), to Harrow School, which his wife's family ran between them.* There was Louisa's brother Henry Drury and his son Benjamin, the Revd Joseph Drury's younger brother Mark and his son William, all clergymen. The Merivales were, of course, frequent visitors to Harrow, and the Merivale and Trollope boys became fast friends. Fanny later wrote

---

* One of the boarding houses at Harrow School is still called 'Druries'.

that Herman was 'always a favourite of mine . . . He had a halo of pretty Drury cousins round him.'[15]

These, then, were the people who would have joined Fanny and her family for an evening of amateur theatricals, a game of whist or an outdoor gastronomic adventure.* However, one neighbour – the new tenant of Julians, in fact – the Revd John William Cunningham, vicar of St Mary's, Harrow, did not entirely approve of the charades which Fanny put on to entertain the young people at her parties. 'Why not, Mr Cunningham?' Fanny asked when confronted by the evangelical clergyman one day. 'Mrs Cunningham has evening parties' – at Julians – 'to which we are always glad to go to hear your daughters play upon the piano.' 'Ah, yes,' Cunningham is supposed to have replied, 'but my daughters always have their backs to the audience.' Later, she was the only non-'pious' lady at a dinner party when the conversation turned to the sale of pincushions for Christian purposes; the mischievous Fanny could not resist repeating her story of Cunningham and the virtuous young ladies at the pianoforte. When confronted by Cunningham, who was present, Fanny justified her indiscretion by declaring, 'with my usual sincerity, "because you deserved it, sir" '.[16]

Fanny was not an irreligious soul: she read aloud with her daughters portions of the Scripture and the Catechism every morning. However, her religious values were formed during the reign of George III, when evangelicalism and Dissent were considered vulgar and ungentlemanlike. Tom recalls that the two or three Dissenting families at Heckfield were considered by the Miltons and their neighbours 'as so many Chinese', 'unaccountably strange and as objectionable'. Fanny believed evangelicalism to be fundamentally hypocritical. And one cannot help but feel that she was entirely justified in her opinion of the Revd Cunningham, especially in the matter of Lord

---

* Fanny writes to Mrs Drury regarding one of her theatre parties, 'will you then have the kindness to place all your young ones in the front row – I reckon that the sofa in front will hold *five little ones*, and their heads will be in the way of no one – I shall reckon upon *twelve* from your house – it will be quite charity to give us a full pit' (undated: Parrish Collection). In another letter she invites Mrs Drury 'to come help me play audience' at a game of charades (undated: Trollope Family Papers, Special Collections, UCLA Library).

Byron's daughter Allegra's grave. Following the death of his illegitimate five-year-old daughter in Italy in 1822, Lord Byron had asked
that the funeral service be read by his old Harrow school friend, Harry
Drury, and a plaque be erected in St Mary's. In an extraordinarily
unctuous speech at a churchwardens' meeting, Cunningham turned
down the natural father's request for a commemorative plaque (on
the grounds, as Anthony later wrote, that it would 'teach boys to get
bastards') and, in the same breath, asked Harry Drury to convey his
admiration of *Cain* to its author, Byron. Drury must have pulled the
rector up short when he replied: 'I think it is the most blasphemous
production that ever came from the press.'[17]

The Drurys detested evangelicalism – and the Revd Cunningham
– even more fiercely than Fanny. Indeed, Tom records that the bad
feeling between them was '*the* leading feature of the social life of
Harrow in those days'. To make matters worse, the Drurys had to
endure Cunningham's sermons at St Mary's, since Harrow School
had no separate chapel at that time. Tom remembers that on one
occasion Cunningham interrupted his own sermon in order to chastise
Mark Drury's two young daughters for either talking or laughing.
Their father, so the story goes, never 'came within speaking distance
of the vicar without growling "Brawler!" in a perfectly audible voice'.
Behind his back, the Drurys would have called the vicar 'Velvet
Cunningham', the sobriquet bestowed by his critics after the publication of his book *The Velvet Cushion* (1814) – a tendentious history
of the Church of England as recounted by a pulpit cushion.

As for Allegra's burial, Harry Drury was furious that he could not
carry out his school friend's wishes. Both the Drurys and Byron
found a staunch ally in Fanny. She had long been an admirer of Byron's
poetry. In *Tremordyn Cliff* Arundel and his sister Lady Augusta discuss
whether Byron's greatest power lay in 'the energy and truth of his
thoughts and feelings, or in his extraordinary faculty of clothing
them aptly in words'. Fanny threw herself into the fray, and put her
literary skills to work on a long 'mock-heroic *Don Juan*-style' poem
satirizing the principal players and events surrounding the debate.
Although witty and often clever, it is not a great work: Fanny goes
over the top both in her abuse of cant and in her praise of Byron.
However, she never intended it for publication – it was simply her

way of lodging a formal protest in a light-hearted, entertaining fashion amongst a small circle of friends. For her efforts Harry Drury presented Fanny with one of Byron's poems written in his own hand.

Fanny could undoubtedly hold her own against the Revd Cunningham's fawning hypocrisy. She was chiefly concerned about his influence on those of an impressionable age. Her son Anthony, by his own admission an awkward and unhappy young teenager, fell under the evangelical clergyman's spell for a time, for he was 'a gentleman-like man with very pleasing manners and a sweet voice'. By the age of nineteen, Anthony knew better: 'I used to talk to Cunningham a good deal at one time, and recall he always used to be very civil to me, but he is a cringing hypocrite and a most confounded liar, and would give his eyes to be a bishop.' Fanny believed that young girls were particularly at risk, and Tom recounts that on one occasion she warned a neighbour's eighteen-year-old daughter, who thought the Revd Cunningham's embrace perfectly innocent, that 'the kiss of peace is apt to change its quality if repeated'. It was probably at this time that Fanny performed to the Drurys' great delight her original verse drama, 'Sign of the Times: The Righteous Rout', a biting satire on an evangelical clergyman.[18]

Like her mock-Byronic poem, this was meant only for the amusement of friends. Yet, it is clear that Fanny had wider ambitions. Years later, when her son Tom was getting nowhere with his writing, Fanny consoled him by reminding him of her own early disappointments: 'cast your eyes back over my literary history: – A MS sent to Colburn, declined; one to Murray returned at the end of six months unopened; another to a man in the Strand, sent back with the assurance that the trade was so bad, no one could publish without loss. All this I bore, and worked up against it all.'[19] What these abortive projects were, novels or poetry, she does not say. However, she must have written them during this period, and her letter makes it clear that her literary aspirations were no secret.

The Revd Cunningham was eventually resurrected by both mother and son as the Revd William Jacob Cartwright in Fanny's *The Vicar of Wrexhill* (1837) and, twenty years later, as the infamous Revd Obadiah Slope in Anthony's *Barchester Towers*. (Cunningham, who died in 1861, would have read both, unless, of course, he thought novel-reading immoral.) Writing only three years after the Trollopes had left Harrow, Fanny could not have done otherwise than deny what many suspected, that Cunningham was indeed the model for the vicar of Wrexhill.* We do not know what Cunningham himself thought, though at least one like-minded clergyman seems to have considered the portrait a compliment, for he insisted that he was the original Revd Cartwright. According to Frances Eleanor Trollope, the basic story in *The Vicar of Wrexhill* – an unscrupulous evangelical clergyman courts a rich widow and, in doing so, divides the family – was suggested to Fanny by her friend Henrietta Skerrett.

Nevertheless, for the detailed portrait of Cartwright Fanny must have had the Revd Cunningham in mind – one has only to compare the initials of the two clergymen, W.J.C. and J.W.C. Indeed, in the course of the novel Fanny makes several sly gibes at Cunningham's expense, some especially for the benefit of her old Harrow friends and allies. Thus, the word 'cushion' – as in *Velvet Cushion* – keeps cropping up in the novel. In one scene the Revd Cartwright, who has in effect taken over the widow's home, asks her son to meet him in *his* library and invites him 'to kneel down on one of these cushions; – of which there are always sufficient, and to spare, in the dwellings of the chosen' (*The Vicar of Wrexhill*). This interview was doubly painful to the young Charles Mowbray, as he later confesses to a friend: 'could you have seen him enthroned in my poor father's library' – a thought no doubt shared by the Trollopes when thinking of Cunningham and his twelve children installed in their beautiful Julians. Harry Drury would have appreciated the local schoolmaster's refusal to bring his pupils to Cartwright's 'Sabbath evening lecture, and Tuesday evening's expounding and Thursday evening's church lecture'. Certainly, anyone who knew Fanny's story about Cunningham and the 'kiss of peace' would have smiled when in *The Vicar of Wrexhill* one naïve young girl insists that Cartwight's caress 'was nothing in the world but a kiss of holy peace and brotherly love'.

We do not know what Thomas Anthony Trollope thought of the

---

* In a letter to her son Tom, and again in her preface to *The Attractive Man* (1846), Fanny emphatically denies that the vicar of Wrexhill was based on Cunningham or any real-life figure (FT to TAT, undated: Parrish Collection).

Allegra episode. Certainly, he was as anti-evangelical as his wife, but he may well have thought that Fanny went too far in her defence of Byron, especially as the poet's reputation was at best dubious. One can imagine Thomas Anthony venturing to check her enthusiasm, in the same way that Plantagenet Palliser tried to discourage his wife Glencora's vehement defence of Phineas Finn, who stood accused of murder. Palliser felt that 'it would have been much better that his wife should not display her interest publicly'. 'But the Duchess, wherever she went', spoke of the case as a 'persecution' and seemed to think that Finn should 'be treated as a hero and a martyr'. Glencora tells Plantagenet:

> 'Out of the full heart the mouth speaks, and my heart is very full. What harm do I do?'
>
> 'You set people talking of you.'
>
> 'They have been doing that ever since we were married; but I do not know that they have made out much against me. We must go after our nature' (*Phineas Redux*).

Perhaps Thomas Anthony, like Palliser, 'was beginning to think that he hardly knew how to manage his wife'.

CHAPTER FOUR

One Fault

Although as local 'charity boys' at Harrow, and later scholars at Winchester, the Trollope boys' tuition was free, clothes and other school provisions, such as boots, waistcoats and pocket handkerchiefs, as Anthony later recalled, still had to be provided and paid for (*An Autobiography*). And then there was tuck money, that is pocket money for the school shop. Thomas Anthony struggled to make ends meet between his law practice and farming, but a bad temper – he was forever insulting his clients – and worse luck – markets were still depressed – meant that the Trollopes had very little ready cash for such expenditures. They had learned too late what the worldly-wise Miss Margaret Hartley knew in *The Blue Belles of England*: 'A young man brought up to the bar, with a fortune just sufficient to live upon, – Does he ever get on?' In an economy drive Nurse Farmer and Fanny, despite her aversion to sewing, sat at home making various garments, including cricket flannels. Fanny thought that they would 'turn out something worthy of a very good tailor'.

Anthony – and the Harrow headmaster, Dr Butler – disagreed. Anthony remembers Dr Butler confronting him on the street and thundering 'whether it was possible that Harrow School was disgraced by so disreputably dirty' – and presumably ill-dressed – 'a little boy as I'. Later, at a private school run by another Drury, the Revd Arthur Drury, in Sunbury, a village situated on the Thames, Anthony 'never had any pocket-money, and seldom had much in the way of clothes'. Frances Eleanor Trollope says that, in answer to his sons' appeals, Thomas Anthony insisted that 'old shoes and trousers should be mended rather than new ones bought'. 'I enclose half a crown from Papa,' Fanny wrote to Tom at Winchester in May 1825, 'a proof at once of poverty and kindness. Without the former it would be more, without the latter it would be nothing. All the world are poor as Job, – and, rather poorer, for Job put none of his sons to public schools, and had no clients who did not pay him. Next year I fear we shall be poorer still, for assuredly there will be *no hay*. We are positively burnt up as if it were a hot mid-summer.'[1]

But, when funds permitted, the Trollopes still took autumn holidays on the Isle of Wight where, on warm October days, one can imagine Fanny advancing the dinner hour from five o'clock to half-past three 'rather than forgo this *al fresco* luxury'. And on rainy days no doubt 'every circulating library on the Island was ransacked' to help pass the time (*One Fault*). The Trollopes also travelled around the English countryside visiting family and friends, including Sir John Trollope, the sixth baronet of Casewick, in Lincolnshire, and in Devon Fanny's cousin on her father's side, Miss Fanny Bent. The children probably looked on visits to Casewick, where the daughters of the house were 'very Missy' and evenings 'very stupid', as a duty rather than a pleasure.[2] Their mother's side of the family, which was a touch eccentric, was much more popular with the Trollope brood, and they always looked forward to staying with Aunt Fanny in Exeter.

'The tie between Fanny Milton and Fanny Bent had always from their earliest years been a very close one,' Tom remembers. Born in the same year, both girls lost their mothers when they were only five years old; both their fathers were clergymen. The families exchanged visits between Sanford, in Devon, and Bristol. As the girls grew older Fanny Bent probably felt herself to be very much the country cousin, for 'young ladies at Clifton' were apt 'to fancy that young ladies in Devonshire must be greatly behind-hand in all things' (*The Widow Barnaby*). In his memoirs Tom fondly remembers his aunt, who had taken a comfortable brick house with gardens in the parish of St Sidwell's, Exeter, in the early 1820s: 'Very plain in feature, and dressed with Quaker-like simplicity and utter disregard for appearance, her figure was as well known in Exeter as the cathedral towers. She had a position and enjoyed an amount of respect which was really singular in the case of a very homely-featured old maid of very small fortune.' 'She was a thoroughgoing Churchwoman and Conservative', and 'she had a strong native sense of humour' – such that she would whisper nonsense verse to an astonished but delighted young Tom while walking up the nave of Exeter Cathedral.[3]

The eccentric, much-loved Fanny Bent appears in one guise or another in the novels of all three writers, Fanny, Tom and Anthony. In *The Widow Barnaby* Fanny describes Miss Betsy Compton, Devon born and bred, as an older woman whose 'dress was always precisely neat and nice as that of a quaker' and who enjoyed reading novels, 'a subscription to a library at Exeter being one of her very few expensive indulgences'. Fanny may have been making a rather sly reference to her cousin's surname when she gives Miss Betsy a slightly crooked back. Amid the society of the 'happily and favourably constituted city' of Sillchester, Tom's lightly disguised portrait of Exeter in *Artingale Castle* (1867), 'Mistress Agnes Artingale held a well-marked and indeed rather a high place' – just as he later remarked of Fanny Bent.

In *He Knew He Was Right*, published two years after *Artingale Castle*, Anthony introduced by far the best known portrait of his aunt: Miss Jemima Stanbury, 'a maiden lady, very much respected, indeed, in the city of Exeter'. Like Fanny Bent, Miss Stanbury was 'a thorough Tory of the old school'. 'In the matter of politics she had long since come to think that everything good was over. She hated the name of Reform.' It is not hard to imagine Fanny Bent disapproving of modern fashions – certainly Miss Stanbury did, especially crinolines and chignons. Indeed the latter did not even like to pronounce this last word, talking rather of ' "those bandboxes which the sluts wear behind their noddles;" for Miss Stanbury allowed herself the use of much strong language'. 'It would have been difficult,' Fanny says of Miss Betsy Compton, 'to find any lady, of any rank, more really and truly independent than Miss Betsy. She felt this, and enjoyed it greatly.' 'A more contented, or, in truth, a more happy spinster might have been sought in vain' (*The Widow Barnaby*).

For the Trollope children, visits to their grandfather's vicarage at Heckfield continued to be deemed 'a great event'. William Milton's mechanical experiments, chiefly pertaining to the 'patent coach', carried on apace. During this period he wrote to the editor of *The Gentleman's Magazine*, hoping to spark off a correspondence on the mysteries of wheel leverage – but to no avail.[4] The large coach-house attached to the vicarage was 'always full of the strangest' – and ugliest, to Tom's eyes – 'collection of models of coaches' and on the 'very pretty evergreen-embowered lawn' there was always 'some model or other intended to illustrate the principles of traction'. One such consisted of two huge wheels, about ten feet high, joined together by a series of cross-bars. Tom, and no doubt the other boys, used to love to 'creep into the interior of this structure' and cause it to move forward by stepping on the bars in 'treadmill fashion'. One day Tom ventured to 'ride' the *rotis volventibus*, as the monstrosity was called, down a steep decline in one corner of the garden; it was not long before 'there was a tremendous smashing of the evergreen hedge, and a black-and-blue little body, whose escape without broken bones was deemed truly prodigious'. Tom learned one of life's important lessons that day: 'Never, Tom,' his grandfather declared, 'put in motion forces which you are unable to control!'

Despite money problems, the Trollopes dined well on roast or boiled meat every day of the week. When presented with a rice pudding and nothing else for dinner at the house of a Harrow neighbour, Mrs Edwards, the outspoken Tom rose in his place to express his indignation. His hostess laughed 'until the tears ran down her cheeks' and fixed him a mutton chop.* Tom and Henry continued to get themselves into trouble. One day they played too near an open drain and contracted typhus. They both nearly died, not so much from the effects of the typhus bacillus as from the calomel, a compound of mercury, prescribed for them by the local apothecary. That same Mrs Edwards of the rice-pudding incident brought her brother, Dr Butt, to examine the boys. Tom by this time was delirious, 'raving about masters coming in at the window to drag me off to the pupil-room' at Harrow. Dr Butt almost certainly saved their lives by

---

* Many years later, when Tom was teaching in Birmingham, Mrs Edwards sought him out in his classroom, and to his mortification, recounted this story to his pupils, with the tears once again running down her face (T. A. Trollope, *What I Remember*, III, pp. 233–4).

stopping the calomel and recommending in its stead port wine.

To entertain her children and their friends Fanny would have organized games – bilbocatch, spillikins, battledore and shuttlecock – on the lawn sloping down in front of Julian Hill, while inside there would have been chess, backgammon and cards. On one occasion, in Tom's first year at Harrow, she had several schoolboys over for a meal and in the evening they all, including Fanny, played a card game called 'commerce'. Fanny was extremely impressed with the twelve-year-old Herman Merivale, who afterwards sat with her by the fireside, reading Dante, Tasso, Ariosto and Spenser, and talking about the Greek poets with her husband. Occasionally there were outings, with or without the children, to London. 'When you are next at home,' Fanny wrote to Tom at Winchester in 1825, 'I shall insist upon your going with me to the National Gallery. It begins to be well worth seeing.'* She had already taken the nine-year-old Anthony the year before. There, as he later recalled, 'I conceived my first ideas of the nature of a picture.'[5]

Somehow or other the Trollopes managed to cut costs (one gathers that the children's school clothes were the main area of saving), for their at-homes carried on as before.

> Let all expenditure, that meets the eye,
> Be pushed to what your utmost means supply;
> And what is wanting to augment the sum,
> Be scraped in quiet privacy at home (*The Mother's Manual*).

Gathered at Julian Hill was the usual eclectic crowd of political exiles, actors, artists and writers, with the addition of Fanny's Harrow neighbours, Lady Milman, Mrs Edwards, the Grants, any number of Drurys – even the Revd Cunningham could be found amongst the sinners. Perhaps like Anthony's evangelical Revd Mr O'Callaghan in *The Bertrams*, Cunningham 'was known to be condescending and

---

* However, the architecture of the building was generally unpopular. In *Uncle Walter* (1852), Fanny's young heroine makes 'a vehement attack on the unfortunate National Gallery, which, truth to say, was rather like "kicking one who had no friends"'.

mild under the influence of tea and muffins – sweetly so if the cream be plentiful and the muffins soft with butter'. Fanny was always adding new names to the guest list, many of whom came, as General Pepe had, with introductions from her old childhood friends. One such visitor was to exert a tremendous influence over Fanny, the radical reformer and proto-feminist Frances Wright.

Between 1818 and 1820 the orphaned, but independently wealthy, handsome and very precocious Scotswoman, Frances Wright, then in her early twenties, toured America with her younger and devoted sister Camilla to gather material for a book. She had dreamed of visiting the new republic since the impressionable age of sixteen, when she first read Carlo Botta's classic account of the revolutionary war. To her, America was 'the theatre where man might first awake to the full knowledge and the full exercise of his powers'.[6] Frances and Camilla travelled with the usual letters of introduction, including one addressed to the New Yorker, Charles Wilkes. He was the nephew of the radical Englishman of 'Wilkes and Liberty' fame, John Wilkes, but he himself was a very conservative American banker who came to disapprove of Frances Wright's more liberal ideas. Through Wilkes the two sisters were introduced to William Milton's old friend, John Garnett, who had made the voyage to America with his wife and young children in 1797.

Only five years apart, John Garnett and William Milton grew up together in Trinity Street, Bristol, where both their fathers were merchants. As young boys they had shared a fascination with all things scientific, but their paths diverged when William Milton went up to Oxford aged eighteen. John Garnett drifted, fell in love a few times, and was finally apprenticed to his father as a merchant in 1773, the same year that William became rector of Heckfield. Nevertheless, the two friends picked up where they had left off when William moved back to Bristol in 1775, and John tutored the Milton children in mathematics and science. Although he became a much respected Bristol citizen, holding the offices of both sheriff and master of the Merchant Venturers, Garnett apparently found it increasingly difficult to reconcile his liberal – even radical – views with the slave trade, which affected every Bristol merchant either directly or indirectly. After a brief sojourn in Kent (just at the time when William

Milton first proposed his plans for a floating harbour, so depriving the clergyman of a loyal ally), John Garnett decided to emigrate to America, as so many others had done before him. 'I love an active useful country life, and the manners and language of Free Men,' he wrote to an old friend in America, General Horatio Gates. 'Give me a line to say, if a good climate, rational society, and a field for honest industry, are to be found near you.'[7]

Frances and Camilla Wright spent several weeks at the Garnetts' New Jersey farm. Frances obviously idolized her host (she had a tendency to worship older men), and she and her sister swore eternal friendship with the two Garnett daughters nearest their age, Julia and Harriet. The Garnett children had received a very liberal education from their father, who encouraged them to view all matters, both scientific and religious, with an open mind. 'In the natural, moral, and political features of your great and growing country,' Frances's aunt wrote to the Garnett sisters concerning her niece, she 'has found objects to fill and gratify her capacious – her magnificent – mind and in you she has met objects of esteem and affection she hardly believed to exist!' As far as England was concerned, Frances later wrote, 'Here all is *retrograde*.'[8]

William Milton and John Garnett had kept in touch over the years, and when in 1816–17 John returned to England with his wife and children for a visit, the two families renewed their close friendship. As well as politics, the two men would have discussed various points of science, for Garnett had also remained a keen amateur scientist, and had even built an observatory on his farm. (He had, in fact, been better appreciated than poor Milton: he was elected to the American Philosophical Society and awarded its Magellan Prize for his work on navigation.) Fanny was thinking of a reunion such as this when she later wrote: 'There is, perhaps, no style of intercourse more agreeable than that which arises between old friends long separated, whom circumstances have so completely severed as to make them look, speak, and feel almost like strangers when they first meet again, yet find, as the renewed intimacy goes on, a thousand topics that pleasantly recall the past' (*One Fault*). Thus when, a few years later, Julia and Harriet wrote to the Miltons, and to Fanny Trollope, urging them to meet this 'angel', as her female friends came to call Frances

Wright, the mistress of Julian Hill welcomed her with open arms.

Like everyone who crossed her path, the Trollopes were enchanted by the charismatic young woman. Frances was a frequent guest at the Harrow farm, where she held court and received her friends and admirers, well-known radicals such as the utilitarian philosopher Jeremy Bentham and Robert Dale Owen, son of the utopian reformer, Robert Owen. In turn, Fanny Trollope introduced her new friend to her own set; General Pepe remembered that he first met Frances Wright 'at the house of Mrs Trollope'.[9] The conversations at Julian Hill at this time must have been dazzling, for there was much to talk about, as a later advertisement for the *Memoirs of the Court of the Regency* by the Duke of Buckingham and Chandos testifies:

> What years those were, from 1811 to 1820! . . . from the accession of the Regent to power to the death of George III: the invasion of Russia, and the war in Spain; the battles of Salamanca and Borodino; the fire of Moscow, the retreat of Napoleon; the conquest of Spain; the surrender of Napoleon; the return from Elba; the Congress of Vienna; the Hundred Days; the crowning carnage of Waterloo; the exile to St Helena; the return of the Bourbons; the settlement of Europe; the public scandals at the English Court; the popular discontent, and the massacre at Peterloo!*

Not to mention the deaths in 1821 of Napoleon and Caroline, the estranged wife of George IV and the focus of royal scandal when she was put on trial for adultery. Slavery would still have been an emotive topic at this time for, although the slave trade had been abolished in 1807, slavery itself continued in Britain's colonies.

Frances Wright had a knack for getting people to do things for her, and the enthusiastic Fanny Trollope was no exception. Besides putting her up at Julian Hill and entertaining her friends there, Fanny forwarded packages, ran errands and generally arranged her affairs in London when the Wright sisters were in Paris or abroad elsewhere.

---

* This advertisement appears at the back of Fanny Trollope's novel, *Fashionable Life* (1856).

Even Thomas Anthony seems to have fallen under Frances's spell. Tom had a vague memory that his father corresponded with Longman (Henry Milton's publishers) on her behalf concerning the publication of her *Views of Society and Manners in America* (1821).

Within a few months of Frances Wright's return from America in 1820, John Garnett was dead. The New Jersey farm, and no doubt his scientific endeavours, had been a constant drain on his purse, and the family were left with almost nothing. By 1823 the Garnetts had decided to sell the farm at a loss, return to Europe and live as best they could on the small income drawn from a few English investments which John Garnett had maintained. As Fanny's brother, Henry Milton, was now looking after the Garnetts' financial affairs, the Miltons would have considered it very much a family matter as to where Mrs Garnett and her three daughters should make their home (the eldest, Anna Maria, recently married, had stayed behind in America). The cost of living was certainly lower on the Continent than in England, and the French were generally less formal and ostentatious – no liveried servants were needed, for example. A Parisian simply strove 'to make his means, be they great or small, contribute as much as possible to the enjoyment and embellishment of his existence'. In any case, the liberal atmosphere in France was more akin to what the Garnetts had left behind in America: 'Even politics, that fearful quicksand which engulfs so many of our social hours, dividing our drawing-rooms into a committee of men and a coterie of women, – even politics may be handled . . . without danger' by women in France (*Paris and the Parisians*). Thus it was that Paris was finally decided upon.

In September 1823, soon after the Garnetts had settled into their new apartments on the rue St Maur, Fanny and Thomas Anthony Trollope paid them a visit. Fanny kept a journal of her month's sojourn in France, which still survives.[10] They set off from Julian Hill at half-past three in the morning in Trollope's gig, and had breakfast at the house of their friend, the painter George Hayter, in time to board the Calais-bound steamer at Tower Bridge. They spent the night in Calais and then continued on to Paris by diligence, arriving in the city very hot and dusty. Understandably, they 'resisted the Garnetts' entreaties to join the party in their salon, of whom Mr

Washington Irvine [i.e. Irving] made one'; the couple preferred to go straight to the apartment which the Garnetts had taken for them and make themselves presentable. Among the Garnetts' Paris circle at this time were the Frenchman Guillaume Hyde de Neuville, who had at one time been the Garnetts' neighbour in New Jersey, and visiting American friends, including the New York banker Charles Wilkes, as well as Washington Irving. On one occasion Irving, whose best-known tales, *Rip van Winkle* and *The Legend of Sleepy Hollow,* had appeared in 1820, called on Mr Wilkes; he notes in his journal 'see Miss Wright there – tall thin talking woman – Mrs Trollop & husband'.[11] In Paris Julia and Harriet Garnett were also reunited with Frances and Camilla Wright, who for the moment had made their home in France.

While her evenings were spent in the Garnetts' salon, the theatre, ballet or opera, Fanny's days were filled with shopping in the Palais Royal and museum-going, from the Louvre to the traveller Denon's famous collection of Egyptian and Japanese artifacts. After a day trip to Versailles, Fanny mused that 'Louis le Grand was the vainest, the most lavish and the most selfish of men.' But the highlight of the Trollopes' stay was an invitation from General Lafayette, popular hero of the American Revolution, to his estate outside Paris, La Grange. It was Frances Wright who first introduced her Harrow friends to Lafayette. Lafayette had expressed a desire to meet the young Scotswoman after the publication of her *Views on Society and Manners in America.* They were duly introduced and, as was her wont, Frances Wright, by then in her mid-twenties, worshipped the man who at sixty-four was old enough to be her grandfather. The admiration was mutual (Stendhal wrote in 1821 that 'in spite of his age [Lafayette] was entirely occupied in grabbing the petticoats of some pretty girl from behind'), and the General opened his home to the Wright sisters.[12]

Through the efforts of Madame de Lafayette, La Grange had remained in the family's possession throughout the upheavals of the French Revolution, when Lafayette had been forced into exile by the Jacobins. It thus retained some pre-revolutionary charm and luxury, while the atmosphere was relaxed and refined. The Trollopes arrived to be greeted by various family members, including Lafayette's five daughters, six grandchildren and their tutors, as well as a number of other house guests. Their apartment consisted of two rooms: in the larger was 'a very handsome bed in recess, with rich crimson satin curtains, and a quilt of the same, covering the bed by day. In the smaller room is a small bed for Monsieur, if it were preferred', Thomas Anthony was politely informed. The dining table was always set for twenty or more, courses were passed around in silver dishes by a host of manservants, and excellent wines were served by the butler. Fanny was so enchanted by it all that at the end of her first day she sat by the window sketching the turrets of the handsome château until a thunderstorm interrupted her. The Wright sisters were supposed to join the party at La Grange, and twice Fanny Trollope set off in Lafayette's carriage to meet the diligence from Paris. However, they got the dates wrong and – 'alas!' – twice Fanny returned without her friends.

The ten-day visit to La Grange passed quickly for Fanny. During the day there were strolls through the extensive grounds, letter-writing and sketching, in the evenings, dancing, music supplied by Lafayette's daughters, dramatic readings and, of course, 'the delightful conversation' of her host. 'We talked much of Pepe – of Fanny Wright' – Frances Wright had introduced Pepe to Lafayette – 'of the revolution – of the various scenes in which he had himself been a principal actor.' He told Fanny that the beheading of Louis XVI had been a tactical error on the republicans' part; the king 'might have been removed in safety and honour from a country no longer in a condition to submit to the yoke'. Despite his moderate stance, Lafayette remained a hero of republicanism, and after the Bourbon restoration in 1815 La Grange became the meeting-place for those with liberal views. The general himself became a leader of the French branch of the Carbonari, an Italian secret society devoted to the overthrow of the Bourbon rulers in Naples. (Thus his interest in General Pepe.) In 1821, only three years before the Trollopes' visit to La Grange, the general had narrowly escaped arrest after an abortive *coup d'état.*

'Nothing,' writes Fanny in her journal, 'could be more interesting than the conversation of this illustrious man; – quiet and simple in manners, open and unconstrained in giving his opinion, gentle and unassuming in listening to the opinions of others. He talked with ease and frankness of the most interesting events of his life.' For his part, Lafayette seems to have been taken with Fanny. He paid her the compliment of rising at five in the morning to see her off and, a few days later, attending the farewell party in Paris which Frances Wright gave for the Trollopes. 'I know not where to find so intellectual, so amiable a set of beings as those I have been living amongst here,' Fanny wrote on the eve of her departure for England.

Although on at least one occasion Thomas Anthony could not leave his bed owing to a bad headache, he seems to have enjoyed Paris and, in particular, Lafayette's hospitality. One evening Lafayette treated his guests to a local *fête de village*. When the dancing began, all the young people from La Grange joined in, as did – no doubt to everyone's surprise – Thomas Anthony. He had something to celebrate: the recent publication of his book, *A Treatise on the Mortgage of Ships* (1823), which was intended to clarify the rather murky legislation on the subject. Trollope's *Treatise* was, 'with his lordship's permission, respectfully dedicated' to Lord Liverpool, at that time president of the Society of Ship-owners as well as prime minister. Lord Liverpool was a Tory, but his policies in this, his second administration, have been described as 'Liberal Toryism', and so no doubt Trollope felt able to court the Prime Minister without betraying his Liberal principles. The barrister would, of course, have been familiar with mortgages as a conveyancer, and he must have come across a few cases dealing with ships which exposed the ambiguity of the law. In any event, with the publication of this book it seems that Thomas Anthony wanted something more out of life than a set of chambers at Lincoln's Inn or a middling farm in Middlesex. Like Lucius Mason in *Orley Farm*, 'he was tormented by a desire to do something, he knew not what, that might be great'. It had been five years since the Meetkerke inheritance had been taken away from him; perhaps the barrister hoped that Lord Liverpool would grant him a government post.

He was probably still waiting to learn the Prime Minister's reaction to his book when, in the spring of 1824, he sat for his friend George Hayter's painting, 'The Trial of William, Lord Russell', which had been commissioned by the Duke of Bedford. Fanny was delighted, and wrote to Tom, 'I shall like to see your father's head there.'[13] No doubt the Trollopes had been regaling their English friends with stories of their visit to Paris and La Grange since their return the previous autumn. Anthony had just started Harrow and both Tom and Henry had been elected to Winchester. All in all, things were looking up for the Trollopes in the early months of 1824. But a double tragedy was about to strike the family which would overwhelm even the resilient Fanny.

Fanny's third son, Arthur, had always been delicate. Frances Eleanor Trollope states that he lived with his grandparents, the Miltons, much of the time, presumably to help his mother out; she had five other children at home, three of them younger, who demanded her attention. Arthur's frail health had not created too much cause for concern. He had entered Harrow at the same time as Anthony, but it was soon decided that he would be better off back with his grandparents, who had left the vicarage at Heckfield and moved into a smaller house in Reading once Fanny's sister Mary had finally married. (She was in her early forties when she married Captain Charles Clyde, RN.) Mrs Milton's opinion was that the little boy was 'not *ill*' though 'hardly stout enough' to go to school. His grandfather, now old and frail, gave Arthur lessons at home. William Milton wrote to Tom and Henry at Winchester in November 1823:

My Dear Boys,
   Feeble as I am, Arthur will not let me rest, unless I take up my Pen to give you a line or two in the Basket. He would hardly have the Face to persevere in this, if He knew (as the case is) that I have nothing more principal to mention, than how incessant He is in his pleasant attentions towards me. He never lets me take my short fine-weather Walks, without placing himself at my Side . . . Arthur has been with us some weeks: in which time I have again taken him through Euclid; & I think there is hardly to be found one, of his Age, more at home in the Matter; no one, I am sure, who more relishes it, & its cognate Subjects. Whatever be his Path through Life; He will, I have no doubt, sometimes find the said Euclid his Staff, sometimes his Lamp.

This scene puts one in mind of old Mr Harding and his little grand-daughter, Posy, who lived with him for a time and to whom he was devoted, playing cat's cradle by his bedside in Anthony's *Last Chronicle of Barset*. Arthur was the only one of William Milton's grandchildren to be mentioned in his will dated 1822. To his 'dear Arthur' he left his ring dial, his set of compasses and his mathematical books.[14]

Within nine months of this letter both Arthur and his grandfather were dead. They passed away within days of each other in July 1824: the eighty-one-year-old William on the twelfth, followed on the twenty-second by eleven-year-old Arthur from tuberculosis and, perhaps, a broken heart, like young Ferdinand in *The Abbess*, who pined for his sister and within a week of her departure, 'to the surprise of the whole household, took to his bed and died, after a low but rapid fever of a few days' continuance'. William Milton had lived, in many respects, a good life. He was loved and respected by his friends and family. Yet, he believed that the world had failed to give him the recognition he deserved for his inventions, in particular, the floating harbour in Bristol. His monument at the back of Heckfield Church – a handsome neoclassical sculpture in marble – reads in full:

Sacred to the memory of the Reverend William Milton, A M formerly fellow of New College Oxford, and fifty-one years vicar of the parish. Eminent both in literature and science, he added to the exemplary discharges of the duties of a Christian minister the elegant pursuits of the scholar and the active prosecution of extensive designs for the public good. He closed an useful and honorable life on the twelfth day of July 1824, in the eighty-first year of his age. As a father, a husband, and a friend, deeply has his loss been felt, and long will his remembrance be cherished.

Fanny adored her father, his humour, his eccentricities, his gentleness, and she would have mourned his passing. But it seemed too cruel that it should have occurred so close to Arthur's death. In an age when child mortality was high, Tom Trollope explains, 'the bereaved father' – or mother – 'of a son who was one of the millions is chastened and humbled in his sorrow by the knowledge that others are suffering his grief; that the blow which has stricken him down but marks him as subject to the lot of mortals, and leaves the world around him to pursue its unaltered course' (*Garstangs of Garstang Grange*). Even so, the death of an eleven-year-old child is a tragedy, and Arthur's death, like Ferdinand's, appears to have been unexpected: 'he was too frail a flower to live! and yet – I had little thought he would have gone so soon'. His sister Juliet 'felt as if she had never loved the sweet boy enough – she remembered his innocent fondness, his engaging gentleness, his winning beauty' (*The Abbess*). Fanny was perhaps again recalling her own state of mind when she describes in *One Fault* the grieving young mother, Isabella Wentworth, standing 'with her dark-browed and repining husband beside the grave, that seemed to receive her heart as the little coffin was lowered into it'.

Death and bereavement loom large in Fanny Trollope's novels, just as they did in her own life. In *The Vicar of Wrexhill* Fanny describes that awful moment when the bereaved must confront the world's sympathy. The Mowbray family, still grieving the loss of their father, 'had all dreaded the moment of reappearing before the eyes of the little village world, and of thus giving public notice, as it were, that they no longer required to be left to mourn in secret: but this painful ceremony came, and was endured, like those that had preceded it'. Harrow could not have been very different. 'The village gentry began to offer their visits of condolence, which, happily however for the tranquillity of the persons chiefly concerned, were performed in the improved manner of modern times; that is to say, every allusion to the recent event being by all but their intimate friends cautiously avoided by all parties.' No doubt Fanny felt that, as with the Mowbrays, 'dreary and heavy was the change that had fallen on them, and it was long ere the mere act of assembling for their daily meals ceased to be a source of suffering'. The death of a child or parent can bring a family closer together; it can also drive them apart.

To Thomas Anthony it must have seemed as if his world was crashing down around him. Nothing had come of his book. Nor had anything come of his father-in-law's will. Besides some plate, the Trollopes inherited a third of William's estate, but not until the debts had been paid, his settlement on his wife Sarah honoured and £300 allotted to Henry Milton (who had by this time a wife, Mary Anne, and twin boys), and then only after taking into account what he had already advanced to the Trollopes on Fanny's marriage. There cannot have been much left. In Fanny's novel *The Old World and the New*, Mary Stormont had never doubted that her father's allowance would continue to be paid to her after his death, but it was not the case: 'I led my dear husband into the same error into which I had fallen.' Fanny may have made this mistake herself. In his state of mind, Thomas Anthony probably believed that his suffering over his son's death was greater than anyone else's. He must have felt like Anthony's bankrupted Ferdinand Lopez when told that his new-born son would not live long: 'Nothing thrives that I have to do with' (*The Prime Minister*).

Arthur's death seems to have driven a wedge between Fanny and her husband: they were unable to console each other. Before their marriage, Thomas Anthony had written to Fanny of his contempt for 'all ardent professions' of emotion; Fanny, however, came to believe that 'few people capable of loving heartily are without the capacity of suffering heartily also' (*The Vicar of Wrexhill*). Of course, it is impossible to know what words passed between Fanny and her husband. Perhaps, like Marmaduke Wentworth in *One Fault*, 'he felt a selfish sorrow' at the death of their young son. Wentworth responds to his wife's open display of grief with the thought: 'Think you, madam, that you alone feel this loss?' 'Those,' he adds, 'who make the greatest display of feeling, rarely suffer the most from it.' Or, was there a moment when, at a loss for what to say to his wife, Thomas Anthony let slip the words, 'Compose yourself'? In *The Old World and the New* these two words had been enough to make the distressed Katherine Smith break off her engagement with Mr Warburton, believing (wrongly) that there was no longer any sympathy, and thus no love, between them. For Fanny, love represented 'all the best feelings that Heaven has given to help us through this vale of tears': 'warm, unselfish, and devoted affection' was 'the only boon worth having, that one human being can bestow upon another'. There was no value in the 'hard, cold, stiff-necked pride' which those like Wentworth – and Thomas Anthony Trollope – called 'independence' (*One Fault*). Fanny, consumed by her own grief, may not have realized the depth of her husband's pain.

Thomas Anthony was angry at everyone: his landlord, Lord Northwick, for bleeding him dry, his children for never doing well enough at school, and his law colleagues for trying his patience. 'The fact was that all the attorneys were afraid of him,' wrote Tom Trollope of Bentham Linacre in *The Garstangs of Garstang Grange*; 'he bullied, and snubbed, and badgered them so intolerably; he proved so undeniably that they knew nothing at all of the matter in hand, and were utter numbskulls and blockheads . . . that they avoided him as the devil avoids holy water; with the result of leaving him at the end of ten years from his call a briefless barrister, though a thoroughly sound and good lawyer.' Tom later described his father in almost exactly these terms.

Thomas Anthony was also angry at his wife. Perhaps he blamed her for her father's disappointing will and their growing debts (Fanny's love of entertaining could not have helped); he may even have held her, in part, responsible for Arthur's death, just as Wentworth had his wife in *One Fault*. He certainly resented Fanny's strength and courage. 'There is nothing perhaps so generally consoling to a man as a well-established grievance, a feeling of having been injured, on which his mind can brood from hour to hour, allowing him to plead his own cause in his own court, within his own heart, – and always to plead it successfully,' wrote Anthony in *Orley Farm*. At the time Fanny probably did not understand all this. Like Mrs O'Donagough in *The Widow Married*, 'she often, indeed, felt that she did not fully comprehend [her husband] – that, although, as she constantly assured herself and [her daughter], she was not in the least bit afraid of him, some feeling which she could not exactly describe, generally in all their little disputes, led her to the conclusion that it might be as well not to defy him'.

The Trollopes' marriage began, slowly and imperceptibly, to come apart. Years later, Fanny drew upon her own experience to portray the breakdown of the Wentworths' marriage in *One Fault*. The beautiful heroine, Isabella Worthington, the daughter of a kind and humble clergyman, marries Marmaduke Wentworth, every inch an aristocrat and a gentleman, but proud, intractable and without humour. Soon Isabella realizes that she is unhappily married, but she cannot say why. 'No terrible event, no fatal discovery of former loves and entanglements, no cruel indication of fading passion, no heart-rending symptoms of indifference', 'nothing of all this had fallen upon her; yet had she endured them all, her spirit could scarcely have been so irremediably wounded and crushed within her as it was now'. 'She felt as if she had married one man, and discovered her husband to be another.'

Like Thomas Anthony, Wentworth suffers from dreadful head-aches – 'as if I had a smithy in my head' – and from a terrible, silent temper. He shows his anger not by swearing oaths but by the 'sternness of his eye – the deep hoarse voice in which he slowly pronounced his reprobation of whatever galled' him. He is not mean or revengeful, 'but instead of having a temper like other men, he has got the devil in him, that never suffers him to rest himself, or let anyone else rest either'. Only once does his anger 'at last burst from him, with a parting violence that resembled the first letting off of steam from a high-pressure engine'. Wentworth demands that his wife obey him, yet is solicitous of her well-being to the point of tyranny. He reproaches his wife Isabella, 'I had hoped that you would have learned that first duty of woman, a gentle and undeviating compliance with the wishes and the will of your husband.' 'Were I indifferent towards you, were I careless, unobservant, or neglectful there might be some shadow of excuse . . . but what shall we say of a woman who, having been treated as you have been, can still exhibit such obstinacy of will as to oppose and positively disobey the commands of a husband so devoted as myself?'

This could as easily be a description of Robert Kennedy, the Scottish aristocrat who marries the intelligent but wilful Lady Laura in Anthony Trollope's *Phineas Finn*. Like his mother in *One Fault*, Anthony portrays his father's silent, uncompromising despotism towards his wife – perhaps in an attempt to understand it. Kennedy's 'wife had not submitted either to his will or to his ways. He had that great desire to enjoy his full rights, so strong in the minds of weak, ambitious men, and he had told himself that a wife's obedience was one of those rights which he could not abandon without injury to his self-esteem.' Lady Laura calls him a 'cold tyrant' and warns her brother, 'there is no tyranny to a woman like telling her of her duty'. No doubt like Anthony's father, 'Mr Kennedy when troubled in his spirits looks at things gloomily, and puts meaning upon words which they should not bear.'

Lady Laura's father hints at the reason for the collapse of her marriage. Kennedy, he states, 'is so hard and dry, and what I call exacting. That is just the word for it. Now Laura has never been used to that. With me she always had her own way in everything, and I always found her fit to have it. I do not understand why her husband should treat her differently.' William Milton, too, had been an indulgent and trusting father. Fanny blamed the failure of the Wentworths' marriage wholly on the husband's 'one fault', his temperament. 'None can doubt it who have ever watched the influence of an ill-tempered husband upon every hour of his wife's existence.' If only Wentworth could 'have restrained the sour irritability of his miserable temper, and the petty ebullitions of the paltry vanity which made him shrink from the avowal of equal rights and equal dignity even with the chosen partner of his greatness, [Isabella] might again have almost fancied herself happy' (*One Fault*).

All these factors must have contributed to the Trollopes' problems, but there was another cause: Thomas Anthony was slowly poisoning himself with calomel,* that same mercury-based drug which had nearly killed Tom and Henry when they contracted typhus. The barrister took it to ease his chronic migraines. Fanny almost certainly associated her husband's increasing moroseness with these headaches: she refers to one character in *The Blue Belles* as a 'melancholy *migraineaire*'. But only Tom, who himself suffered from migraine between the ages of fifteen and forty, realized that calomel had had the effect of shattering his [father's] nervous system in a deplorable manner'; and so it would have, for chronic mercury poisoning, as well as damaging the liver and kidneys, causes irreversible brain damage, the symptoms of which are irritability and irrationality.

The deaths of her son and father left Fanny feeling weak and vulnerable. She found it difficult to look to her husband for comfort, and so she came to rely upon her close female friends. Although Julia and Harriet Garnett were both nearly fifteen years her junior, Fanny had always found 'the genuine liking and affection of the young . . .

* Mercurous chloride.

a very delicious incense to the old' (*Town and Country*). From the Isle of Wight, where she had gone to recuperate following the funerals (as does Isabella Wentworth after the death of her child), Fanny replied to Julia Garnett's letter of sympathy: 'I think you will *know* how I have felt it, without my attempting to tell you – most sweet, most touching are the words of affection when the heart is heavy with sorrow.' Betraying her anxiety concerning Thomas Anthony, she adds: 'I long to show these dear pages to my good husband – his heart too will thank you for them – and his heart too will yield to their eloquence – or I much mistake.' 'I have indeed suffered much of late,' Fanny concludes, 'and nothing does, or can soothe such suffering so effectually as the kindness of old and valued friends.'[15]

But the bereaved mother sorely missed the company of one of her most valued young friends, Frances Wright. When earlier that same year (1824) Lafayette had received an invitation from President Monroe and Congress to visit the States, he desired the young heiress to go with him; she, in turn, wanted him to adopt her and Camilla as his daughters. Perhaps not surprisingly, Lafayette's family regarded Frances Wright as a threat, and they refused to allow her to travel with the general. However, when he fell ill on the eve of his departure, his family gave in and the Wright sisters accompanied him to America – sailing out, however, on a separate ship. At first, Fanny Trollope disapproved of her young friend's conduct in the matter; but in her fragile state of mind following Arthur's death she came to regret ever having doubted the motives of 'that angel friend that seems dearer as every hour bears her farther from me'. In the same letter written from the Isle of Wight, quoted above, she confesses to Julia:

> my sorrowing heart tells me I have been [unjust] to my sweet Fanny – and oh! Julia how painful is this feeling. This is a pain *you* can never feel. – It was but on one point that I can thus accuse myself. – It was upon hearing that she had so suddenly left England – It *seemed* as if she had acted rashly, intemperately – but *data* were wanting – you waited not for these – but with the full entire confidence of undoubting affection, felt she must be right because she was Fanny. Dearest Julia your affection has been a faithful lodestar – it has not misled you. She *was*

right. She *is* right now – and I shall not easily be led to doubt it again – Most singular in truth has been, and must be her position. The very acts that in all other women we should deem wrong – are in her a great and ever-powering duty.

In *The Vicar of Wrexhill* Fanny Trollope describes how Mrs Mowbray's recent bereavement had exposed a 'weakness that induced her to seize gladly and gratefully any hand extended to lead her, and which, while it made her distrust herself, gave most sovereign sway and masterdom to any one ready and willing to supply the strength and decision of purpose which she wanted'. In the novel, it is the unctuous evangelical Revd Cartwright who exploits the widow. In much the same way, the charismatic and single-minded Frances Wright was to change for ever the course of Fanny Trollope's life.

CHAPTER FIVE

The Old World and the New

Such was Frances Wright's personal magnetism that her second sojourn in America, between 1824 and the late summer of 1827, left her Paris friends, the Garnett sisters, feeling destitute and aimless. In a letter Frances exhorted Julia Garnett to take up some occupation, for 'without some fixed and steady occupation of labour – of business – of study – something which keeps in habitual exercise our physical or mental energies and the better when it is both, it is impossible to make our existence glide smoothly – we must know moments nay hours of vexation and lassitude'.[1] Fanny Trollope also sorely felt the loss of Frances Wright's companionship, but it was not in her nature to languish: her great consolation always was to take up some occupation or cause on another's behalf. 'As long as there was something useful to be done, and some one she loved to do it for', Katherine, the heroine of *The Old World and the New*, 'could not be very miserable, for her energetic activity stood in the place of happiness'. Fanny continued to host at-homes, devise charades, stage amateur theatricals, organize picnics and teach her children Italian so that they could share her love of Dante.

Just at this time Fanny threw herself into the efforts of her old Hampshire friend, Mary Russell Mitford, to see her play *Rienzi* performed on the London stage. In 1824–5 the actor William Charles Macready had encouraged Mary Mitford to revise the play – mainly to enhance his own leading role – for the Drury Lane Theatre. The dramatist was, understandably, annoyed when nothing came of

Macready's promises. Macready, for his part, was horrified when an article damning the arrogance of the *'great actors'*, and citing his treatment of Miss Mitford and her play, appeared in *Blackwood's Magazine*. He even claimed in later life that the article, written by a friend of the dramatist but without her knowledge, had ruined his reputation.[2]

It was at this point that Fanny Trollope stepped in, for she was a great admirer of Mary Mitford's work. In the spring of 1826 Fanny read *Rienzi* and asked her friend Lady Milman's son, Henry, himself a dramatist and at this time a neighbour of Miss Mitford near Reading, to do the same. Fanny thought that her friend Macready would make a 'glorious "Rienzi." ' She knew of Macready's unhappiness over the *Blackwood's* article; but, she was equally aware of the rivalry between Macready and his fellow actor Edmund Kean. Fanny reckoned that she could set one against the other. She reassured Mary Mitford in a letter, 'Trust me, dear William would rather eat his heart than see Kean appear in "Rienzi." ' The ensuing correspondence between the two women reveals a series of deliciously farcical moments. Fanny writes that she saw her friend Kean, but *'nobody* knew what he intended to do', not even his wife. Fanny then lured Macready to pass a day at Julian Hill, but to no avail. To begin with, Fanny never had a moment alone with the actor, for 'Mr T[rollope] had brought down a young Oxonian with him, who never quitted us'. Macready must have appreciated the respite, and he refused to be drawn. 'I never saw anything to equal the ice-case into which he retreats the instant a word is uttered relative to his profession, and I confess myself unable to pursue him into it. I got from him that his movements for *next* year . . . depend entirely on Kean; if he acts in London, Mr Macready will act in America, and *vice versa*. Thus they cannot be *pitted*, as I had hoped, one against the other.'

Nevertheless, Macready still wanted to play Rienzi but was wary of dealing directly with Miss Mitford. Fanny volunteered to act as intermediary. In the summer of 1826, when Fanny found herself in Paris at the same time as Macready, she proposed to him that they meet *'seul-à-seul'* in the Bois de Boulogne. 'This is where the duels are usually fought,' she writes to Miss Mitford; 'our meeting, I flatter myself, will be of a different kind.' In the end, Kean spent the 1827 season in London, and Macready took *Rienzi* on tour to America. Fanny was disappointed that her mission had only partially succeeded, but at the end of 1826 she was at last able to rejoice at her friend's success on the London stage with another historical drama, *Foscari*. Mary Mitford reported that Fanny 'between joy for my triumph and sympathy with the play, has cried herself half blind'. It is not surprising that Mary Mitford later remembered her old friend Fanny as 'a lively, brilliant woman of the world, with a warm, blunt, cordial manner, and many accomplishments'. *Rienzi* finally had its début in London at Drury Lane at the end of 1828: Fanny, however, was not to see it performed until 1831 – in New York. But this is getting ahead of our story.

There were other causes to take up in the absence of Frances Wright. Fanny wrote to Mary Mitford in the spring of 1827, asking that she use her influence to get the artist Auguste Hervieu and his painting 'Love and Folly', recently accepted by the Royal Academy, 'spoken of in *The Times* and perhaps in some other publications'. Hervieu, by all accounts a highly-strung young man given to emotional outbursts, was yet another political exile whom Fanny had befriended, one 'among the many young Frenchmen who have been exiled for wishing for more freedom than the Bourbon fools and knaves allowed'. 'His father,' Fanny explains to her friend, 'a colonel in the emperor's army, died in the retreat from Moscow, and left him no inheritance, but debts. His only surviving relative is a rich priest – a Jesuit – whom, as you may well imagine, he has utterly offended.' The thirty-three-year-old artist, wanted on the Continent for his underground activities against the monarchs of France and Spain, was 'totally and entirely *alone*, and unknown'. 'How he has contrived to live, I know not,' Fanny continues; sometimes he must even go 'without his dinner to buy colours'. Hervieu may have exaggerated his plight when he saw what an eager listener Fanny was. By the time he met the Trollopes, Hervieu had been in England for six years and had already exhibited three paintings at the Royal Academy.

However, fame was not to come to the young Frenchman – at least, not in 1827. 'Not all the patronage of all the puffers can avail if the picture be badly hung,' Fanny later reported to Mary Mitford, and 'les academiciens *have* hung it in such a place, that had they hung it the front to the wall it would have made no difference.' Hervieu soon became a familiar face in the Trollope household, for Fanny engaged him as a drawing-master for the children. He joined in the Trollopes' amateur productions of Molière, coaching them on their French pronunciation. Tom remembers Hervieu drawing caricatures while they were all listening to Thomas Anthony reading the dreaded *Grandison*. The artist also drew sketches of the children and from time to time presented them with little gifts. He sent Tom, then at Winchester, a thin volume with the following note, revealing the state of his English: 'My dear Thom, if this Anacreon can please you, I do offert you.' Fanny and her husband occasionally took Hervieu along to social engagements, no doubt in an attempt to forward his career. She writes to Mary Mitford of one such event at the house of the writer Letitia Elizabeth Landon: 'It was really a very smart party, though *some of us* did look rather queer. You need not talk of our democratic friend to any of our dear good Tory ones. They would groan in spirit, and think that Trollope, his wife, and all his children were going to destruction.'[3]

Fanny also occupied herself with a little translating and a little matchmaking. General Pepe had remained in close touch with the Trollopes. In early 1825 he wrote to Fanny, expressing his sympathy at the news of Arthur's death. 'You are constant in friendship, and I hold constancy to be a great virtue in a lady,' he remarked in the same letter. Pepe paid Fanny's mastery of Italian a great compliment by asking her to translate into English verse an ode written by Vittorio Alfieri in honour of Lafayette when he, 'forsaking all the pleasures of Paris and the Court, had gone over to America to assist in the sacred cause of that country's independence'. The two generals had much in common, from a love of soldiery to a hatred of tyranny. Pepe notes in his memoirs that 'the poet, Thomas Campbell, assured me that the translation possessed much merit'. Pepe had the ode published in the English papers, several of which he sent to Lafayette.[4]

Julia Garnett had also found something to take her mind off her friend Frances Wright's prolonged absence. Over the course of the 1826–7 Paris season, Julia spent a lot of time in the company of the young Hanoverian historian, Georg Heinrich Pertz, whom she had

97

first met at one of Lafayette's soirées. When Julia learned that he was to visit London in the spring to work in the British Museum, she wrote a letter of introduction on his behalf to Fanny Trollope. Julia's letter must have been quite revealing – or perhaps the older and more worldly of the two could read between the lines, for Fanny wrote to her friend: 'I long to see him [Pertz] – Julia mark my words – *you love him.* I see it, I'm sure of it – If he loves you, I hope he will tell me so – and then we shall be *very very* dear friends – Now do not write off by the post to contradict all this – *for I shall not believe you.*' Needless to say, Fanny welcomed the young Georg with open arms, and he became a frequent visitor to the Trollope household that summer – as was Julia, for Fanny, having approved of Julia's choice, did not waste much time in inviting her young friend to stay at Julian Hill.

Georg Pertz later recalled: 'Usually I came on Friday or Saturday from London, and returned thither early on Monday. About three weeks after Julia's arrival, Mrs T. had got up a dramatic evening entertainment, in which I had to marvel at Julia, in English speech and dress, in the role of Roscolana in the *Malade Imaginaire*' – another Molière play. The serious-minded Georg had thought to wait to propose to Julia until his academic post in Germany had been decided, but Fanny's machinations proved too much and, 'as a powerful bud, illuminated by the sun of July, breaks its casing and unfolds its priceless blossom, so did my love break through this last boundary, and on the 3rd of August she made me the happiest man by acknowledging her love for me'.[5] Anthony Trollope may have been thinking of his mother's matchmaking when in *Phineas Redux* he has Glencora Palliser bring together Madame Max Goesler and Phineas Finn. Like Fanny, Glencora 'was one of those women whose minds were always engaged on such matters, and who are able to see how things will go. It must not be asserted of her that her delicacy was untainted, or her taste perfect; but she was clever – discreet in the midst of indiscretions – thoughtful and good-natured. She had considered it all, and given her orders with accuracy.'

In early 1825 all the Trollope boys were at boarding-school: Tom and Henry were still at Winchester; Anthony, who had spent two miserable and unsuccessful years at Harrow, was just starting at

Sunbury, a private school south-west of London run by the Revd Arthur Drury. Fanny was a lively correspondent. She loved to write to the boys in French and Italian – so much so that Tom finally petitioned that '*some* English' appear in every letter. Like her father, Fanny had a knack for figures, and she often sent Tom mathematical puzzles which she had devised. Dr George Frederick Nott, the Winchester prebendary who had heard young Tom's outburst against his Anabaptist nurse in Keppel Street, had the two oldest Trollope boys, then aged fourteen and thirteen to dinner one Sunday afternoon. He paints a charming picture of the visit for their mother: 'As soon as dinner was over, and a little chat had passed, I took up my pen to finish a letter, and I begged they would amuse themselves till tea time with a Book.' One chose Dryden, the other a tract of sermons. 'Bravo quoth I,' he continues.

> The choice augurs well. But I doubt how far the body will keep pace with the Mind. Just as I thought. A warm fire, a good dinner, and a rare arm Chair were too much for their love of literature. In five minutes they were fast asleep: and so comfortable did they seem that I had not the heart to wake them 'till tea was quite ready, and there was no more than time to drink it before they were obliged to go into College. I again assure you that I was pleased highly with their manners and conversation, and not a little surprised at being asked by the eldest what I thought of Dante, and whether I did not consider the third, the finest book of the Inferno. Savvy fellow!

Winchester had not made Tom any less precocious. The next year he was created 'candle-keeper', a title – attended by certain privileges but no duties – which was bestowed upon the seven boys who had been in the college longest. Fanny had an irreverent side to her and never allowed herself, or her children, to take such outmoded traditions too seriously. She has her tongue firmly in her cheek when she writes to congratulate Tom: 'Hail! All hail! As Volumnia bowed low before her Coriolanus, so do I now bow low before my – Tom. Oh dreadful bathos! No; before my great Adolphus, that lion of the West! And as Volumnia knelt to her son for mercy on the Romans, so do I kneel to thee for mercy on thy fags.'[6] One wonders if Tom and Henry got into trouble at Winchester by aping their mother's unconventional views. In *The Ward of Thorpe Combe*, written years later, Fanny includes a conversation calculated to make her sons smile. 'I know nothing that makes so decided a difference as a good school and a vulgar one,' comments an elderly spinster. The vulgar schools turn out to be 'Winchester, Westminster, Harrow, Shrewsbury, Rugby, and all the rest of them', Eton being the only good one.

Despite her apparent good humour, all was not well in the Trollope household. Reflecting on her own troubles, it may have struck her, attending an evening soirée, 'how little we are apt to think as we enter some crowded rendezvous of fashion, and throw a light glance over the light throng entering with us, – how little at such a moment are we apt to think of the various cares, sorrows, fears, and anxieties, that may be entering along with them; they all look so smilingly, or so proudly, or so richly, or so beautifully, that it never enters one's head to remember that every bosom there . . . has each its own little museum of cares, which, if laid bare before us, would make the outward coating seem wondrously flimsy' (*Hargrave*).

The Trollopes' finances had gone from bad to worse. Although the manufacturing base, including trade, transport and building, began to prosper in the 1820s, agriculture, even with the Corn Laws still in place, remained depressed for the next decade. The value of livestock was also hit. *The Farmers' Magazine* for February 1822 explained: 'Many respectable agriculturalists, who were lately considered as opulent, are now selling off to prevent either ruin, or are sold up by their landlords under a distress of rent. So many and frequent are the instances of distress, that it has become a common topic of conversation – "Who will fall next?" '[7] The Trollopes were no exception.

And then there were the social pressures. Thomas Anthony had grown up believing that he, as the grandson of a baronet and once heir-apparent to his uncle Meetkerke's property, had certain standards to uphold and obligations to fulfil. To be a gentleman was everything, and Thomas Anthony wanted his sons to look, feel and act as true gentlemen. But how difficult it was to find the money to clothe and educate them properly, while still maintaining that fragile veneer of respectability – the sort of respectability which had a price tag attached to it. Miss Matilda Perkins, also a member of the impoverished gentry, remarks in *The Widow Married*: 'There is nobody of any fashion, as we all know, who does not leave bills everywhere.' No doubt thinking of her own experience, Fanny says of the English 'if no bills were run up at Gunter's, or at Howell and James's, because it was worse than death to be outdone, – we should . . . be a happier and a more respectable people' (*Paris and the Parisians*). There were so many people, 'possessed of many natural advantages', who 'endanger them all by the silly practice of spending a little more money than they have got', and 'they can never again find themselves really and truly at ease in their circumstances' (*The Life and Adventures of a Clever Woman*). Mrs Markham, the daughter of a gentleman who happily settles for a 'toy of a house' in secluded Devon when she marries a lieutenant with a small pension, had realized early on that respectability in the eyes of the world reflected more one's expenditure than one's dignity or self-worth. Whenever she saw a couple

> straining and striving to bring up a large family respectably, i.e. not according to their own station, but to that of the rank next above them – she was wont to say, 'Quite a mistake – quite a mistake, indeed! – They have blundered sadly, those gentlemen and ladies; for when, in the matter of keeping house, people set out wrong, it is curious to see how altogether out of the way they get before they come to the end of their journey.'

As for his law practice, Thomas Anthony was caught in the same embarrassing predicament as the young barrister, Frank Greystock, in Anthony Trollope's *Eustace Diamonds*. He explains: 'it is so hard with us. Attorneys owe us large sums of money, and we can't dun them very well. I have a lot of money due to me from rich men, who don't pay me simply because they don't think that it matters. I talk to them grandly, and look big, as though money was the last thing I thought of, when I am longing to touch my hat and ask them as a great favour to settle my little bill' – but this was not the behaviour of a gentleman. Thomas Anthony continued to argue with clients as well as family and friends until nearly everyone was afraid of him.

Anthony could have been describing his father at this point in his life when he wrote of Mr Wharton in *The Prime Minister* that he was 'a thorough lawyer . . . no one doubted his law. He had once written a book – on the mortgage of stocks in trade; but that had been in early life, and he had never since dabbled in literature.'

Anthony then says of Wharton: 'He was certainly a man of whom men were generally afraid. At the whist-table no one would venture to scold him. In the court no one ever contradicted him. In his own house, though he was very quiet, the servants dreaded to offend him.' In his memoirs, Tom Trollope makes clear that here too Anthony was thinking of their father. 'He was very fond of whist,' Tom wrote of Thomas Anthony, 'and was I believe a good player. But people did not like to play with him.' An old family friend once told Tom, 'Many men will scold their partners occasionally. But Trollope invariably scolds us all round with the utmost impartiality; and that every deal!' The same bad temper which had affected Thomas Anthony's marriage also damaged his career and his relationships with his children. Tom continues, 'he was, in a word, a highly respected, but not a popular or well-beloved man. Worst of all, alas! he was not popular in his own home. No one of all the family circle was happy in his presence', yet 'he was as affectionate a father as any children ever had'.

Anthony, too, remarked that Thomas Anthony's temper was 'so irritable that even those he loved the best could not endure it. We were all estranged from him, and yet I believe that he would have given his heart's blood for any of us' (*An Autobiography*). Of the Duke of Omnium, formerly Plantagenet Palliser, one of several characters modelled on his father, Anthony writes: 'He was a man so reticent and undemonstrative in his manner that he had never known how to make confidential friends of his children' (*The Duke's Children*). In *Orley Farm*, Anthony has his father in mind when he muses: 'There are men, and excellent men too, from whose minds the cares of life never banish themselves, who never seem to remember that provision is made for the young ravens. They toil and spin always, thinking sternly of the worst and rarely hoping for the best. They are ever making provision for rainy days, as though there were to be no more sunshine. So anxious are they for their children that they take no pleasure in them, and their fear is constant that the earth will cease to produce her fruits.'

Thomas Anthony was just such a one. He desperately wanted his sons to succeed, and to him, success meant New College, Oxford. Fanny remarked of the Worthington family in *One Fault* that 'one of the topics which added to the enjoyment of that happy evening was the certainty which many vacancies for the following year afforded, that Charles would "get New College" as the phrase goes'. Thomas Anthony was obsessed by this ambition for Tom, Henry and Anthony. In her biography of Fanny, Tom's wife, Frances Eleanor Trollope, describes Thomas Anthony's letters to his sons at Winchester as being 'extraordinary from their minute and reiterated questions about every detail of their progress at Winchester'.

> The mere reading of these old letters seems to arouse a kind of irritable antagonism. Nothing is taken for granted. Everything is discussed and enquired into, with the most wearisome insistence. In short he *worries* the boys unsparingly and unceasingly, unconscious that he risks creating a revulsion of feeling that may frustrate the very object he has at heart. His aim is solely their benefit. No father could display more single-minded devotion to the welfare of his family than did Thomas Anthony Trollope. But he never put himself for a moment in the boys' place.

'What he had to say, he reasoned, was right and just; it was proper that he should be kept informed of their progress; it was his duty to urge them onward.'

Thus, as far as Thomas Anthony was concerned, it was nothing short of disaster when Henry left Winchester in 1826 before completing his studies – 'to the anger of his father,' as Frances Eleanor Trollope notes, 'and the deep sorrow and mortification of both parents'. Tom, who had always been a good student, had been able to cope with the pressure their father exerted. Henry, by far the most outgoing of the Trollope boys – and the most like his mother, full of spirit and romance, enthusiastic and fun-loving – could not. As Frances Eleanor Trollope explains, 'Henry was idle.' He 'had a bright intelligence and a warm heart; but he was of a haughty, exacting, and irritable temper' – taking after his father.[8]

Fanny was no doubt recalling Henry's plight when she wrote *Uncle Walter*, which opens with a description of two brothers, aged thirteen and fourteen. Their schoolmaster, Dr Porsonby, writes to their father

> explicitly declaring that he feared it was but too clear that his [in this case] eldest son was wholly averse to intellectual pursuits, his utmost efforts having proved unavailing in leading him to perceive in 'Virgil' higher beauties than were to be found in 'Robinson Crusoe,' which in truth was the only book he ever seemed to open willingly. He had brought with him from home, as it appeared, a copy of that idle work ... On other points, however, the Doctor seemed quite ready to avow that Master Walter Harrington was not a bad boy; far from it indeed, for he manifested many amiable qualities, and was a particular favourite with Mrs Porsonby.

The other Harrington boy – named Henry, though clearly based on Tom at that age – is a model student, and the only book he ever had in his hands, besides the prescribed classics, 'was a little work that contained detailed information respecting all the scholarships and fellowships in the University of Oxford'.

There must have been terrible clashes between the spirited Henry and his overbearing father, clashes which the young Anthony remembered. Quarrelling fathers and sons abound in his fiction: Larry and Thady Macdermot in his very first novel, *The Macdermots of Ballycloran*, Daniel and John Caldigate in *John Caldigate*, and Adolphus and Dolly Longstaffe in *The Way We Live Now*. 'My father annoys me by everything he says and does, and I annoy him by saying and doing nothing,' Lord Chiltern says of his father, Lord Brentford, in *Phineas Finn*. Yet, his parents could not afford to allow the fifteen-year-old Henry to do nothing. He needed a career, but without further costly tuition the professions would be closed to him. The Trollopes hit upon the idea of placing Henry in a Paris counting-house to learn something about finance. They reasoned that in the French capital he could live more cheaply than in London and perfect his French, yet still be amongst close family friends.

Fanny threw herself into the problem of Henry's future with such devotion and energy that it is hard not to see it as an attempt to overcome her sense of loss following Arthur's death. That summer of 1826 Fanny and Thomas Anthony accompanied Henry to Paris and stayed several weeks to see that he settled in to his new life. In his mother's company he met a fascinating array of people, mainly through the Garnetts, which included the philosopher Benjamin Constant, the American novelist James Fenimore Cooper and the historian Sismondi, Julia and Harriet's cousin by marriage. General Lafayette, who had recently returned from his triumphant tour of America, invited the Trollopes back to La Grange. 'Henry particularly wished for you and talked of you,' Fanny wrote to Tom from Paris, 'when he was swallowing grapes by wholesale in General Lafayette's vineyard.' He also wandered into Lafayette's orchard, where cider was being made, and consumed as many apples 'as were convenient'.

Before returning to Harrow, his parents placed Henry in the charge of a Protestant Swiss family in Paris, the Monods, and paid for dancing and gymnastic lessons.[9] At first Henry's letters home are cheerful enough. He does not find French cookery as oily as he expected, nor does he find things as cheap as he had hoped. Although it had been twelve years since Waterloo, Henry notes that, walking along the Paris streets, 'it is not uncommon to hear the boys halloa out "Voici le petit goddam! *Nous battrons les Anglais avec des manches à balai!*" '* He enjoys the *Fête du Roi*, when 'in the evening the whole of Paris was illuminated, and the theatres', free to the public, 'were open the whole day'. Outdoor music could be heard continually, emanating from stages built specially along the Champs Elysées. 'And to crown all, a great balloon, and in the evening at dark, some admirable fireworks. A thousand rockets were let off at once.' Henry then describes catching sight of the seven-year-old Duke of Bordeaux, at that time heir to the throne, '*looking out of his carriage window and making faces*'.

---

* 'Look at the little Brit! *We shall fight the English with broomsticks!*'

It seems to have been a great weight off his father's mind, knowing that Henry was in a position to begin to earn his own living. Thomas Anthony even allowed himself to be commandeered into the 'corps dramatique' for Fanny's production of Molière's *Femmes savantes* in French. However, Henry soon became unhappy and homesick. After a year, he was finally given leave to return home for the summer holidays of 1827. The indefatigable Fanny writes to Tom at Winchester: 'I enclose you Henry's last letter. I hope you will share the delight he anticipates from the family reunion, I expect to enjoy it myself, not a little. I have already been planning sundry "drolleries" to amuse us all. As I am to stay at home all the long vacation, I hope to be very happy there. We must have our French play again, and "Chrononhotonthologos"* into the bargain. I flatter myself that you will this year find some fruit left you; — at least the gooseberries, currants, peaches, nectarines, and apricots, all promise largely.'[10] By the end of the holiday Henry was loathe to return to his dreary Parisian office, but there was nothing else for it. At least he had his mother's visit to look forward to in September for Julia Garnett's wedding, which was to take place at the American Embassy. Frances Wright, just recently returned from her long sojourn in America, was to be one of the guests of honour.

Frances Wright's second trip to America in 1824–7 had not turned out quite the way she had planned. Within just a few months General Lafayette and his 'adopted daughter' had fallen out and gone their separate ways. Frances wrote to the Garnetts in October 1824 that 'the enthusiasm, triumphs & rejoicings exhibited here before the countenance of the great & good Lafayette have no longer charms for me'.[11] She had become too outspoken and her views too radical for the sixty-seven-year-old Frenchman. Her friends back in Paris believed that she had fallen under the baleful influence of Robert Owen, the Scottish reformer, who had also journeyed to America in 1824, to drum up support among statesmen and frontiersmen alike for his utopian community of New Harmony, Indiana. Owen espoused radical equality and socialism; in addition, he favoured the abolition of

* An eighteenth-century burlesque by Henry Carey.

that awful 'Trinity of Man's oppressors', 'Private Property, Irrational Religion and Marriage'.

Frances Wright's views on slavery had also altered somewhat since the publication of her *Views of Society and Manners in America* (1821). On her first transatlantic visit, Frances, aged only twenty-one, had been greatly influenced by her American friends and had, for the most part, assumed their prejudices. Thus, in her book she claims that the Unites States was the first country to abolish the slave trade. This was being economical with the truth: in 1794 the government had prohibited only the export of slaves from the country. Britain was the first nation to abolish the slave trade altogether, in 1807. (Slavery had been illegal in England since 1772.) Concerning the emancipation of slaves, Frances had written that 'this neither can nor ought to be done too hastily. To give liberty to a slave before he understands its value is, perhaps, rather to impose a penalty than to bestow a blessing.' She then adds, 'Poor, ignorant, and lazy, it is impossible that they should not soon be vicious.'

By 1824, Frances Wright had become impatient with what she saw as most Americans' complacent view of slavery as a necessary evil. She conceived the idea of establishing a community for the education of slaves in preparation for their eventual emancipation. Frances travelled over 600 miles on horseback with her sister Camilla to look for suitable land, visiting Owen's New Harmony along the way. By the end of the journey, poor Camilla was suffering terribly from a boil on her back caused by the pressure of her corset bone. Frances consulted Robert Owen's son, Robert Dale Owen, who was to take part in the enterprise, before settling on 200 acres in the backwoods of Tennessee. She then purchased about twenty slaves to help build and finance Nashoba. Once the community was up and running, these slaves would be the first to benefit from her educational programme. By early 1826 there were a handful of like-minded reformers at Nashoba besides Frances Wright and her sister Camilla: Eliza and George Flower, formerly of New Harmony, and James Richardson, a Scotsman with a medical background. George Whitby had drifted over from a nearby Shaker village and, before that, he too had been a New Harmonian.

Once back in Europe in late July 1827, Frances Wright immediately set about recruiting more people to join her great enterprise. As Robert Dale Owen put it: 'The more I see of the old world the less I feel inclined to remain in it. But I should like to rescue out of it a few rational beings who are too good for it & would be much happier in the woods.'[12] Frances had every reason to believe she would succeed. Since at least the 1790s the abolition of slavery and the slave trade had been an important, even fashionable, cause amongst the educated classes in England; and utopianism was in the air. Ideal communities, like New Harmony, were springing up all over America. In fact, the United States itself was considered a utopia writ large: 'A frame of government perfect in its principles ... brought down from the airy regions of Utopia.'[13]

Frances approached Mary Shelley, who politely but firmly turned down the invitation. Since the spring, while still in America, she had been trying to persuade the Garnett sisters to come to Nashoba. She was especially keen that Harriet join her after her sister's wedding – though the reformer did not think marriage would necessarily be an obstacle for Julia: 'You know where you have another home and another fond friend to share it with,' she wrote somewhat tactlessly to the bride-to-be. Harriet later confessed to her sister: 'I should have joined Nashoba from the love I bear to my Fanny [Wright], without approving God knows of its principles.' But Harriet wanted to remain near her family, and her mother was too old to take up residence on the American frontier. In any case, the Garnetts liked Paris and all it had to offer: 'the cards and conversation, tea, English plum cake, sirops & orgeat', wrote Harriet. They were reluctant to give up the Paris salons of, among others, the elegant and urbane Madame Juliette Récamier, where they met such luminaries as, in addition to those already mentioned, Stendhal and Chateaubriand. Apparently, Stendhal was attracted to Harriet, and Prosper Merimée pined after Julia though he was ten years her junior. More importantly, respected friends such as Lafayette and Sismondi urged the sisters to resist the temptation to throw in their lot with such a loose cannon, 'even for the sake of the cause' of emancipation. Harriet found it difficult to say 'no' to the formidable Frances Wright, so she and her family began to look for excuses and delays. An aunt of the Wright sisters confronted the Garnetts with the astute observation that they had 'even taken a *lease* of a house in Paris, that it might operate as an obstacle to your going to America, lest you should be tempted'.[14]

Fanny Trollope, too, was worried by her young friend's increasingly unorthodox opinions. In the spring of 1827 Frances Wright had also been writing to the Trollopes. She wanted their help in publishing a paper setting forth the principles of Nashoba – not only those of equality, but also of free love and freedom from religion. Fanny confided to Julia, 'it would be utter madness to print it here – contempt, ridicule, and reprobation would be the result . . . Dear noble, simple-hearted Fanny dreams not of the light in which her declared opinions against religion would be viewed.' However, the impressionable Henry had no such doubts concerning the charismatic Miss Wright and her principles. As a frequent visitor to the Garnetts' apartments in Paris, he would have heard the Garnetts debating whether or not to join Frances Wright in her American crusade. Once she was back in Paris, Henry clearly became caught up in the reformer's enthusiasm, and he began to think that signing on as an instructor at Nashoba might be the means of his escape from the dreaded Parisian counting-house. As Tom remembered it, Miss Wright proposed to Fanny that she bring Henry to America. Certainly Miss Wright would have encouraged the young man's zeal. Henry did his best to persuade his mother that his future lay in America, 'a country where the dream of sages, smiled at as utopian, seems distinctly realized', as Miss Wright had written six years earlier in *Views of Society and Manners in America.* Thomas Carlyle called it 'that asylum or rather hiding place for poverty and discontent'.[15]

The two women had not seen each other for nearly three years when Fanny met Frances Wright at Julia Garnett's wedding that September. (Thomas Anthony had stayed behind in Harrow to supervise the harvest.) It did not take long before the English matron fell once again under Frances's spell. Returning home after the festivities, Fanny was delighted to have her young friend as a travelling companion on top of the London diligence, and subsequently as a guest at Julian Hill. Fanny wrote to Julia in October:

Never was there I am persuaded such a being as Fanny Wright – no never – and I am not the only one who thinks so – some of my friends declare that if worship may be offered, it must be to her – that she is at once all that women should be – and something more than woman ever was – and I know not what beside – and I for my part applaud and approve all they say – Miss Landon to whom I had mentioned her being here has written to ask leave to look at the most interesting woman in Europe – I honor the little Sappho for the wish & have granted it.

Evidently, Miss Wright did not always return the esteem in which the Trollopes' friends held her. 'I said to Fanny [Wright] just now,' Fanny continues in the same letter, 'what will you do if Capt Kater calls to see you – She looked up as mild as an angel, and said "I shall mind it no more than if a jackass came to look at me." I assure you I fully expect that he will do so.' It was at this time that Auguste Hervieu painted the portrait of Frances Wright which Tom Trollope recalls in his memoirs: 'She is represented standing, with her hand on the neck of a grey horse (the same old gig horse that had drawn my parents and myself over so many miles of Devonshire, Somersetshire, and Monmouthshire . . .), and, if I remember rightly, in Turkish trousers.' Tom remembered his mother's friend as 'very handsome in a large and almost masculine style of beauty, with a most commanding presence, a superb figure, and stature fully masculine. Her features both in form and expression were really noble.'*

It soon became clear to Fanny that Henry's enthusiasm for the American enterprise was not going to abate. She wrote to Harriet, 'Does poor dear Henry still continue to dream of Fanny Wright and Nashoba? More improbable things have happened than that his wish should be listened to – but I dare not tell him so as yet – as his father has by no means made up his mind on the subject.'[16] Henry's attitude may have been that of young Henry Hamilton who proposes to 'persuade my father to let me try what I can do to help myself in the

---

* In *The Bertrams* Anthony is perhaps recalling Miss Wright's striking image when describing Mrs Hunter, 'got up with considerable attention as to oriental costume', who 'seemed to think a good deal about her trousers'.

new world' – in his case, Australia. 'If my poor father gets rid of me for a hundred a year, he will have no reason to complain; and I shall be quite ready to accept this in full of all my demands upon him.' However, his friends call it 'your very romantic and, as it seems to me, your very ill-advised project' (*Fashionable Life*).

His mother was not one of those who told Henry that the project was ill-advised. In fact, she had reasons of her own which led her to think seriously about joining her son in his American venture. The Trollopes' marriage, under so much strain for so many years, was on the verge of collapse. One can only guess what Fanny had endured, but certain moments in her novels, especially *One Fault*, which portrays the breakdown of a marriage, seem so genuine that it is hard not to believe that Fanny was writing from personal experience. Wentworth 'would have deemed it a wilful and pernicious blindness, had he suffered two minutes delay in the arrival of dinner, . . . or the unlucky slapping-to of a door, . . . or the late arrival of the post, . . . or a soup too salt, or not salt enough, . . . or a clock too fast, or too slow; . . . or ten thousand other things of like importance, to pass without feeling and expressing unbounded indignation' (*One Fault*). Isabella has to endure her husband's 'silent look of estrangement'. In *A Romance of Vienna*, Count Alderberg derides his wife with some harsh words 'spoken with his head bent over an empty coffee-cup, on the bottom of which he was curiously making landscapes of coffee-grounds by the aid of a teaspoon'. Fanny must have lamented what was happening not only to her husband but also to herself. She observes in *One Fault*:

> Many women who have for years been made miserable by the temper of a husband . . . will at last learn to suffer from the evil influence only when its cause is near at hand, making their lives resemble a chess-board, the black squares representing the hours when their vowed partner is present with them, and the white ones those when he is not . . . [Isabella] had grown artful too; she knew it, and she wept to think of it.

Fanny learned more than artfulness; she learned to be angry and to draw strength from that anger. 'We are often told that the first falling in love is an important epoch in existence, and that the whole character frequently appears changed by it. Perhaps the first time of falling into anger, may also be an important epoch, and produce as great a change' (*Fashionable Life*).

And with every setback and failure, Thomas Anthony's temper grew worse, so much so that the fact could no longer be hidden from others. In *One Fault* Wentworth's 'extreme sensitiveness to external appearances had generally served as a sufficient curb upon his temper, to prevent his being pointed out as a tyrant'. 'But with all the restraint, and all the caution it was in his power to use, it was not possible wholly to conceal the habitual sourness, the ready irritation, the fretful complainings that made so essential a part of his daily history.' 'Dinner parties and evening parties, . . . morning calls and accidental meetings innumerable, may come and go, yet still leave the parties very profoundly ignorant of the inward and spiritual dispositions of each other; but living in the same family is quite a different affair, and no husband, or wife either, can pass this ordeal without showing to observers of tolerable acuteness whether they live well together or not.'

Julia Garnett and Frances Wright had both been house guests of the Trollopes over the summer and autumn of 1827, and these close female friends of Fanny would have noticed that all was not right between husband and wife. Yet, like Isabella Wentworth, Fanny had 'decided that as the fate she had chosen for herself admitted of no remedy, it would be equally weak and wicked to render her husband hateful in the eyes of her family and friends, by disclosing what must make them miserable, without in the least degree alleviating her own unhappiness' (*One Fault*). Elsewhere in the novel she adapts Hamlet's line: 'One *may* smile, and *smile*, and be a wretch!' In her voluminous correspondence Fanny only once alludes to Thomas Anthony's temper. To Harriet she confides that the scheme to go to America 'is the more agreeable to me because it promises me frequent intervals of tranquillity in the absence of Mr T.: – He is a good honorable man – but his temper is dreadful – every year increases his irritability – and also, its lamentable affect upon the children – you will not find it difficult to remember this and I will not dilate upon it.'[17]

Fanny's obvious devotion to Frances Wright almost certainly put further strain on the Trollopes' marriage. Frances may have tried to persuade Fanny to come away with her on witnessing her host's dreadful temper. A forty-eight-year-old mother of five might not have seemed an ideal candidate for Nashoba, but the tireless reformer longed for 'one of my own sex to commune with & sometimes to lean upon in all the confidence of equality and friendship'. Much later, Frances Wright claimed that she 'at first used every argument to dissuade her from an enterprise from which I thought her unfit'. Thomas Anthony saw it differently. His version was that Miss Wright 'induced' his wife to go with her.[18] In Fanny's eyes, however, the journey to America presented her with the perfect opportunity to live apart from her husband without the stigma of a formal separation. 'The disgrace which such a separation would be likely to bring upon her ... family was probably the leading idea in her mind, as she resolved against it' (*Town and Country*).

But escape was not her sole motivation. She found Miss Wright – her ideas, and her friends – stimulating. The free-thinking Fanny had for some time felt intellectually isolated, not only from her husband but also from most of her English acquaintances. Fanny had written to Julia in the spring of 1827: 'Oh how I wish for you! How completely have you spoiled me for every body else – strange that you should be the only friends, you & Harriet, to whom I can venture to say just every thing I think upon every subject – yet so it is. I feel sure that my opinions on many points are sound and enlightened ... and yet I dare no more venture to give breath to my opinions, than I would set fire to the castle at Windsor – all this makes society very flat, stale and unprofitable – Heaven knows I do not want to be talking ... radicalism – nor infidelity – but I should like to live among human beings who would not look upon reason as crime, nor on free discussion as treason and blasphemy.' Thus Fanny allowed herself to believe that by going to America she would not simply be running away from troubles at home, but would be pursuing the utopian dream, albeit someone else's dream. On 8 October she wrote to Harriet,

> will it be possible to let this 'angel' (yes Harriet you are right she *is* an angel) will it be possible to let her depart without

moving to follow her? I think not. I feel greatly inclined to say 'where her country is, there shall be my country' – The more I see of her, the more I listen to her, the more I feel convinced that *all* her notions are right. – She is pointing out to man a short road to that goal which for ages he has been in vain endeavoring to reach. Under her system I believe it possible that man may be happy – and we have had proof enough that he can not be so under any of those already tried.[19]

But the most compelling reasons for departure were financial. The final straw had come earlier that autumn. The Trollopes had already retreated once, from Julians to Julian Hill; Thomas Anthony now declared that further cutbacks were necessary, and that the family would have to move from their cherished 'cottage' to a run-down farmhouse in Harrow Weald, on the other side of Harrow-on-the-Hill. 'My final determination to accompany Fanny [Wright] to Nashoba,' Fanny explained to Julia, 'was brought on by Mr. T's telling me on my return to Harrow that he was determined upon letting our house there, for the purpose of retrenching our expenses. He proposes one or two plans of retirement – at which my heart sickened – and I used all my power to persuade him that a year or two passed at Nashoba would repair our affairs more completely than any other.'[20] Fanny's desire was to break 'up her English home without pleading broken fortunes to all the world', as her son Anthony astutely observed in his autobiography. 'To have pleaded poverty as a reason for declining to mix in the society she loved would have required more courage than Mrs Maxwell possessed,' Fanny wrote in *Tremordyn Cliff*. Anthony claimed, somewhat unkindly, that his mother's life up until this time had been 'easy, luxurious, and idle' (*An Autobiography*). Fanny was perhaps closer to the truth when she remarked in *The Old World and the New*: 'There had been nothing like extravagance in their manner of living, but there had been ease and comfort; and it is precisely under these circumstances that retrenchment, sudden retrenchment, is the most difficult.'

Fanny would have carefully considered the alternatives before her, as did the Stormonts and their cousin Katherine Smith in this same novel, written twenty years after these events. They felt that simply

1. 'The Cloakroom of the Clifton Assembly Rooms' by Rolina Sharples, 1817–20. The young Fanny Milton attended the Assembly Room balls in Clifton. Years later a certain peer of the realm said to Anthony Trollope of his mother, 'I danced with her when she was Fanny Milton, and I remember she had the neatest foot and ankle I ever saw!'

2. 'Russell Square, and Statue of the Duke of Bedford', 1827–30. First as a single woman, then as a young mother, Fanny lived in Keppel Street, off Russell Square, where handsome dwellings were springing up 'as white and bright as new-born mushrooms'. In Jane Austen's *Emma* a character says of this neighbourhood, 'We are so very airy!'

3. Portrait of Henry Milton by John Lucas. Mary Russell Mitford wrote of Fanny's younger brother Henry that he was 'one of the best judges of art in England', and described him as 'a lively, agreeable, enthusiastic person, who always carries things his own way'.

4. Portrait of Mary Russell Mitford by John Lucas. Fanny's girlhood friend, the popular author Mary Russell Mitford, was also a close friend of Elizabeth Barrett Browning. Tom Trollope described her as a 'genuinely warm-hearted woman' who 'gushed' when she spoke.

5. Julians, Hertfordshire. The estate of Adolphus Meetkerke, which Fanny's husband Thomas Anthony expected to inherit from his uncle. The Trollopes' eldest son, Tom, was raised to believe that 'I was to be the future owner of Julians, and live on my own acres.'

6. Detail from 'The Trial of William Lord Russell 1683', an engraving after the painting by George Hayter, 1824. Thomas Anthony Trollope sat for one of the lawyers pictured above – possibly the lawyer in the bottom-left-hand corner. Fanny wrote to Tom, 'I shall like to see your father's head there.'

7. 'Orley Farm', engraving by John Everett Millais. Anthony based Orley Farm on Julian Hill, the Trollopes' home at Harrow for nearly twenty years. 'This place, just as it was when we lived there, is to be seen in the frontispiece of that novel.'

8. Portrait of Frances Wright by Auguste Hervieu, 1827. The French artist Hervieu painted this portrait of the reformer, standing next to the Trollopes' old grey gig horse, at Julian Hill. Tom Trollope recalled that his mother's friend had 'a most commanding presence, a superb figure, and stature fully masculine'.

9. 'Philosophical Millinery Store', Hervieu's illustration for *The Domestic Manners*, 1832. The proprietor of the New Orleans millinery shop, Miss Mary Carroll, promulgated abolition and reform while selling hats. Pictured above, in front of the counter, are Fanny Trollope, the utopian William Maclure and Frances Wright.

10. 'Settlement of Nashoba', Hervieu's illustration for *The Domestic Manners*, 1832. 'One glance,' Fanny recalled, 'sufficed to convince me that every idea I had formed of the place was as far as possible from the truth. Desolation was the only feeling – the only word that presented itself.'

11 & 12. Two views of the Trollopes' Cincinnati Bazaar: above, a daguerreotype of the Cincinnati river front, *c.* 1847, in which the dome and turrets of the Bazaar are clearly visible; below, a contemporary woodcut showing the entrance to the Bazaar on Third Street. Fanny's Cincinnati friend, Timothy Flint, called it a 'Turkish Babel'.

13. 'Cincinnati Ball Room', Hervieu's illustration for *The Domestic Manners*, 1832.
'The gentlemen had a splendid entertainment spread for them in another large room',
while the ladies 'sat down on a row of chairs placed round the walls, and each making
a table of her knees, began eating her sweet, but sad and sulky repast'.

14. 'The Trollope Family, from a sketch taken from life, made in Cincinnati in 1829'.
This 1832 caricature, which reflects America's hostile reaction to *The Domestic Manners*,
depicts Mrs Trollope and her two daughters looking on as her son Henry sits for
Hervieu's historical painting, 'Lafayette's Landing at Cincinnati'.

15. Watercolour portrait of Mrs Trollope by Miss Lucy Adams, *c.* 1832. This sketch was made soon after the publication of *The Domestic Manners of the Americans*, when, as Fanny wrote to her son Tom, 'I awoke one morning and found myself famous.'

to move elsewhere in England would not improve their situation much, yet they dreaded to 'add another idle English family, to the many which have already established themselves in France, Italy, and Germany', for 'the most striking feature in the existence of all these European emigrants is idleness'. 'The scheme I would propose,' declares Katherine, 'would involve the necessity of ceaseless exertion and industry. – In a word, my cousins, were our movements to be regulated by me, we should be sailing, bag and baggage, for the United States of America within a month.' Fanny hoped – she sincerely believed – that, while helping Henry to establish himself in America, she could live more cheaply for a time in Miss Wright's backwoods community, thus taking some strain off the family finances. She would certainly not be the first English person to travel to America – she had only to think of John Garnett and his family. Indeed, 'the subject of emigration had been one of the great social questions . . . of the age' (*The Old World and the New*).

It is not hard to imagine that Fanny found it difficult to broach the subject of America with her husband; perhaps, like Glencora Palliser, she 'never could find the proper moment for doing this, having, with all her courage – low down in some corner of her heart – a wholesome fear of a certain quiet power which her husband possessed' (*The Prime Minister*). But Fanny was not one to sit still and do nothing. Like her heroine Clara Holmwood in *Fashionable Life*, she felt that 'the misfortune which has fallen upon me is not, in my opinion, of a nature to be relieved by patience. I think it must be met with resolution, and endured with courage.' It may be that she 'chose to make the disclosure' to her husband during 'the hour when men are generally supposed to be in the most amiable frame of mind possible, namely, when hunger, but not appetite, has been satisfied, and digestion not fully begun; that is to say', while he was 'enjoying his walnuts and his wine' (*The Widow Barnaby*). After, no doubt, many entreaties and reasoned arguments, Thomas Anthony finally agreed to her plans, but Fanny was not at all sure that he would not change his mind. Her time of departure was not absolutely fixed until five days before sailing: 'She expected always something would prevent her voyage and wished it therefore not known or talked about,' Frances Wright later wrote to Harriet Garnett. Fanny knew people would disapprove and perhaps feared that their efforts to dissuade her might weaken her resolve. Captain Kater, for one, had told her 'with affectionate sadness that "he saw I was hopelessly mad" '. They parted, however, 'the best of friends – and he confessed that if he were younger and a little less sick, he should like to go too'.[21]

Fanny's entourage was to include, besides herself and Henry, her two daughters, aged nine and eleven, William Abbot, a young farmer who had worked for the Trollopes, and Hester Rust, to whom Fanny paid tribute in the person of Katherine Smith's maid, Rebecca, 'a treasure past all price: excellent as cook, dairy-maid, bread-maker, brewer, and universal good manager in all ways' (*The Old World and the New*). Fanny still believed that Harriet Garnett would soon follow. 'Next year,' she writes, 'perhaps we shall be amusing each other at Nashoba.' Thomas Anthony moved into the Harrow Weald farm-house, occupying only two rooms; the furniture which he did not need was to accompany Fanny on the voyage, no doubt to make the backwoods of Tennessee feel more like home. Fanny deliberately left Tom and Anthony behind to finish their education in the hope that, unlike Henry, they might gain a place at university and go on to a profession. Anthony was to join Tom at Winchester shortly before the Trollopes' home was broken up. She had already written to entreat Tom to take care of his somewhat 'idle' but 'good-hearted' little brother: 'I think you will find advice and remonstrance better taken by him than by poor Henry. Greatly comforted am I to know that Tony has a praefect brother.'[22] Fanny may have had Anthony in mind when, in *One Fault*, she describes in loving detail the gentle but awkward Alfred's departure for Winchester: the family dog, Neptune, 'received his last adieu, patted, and gently pushed back at the same time, that he might not quit the house and follow him.'

At last, on 4 November 1827, Fanny and her companions, together with Frances Wright, set sail from Tower Bridge aboard the *Edward*. Thomas Anthony accompanied Fanny to the boat – Harriet Garnett wrote that he was in good spirits at the time of their departure. Mary Shelley was at Tower Bridge also, to see Frances Wright off. At the very last minute Hervieu decided to sign on as drawing master at Nashoba: he boarded ship only hours before its departure. The Garnetts did not know of his whereabouts – or that of his portrait of Frances Wright – until months afterwards. 'No news of Hervieu & the picture,' Harriet wrote Julia in December. 'Can he too have gone to Nashoba? I hope he has not taken the picture with him.' The captain was waiting for the tide, 'we were all on board, and his vessel under weigh, before any efforts could be made to overtake us', the Englishman Edward Gordon writes from aboard ship in Fanny's first novel, *The Refugee in America*. 'I gave the servants their choice of returning on shore, or going with us, and both decided upon following our fortunes.' Fanny Trollope wrote to Julia Pertz from aboard ship:

I have left the people making great eyes at me – but I care but little for this. I expect to be very happy, and very free from care at Nashoba – and this will more than repay me for being the object of a few *'dear me's!'*[23]

CHAPTER SIX

The Refugee in America

'Don't you think, Emily, that you should like to run up and down the deck of a great, large ship?' the young Emily Hubert is asked in *The Widow Married.* This is certainly how Fanny Trollope's two daughters, Cecilia and Emily, would have amused themselves as the *Edward* sailed down the Thames. The sixteen-year-old Henry, meanwhile, would have explored every nook and cranny of the vessel, pestering the captain and sailors with all sorts of questions. Their mother, along with her adult companions, Frances Wright and Auguste Hervieu, might have been in more pensive mood: 'though each of the three thus seated together were as far removed as they well could be from a state of mental activity, they neither of them felt disposed to converse. When the heart is really very full, most people feel it a greater relief to think than to talk; and thus they marked in silence the skilful and rapid progress of their noble bark through the innumerable host of ships that crowded the river' (*The Old World and the New*).

The transatlantic crossing was not entirely uneventful: their ship was pursued by pirates in the Gulf of Mexico. But, on the whole, Fanny found the voyage somewhat tedious and unsettling – in more ways than one. She later wrote to Harriet Garnett:

I was a very poor creature during the voyage and persuaded myself repeatedly that it was my weakness of mind and body that made me deem Fanny [Wright] too eccentric, when I saw

118

her sitting upon a coil of rope in the steerage, reading to a sailor occupied in patching his breeches on another, some of the wildest doctrines of equality and concubinage that pen ever traced on paper – writing such, and reading them aloud, was her chief occupation during the voyage – and I often recurred to the idea that had tormented us at Paris, that she was not in her right senses.[1]

But there was no turning back and, on Christmas Day 1827, after seven long weeks, the *Edward* arrived at the mouth of the Mississippi and 'passed from the bright blue waves, whose varying aspect had so long furnished our chief amusement, into the murky stream which now received us'. 'I never beheld a scene so utterly desolate as this entrance of the Mississippi,' Fanny wrote. 'One only object rears itself above the eddying waters; this is the mast of a vessel long since wrecked in attempting to cross the bar, and it still stands, a dismal witness of the destruction that has been, and a boding prophet of that which is to come.' For miles there were only 'mud banks, monstrous bulrushes, and now and then a huge crocodile* luxuriating in the slime', as well as 'vast quantities of driftwood'. 'We began to feel that our walk on the quarter-deck was very like the exercise of an ass in a mill; that our books had lost half their pages, and that the other half were known by rote; that our beef was very salt, and our biscuits very hard; in short, that having studied the good ship, *Edward*, from stem to stern till we knew the name of every sail, and the use of every pulley, we had had enough of her' (*The Domestic Manners*).

Their final destination, Nashoba, was in Tennessee, then on the western frontier of the United States, and the easiest and most direct route was not to travel westward by coach from New York or Boston, but to sail up the Mississippi to the port of Memphis, Tennessee. After three days of negotiating sandbars and dodging driftwood, Frances Wright and her party left the *Edward* at New Orleans, the bustling gateway to the Mississippi, to await the paddle-steamer which would take them on to Memphis. New Orleans and the other towns along the Mississippi were truly of another world. The streets

* In fact, alligators, not crocodiles, are endemic to North America.

abounded 'in verandas, balconies, and awnings . . . fine orange-trees fill the air with their perfume . . . the whole scene animated by the variety of its living groups; among which, creoles, quadroons, and negroes are found in nearly equal proportions; while not unfrequently a party of Indians, more picturesque than any of them, may be seen sadly and silently gazing upon the wide expanse that was once their own' (*Jonathan Jefferson Whitlaw*).

While in New Orleans, Fanny and her children ventured outside town to explore the luxuriant, almost tropical, forest with its branches draped in Spanish moss. She also visited the 'philosophical milliner' Miss Mary Carroll, an abolitionist and friend of Frances Wright, who promulgated Miss Wright's doctrines while selling hats. At Miss Carroll's shop Fanny met the Scottish-born geologist turned utopian, William Maclure. In early 1826 Maclure, together with other eminent scientists and educators, had travelled by boat, dubbed the 'Boatload of Knowledge', to join Robert Owen's community of New Harmony, Indiana. By June 1827 Owen's socialist experiment had failed, but Maclure's 'School of Industry' carried on at New Harmony. Sitting at the hat counter, Fanny noted that 'in the course of five minutes' Maclure 'propounded as many axioms, as "Ignorance is the only devil;" "Man makes his own existence;" and the like' (*The Domestic Manners*).

On New Year's Day, 1828, Frances Wright and her entourage boarded the steamboat, *Belvidere*, destined for Memphis. After five days in New Orleans Fanny and her children had begun to find the heat – and the mosquitoes – very disagreeable, but not more so than the condition of the carpet on the *Belvidere*, which required 'the pen of a Swift to do it justice'. Yet this was nothing compared to

> the total want of all the usual courtesies of the table, the voracious rapidity with which the viands were seized and devoured, the strange uncouth phrases and pronunciation; the loathsome spitting, from the contamination of which it was absolutely impossible to protect our dresses; the frightful manner of feeding with their knives, till the whole blade seemed to enter into the mouth; and the still more frightful manner of cleaning the teeth afterwards with a pocket knife, [which] soon forced us to feel

that we were not surrounded by the generals, colonels, and majors of the old world. [Fanny had discovered that all American men seemed to boast some sort of military title.]

Nor was there any polite dinner conversation to be had: 'the only sounds heard were those produced by the knives and forks, with the unceasing chorus of coughing, &c.'. To Fanny's horror, the *Belvidere* ran aground somewhere between New Orleans and Memphis. They had to endure 'two breakfasts, two dinners, and a supper . . . with the Ohio and Kentucky gentlemen, before they moved an inch' (*The Domestic Manners*).

At long last Fanny and the rest of the ship's passengers 'had the pleasure of being told that we had arrived at Memphis' – at midnight in the pouring rain. The small town stood on a high bluff above the river and, as they made their way up the steep muddy road on foot, 'shoes and gloves were lost in the mire'. Frances Wright 'was anxious to get home, and we were scarcely less so to see her Nashoba'; so, after only two nights in Memphis, Frances set off on horseback through fifteen miles of dense forest. The rest of the group, including the Harrow furniture, followed in a wagon, enduring numerous bumps and bruises when the 'road' soon became nothing more than a passage cleared of trees, but not of the tree stumps. Finally, the party arrived at Nashoba. Fanny's doubts about Frances Wright, so long suppressed, proved to be all too well founded. 'One glance,' Fanny recalled, 'sufficed to convince me that every idea I had formed of the place was as far as possible from the truth. Desolation was the only feeling – the only word that presented itself' (*The Domestic Manners*). The entire settlement consisted of three roofless log cabins in a forest clearing. 'The Frances Wright of Nashoba, in dress, looks, and manner, bore no more resemblance to the Miss Wright I had known and admired in London and Paris than did her log cabin to the Tuileries or Buckingham Palace,' Fanny later wrote. Eliza and George Flower and the Scotsman, James Richardson, had long gone; the only white inhabitants to be found were Frances's sister Camilla and Richeson Whitby, who had married in Frances Wright's absence. 'The Nashoba bride dear Cam,' wrote Harriet to her sister, 'who like other philosophers does not act according to her principles.' Months afterwards Fanny Trollope heard rumours that the Flowers had left as a result of Eliza's well-founded jealousy of Frances Wright's relations with her husband and that Camilla had lived with Whitby, whom she calls a 'surly brute', for five months before they succumbed to convention and married. The only time Fanny saw the slaves whom they were supposed to educate was when the poor souls brought logs for the fires. 'The food was scanty and far from wholesome – no milk or butter, bad water, very little bread and no meat but pork.'[2]

But what upset Fanny the most was the state of Camilla's health. She and Whitby both looked 'like spectres from fever and ague' – that is, malaria. Fanny had no money left, but fearing for her children's health, she resolved to quit the place. Fanny was not the only disappointed person in the group. When Hervieu discovered that no school had yet been formed, he flew into a rage. 'He wept with passion and grief mixed.' In *The Refugee*, Fanny describes the despair of another Frenchman, M. de Clairville, who had been attracted by the prospect of a better life in 'Perfect Bliss', a backwoods utopia on the Red River: he was told 'to hew down a tree, cut it into rails, and fix it as a zig-zag or serpentine fence. The poor Frenchman, whose visions had been of scientific lectures, amateur concerts, private theatricals, and universal philanthropy, was startled.' Frances Wright merely remarked to Harriet Garnett that she had soon found Hervieu 'to be totally unsuited for anything but his art'.[3]

The distraught Hervieu had immediately set off back to Memphis to make some money painting society portraits. After ten days Fanny followed his example and made the fifteen-mile trek back to Memphis – presumably with her chairs and tables in tow – where she considered what to do next. Whatever Fanny said to Frances Wright, the reformer seems to have accepted her departure with a good grace: the Nashoba journal records a loan of $300 'to Mrs Trollope to assist her in removing from Nashoba to some place in the western world better suited to her future plans for herself and her children'.[4] Fanny soon decided to continue up river with her family and dependants to Cincinnati, on the banks of the Ohio River. Perhaps, as in her novel *The Refugee in America*, a steamboat captain recommended that she make the city her 'winter headquarters, as offering a specimen of the rapid progress of society' and thereby 'highly interesting to a stranger'. Fanny was clearly determined, like her heroine Katherine Smith, 'by courage, enterprise, and industry', so far to 'increase my fortune as to enable me to command the comforts to which I have been accustomed, without compromising either my sincerity or my independence. I could not do this in England', 'but I might do it in the United States' (*The Old World and the New*). Hervieu, meanwhile, had painted everyone worth painting in the small town of Memphis and decided to accompany the Trollopes to Cincinnati aboard the steamboat *Criterion*.

Cincinnati was, indeed, the fastest-growing city in America at this time: within a period of thirty years it had been transformed from wilderness into a prosperous port city of 20,000 citizens. Its position on the Ohio river, which flows from Wheeling, West Virginia, westwards to join the Mississippi, put Cincinnati at the crossroads of an expanding America. It became the nation's stockyard, as hordes of pigs passed from steamboat to slaughterhouse – thus earning it the name 'Porkopolis'.* From its docks not only pork, but also flour, whiskey, and other goods travelled west and south, as far as the West Indies and South America, and factories sprang up, producing everything from steam-engines to hats. The city also enjoyed some cultural life, for many of its inhabitants – and institutions – were recent imports from the more refined east coast of America. Thus, by the 1820s Cincinnati could boast of music societies, theatres, a Mechanics Institute ('for the cultivation of the arts and sciences'), a medical college and hospital, schools, churches, newspapers and circulating libraries. It never lost its porcine sobriquet, but it also came to be called the 'Athens of the West' and the 'Queen City'.[5]

Fanny had high hopes as the *Criterion* entered the Ohio river, dubbed 'La Belle Rivière' by the New Orleans French. She was leaving behind, 'I trust for ever . . . that murky stream which is as emphatically called "the deadly" ', the Mississippi, where 'it is said that nothing that ever sunk beneath its muddy surface was known to rise again'. 'So powerful was the effect of this sweet scenery, that we ceased to grumble at our dinners and suppers; nay, we almost learnt to rival

---

* Even today, a billboard outside Cincinnati greets visitors with the slogan 'Pork, the other white meat'.

our neighbours at table in their voracious rapidity of swallowing, so eager were we to place ourselves again on the guard,' that is, the gallery which runs round the cabins, 'lest we might lose sight of the beauty that was passing away from us' (*The Domestic Manners*). Fanny's first impressions of Cincinnati, 'with its busy prosperity . . . magnificent position . . . noble quay, the widely-spreading streets, and magnificent market' were favourable (*The Old World and the New*). Situated on a pretty bend in the river and surrounded on three sides by lush green hills – 'the seven hills of Cincinnati' – it is still an attractive city. To Fanny in 1828 its streets, laid out like most American cities on a grid pattern, looked neat and tidy.

The Trollopes found a house to rent in Race Street, very near the centre of town, which looked pleasant and comfortable, no doubt made more so by her English furniture. However, the house was 'devoid of nearly all the accommodation that Europeans conceive necessary to decency and comfort. No pump, no cistern, no drain of any kind, no dustman's cart, or any other visible means of getting rid of the rubbish.' Their landlord soon set them straight: they must throw their garbage into the middle of the street, 'and the pigs soon take them off'. After all, this was Porkopolis. 'In truth,' Fanny observes, 'the pigs are constantly seen doing Herculean service in this way through every quarter of the city', 'though it is not very agreeable to live surrounded by herds of these unsavoury animals'. 'If I determined upon a walk up Main-street, the chances were five hundred to one against my reaching the shady side without brushing by a snout fresh dripping from the kennel.' Nevertheless, it had been three full months since Fanny had seen any sign of civilization, except for something of the kind in New Orleans, and in Cincinnati 'the sight of bricks and mortar was really refreshing, and a house of three stories looked splendid' – not to mention a brick church (*The Domestic Manners*).

Henry did not accompany his family all the way to Cincinnati; instead he disembarked, probably at Cairo, Illinois, where the Ohio and Mississippi meet, to join another boat travelling up the Wabash river to Maclure's School of Industry at New Harmony, Indiana. Fanny had been impressed by Maclure's educational programme when she met him in New Orleans. She evidently thought that Henry might benefit from a few terms at New Harmony, where pupils paid for their room and board by manual labour, which they alternated with learning. Maclure's notion was to teach the young men and women useful, rather than intellectual, pursuits: carpentry, agriculture, shoemaking, dressmaking, cooking, engraving and printing.

However, as far as the sixteen-year-old Henry was concerned, the School of Industry was nothing more than a work-camp. Because of ill-health, Maclure spent most of the year in Mexico, leaving a Frenchwoman, Mme Marie Fretageot, in charge of the school. Fanny later claimed that Mme Fretageot 'threw out all that related to the intellectual part of the business', and drew wealth 'from the thews and sinews of the youths they had collected', many of whom, like Henry, 'had been sent from a distance by indigent parents, for gratuitous education, and possessed no means of leaving' (*The Domestic Manners*). Henry arrived at the coldest, bleakest time of the year, late January. New Harmony would have been deep in snow, and the students' sleeping quarters, a clapboard meeting-house, draughty and uncomfortable. True to form, within just a few weeks Henry was miserable and wrote to his mother that he 'had not only to earn his bread, but to make it, and bake it, and to labour in the fields all day'.[6]

With Hervieu's help Fanny scrounged enough money to pay for Henry's fare to Cincinnati. The $300 which Frances Wright had loaned her was fast disappearing. Nevertheless, Fanny felt that she might yet make a success of her American venture. The cost of living was relatively low and she believed that opportunities abounded in the fast-growing city. Fanny began to look on Cincinnati as the 'remote but very pretty nest' where she would sit 'to hatch golden eggs for my son Henry'.[7] Over the following months the Trollopes embarked on a number of money-making schemes, the progress of which can be followed in the columns of *The Cincinnati Gazette*. Fanny's first thought was that Henry's classical education, such as it was, would be a rare and valued commodity in a frontier town. On 28 March 1828 she placed the following advertisement in *The Cincinnati Gazette*:

Mr Henry Trollope, having received a completely classical education, at the royal college of Winchester (England), would be happy to give lessons in the Latin language to gentlemen at their own houses. By an improved method of teaching, now getting into general use in Europe, Mr H. Trollope flatters himself he shall be able to give a competent knowledge of the Latin tongue in a much shorter space of time than has hitherto been considered necessary.

Terms: Fifty cents for lessons of one hour.

Despite Fanny's skill in the copywriter's art, no pupils were forth-coming.

Fanny's next idea was to put her experience of amateur theatricals to good use. She had noticed that there was not much to do in the frontier town. 'I never saw any people who appeared to live so much without amusements as the Cincinnatians' (*The Domestic Manners*). Soon after her arrival in the city she had made the acquaintance of a Frenchman, Joseph Dorfeuille, who ran the Western Museum. The museum had originally been established to promote science and natural history, and boasted a collection of prehistoric remains, Indian relics, fossils, mineral specimens, bones and stuffed animals (the young John J. Audubon had worked there as a taxidermist). However, as Fanny Trollope wryly noted, Dorfeuille could not 'trust to his science for attracting the citizens' (*The Domestic Manners*). 'He collected anything and everything that he thought would excite the curiosity of the people and induce them to pay their quarter dollars for admission,' Tom recalled. Fanny had a feel for what might prove popular, and she suggested to Dorfeuille a new and unusual attraction for the museum: 'The Invisible Girl', a mock-Delphic oracle. Fanny's inspiration probably came from a popular London entertainment: 'The Invisible Girl: The Oracle of Leicester Square'. Hervieu designed the stage set, an exotic combination of motifs from ancient Egypt and the witches' scene in *Macbeth*, and Henry, donning a toga and veil, prepared to spout a garbled mixture of Latin, French, German and Italian in reply to visitors' questions. *The Cincinnati Gazette* declares:

The proprietor of the WESTERN MUSEUM is now able to tender to the public, the gratification of receiving the responses of the '*Invisible Girl*.' As he has spared no expense in preparing this most interesting philosophical experiment, he relies upon his fellow citizens for a fair demonstration of a disposition to remunerate him for an attempt to present to the world, a subject in which science and taste have been equally consulted [12 April 1828].

It was a huge success. A townsman later declared that Henry 'under the guise of the invisible woman puzzled the wise-acres of the community for weeks'.[8]

The popularity of 'The Invisible Girl' led Dorfeuille to back a second, even more spectacular show conceived by the Trollopes in collaboration with a twenty-two-year-old artist working at the time for Dorfeuille, Hiram Powers. Seeing that the good people of Cincinnati had 'a most extravagant passion for wax figures', Fanny devised the 'Infernal Regions', featuring scenes from her favourite work of literature, Dante's *Divina Commedia*, with mechanical wax figures sculpted by Powers and transparencies painted by Hervieu. 'Wax, paint and springs', as well as an electrical current that occasionally gave the spectators a jolt, 'have done wonders', Fanny remarked (*The Domestic Manners*). Perhaps she had picked up some ideas from Madame Tussaud's in London. In any case, the show was a huge hit and continued to draw crowds at the Western Museum for at least another thirty years. W. H. Venable, writing in 1891, remembers going to see the 'Infernal Regions' as a boy: 'I recall even yet the feeling of terror with which I beheld the glaring eyes of the frightful female named Sin, who sat hard by the infernal gates, and who jumped at me with a horrid cry.'[9]

With two popular successes behind them, things seemed to be going reasonably well for the Trollopes. By the middle of the summer (1828) Fanny had found a pretty cottage, cool and airy with green Venetian blinds, in a wooded area called Mohawk, which lies below one of 'the seven hills', about a mile and a half from the centre of the city. This suited Fanny much better: she could cultivate her own vegetables and keep a cow. In *The Domestic Manners* she pays tribute to the good neighbours she enjoyed in Mohawk. Twenty years later she again recalled their many kindnesses to her and her family: 'a good neighbour in the forest ... is a treasure beyond all price, and

can, in fact, only be justly estimated by those who have first known
the want of such a blessing, and then enjoyed the possession of it'
(*The Old World and the New*). In this house Fanny was also able to
entertain more easily, as far as her very modest budget allowed, and
with Henry's help she organized theatricals and charades, often
followed by dancing. One contemporary describes a party given by
Fanny for about a hundred guests, 'and a handsome one it was',
during which Henry played Falstaff in a performance of *The Merry
Wives of Windsor*. 'Falstaff's good, round belly was found to be lined
with sack instead of capon, and the play was incredibly funny, for
he was very drunk, and had a small feather-bed tucked under his
waistcoat.' Henry's talents extended to satiric verse, some of which
survives in a notebook which he kept while in America. One can
imagine Henry entertaining his mother and sisters with his ode to
the butcher, Mr Everett, entitled 'Remember me – or the humble
Supplication of Mrs T— of Cincinnati to Mr E—'

> Remember me – for oh t'is sweet
> To taste the juices of thy meat.
> Remember me dear butcher pray,
> Remember my beef steak today;
> Not when the slaughtered doth fall,
> But when the fat meat spreads thy stall;
> When rounds and rumps before thee lie,
> And ribs and loins hang up on high;
> When round the eager crowd you see –
> Sweet Butcher then remember me.[10]

By this time the Trollopes counted among their friends and
acquaintances in Cincinnati, besides Hiram Powers and Joseph Dorfeuille, the English comedian Alexander Drake and his American
wife, also an actor; the jovial, florid and rotund Dr William Price, an
avowed atheist and former resident of New Harmony, his 'foolish
friendly little wife' and their two daughters; the Harvard-educated
Timothy Flint, editor of the short-lived *Western Monthly Review*
(1827–30), whom Fanny thought 'the most agreeable acquaintance
I made in Cincinnati, and indeed one of the most talented men I ever

met' (*The Domestic Manners*); Morgan Neville, a lawyer and journalist, whose father had been an aide-de-camp to General Lafayette; the ambitious Nicholas Longworth, who made a killing in Ohio real estate and later became Powers's Maecenas, eventually sending him to Italy,* and the musician Joseph Tosso, born in Mexico City of Italian parents, who had studied in Paris. Tosso's initial reaction to Mrs Trollope may have been typical of his fellow citizens. Apparently the musician for a long time avoided an introduction to Fanny because he detested her ugly bonnets and shawls – 'a green calash and a long plaid cloak dragging at her heels', as *The Cincinnati Mirror* claimed. When they did finally meet, Tosso found her very clever and so charming that he ended up speaking with her for two hours. He later remarked that the English matron had a soul 'as big as an ox'.[11]

Nevertheless, Fanny was not happy in Cincinnati. She found the general society of the place dull and inhibiting. 'They have no public balls, excepting, I think, six, during the Christmas holidays. They have no concerts. They have no dinner parties. They have a theatre, which is, in fact, the only public amusement in this triste little town', but it was very poorly attended. It was only 'in the churches and chapels of the town that the ladies are to be seen in full costume', she wryly observes in *The Domestic Manners*. 'Were it not for the churches, indeed, I think there might be a general bonfire of best bonnets, for I never could discover any other use for them.' And even when the ladies managed to attend gatherings outside consecrated ground, their presence 'rendered it impossible in [the men's] opinion to continue the conversation in the same strain'. The gentlemen were 'well informed and agreeable; but as to bringing any intellect into a discourse with ladies, that was quite out of the question'. Fanny undoubtedly admired individual Americans, such as Timothy Flint, but

> whatever may be the talents of the persons who meet together
> in society, the very shape, form and arrangement of the meeting
> is sufficient to paralyze conversation. The women invariably

---

* Longworth's money was not wasted. Hiram Powers became the most celebrated American sculptor of the nineteenth century.

herd together at one part of the room, and the men at the other
. . . the gentlemen spit, talk of elections and the price of produce,
and spit again. The ladies look at each other's dresses till they
know every pin by heart; talk of Parson Somebody's last sermon
on the day of judgement, on Dr T'otherbody's new pills for
dyspepsia, till the 'tea' is announced, when they all console
themselves together for whatever they may have suffered in
keeping awake, by taking more tea, coffee . . . It always appeared
to me that they remained together as long as they could bear
it, and then they rise *en masse*, cloak, bonnet, shawl, and exit
(*The Domestic Manners*).

Fanny might have been able to break the ice somewhat with her
theatricals, but this sort of society was not what she was used to in
London drawing-rooms or Paris salons. Even picnics were discouraged: apart from the presence of mosquitoes and termites everywhere,
it was 'considered very indelicate for ladies and gentlemen to sit
down together on the grass'. A family outing in the woods near their
home turned into a nightmare when Fanny and her children suddenly
came upon a slaughterhouse: the pretty brook was red with pigs'
blood, the stench was unimaginable, and discarded pigs' tails and
jawbones lay about everywhere. Fanny reflects on this episode in
The Domestic Manners: 'I am sure I should have liked Cincinnati much
better if the people had not dealt so very largely in hogs.'

Timothy Flint, Fanny's much-admired friend, later wrote that the
Englishwoman had owed her 'uncurteous' reception in Cincinnati to
'the habit of the ladies there of estimating people according to their
show and dress. Had she come with numerous letters [of introduc-
tion], and been an elegant figure dressed in the most approving
fashion, there is no doubt that she would have made her way in every
circle.' Fanny had no letters of introduction because she had never
expected to end up in Cincinnati. She struck the curious residents as
'a short plump figure, with a ruddy, round Saxon face of bright
complexion', 'of appearance singularly unladylike, a misfortune
heightened by her want of taste and female intelligence in regard to
dress, or her holding herself utterly above such considerations'. 'My
dear,' one woman is reported to have said, 'she never could *get in*.

Her manners were bad and she had no refinement. After seeing how she behaved in market no one could think of asking her inside a drawing-room.' Cincinnati society, so desperate to be thought refined and fashionable by the world at large, could not abide anyone who did not strictly conform.

The story of the French widow in *The Refugee in America* mirrors Fanny's own experiences. Mme de Clairville had left Europe with her husband, bound for the utopian community of Perfect Bliss. It proved a disaster. M. de Clairville soon died of overwork and a broken heart. His wife, who was left destitute, took refuge in the small but growing city of Rochester, New York, clearly a portrait of Cincinnati, where she eventually meets and befriends the Gordon party. 'From that moment, she had buried her sorrows and her anxieties, her hopes and her fears, at the very bottom of her heart; and no one at Rochester knew anything more about her' than that she had to make the most of a small income. She was not a great person at Rochester for 'the ladies had discovered that she had but two visiting gowns in the world' and 'no one ever saw even a new ribbon about her since the day of her arrival, now nearly six months ago'. This is basically how Fanny Trollope was described to Frederick Marryat when he visited Cincinnati some years later: 'When Mrs Trollope came here, she was quite unknown, except inasmuch as that she was a married woman, travelling without her husband. In a small society . . . it was not surprising, therefore, that we should be cautious about receiving a lady who, in our opinion, was offending against *les bienséances*.'*[12]

Perhaps most damaging of all, Mrs Trollope's exact relationship to the French artist Hervieu, 'naturally furnished much tea table conversation'.[13] Despite the whispers, there was nothing untoward in their friendship. Fanny had tried her best to advance Hervieu's career back in England and the grateful artist, with no family of his own, was devoted to the whole Trollope clan. In Cincinnati he and Henry had become inseparable friends as well as artistic collaborators and, eventually, business partners. In *The Refugee* Fanny describes the ladies of Rochester, who gossiped 'in that spirit of peculiar malevolence which she denominated Christian charity'. With a

* 'the proprieties'.

wonderful command of American idiom, she writes: 'it was in vain that one expected, another guessed, a third calculated, and a fourth reckoned' how the Gordon party, Edward Gordon and his attractive daughter, Caroline, a single young man and a French widow, fitted together. One local resident thought that Caroline must have run away from her husband, another that she was a bankrupt, fleeing creditors back in England; or worse, that they were forgers, bank robbers or political exiles (though 'they seemed not the kind of stuff of which demagogues and radicals are made').

Mme de Clairville also shares many traits with her compatriot, Hervieu. Like Hervieu, she retains a heavy, somewhat comical, French accent. The locals cannot understand the friendship which has developed between the wealthy Gordons and the impoverished Frenchwoman: 'Why *do* they take her about with them?' 'At first, Madame de Clairville had not been included in the invitations' issued to the well-heeled English family, 'but Miss Gordon made it speedily understood that she went no where without her'. One can imagine Fanny, newly arrived in Cincinnati, insisting that the Frenchman travelling with her family be included in all their invitations. She describes a delicious moment in *The Refugee* which may well have been based on a real incident between Hervieu and Henry, or perhaps Fanny herself. While Caroline Gordon is observing some absurd Americanism at a small gathering, 'she ventured to look at Madame de Clairville, and the eloquent manner in which her friend took a pinch of snuff, in answer to her appeal, almost atoned for the dullness of the meeting'.

Her daughters would also have provided Fanny with moments of mirth. No doubt she listened to 'the speculations of little Emily on their [neighbours], which partook largely of the peculiar vein of observation in which children sometimes remark on what appears ridiculous to them, with a freshness and keenness of quizzing that might be sought for in vain in the sallies of the most practised proficients in the art' (*The Widow Married*). Nevertheless, she knew that her little girls too were unhappy. The eleven-year-old Cecilia wrote at the end of her mother's letter to her brothers back home, 'Cincinnati is a very pretty little town, but I heartily hope papa will come and take us away from it!' In addition, their physical well-being remained of great concern to Fanny. Cincinnati was not a healthy place: apart from the shortcomings in the city's garbage disposal, there were no drains. In May–June of 1828, with the warm weather – and the mosquitoes – both mother and son succumbed to bouts of malaria. She writes to Tom: 'You would hardly know Henry and me, we are both so thin.'[14]

What made matters worse, money was in short supply despite their successes at the Western Museum. Dorfeuille would have creamed off most of the profits from the 'Invisible Girl' and the 'Infernal Regions'. By May 1828 Fanny had sent eight letters to her husband asking for financial assistance. She sent these by various different means – people passing through Cincinnati on their way eastwards or via certain coffee-houses with transatlantic connections. Yet she had not received one line from Thomas Anthony in return. In *The Refugee in America* an important letter has been dispatched two months previously, 'the reply to which was to regulate their future movements, but two more must pass away, before they could reckon with certainty upon receiving his answer'. Fanny wrote to her sons Tom and Anthony at Winchester: 'I cannot express to you the dreadful anxiety to which this silence gives birth. Is your father ill? Is he dead? Have his affairs fallen into such confusion that he has not been able to procure the money necessary to send us a remittance?' 'Our situation here would be dreadful, were it not for M. Hervieu's grateful, and generous kindness. It is more than a month that we have not had a mouthful of food that he has not paid for. How are you both, my darling boys? ... Dear Tom, dear Anthony, do not forget us!'[15]

Besides his part in the 'Invisible Girl' and the 'Infernal Regions', Hervieu had tried his hand at teaching in order to secure an income large enough for himself and his friends. An enterprising German, Frederick Eckstein, established an Academy of Fine Arts in Cincinnati and offered Hervieu a good salary to teach drawing. However, when the artist remonstrated against his pupils' constant talking and running around in class, Eckstein refused to impose discipline, fearing that he would lose their parents' custom. Hervieu stormed out: 'Eh bien, Monsieur, I must leave the young republicans to your management' (*The Domestic Manners*). He then set up his own rival school of drawing, assuring the public that in 'insisting' on certain regulations, 'the principal of which was to induce silence during the lessons, he was actuated solely by his earnest wish for the rapid improvement of his pupils' (*Cincinnati Gazette*, 8 April 1828). One wonders how successful he was in this enterprise, for Hervieu certainly did not have a high opinion of American youth. He scribbled in one of Fanny's American notebooks: 'Jamais les parens americains ne reprimandent leurs enfans.'*[16]

So unhappy and unsettled was Fanny at this time, especially at the thought that Henry still had no prospects, she could not bear to write to her friends in Europe. A mutual American friend told the Garnetts that Fanny was 'out of spirits'. She later explained to Harriet Garnett that her silence had stemmed 'from the feeling, oppressively strong, that in telling you all I have seen and all I have heard, I should be giving you the greatest pain'. Ignorance and uncertainty fuelled the speculation and gossip back home which had begun immediately after Fanny's furtive departure from London. 'I am shocked at so bold and unnatural a step,' Mrs Garnett wrote to her daughter Julia: 'She has told her Harrow friends by a note after she left it, that it is a visit to . . . Nashoba & to see Niagara, place her children at school & return with her husband in one or two years. But the gossip of Harrow will perhaps tell another story.' 'All Harrow is in amaze at Mrs T.'s departure,' Harriet added to her mother's letter to Julia. 'Imagine the surprise of the Milmans & all that will be said.' Two weeks later she again wrote to her sister:

I can scarcely yet believe that Mrs T. is actually on her way & Trollope alone in his old age in London. How will he bear the reports that must at last reach him of Nashoba? . . . But the step once taken there is no return, at least for a woman. The grates of the most rigid convent are not so insurmountable a barrier betwixt the world & the nun they enclose, as public scorn makes against a woman who has joined such a community as Nashoba.

The condemnation was universal, according to Harriet. Marianne Skerrett, whom Fanny had known since girlhood, wrote 'to say that

---

* 'American parents never discipline their children.'

all Mrs T.'s friends were grieved & shocked at her going to America & that she parted with coldness from them all & also from her brother. Macready endeavoured to persuade her not to go – in vain.'[17]

Fanny would have been surprised – and hurt – had she heard the Garnetts go on in this vein; after all, Harriet had led both her and Frances Wright to believe before their sailing that she was seriously thinking of joining them at Nashoba the following year. If anything, Mrs Trollope assumed that the Garnetts would criticize her for abandoning Nashoba, and Frances Wright, so suddenly. Indeed, in this she was not wrong, for consistency was never the Garnetts' strong point. Only a few months after Harriet had expressed such dismay at Fanny's departure for the infamous Nashoba, she is writing to Julia: 'You will be astonished and grieved at Mrs Trollope's having so immediately left Nashoba. Poor dear Fanny [Wright], how great must be her disappointment!' And a week later: 'Poor Fanny! How could Mrs Trollope leave her?' 'The more I think of it – of [Mrs Trollope's] enthusiasm for the cause, of all the sacrifices she made to accompany Fanny, of the difficulties she conquered, of the public opinion she braved, the more astonishing does it seem to me that she should so soon have been discouraged.'[18] Fanny Trollope might have answered Harriet with the thought, which she confided to her readers ten years later: 'Let no one ever profess, or ever secretly plume themselves upon any strong determination of never doing this, that, or the other . . . for fate often seems to delight in taking vengeance for such presumption, and to force the self-confident boaster into doing precisely that, against which his protestations had been the most vehement' (*One Fault*).

At last Fanny received a letter from her husband: he was still planning to come out to Cincinnati that autumn (1828) with Tom, who had recently left Winchester and was twiddling his thumbs, waiting to be offered a place at New College. Their son Anthony would stay behind, attending to his studies. The Trollopes' friends were not slow to give advice to Thomas Anthony before his departure. Harriet was of the opinion that it would be highly imprudent 'in poor Mrs Trollope should she remain in America and let her husband return without her', and wrote him a letter to that effect. Just before he was due to sail, Marianne Skerrett 'asked him closely if he meant to bring her back and he said he did not know, neither would he give any idea of how long his return might be off'. 'I wish to see them all again,' Miss Skerrett told Harriet, 'except one, I can't say I want to see Mr Hervieu back.'[19] All of this must have been wormwood to the intensely private barrister. He was probably relieved when he and Tom boarded the *Corinthian* at Plymouth and set sail for New York on 1 September 1828.

Owing to what Tom called his father's 'Spartan contempt for comfort', they travelled steerage. In the bowels of the ship there was no privacy, insufficient ventilation, and the whole place was 'dirty to a revolting degree'. Thomas Anthony took to his berth and rarely left it during the five-and-a-half week voyage, 'suffering from his usual sick headache more or less during the whole time'. Tom could not face his quarters and slept on deck every night. They were met in New York by Charles Wilkes, whom the Trollopes had met in Paris through the Garnetts and the Wrights. He was a very good friend to Fanny throughout her American sojourn. He forwarded letters to England and managed the transfer of funds from England to America; he even advanced some cash at her request 'in consideration of the forlorn situation into which this wild goose expedition has thrown me'.[20] Fanny commemorated him in *The Refugee in America* as 'the good-natured New Yorker who forwarded a letter to the Continent' which Mme de Clairville could not afford to post.* From New York Tom and his father travelled west through untouched forest and over 'corduroy' (log) roads and tree stumps.

Meanwhile, Fanny writes in *The Domestic Manners*, 'we were now in daily expectation of the arrival of Mr T.; but day after day, and week after week passed by, till we began to fear some untoward circumstance might delay his coming till Spring; at last, when we had almost ceased to look out for him, on the road which led from the town, he arrived, late at night'. With the exception of Anthony, Fanny now had her family around her again. Away from his cares

---

* On news of his death in 1833 Fanny wrote to Julia Pertz, 'I have lost a friend in him, who, though known late in life, had become dearer to me than I can tell you. Indeed I have never known anything like him, nor can I ever hope to meet one like him again' (17 November 1833: Garnett–Pertz Papers).

and creditors, Thomas Anthony's mood seems to have improved, and the five or six months that her husband and son stayed in Mohawk were the happiest for Fanny during her three-and-a-half year stay in the United States. She was able to see her surroundings through fresh eyes, and it all became 'doubly interesting' to her. To an English schoolboy 'it was indeed a new world'. As United States history was most definitely not on the public-school curriculum, America 'is hardly better known than Fairy Land; and the American character has not been much more deeply studied than that of the Anthropophagi: all, therefore, was new, and every thing amusing' (*The Domestic Manners*). Tom warmed to the Americans' 'frank and unconstrained manner', which had 'the effect of making me less shy with them than with others'.

We do not know whether Thomas Anthony conveyed Harriet Garnett's words of advice to his wife. If so, they probably fell on deaf ears, for Fanny had thought of a project which she hoped and believed would set up Henry – and Hervieu as his partner – for many years to come. Fanny's idea was to build on the success of the 'Invisible Girl' and the 'Infernal Regions'. Besides Dorfeuille's Western Museum, there was no other suitable venue for such entertainments. She felt Cincinnati could benefit from a social centre which would provide exhibition, lecture and reading rooms, a theatre, panoramic rotunda, coffee-house and other refreshment areas, a ballroom with musicians' gallery, and rooms for private parties. She reckoned that such a building would produce a steady income: revenue would come in not only from the various shows and exhibitions which the Trollopes would put on, but also from renting out rooms to local groups. Fanny intended that the very design of the building would divert and entertain visitors. On the façade Greek columns would frame 'arabesque' windows below a scalloped Gothic battlement topped by a large Turkish dome or rotunda. The rear elevation would be predominantly Egyptian in style. The interior was to be along similar lines, with Hervieu providing most of the decoration.

Although this design may sound outlandish, such an eclectic mix of architectural styles could be seen in many buildings in Regency England, notably the Royal Pavilion at Brighton. Fanny's idea may have been directly inspired by the immensely popular Egyptian Hall, an exhibition space which had opened in London in 1812.* The Egyptian style had come into vogue following Napoleon's campaign in north Africa, and both the Egyptian Hall and the Trollopes' plan copied details from Dominique Vivant Denon's illustrated *Voyages dans la Basse et la Haute Egypte* (1802).† Fanny had, in fact, seen Denon's exhibition of Egyptian artifacts on her trip to Paris in 1823. The Egyptian Hall's creator, the English collector William Bullock, had recently settled in the Ohio valley with plans to build his own utopia, to be called Hygeia. He entertained Mrs Trollope at his mansion soon after her arrival, and it is entirely possible that over dinner someone said, merely in passing or even in jest, that a building like the Egyptian Hall would be an ornament to the 'Queen City'.²¹

Fanny's was an ambitious project, but she probably felt she already had some experience in these matters, having helped to oversee the construction of Julians in Harrow. Thomas Anthony agreed to advance her $6,000 to cover the building costs; he also had an improvement to make to the scheme – to outfit one floor as a sort of department store. As Fanny later explained to Julia Pertz, he introduced the idea of a '*Bazaar*, the letting the stands of which, he calculated, would be very profitable. It was objected that the people having never seen such a thing, would not be likely to take to it. – To this he replied that he would *teach them* what it was, by sending out things to fit out the room at first – this frightened me, as I knew we none of us understood any thing of buying and selling – but he was determined on making the experiment.'²² Perhaps Thomas Anthony hoped to emulate the Burlington Arcade on Piccadilly which Lord George Cavendish (afterwards Earl of Burlington) had built in 1819 for just such a purpose.

Despite her initial objections, Fanny agreed to her husband's 'improvements' and in January 1829 the Trollopes chose a site, that

---

* In *Town and Country*, her novel which opens in 1811, Fanny has one of her characters propose a visit to 'the Esquimaux family, exhibiting at the Egyptian Hall'.

† *Cincinnati Mirror*, 3 (1833) states that the Bazaar's Egyptian columns were modelled on the temple of Apollinopolis at Etfou, illustrated in Denon's *Voyage* (plate xxviii).

of the original town fort which overlooked the Ohio river, and paid over $1,500 for the land. Mr Trollope signed the deeds, as Henry was not yet of age and the law prohibited married women from owning property, and promised to dispatch a consignment of merchandise from Europe to fill the Bazaar stalls. 'Mr Trollope has entered into an equal division with Henry of all profits proceeding from this institution till he shall be of age, after which he is to have the whole, as long as he chooses to remain here to superintend it. When he leaves it, which he hopes to do in ten years, Mr Trollope hopes to sell it to advantage. The rapid, and almost daily increase of this extraordinary city certainly warrants the expectation.' Thus Fanny wrote in a letter to Harriet, for her optimism had returned and she felt she had something positive to say.

She was even looking several years ahead: Thomas Anthony would return in a year to take her elder daughter Cecilia back with him so that she could attend a good school in either Paris or London. As for herself, she had promised Henry that she would remain in Cincinnati for another two or, at the most, three years. 'Eighteen is too young to be left.' All in all, Fanny remarked, 'we are extremely pleased with our present situation, and for myself I can truly say, that I had much rather have seen all I have, and all I still hope to do, of America, notwithstanding all contretemps, than to have remained at Harrow, living beyond our income. We are now living upon about one fourth of it and our encumbrances will we think be removed by the time I have fixed as that of our intended return.' 'Henry is grown very tall and a great dandy,' Fanny informs Harriet on a more personal note. 'Cecilia is tall too, and folks call her pretty, which is one reason why I am anxious that she should leave this land of early flirtation for an European school. Emily is just what you last saw her, a little taller, a little more advanced in mind, but as much a child as ever.'[23]

In early February 1829 Tom and his father prepared to return to England. Fanny and the girls procured 'buffalo robes and double shoes' for the long, cold journey eastwards. They delayed their departure, however, by a few days in order to be able to meet the newly elected President, Andrew Jackson. Jackson, who was perceived to be the champion of the common man and of states' rights, was proceeding by steamboat from his home in Tennessee to

Washington. In *The Domestic Manners* Fanny notes that Jackson 'had been decidedly the popular candidate at Cincinnati' over John Quincy Adams, a federalist and member of the east-coast élite. 'For months past,' she adds, 'we had been accustomed to the cry of "Jackson for ever" from an overwhelming majority.' Thomas Anthony and his two sons duly joined the ranks of Cincinnati's most prominent citizens to shake hands with the tall grey-haired man with 'harsh gaunt features', and travelled with him on the same boat up the Ohio, heading eastwards. In New York Thomas Anthony and Tom bought first-class tickets and boarded ship bound for home.

On his return to England Thomas Anthony sent out $2,000 to cover the initial building costs, which he apparently raised from the sale of some land in Gloucestershire.* Back in Cincinnati, construction soon began on the Bazaar; however, nothing went according to plan. '*Everything* from the time you left us,' Fanny wrote to Tom, 'went wrong, spite of exertions – nay hard labour, on our part that would pain you to hear of.' According to a contemporary editor, 'in building a "green horn" is snuffed like carrion by every rogue within cheating distance', and Fanny was no exception. An observer reported that 'every brick in her Babel cost her three prices' and the man, 'a countryman of her own, by the by', whom she paid in advance to lay the gas pipes (the Bazaar was to have the first gas lights in Cincinnati) 'evaporated with the cash'. She hired another 'cowboy builder' who completed the job. Her initial building estimate of $6,000 was soon $8,000 and rising. Despite all her problems, Fanny proved adept at drumming up favourable publicity. While it was still under construction, the *Cincinnati Chronicle* gave its readers a detailed description of the structure that was rising on the banks of the Ohio. After dilating at length on the many wonders of the new edifice, the *Chronicle* continues:

> The Bazaar, which when finished, will not have cost less than fifteen thousand dollars, is owned by Thomas A. Trollope, Esq.,

---

* In 1829 Thomas Anthony sold some land in Gloucestershire, which he had bought two years earlier, making a profit of £430 (Gloucester Record Office, D34/IX/95, 96). The exchange rate at this time was roughly $4.8 to the pound.

of London, who deserves much credit for the taste and public spirit that induced the erection of a building so ornamental to our city.[24]

Meanwhile, Fanny was eagerly awaiting the remaining $4,000 which Thomas Anthony had promised. She was horrified when, instead of a banker's draft for that amount, she received '$4,000 worth of the most trumpery goods that probably ever were shipped' to America.* She had earlier advised her husband that they should limit their initial outlay for merchandise to only £150. 'He had exerted himself extremely,' Fanny later wrote, 'to procure these goods, and . . . flattered himself they would sell well, and speedily, and so enable me to pay for the completion of the building.' Thomas Anthony probably thought he was being clever in sending goods rather than money, for he believed the merchandise would turn a handsome profit and thereby provide his family with a useful financial cushion. But he had not done his market research. He had bought certain 'French articles of finery' which another, more conveniently located Cincinnati shop already stocked in a much larger and better assortment. Fanny later confided to Julia that it was 'the sight of those dreadful and utterly unsaleable goods, and the consciousness of the money to be paid', which sent her to bed for eleven weeks, often delirious, with malaria.[25] In bed she read the whole of James Fenimore Cooper, and 'I never closed my eyes without seeing 'bloody scalps floating round' and Red Indians stealing up noiselessly; 'an additional ounce of calomel hardly sufficed to neu-tralize the effect' (*The Domestic Manners*).

Fanny was now deep in debt. Desperate for some return on their investment, she opened the Bazaar for business in mid-October 1829, even before it was finished. Judging from the notice Fanny placed in the *Cincinnati Gazette* on 17 October, the first day of business was marred by problems with the lighting.

---

* In his *Autobiography*, Anthony refers to his father buying pocket-knives and pepper boxes.

BAZAAR

The public of Cincinnati are respectfully informed that in consequence of an imperfection in the Gas pipes, an unpleasant smell is emitted. The proprietors, therefore, have determined to suspend the use of Gas, till the error shall have been corrected.

The establishment will be lighted up at present with Oil and Spermaceti. The exhibition of the Great Room will continue from 9 o'clock in the morning till 9 at night. – Admission, 25 cents.

The display of Fancy Goods in the lower part of the Bazaar will take place on Monday and be open daily from 9 o'clock in the morning till 9 at night.

The customers did not flock. At some point, in an attempt to recoup their losses, Henry sold most of the merchandise at auction 'for what he could get, in order to pacify the workmen'.[26] Fanny then tried to rent out the stalls to local merchants, but to no avail. The English actor Joseph Cowell, on tour in the United States, recalls the conversation which he had with a compatriot who had opened a haberdashery stand in the Bazaar and had sold only a few pairs of socks in the course of a week. Mrs Trollope was so desperate to make the place work, the merchant confided, that 'any of her own country as apply, she furnishes 'em with a few things, and gives 'em half the profits and a cold cut, and a cup o' tea, to try and get the place into notice'. 'Nothing answers that's rational in this outlandish country, as Mrs Trollope says ... D'ye see them 'ere spitboxes?' he asked Cowell. 'Well, she can't begin to persuade 'em to make use on 'em; they will squirt their backer on one side, which teases the old woman half to death.'[27]

Fanny tried other ploys to lure the townspeople into the Bazaar. She organized theatrical evenings, composed of songs and recitations, with the help and no doubt encouragement of the actor Alexander Drake and his wife, as their own theatre in the city had not been a commercial success. But the people of Cincinnati, particularly its preachers, were downright puritanical when it came to theatre, feeling it revealed man's baser nature. And, according to Fanny, they were right – in regard to audiences at least. The spitting amongst male spectators was incessant and the mixed smell of onions and whiskey on their breath unbearable. Men lounged on the balcony, 'the entire rear of the person presented to the audience', and threw cracked nutshells and other debris into the pit. 'The noises, too, were perpetual, and of the most unpleasant kind; the applause is expressed by cries and thumping with the feet, instead of clapping' (*The Domestic Manners*). Fanny's friend Macready later concurred. After a two-day stopover in Cincinnati he left 'very much *disgusted* with the house which was very bad. I am sick of American audiences; they are not fit to have the language in which Shakespeare wrote.'[28]

The *Cincinnati Gazette* (28 November 1829) said of the first of Mrs Trollope's evenings that it was 'very handsomely *got up*'. 'The audience, however, was very small.' The paper urged the proprietors not to 'feel discouraged, for it is not at all the *fashion* of our *fashionables* to attend the first evening of any public amusement'. Joseph Cowell was to appear with the Drakes in the second theatrical venture. 'A green baize curtain was fastened from the ceiling across the middle of the platform, to form *the stage* and *behind the scenes*, where we were huddled together, with two chairs between us, before the audience arrived.' The Trollope family almost outnumbered the rest of the dismal audience.

Cowell recalls with horror how 'a very loud sneeze, which a young lady favoured me with during the third verse of my song, caused a whispering titter; and the one that usually follows, being interfered with by a friend or pocket-handkerchief, went the wrong way, and the very odd kind of noise it assumed caused a general laugh, during which I finished my song, and made my escape through the slit'. Mrs Trollope and another gentleman, who had been Cowell's tailor back in Philadelphia, of all things, tried to prevail on Cowell to return on stage to perform another song. 'I knew it was useless to refuse,' Cowell states; 'everybody knows that tailors will never take no for an answer, even when they dun you for their bill; so following the example of their customers, *I lied*. But fearing that his perseverance might induce him even to follow me to my hotel, I took shelter in a tavern at the corner of Market-street and Broadway; had a chat with ... the proprietor, and sipped gin-and-water till the lights were extinguished in Mrs Trollope's turret, and the show and all danger over.' The *Cincinnati Gazette* (5 December 1829) dryly reported a few days later 'the company, though not so large as could have been wished, was fashionable'.

For his part, Hervieu hoped to attract visitors to the exhibition hall with the display of his latest masterpiece, an historical scene entitled 'Lafayette's Landing at Cincinnati', commemorating the American hero's visit to the city on his tour of the United States in 1824. It met with general public approval, with the exception of one individual who, signing himself 'X' in the *Cincinnati Gazette*, griped that Hervieu's 'historical' painting should rather be labelled '*imaginative*'. This was a fair comment to make, as Hervieu, in an effort to flatter Cincinnati's brightest and best, painted most of them into the picture, whether they were there in 1824 or not. Local dignitaries, the governors of Ohio and Kentucky, various generals and colonels, the lawyer Daniel Gano, who happened to be the Trollopes' Mohawk landlord, and Timothy Flint, as well as their particular friends, Hiram Powers and Joseph Dorfeuille, were all included. Timothy Flint, not surprisingly, wrote a very full and favourable review of the work in his *Western Monthly Review*. (Flint declared that any objections to his presence in the painting, despite the fact that he did not arrive in Cincinnati until 1827, should be considered 'hypercritical'.) As far as Flint was concerned, Hervieu's revolutionary background, 'his youthful dreams' of 'liberty and the glories of a free country' stood him in good stead on American shores.[29]

But a painting could not save the Bazaar. The location, on the edge of town and a quarter of a mile from the city's commercial centre, was blamed. The exotic architecture, no doubt badly executed, seemed to attract only ridicule from locals and visitors alike. Fanny had hoped it would be 'the chief lion of the city', instead, it turned out to be its greatest white elephant. Timothy Flint later described the Bazaar as a 'Turkish Babel'; Fanny's compatriots, Harriet Martineau and Captain Marryat, were to call it 'the great deformity of the city' and '*preposterous*'. One architectural historian has pointed out that 'in such a city of brick boxes with Neoclassical trim, Mrs Trollope's Bazaar was indeed an architectural monster'; 'it stood out like a belly dancer in a procession of Greek maidens'.[30]

Only a few weeks after the Bazaar's opening, the following sad little notice (almost certainly drafted by Fanny as Hervieu's English would not have been up to it) appeared in the *Cincinnati Gazette* on 19 December 1829:

Mr A. Hervieu presents his respectful compliments to the Ladies & Gentlemen of Cincinnati. It was his earnest wish to have offered to them such an entertainment on every Thursday evening as might have obtained patronage. Painting, poetry, and music were put in requisition at the great room of the Bazaar to gratify their taste and to win their favor – but he has failed. On Thursday evening last, half a dozen gentlemen from a steam boat were all who presented themselves. He therefore respectfully withdraws the attempt.

The building was being finished on credit, and the workmen were now 'clamorous for payment . . . The bills came in, infinitely higher than we calculated upon' – and after an ineffectual attempt to let the Bazaar, *'every thing* was seized by the creditors', as Fanny later explained to Julia Pertz. She confided to her son Tom that *'every bed had been seized,* and that we – your sisters and myself – were sleeping together in one small bed at Major L.'s and boarding there, as well as Henry and Hervieu who both lay on the floor in the kitchen, *for the value of my parlour carpet'*. The Garnetts heard from Camilla Wright that the Trollopes, whose original estimate had apparently been $6,000, had 'sunk $20,000 in this building which they now find will not answer'; Timothy Flint later claimed that they had lost $17,000* at a single stroke.[31]

The Trollopes had lost all credibility in Cincinnati. Lafayette, who had been under the mistaken impression that Mrs Trollope had established herself in New York, eventually wrote a letter of introduction on her behalf to Morgan Neville, the son of his former aide-de-

---

* According to Flint, the building had cost $24,000, of which the Trollopes 'actually paid some twelve or thirteen thousand' plus 'four or five thousand dollars more in French articles of finery' ([Flint,] 'Travelers in America', *Knickerbocker, or New York Monthly Magazine*, 2 (1833)).

camp, in Cincinnati; the old general always enjoyed using his influence to help his female friends. Although this did not arrive until after Thomas Anthony's departure from the city, Fanny was appreciative: 'Such an introduction is worth something in this country ... They contain *in fact*, the first certain assurance that we are not a set of very accomplished swindlers!'[32] Nevertheless, it was all too late: the damage had already been done.

Evicted from the pretty cottage at Mohawk, bankrupt, with no funds forthcoming from England, Fanny and her children were utterly destitute. 'Had not Hervieu's labours enabled him to furnish us with money to live upon – I know not how we should have escaped *starving* in that land of plenty.' But, by far the worst of it was living with the knowledge of failure: 'Guess what I must have suffered,' Fanny later confessed to Julia, 'at finding that all the pecuniary efforts poor Trollope had been making to place [Henry] well, and permanently, at Cincinnati, were utterly thrown away!' The Bazaar débâcle took its toll not only on Fanny, but also on Henry. Fanny had not yet fully recovered her strength when Henry too fell ill with malaria. He could not seem to shake it off: 'he took the ague and fever so seriously that he soon looked like a walking corpse', Fanny wrote in this same letter to Julia. 'Everyone said that his native air was all that was left to try for him, and you will easily believe, dearest, that this sentence once pronounced I decided that *coûte que coûte** he should have it.'[33] The idea had been that Thomas Anthony would return to Cincinnati in May 1830. She wrote to him, asking that he abandon his plans and, instead, send the money to pay for their passage home to England. It was then midwinter, and Fanny hoped to start as soon as the ice on the frozen Ohio had broken up sufficiently to make the river navigable.

For the whole of February there was nothing to do but nurse Henry, wait for an answer to her pleading letters, and watch for the departure of the ice on the river, which 'was to be the signal of ours', or so Fanny hoped (*The Domestic Manners*). She had time to reflect on the advice of her friends who had told her before she left England that none of the advantages proposed in her plan to live abroad was

* 'whatever it costs'.

'equal to the value of the vicinity and protection of "her own people" '
(*Tremordyn Cliff*). 'The remembrance of all this now came bitterly to
the heart of Mrs Maxwell. How impossible would it have been had
she not withdrawn herself from the protection of *"her own people,"*
that the misfortune she now groaned under, could have fallen upon
herself and her innocent child!'

CHAPTER SEVEN

The Domestic Manners of the Americans

By March Fanny had finally received a letter from her husband, but he had no help to offer. When Thomas Anthony read her account of the Bazaar's failure, as Fanny explained to Julia Pertz, 'he declared he had no more money to send – that he was ruined by the transaction which *we* had managed wretchedly'. Instead, on 13 March 1830 Thomas Anthony went down to the American consulate in London to draw up a document, handing the property over to a joint stock company, consisting of himself and other creditors. By doing so he hoped, after the debts had been paid, eventually to salvage something from his investment. He assigned the Trollopes' Cincinnati acquaintance, Morgan Neville, to act as his attorney.[1] In *The Old World and the New*, Fanny tells the tale of a German whose attempts to build a palatial residence in the Ohio valley had led to his ruin. 'He had creditors in all directions, and though the poorest labourer he employed lived with much more luxury than he permitted to himself – in order to pay a little to one, and a little to another, and so "get along," till better times arrived – he broke down at last, and placing all his affairs in the hands of a Cincinnati lawyer, he shipped himself back to the old world, only too happy to give up his visions of parks and palaces.' Fanny wryly adds, 'whether the lawyer was honest or not I cannot say; but it really mattered very little, for the clamour for ready money among the creditors was such, that there was no possible mode of quieting it, save by immediately offering the whole property for sale'. The moral of the story: 'Nothing is so difficult as to get along in the United States without ready money. Nothing is so easy with it.'

On 18 April, a month after Thomas Anthony had acknowledged the failure of the Bazaar before witnesses at the American consulate, Tom was awakened at half-past midnight by a knocking at the door of the Harrow Weald farmhouse. It was Henry. He had spent all the money remaining to him on the coach fare from Liverpool, where his ship had docked; the sickly youth had then had to walk the sixteen miles from London to Harrow. The next day, Tom wrote in his diary, was 'consumed in talking to him'. It appeared that when Fanny realized that no money would be forthcoming from her husband, she again had to turn to Hervieu for help. The ever-faithful Frenchman had supplemented what little money Fanny had with his own modest earnings to enable Henry to return to England without further delay. The son almost certainly did not get a warm welcome from the father. Thomas Anthony wrote angrily to Fanny that he did not like to think 'himself under the greatest obligations to Hervieu'. He chose to blame Henry for mismanagement rather than admit that his wife and children were left destitute in a strange land. He wrote to Fanny, after she had made all the facts known to him, that he could not 'imagine why it was necessary for Henry to set off immediately'. 'How is it possible,' he writes in a later communication, 'that you are dependent on Hervieu for your living, when I have sent out goods to the amount of £2,000.'*[2]

The home at Harrow Weald to which Henry had returned was, according to Anthony, 'one of those farmhouses which seem always to be in danger of falling into the neighbouring horse-pond. As it crept downwards from house to stables, from stables to barns, from barns to cowsheds, and from cowsheds to dung-heaps, one could hardly tell where one began and the other ended!' Tom did not remember it as 'tumble-down' but, certainly, it was 'shabby' and 'forlorn enough'.[3] 'Our table was poorer,' Anthony adds, 'than that

---

* That is, $9,600. Fanny had written to Julia Pertz that her husband had sent out $4,000 worth of 'the most trumpery goods'. Either Thomas Anthony was over-estimating the sale value of the merchandise or he confused the figures.

of the bailiff.' 'The furniture was mean and scanty': there were no more than three beds, for Tom had to give his over to Henry that first night, and they were without pillows. Thomas Anthony, becoming every day more morose and incapacitated, had given up his law practice altogether by the beginning of 1831, though he retained his chambers.* When he was not out working in the fields or, as was more often the case, in bed with one of his sick headaches, he lived in the parlour 'shut up among big books' (*An Autobiography*).

Thomas Anthony no doubt cursed the day in 1813 when he had signed that disastrous lease on the original Harrow property, which, although he had vacated the house in 1827, still 'tied him to the stake', as Tom recalls him saying. The price of grain had continued to fall; several bad harvests followed back to back; Middlesex farmers brought home their sheep unsold from Kingston market. In 1828, in the midst of all this hardship, the government of the day relaxed the Corn Laws, taking away what little financial protection the farmers had. One small landowner in nearby Roxeth hanged himself the next year. Things could only get better, but they did not: in 1830 a sudden slump in the economy hit both industry and agriculture. Landlords everywhere were giving rebates on agricultural rents, but not Lord Northwick.

The correspondence over the Christmas and New Year period of 1830–1 between Northwick, who was more often than not at his other great house in Worcestershire, his bailiff Quilton and Thomas Anthony Trollope, tells a sorry tale.† Again and again Thomas Anthony asks that he be given time to sell his grain at market and pay his lordship in instalments – otherwise, 'it must be my ruin'. The rather soft-hearted Quilton wrote to Northwick that more often than not, when he went to collect the rent, the barrister was ill in bed. But the irascible Northwick showed no mercy; he had his own worries. By 1831–2 he had incurred large debts in building a fabulous art collection, as well as a special gallery to house it.† He was also having

---

* The last appearance of Thomas Anthony Trollope in the *Law Lists* occurs in 1830.

† Northwick bought paintings by Botticelli, Fra Angelico, Breughel, Titian, Rubens, Rembrandt, Holbein, Callot, Claude, Poussin, David, Gainsborough and Van Dyck. Many of Northwick's purchases now hang in the National Gallery.

problems with other tenants. In 1830, objecting to an 'obnoxious' threshing-machine belonging to one of them, he sent his servants to remove it. This resulted in his men being found guilty of 'riot and assault' by the local justices. Northwick was furious. The affair was taken up by the press and eventually came before the Home Secretary, Lord Melbourne. Northwick published a fifty-five-page pamphlet in his own defence, accusing the papers of 'the subversion of all lawful authorities, to excite the lower orders' and attempting to incite 'revolution and murder'.* Northwick then began to get threatening letters from 'Captain Swing', the *nom de guerre* of rural agitators, who declared that the landlord had 'ground the labouring man too long'. Thus Northwick was not in a conciliatory mood when he received a letter drafted by Trollope and signed by three other tenants, asking that rents be reduced. The somewhat paranoid peer accused Trollope of heading a conspiracy against him and 'ill-requit[ing] the kind feelings I have always manifested toward him'. The barrister replied that there was no conspiracy: he and the other men had happened to see each other in the church vestry on a Sunday, when the subject quite naturally came up.

Often Thomas Anthony was so ill he asked Henry to write to Northwick on his behalf. On at least one occasion, the semi-literate Quilton wrote to Northwick that he had come across the barrister 'at the Post Office waiting the arrival of your lordship's letter to me & beg to see it & he read the greatest part of it'. Thomas Anthony was finally able to fend off his landlord with the help of a London friend who loaned him £150, 'preferring this to signing a bill for the amount'. He reminds Northwick that he has paid all his rents over seventeen years 'but for the last half year', owing to 'the heavy & almost ruinous losses I have sustained particularly [in] the last two years'. Anthony recalls that 'we all regarded the Lord Northwick of those days as a cormorant who was eating us all up' (*An Autobiography*). Anthony's contribution to the struggle seems to have been to distract the enemy, or his daughter at any rate, by 'making innocent love' to Miss Quilton in the kitchen.

When Fanny left England in the autumn of 1827 she had

* Privately printed in Oxford [1831].

commended Anthony to the care of his elder brother, Tom, at Winchester. To her mind, the College had an 'admirable arrangement', 'by which much of the instruction, and, even, discipline of the little boys is entrusted to the elder ones,' and is 'accompanied by the payment of two guineas, I believe, for each pupil ... producing an income sufficient to be of most essential relief' (*One Fault*). Anthony did not see it this way. He later wrote of Tom that 'in those school-days he was, of all my foes, the worst'. 'In his capacity of teacher and ruler, he had studied the theories of Draco', and 'as a part of his daily exercise, he thrashed me with a big stick'. Perhaps Tom was the sort of public school boy who was both 'rough and kind; affecting perhaps more roughness than naturally belonged to him, from a mistaken notion that it made him look bold, and English, and manly' (*The Blue Belles*).

The school holidays were no better for Anthony. Tom probably spent the greater part of them with his schoolmates, for he had a great many Wykehamist friends. But for Anthony, 'there was often a difficulty about the holidays, – as to what should be done' with him (*An Autobiography*). His father apparently neglected to arrange for Anthony to spend time with the Trollopes' many friends and relations, leaving the boy to mope around his dingy rooms at Lincoln's Inn, 'each of them brown with the binding of law books and of the dust collected on law papers, and with the furniture that had been brown always, and had become browner with years' (*Phineas Finn*). Thomas Anthony also overlooked the need to pay his youngest son's bills at Winchester before he and Tom went off to America in the autumn of 1828. As a result, the school tradesmen, who provided the boys with everything from boots to pocket handkerchiefs during term time, refused to extend any further credit to Anthony. He became a 'pariah' amongst his peers.

Within a year of his return to Harrow, Thomas Anthony found he had to provide not only for Anthony's living expenses away from home but also those of his other two sons, Tom and Henry. Tom's New College place had never materialized but, determined that his sons should have a university education, Thomas Anthony enrolled his eldest son at St Alban Hall, Oxford, in October 1829. Henry entered Caius College, Cambridge, the next autumn. The financial strain proved too much, and just before that dismal Christmas of 1830, when Lord Northwick's demands for arrears were at their height, Thomas Anthony took his youngest son Anthony out of Winchester and enrolled him once more as a free day boy at Harrow School. It was just at this period, Frances Eleanor Trollope remarks, that Mr Trollope 'seems to have been absolutely a prey to a sort of monomania on the subject of allowing his sons any money'. Anthony's fellow Harrovian at this time, William Gregory, recalled many years later that Mr Trollope's financial troubles were well-known. An edict went round the school that he 'had been outlawed, and every body believed it was the duty of a loyal subject of the crown to shoot or otherwise destroy "Old Trollope" if possible. Fortunately, he never appeared among us.'[5]

Anthony was only twelve when his mother sailed to America. Her departure was shrouded in mystery. In any case, he was too young to understand her reasons for leaving: her grief at the deaths of her son and father, her distress over her husband's state of mind, her financial worries and her anxiety over Henry's future. All Anthony knew at the time was that he felt miserable and abandoned. Tom, at least, had been able to pay an extended visit to his mother and siblings in Cincinnati after the first year. Anthony's recollection of his mother's face and voice would have inevitably grown rather hazy over the years. Fanny felt this to be the case, and wrote to Tom in the late summer of 1830, 'My poor dear Anthony will have outgrown our recollection! Tell him not to outgrow his affection for us. No day passes, – hardly an hour – without our talking of you all.'[6]

Whereas Tom and Henry's natural sympathies lay with their mother, with whom they had shared so much pain as well as happiness, Anthony's heart went out to their father – the only parent he knew between the ages of twelve and sixteen. He came to believe that Fanny had abandoned not only her twelve-year-old son but also her husband – both equally vulnerable. Anthony no doubt asked himself, as did Lucius Mason in *Orley Farm*, 'Was it not her position in life to be his mother? Had she not had her young days?' Yet Lady Mason 'had been preparing for herself in the world new hopes, a new home, and a new ambition'. Anthony's message is always the same in his novels. 'Wives,' thought Mrs Low, 'should never leave their husbands on any pretext; and, as far as she had heard the story, there had been no pretext at all' in Lady Laura Kennedy's case (*Phineas Redux*). Grace Crawley says to her mother, 'When there is unhappiness, people should stay together; – shouldn't they, mamma?' (*The Last Chronicle of Barset*).

Most tragic of all, the young Anthony sensed that, as Mrs Garnett wrote to her daughter Julia, 'with all his oddities, [Thomas Anthony] doted on his Fanny'.[7] Forty years later, Anthony has Nora Rowley remark concerning her sister Emily's morose and difficult husband, Louis Trevelyan: 'You know that he is good at heart – that nobody on earth loves you as he does' (*He Knew He Was Right*). In his *Autobiography* Anthony states that with *He Knew He Was Right* he intended 'to create sympathy for the unfortunate man who, while endeavouring to do his duty to all around him, should be led constantly astray by his unwillingness to submit his own judgement to the judgement of others'. There are numerous parallels between Louis Trevelyan and Thomas Anthony. Both men eventually drive away those they love by their irrational anger and jealousy: 'The companionship of his wife had once been to him everything in the world,' Anthony writes of Trevelyan; 'but now, for many months past, he had known no companion.'

Like Trollope, Trevelyan has to endure the ignominy of being cautioned by friends about his wife's unconventional behaviour. Thinking himself disgraced, he avoids the company of friends and hides himself away in furnished chambers in Lincoln's Inn. 'He could not divest his mind of the injury which had accrued to him from his wife's conduct'; 'what was he to do with the wretched woman . . . whom no most distant retirement would make safe from the effects of her own ignorance, folly, and obstinacy?' For days Louis Trevelyan 'had eaten alone, and sat alone, and walked alone'. The young Anthony would have been his father's only companion when he was home from Winchester for the holidays, and when he was again a day boy at Harrow while Tom and Henry were at university. Trevelyan had sometimes thought 'that he would be happy in the love of his child' – his only son whom he took to live with him. Anthony had clearly felt himself to be as helpless as the toddler Louis junior in alleviating his father's suffering: 'to repay him for his kindness his boy was always dumb before him'.

'I certainly must be composed of very elastic materials for spite of sickness, embarrassment, and sorrow, I still am in good spirits, and full of hope for the future,' Fanny wrote to Julia Pertz on 12 March 1830.[8] The contrast between husband and wife could not have been greater:

> Of all the numerous heaven-born host of innate blessings bestowed upon us by the tender prophetic love of our Divine Creator, a constitutionally active mind is perhaps the greatest. That last, lowest, deepest misery of despondency, a sinking languid spirit, is, almost of necessity, unknown to it. To an active mind all things possible are, more or less, within its reach, and even if this storehouse of hope should fail, then things impossible will give exercise to faculties, less healthful and profitable perhaps, but not always less enjoyable and consolatory (*The Old World and the New*).

By the end of February the ice had broken on the Ohio, and the Trollopes together with Hervieu had been able to travel up river to Wheeling, Virginia. With them went Fanny's loyal English maid Hester Rust, 'an excellent creature'. The farm labourer who had come out with the Trollopes, William Abbot, had found a good job in Memphis and stayed behind. At Wheeling, the party probably split up; they had money enough for only one transatlantic passage, so Henry would have continued on his own to New York to catch his boat home. The rest travelled by coach across the Alleghenies towards Washington, DC. The hotels left something to be desired: Fanny 'found linen on the beds which, they assured us had only been used *a few nights*' (*The Domestic Manners*). Nevertheless, Fanny's spirits seemed to rise in proportion to the distance she put between herself and Cincinnati: 'every thing I have seen since I began to climb the Allegheny mountains has delighted me – and to confess the truth it is the first time I have been delighted since I came to America'.[9] A product of the Romantic era, Fanny fully appreciated the untamed

American landscape, 'the tall stalks of Indian corn, waving their tassels in the breeze of night; the dark impenetrable wall of forest . . . the loud, deep, unceasing croak of the bull-frog, and at intervals, the hollow, painful howl of the distant wolf' (*The Refugee*).

Fanny's intention was to visit Stonington, Maryland, where Anna Maria Stone, Julia and Harriet Garnett's eldest sister, had remained with her husband. Stonington was not too far from Washington, where Hervieu expected to make his reputation by exhibiting his canvas 'Lafayette's Landing in Cincinnati'. Fanny too had a plan which she hoped would enable her to salvage something from the wreckage of their American sojourn. Since her arrival in Cincinnati, two years earlier, Fanny had been gathering material for what was to become *The Domestic Manners of the Americans*. She had tried her hand at writing before, back in England, and had even sent a few manuscripts round to London publishers, though without success. She realized, however, that a book relating her experiences of the American frontier might just find its way into print. She wrote to her son Tom in the summer of 1828, only a few months after she had arrived in Cincinnati: 'I amuse myself by making notes, and hope some day to manufacture them into a volume. This is a remote corner of the world, and but seldom visited, and I think that if Hervieu could find time to furnish sketches of scenery, and groups, a very taking little volume might be produced.' To Mary Russell Mitford she exclaimed: 'Oh! my dear friend, had I but the tenth of an inch of the nib of your pen, what pictures might I draw of the people here! – so very queer, so very unlike any other thing in heaven above or earth below! – but it may not be. I can look, and I can laugh, but the power of describing is not given to above half a dozen in a century.' Fanny borrowed her sons' notebooks (two have Tom's initials and one is inscribed 'H. Trollope' with the words 'Noli me tangere, Nemo me Impune Accessit'* on the cover) to jot down American descriptions, scenes and conversations in between remedies for dysentery, snake bites and malarial fever. (The latter was for Henry's benefit: 'One

---

* 'Let no one touch me.' '*Nemo me impune accessit*' ('no one approaches me with impunity') appears to be Henry's pun on '*nemo me impune laccessit*' ('no one provokes me with impunity'), the motto of the Stewart royal family.

spoonful every 2 hours when the fever is on him.') Fanny also had some help with her research: in a rounded, childish script someone, probably her daughter Cecilia, has copied down a description of an Indian summer.[10]

Two of her female characters who follow Fanny out to America also set about writing books describing all they have seen. In *The Refugee* Caroline, like Mrs Trollope before her, attends the debates in the Senate 'for the purpose of collecting attitudes for her book of sketches on the American graces'. An American lady tells the Widow Barnaby that, if someone were to write a book of travels contradicting all the previous lies about the United States, the author's name would be rendered 'as glorious throughout the Union as that of General Lafayette himself. And as to dollars! Oh, my! There would be no end to the dollars as would be made by it.' So, the widow 'set about her task in good earnest, settling her chair, placing a whole quire of paper before her, and fixing a steel pen to her fancy'. Like Fanny, she begins by writing down 'the heads of various subjects to which she immediately intended to direct her attention'. With a lovely touch of self-irony, Fanny goes on to describe Martha Barnaby's moment of epiphany: 'now the important business was actually begun, and Mrs Allen Barnaby in turning over the first page of her book turned over a new page in her own history also; and she felt this – felt that her genius had now brought her to another epoch of her fate, and she doubted not but that she should date from it the growth and the ripening of honour, profit and renown' (*The Barnabys in America*).

Even as early as June 1828 Fanny had begun approaching American publishers. She sent a partial rough draft of the book to her friend Charles Wilkes in New York, asking him to pass it on to a New York publisher whom he knew. She wanted the publisher's 'opinion as to the *finishing up* and *writing fair* the remainder as I should not like to take even this much trouble, if he were not likely to publish it, when it was done'. Nothing came of the attempt. But by the spring of 1830, when all her other hopes and dreams of the previous two years had been shattered, Fanny returned to the idea of a book, the writing of which clearly became a source of comfort. 'You know enough of composition,' she wrote to Tom from Stonington, 'to be aware that nothing more completely occupies the mind; and Hope – that quits us the last, perhaps, of all our friends – tells me that it is *possible* my book may succeed.'[11]

Fanny was encouraged by the reception of Basil Hall's *Travels in North America*, which had appeared in America in 1829. She wrote to Mary Russell Mitford on 28 July 1830 that the Englishman's book 'has put the Union in a blaze from one end to the other. I never on any occasion heard so general an expression of contempt and detestation as that which follows his name.' If only her travel book could be as talked about – and successful – as Hall's. In Stonington the work began to take shape: the first half would be a detailed picture of Cincinnati and its citizens, the second half a more conventional travel book, with descriptions of the cities and scenery she visited after her departure from Cincinnati. She knew that the book would not be flattering to the Americans, for she wrote to Julia at this time that 'it will make Harriet angry – and perhaps you will shake your dear little head, but I have described things exactly as I have seen them and have only omitted what I thought it invidious and ill-natured to mention – never any thing that could be admired and approved'.[12]

In the meantime, however, the Trollopes still had to find the means to live. Their good friend Mrs Stone, by this time a widow with a large family, had herself fallen on hard times, and was obliged to charge her friends a weekly rent of $8.25. Fanny and her daughters now had to rely entirely on Hervieu's generosity. As she wrote to Julia Pertz, 'painting is a poor business in America – but this excellent and devoted friend continued to support us by it, for *two years*'. Hervieu's historical painting (sadly, now lost) was well-received in Philadelphia as well as the capital, but it did not bring him fame and fortune – the exhibition did not even pay for itself. The artist went back to doing society portraits and drawing lessons. The ghastly Garnetts, as they perhaps should be called, had written of Fanny's indiscretions to Mrs Stone, who agreed with them that it was regrettable she had entered America 'at the back door'. Nevertheless, she was a good friend to the Trollopes and did all she could for them, including nursing Fanny when she once more fell dangerously ill in the autumn of 1830. The doctor advised that she leave the Stones' 'cold frame house' and move to the slightly gentler climate of Alexandria, Virginia.[13]

By the spring of 1831 Hervieu had saved enough to take himself and his friends up the coast to New York. Fanny liked the eastern cities: she thought 'the whole aspect of Washington . . . light, cheerful, and airy': its buildings full of majesty and beauty; its streets void of 'all sights, sounds, or smells of commerce' – or pigs, she might have added. Fanny predicted that New York would one day cover Manhattan Island and rise, 'like Venice, from the sea'. It was here that she finally saw Mary Russell Mitford's play, *Rienzi*, along with the spitters and a mother 'performing the most maternal office possible' (*The Domestic Manners*). 'Not even the bad acting,' Fanny wrote to the author back home, 'could spoil it.'[14] Her visit to Philadelphia was somewhat marred when, upon entering the Antique Statue Gallery at the Pennsylvania Academy of Fine Arts, she was informed that 'the ladies like to go into that room by themselves, when there be no gentlemen watching them'. The English matron did not like being made to feel that she had been granted permission 'to steal a glance at what was deemed indecent'. She found some of the casts defaced 'in a most indecent and shameless manner', clearly by rowdy young men unaccompanied by either their wives, sweethearts or mothers (*The Domestic Manners*).

At this period no European visitor to America would have felt his or her trip complete without seeing Niagara Falls: John Quincy Adams, Jackson's presidential rival, once remarked that the falls were the chief 'icon of the American sublime . . . vast, unmeasurable, unconquerable, inexplicable'.[15] Fanny was no exception. Her husband and Tom had also visited them before returning to England, but, all too typically, their stay was 'in great measure spoiled' by one of Thomas Anthony's migraines. According to Tom, his father 'dragged himself painfully to the usual spot to view the Falls, and having looked, returned to bed'. Fanny, on the other hand, climbed 'the giddy stairs which scale the very edge of the torrent . . . on which, shudder as you may, you must take your stand or lose your reputation as a tourist' (*The Domestic Manners*).

Not surprisingly, Fanny met a fellow Englishman at Niagara, Captain Thomas Hamilton, an author of some repute. Fanny had written to Tom earlier from Stonington that Cecilia was 'literally without shoes', and his sisters did nothing but 'mend, – and mend, – and mend'. However, Hamilton's description of the Trollopes, relayed to a third person through his cousin Walter Stirling, shows just how conspicuous their poverty had become. In his cousin's opinion, Stirling writes, Mrs Trollope was 'a very eccentric person – She was then travelling with her 2 daughters, merely girls, and a Frenchman. In what capacity this latter attended her, Hamilton could not make out, but from the odd appearance of matters, and her apparent poverty, which hardly admitted her and her daughters being decently dressed, it was conclusive against her being taken notice of by respectable ladies, or treated as one herself. – It is perfectly evident she could [not] have seen anything of society in the Atlantic States, and she had no introductions, or the means of mixing in good company.' Nevertheless, Stirling adds, 'I understand Mrs Trollope is a woman of very good family & education, & I believe of good character, notwithstanding her connection with Miss Wright, & her French *compagnon de voyage* at Niagara.'[16] Did Fanny notice the look of disapproval in Captain Hamilton's eyes and cry inwardly that she and her family had been brought so low? At least she would have found consolation in the work at hand, for, by this time, June 1831, she had nearly completed her research.

Niagara was to be the Trollopes' last tourist destination in America. Cecilia was now nearly fifteen, and Fanny had gathered more than enough material for her book. However, she later explained to Julia, 'with all the exertions Hervieu could make, he never could get enough before hand, to realize a sum sufficient to bring us home. I wrote to Mr Trollope and told him that for my dear girls' sake I was *determined* upon returning to England – and that if he was unable to furnish me with the means, I would apply to his family for them.'[17] The blackmail succeeded: Thomas Anthony at last sent out £80. The next step was 'the important business of securing our homeward passage'. 'One must know what it is to cross the ocean,' Fanny remarked,

before the immense importance of all the little details of accommodation can be understood. The anxious first look into the face of the captain, to ascertain if he be gentle or rough; another, scarcely less important, in that of the steward, generally a sable one, but not the less expressive; the accurate, but rapid glance of measurement thrown round the little state-rooms; another at the good or bad arrangement of the stair-case, by which you are to stumble up and stumble down, from cabin to deck, and from deck to cabin; all this, they only can understand who have felt it.

Fanny packed up her 'six hundred pages of griffonage',* as she calls her manuscript, and boarded ship (*The Domestic Manners*). She disembarked at Woolwich in August 1831, after an absence of nearly four years. 'At last the boat was alongside, which was to convey' the weary travellers 'to those dear dirty steps, beside the Custom-house of London, the stumbling up of which has occasioned joy and gladness to so many hearts' (*The Widow Married*).

As much as she had wished for the reunion with her husband and sons, Fanny must have been filled with trepidation when the moment finally arrived. Communication between husband and wife since Thomas Anthony's departure from Cincinnati in early 1829 had been almost non-existent. 'The two years and two months of his absence had dragged themselves away, without either having had any direct tidings of the other. Under such circumstances there is no confidence, however strong, which can prevent some feeling approaching to doubt and dread, lest the first glance of the long absent eye should be less full of love than the last,' so Fanny wrote of Lieutenant Markham and his fiancée in *The Blue Belles*. But Fanny's delight at being amongst her family, especially all her children once more, helped her to overcome her fears. 'The first long evening, aye, and despite pale faces and fatigue, the greater part of the night, was passed in that delightful confusion of questions asked, and answers not waited for, of narratives began, but never ended; of tears that celebrate excesses of joy, and smiles that speak of sorrows past, which marks the perfection of contentment, setting ceremony, order, and common sense at defiance' (*The Refugee*). As she wrote to Julia

* scribblings.

on her return, 'my dear children are *all* devoted to me – I never saw *more* attached or affectionate children – this is my greatest comfort'.[18]

Tom says that his mother set about straightaway brightening the gloomy Harrow Weald farmhouse with the help of some young girls whom she invited round. Pillows were conjured up and, presumably, beds for herself and the girls. However, Fanny soon realized that the need to make money from *The Domestic Manners* had become even more imperative, for the situation with her husband had become desperate. Fanny tells Julia that although everyone was in good health, 'there are other circumstances less agreeable, attending my return. Mr T. assures me that his affairs are in the greatest disorder – that he has lost *more* than £500 sterling per ann: by his farms for many years past. That he has endeavoured to redeem this by many speculations, *all* of which have failed.'[19] He continued to blame Henry and, no doubt, Fanny for the Cincinnati débâcle. 'What am I to do?' Thomas Anthony might have exclaimed to his wife, as did Plantagenet Palliser. 'How am I to free myself from the impediments which you make for me? My enemies I can overcome – but I cannot escape the pitfalls which are made for me by my own wife.' 'I sometimes think,' Glencora replies, 'that I should have been the man, my skin is so thick; and that you should have been the woman, yours is so tender' (*The Prime Minister*).

Fanny threw herself into her work. She locked herself away at the top of the house, in what became known to her family as 'The Sacred Den', to finish writing and revising *The Domestic Manners*. The room was probably like that described in *Mrs Mathews*, an 'oddly-shaped and oddly-furnished apartment', with a 'queer, narrow twisting little staircase which led to it'. 'So sacred' was it that 'none ever ventured to enter', except when invited (*Tremordyn Cliff*). She soon honoured her old Harrow friends the Milmans with such an invitation, having granted them a sneak preview of *The Domestic Manners* in an early version. 'Yesterday the whole Milman family mounted the stairs to my room, clamorously calling for "More book! More book!" Imagine me, if you please, looking extremely modest, but being vastly delighted,' she writes to Tom at Oxford. 'The old Lady Milman told me that if I had been hid behind the door the evening before,

I might have been well contented with what I heard, which was what could rarely happen to authors so placed! All this is very encouraging.'[20]

The next task Fanny set about was to find a publisher. Mary Russell Mitford gave her an introduction to Whittaker, Treacher & Co., who agreed to consider her manuscript. For a second opinion Whittaker sent it to Basil Hall, whose best-selling travel book Fanny hoped to emulate. To her delight, he wholeheartedly recommended the book for publication and lent his full support to its author. Hall's volumes – and the public's reaction to them – had helped her to realize her own book's weaknesses and, more importantly, its strengths. In a letter to Miss Mitford she is privately critical of Hall's volumes. Her censure, however, is not aimed at Hall's general points, with which she has much sympathy, but with the shallowness of his account. Hall, armed with those all-important letters of introduction as well as his reputation as an author, had been 'received in full drawing-room style', Fanny remarked. 'He saw the country in full dress, and had little or no opportunity of judging of it unhoused, unanointed, unannealed, with all its imperfections on its head, as I and my family too often had' (*The Domestic Manners*).

Unlike more distinguished travel writers such as Hall, Fanny does not collect statistics, but domestic detail and personal anecdotes. She does not dine with US senators but visits the humble home of a backwoodsman and his wife. Fanny came to realize that this was her great skill: to describe the minutiae of life in America. Furthermore, as Frances Eleanor Trollope was later to say of her mother-in-law, she possessed that ' "deep-seated habit of direct fellow-feeling with individual fellow-men," which George Eliot says is so indispensable to our morality'.[21] It was this quality which allowed Fanny to see through the layers of prejudice and received wisdom in America straight to the truth of the matter, often illustrating her point with a single, telling anecdote – one might even say a 'snapshot' of the society which she viewed.

Fanny did not spare Cincinnati: she describes the pigs in the streets, the disgusting spitting, the horrendous table manners and the citizens' almost comical prudishness, and she does so in a highly entertaining way. But Fanny does not merely describe; she digs deep into the fabric of American society. She blamed the lack of refinement in America on the low esteem in which women are held, guarded, as they are, 'by a seven-fold shield of habitual insignificance'. Fanny's description of a day in the life of a well-to-do lady in Philadelphia, although it offers no explicit criticism, is a devastating commentary – skilfully written – on the role of women in America. 'She has a very handsome house, with white marble steps and door-posts, and a delicate silver knocker and door-handle; she has very handsome drawing-rooms . . . she is always very handsomely dressed; and, moreover, she is very handsome herself.' But, she cannot escape the daily, incessant tedium of her existence. At about three o'clock she begins to await her husband's return: 'He comes, shakes hands with her, spits, and dines. The conversation is not much, and ten minutes suffices for the dinner.' The husband then goes off to his club for the rest of the evening – 'And so ends her day.'

Religion in America, according to Fanny Trollope, did nothing to relieve the oppression of women but, in fact, contributed to it. She remarks on the unusual 'influence which the ministers of all the innumerable religious sects throughout America, have on the females of their respective congregations': 'it is from the clergy only that the women of America receive that sort of attention which is so dearly valued by every female heart throughout the world'. Fanny describes both a revival meeting in Cincinnati itself and a 'camp-meeting' in the wilds of Indiana. The revival meeting was more typical (and not unfamiliar today). After a fire-and-brimstone sermon, a number of young girls 'came tottering out, their hands clasped, their heads hanging on their bosoms, and every limb trembling . . . Young creatures, with features pale and distorted, fell on their knees on the pavement, and soon sunk forward on their faces; the most violent cries and shrieks followed, while from time to time a voice was heard in convulsive accents, exclaiming, "Oh Lord!" "Oh Lord Jesus!" "Help me, Jesus!" and the like.' The preachers walked about these girls, offering them 'whispered comfortings, and from time to time a mystic caress'. Freedom of religion was hailed as one of the most enlightened principles of the Constitution. However, Fanny has a different view: 'a religious tyranny may be exerted very effectually without the aid of the government, in a way much more oppressive than the paying of tithe'.

In Fanny's eyes, these evangelical clergymen were guilty of a sin far greater than a lack of refinement, and that was an excess of hypocrisy. Indeed, this is the fundamental criticism which she extends to the whole of American society. And nothing to her more clearly illustrated the hypocrisy pervading 'the land of the free' than the institution of slavery. One incident in particular which Fanny recounts conveys, in a way that no abstract argument could, the ruinous effect which slavery had on the hearts and minds of Americans, even children. On the farm in Alexandria, Virginia, where she boarded during the winter of 1830–31, a very young slave girl had unwittingly eaten a biscuit which had been sprinkled with arsenic and left (irresponsibly) on a shelf to dispose of some rats. Fanny immediately mixed some mustard and water and made the girl swallow it to expel the poison. She then sat down and 'took the little sufferer in my lap', observing 'a general titter among the white members of the family'. 'The youngest of the family, a little girl about the same age of the young slave, after gazing at me for a few moments in utter astonishment, exclaimed, "My! If Mrs Trollope has not taken her in her lap, and wiped her nasty mouth! Why I would not have touched her mouth for two hundred dollars!" ' When Fanny later inquired after the slave girl, who was still in great pain, 'another young lady of the family, the one by whose imprudence the accident had occurred, met my anxious enquiries with ill-suppressed mirth – told me they had sent for the doctor – and then burst into uncontrollable laughter'.

The clarity and humanity of Fanny Trollope's observations appear all the more refreshing when compared to Frances Wright's blinkered view of the United States, as propounded in her *Views of Society and Manners in America* (1821). The great campaigner for equal rights between men and women felt there was no reason to regret the annihilation of the American Indian, for 'the savage, with all his virtues, and he has some virtues, is still a savage . . . holding a lower place in creation than men who, to the proud spirit of independence, unite the softer feelings that spring only within the pale of civilized life. The increase and spread of the white population at the expense

165

of the red is, as it were, the triumph of peace over violence.' With breathtaking ignorance Frances Wright then talks of the 'wise and humane' treaties between the federal government and the Indians, which 'have never been violated'. In fact, the newly established nation was greedy for land: treaties were disregarded, and both Washington and Jefferson, as governor of Virginia, had sent out troops to exterminate the Indians.[22] Fanny Trollope, however, was not fooled, and found the American government to be 'treacherous and false almost beyond belief in their intercourse with the unhappy Indians'. She goes on to make one of the most powerful and outspoken declarations in *The Domestic Manners*:

> Had I, during my residence in the United States, observed any single feature in their national character that could justify their eternal boast of liberality and the love of freedom, I might have respected them, however much my taste might have been offended by what was peculiar in their manners or customs. But it is impossible for any mind of common honesty not to be revolted by the contradictions in their principles and practice . . . you will see them with one hand hoisting the cap of liberty, and with the other flogging their slaves. You will see them one hour lecturing their mob on the indefeasible rights of man, and the next driving from their homes the children of the soil, whom they have bound themselves to protect by the most solemn treaties.

For Fanny Trollope that sacred American phrase 'All men are created equal' was merely 'mischievous sophistry'. She was clear-sighted enough to perceive that true equality was an impossibility in the United States of the 1820s: deep-seated prejudice barred racial equality, and economic equality was simply a nonsense. In her notebooks she had commented that the really poor 'are constantly kept in a state of irritation by feeling that their boasted equality is a falsehood. It is a delusion which their pride leads them to wish at while their penury goads them to hate the solid reality of inequality which exists in America exactly as much as it does elsewhere.' She does, however, acknowledge the equality of opportunity which was open to Americans. Indeed, 'this is the only feature in American society that I recognize as indicative of the equality they profess. Any man's son may become the equal of any other man's son, and the consciousness of this is certainly a spur to exertion; on the other hand, it is also a spur to that coarse familiarity, untempered by any shadow of respect,' which Fanny, who was in this regard at least a child of her time, found so disconcerting. 'This is a positive evil, and, I think, more than balances its advantages.'

Mrs Trollope had gone out to America something of a liberal; she returned to England very much a conservative. As she wrote to Mary Russell Mitford, 'I know your good father ... is a bit of a radical – so I was, too, once, but the United States offer a *radical* cure for this.'[23] She wrote the following passage no doubt with Frances Wright's visits to her beloved Harrow home in mind: 'the theory of equality may be very daintily discussed by English gentlemen in a London dining-room, when the servant, having placed a fresh bottle of cool wine on the table, respectfully shuts the door, and leaves them to their walnuts and their wisdom; but it will be found less palatable when it presents itself in the shape of a hard, greasy paw, and is claimed in accents that breathe less of freedom than of onions and whiskey. Strong, indeed, must be the love of equality in an English breast if it can survive a tour through the Union.' 'Were I an English legislator,' Fanny comments earlier in the book, 'instead of sending sedition to the Tower, I would send her to make a tour of the United States. I had a little leaning towards sedition myself when I set out, but before I had half completed my tour I was quite cured.' She concluded at the end of *The Domestic Manners of the Americans*: 'I do not like them. I do not like their principles, I do not like their manners, I do not like their opinions.'

Fanny was not only perceptive, she was also astute. On her return to England in the autumn of 1831, the issues of democracy and equality were very much in the air. The new Whig administration of November 1830 was determined to satisfy the growing demand for parliamentary reform by abolishing the 'rotten boroughs', creating new seats to represent the growing towns, and extending the franchise. In an atmosphere of intense political crisis arguments raged for and against the Reform Bill which Lord John Russell had first put forward in March 1831. When in September the House of Lords threw out this early version of the Bill, radical newspapers appeared with the black edges of mourning and at Bristol, Fanny's birthplace, the mob ran riot for two days and destroyed half of Queen Square, near to where her mother's family, the Gresleys and the Hellicars, lived. In her sketches of contemporary country life, *Our Village*, Mary Russell Mitford describes 'the open and noisy meetings of determined men at noontide in the streets and greens of our Berkshire villages, and even sometimes in the very churchyards', 'their daylight marches on the high road, regular and orderly as those of an army'. 'Nor were the preparations for defence . . . less shocking': 'The hourly visits of bustling parish officers, bristling with importance', 'the soldiers, transported from place to place in carts the better to catch the rogues'. But, she adds, worst of all were the rumours of death and destruction. Hervieu is typically melodramatic in a letter to Tom: 'Certes I could not choose a worse time to write to you. I have been for nearly three weeks vexed beyond the power of my mild temper. First this cursed Reforme Bill . . . then the lithographic stone from France is not yet here, your poor Mamma has been floating about from incertitude to incertitude, cholera morbus and revolution spread their wings over everything we meet, – yes, we must all go to the devil at last!'[24]

Whittaker had arranged for *The Domestic Manners of the Americans* to be published in January 1832, just a few days after a favourable anonymous piece on the book (written by Basil Hall) was due to appear in *The Quarterly Review*. However, articles on the recent Bristol and Manchester riots overwhelmed the January issue, and to Fanny's annoyance, the publication of her book and Hall's review were postponed until March. The delay was fortuitous – and possibly even deliberate on Whittaker's part, for by March the debate over the Reform Bill was approaching its climax. The Bill's supporters held up America as a beacon of democracy and an example to be followed. The United States had long been regarded as the great democratic experiment, and every travel book about the country was received as if it were a 'party pamphlet', as John Stuart Mill remarked.[25] British periodicals had been fuelling the controversy since the 1810s, with the conservative *Quarterly Review* and the liberal *Westminster Review* predictably taking opposing views on the virtues and vices of the American republic.*

It was in this politically charged atmosphere that Fanny Trollope sat down in her 'Sacred Den' to write the final version of her preface to the book, dated 'Harrow, March, 1832'. As the liberal *Edinburgh Review* would rightly observe, this was nothing more nor less than 'an express advertisement against the Reform Bill'.[26] Fanny felt very strongly that American democracy, so seriously flawed, should not be hailed as a paradigm of government, and she was happy to lend support to the Tory cause – she later described the political division as a 'yawning gulf which divides the conservative from the destructive' (*The Widow Married*). But, more importantly, Fanny needed this first book, which was, after all, from the pen of an unknown woman writer, to be a financial success. Therefore, encouraged and guided by Basil Hall and her publisher, she deliberately threw *The Domestic Manners* into the political fray with an inflammatory preface, hoping that the ensuing fracas would make it a bestseller. The Tories, unlike the radicals, did not have much effective propaganda at their disposal, and they had only to read Mrs Trollope's opening words to know that here was the ammunition they needed for their final assault on the Bill. She begins:

> Although much has already been written on the great experiment, as it has been called, now making in government, on the other side of the Atlantic, there appears to be still room for many interesting details on the influence which the political system of the country has produced on the principles, tastes, and manners, of its domestic life ... by describing, faithfully, the daily aspect of ordinary life, she [Fanny writes in the third person] has endeavoured to shew how greatly the advantage is on the side of those who are governed by the few, instead of the many. The chief object she has had in view is to encourage her

---

* In *Paris and the Parisians* (1836) Fanny tells the story of a nurse who kept *The Westminster Review* among the baby linen and read while nursing her mistress's child. Her fiancé had given it to her, saying 'it is no more than what it is the duty of everybody to understand'.

countrymen to hold fast by a constitution that ensures all the blessings which flow from established habits and solid principles.

On 19 March 1832, three days before the Reform Bill was due to have its third and final reading in the House of Commons, and nine days after its author's fifty-third birthday, *The Domestic Manners of the Americans* was finally published. For Fanny, her husband and their five children, everything now depended on its success.

CHAPTER EIGHT

Fashionable Life

'I awoke one morning and found myself famous,' Fanny wrote to her son Tom, echoing Byron. 'You would laugh did you know to what an extent I am lionized.' The publisher of *The Quarterly Review*, John Murray, predicted that *The Domestic Manners of the Americans* would 'sell like wildfire!' – and so it did. Within a year the book had run through four editions. John Gibson Lockhart, the *Quarterly*'s editor and Sir Walter Scott's son-in-law, told Fanny's old Harrow friend Henry Milman that 'it was the cleverest woman's book which he had read for a long time'.[1]

Amid a flurry of social engagements Fanny was introduced to 'half the poets, painters, wits and wonders that were in town' and was 'abundantly complimented'. The seasoned bluestockings, the Berry sisters, besought Basil Hall to bring Fanny along to one of their soirées in Curzon Street. Fanny obliged, and there, she wrote to Tom, 'the Countess of Morley told me she was certain that if I drove through London proclaiming who I was, I should have the horses taken off and be drawn in triumph from one end of town to the other! The Honourable Mr Somebody declared that my thunder storm was the finest thing in prose or verse. Lady Charlotte Lindsay *implored* me to go on writing – never was anything so delightful. Lady Louisa Stewart told me that I had quite put English out of fashion, and that every one was talking Yankee talk.' 'Go the whole hog' and the other quaint Americanisms which Fanny had mimicked so well in *The Domestic Manners* became all the rage among the English élite. 'The presence of a lion of some sort' was a 'necessary phenomenon of a London or Paris drawing-room' (*Vienna and the Austrians*). And where the lions go, the 'lion-huntress' follows, as Henry irreverently dubbed a woman who sent numerous invitations to Mrs Trollope, claiming that her son and Tom had been great friends at Winchester, though the latter had only the haziest recollection of his schoolfellow.[2]

The Domestic Manners met with most of her friends' approval. Captain 'Pendulum' Kater wrote Fanny 'a volume of panegyric', and even Captain Hamilton, who had been dismayed by Mrs Trollope's 'odd appearance' and 'apparent poverty' at Niagara Falls, was happy to inform her 'that his two neighbours on the Lakes, Southey and Wordsworth, are both *delighted*'. Where there was criticism, her more loyal friends were quick to leap to Fanny's defence. When an American stated before the Revd Isaac Fidler, a friend of her brother Henry, that *The Domestic Manners* was 'a tissue of illiberal falsehoods', Fidler called upon him to get his copy and declared that if the American could find one false claim, 'he would do penance for his countrywoman, and eat her book'. Some years later, when Fanny's fellow author, Harriet Martineau, began to abuse Mrs Trollope's views on the young republic at a dinner party, Henry Milman 'put in a word for her'. Miss Martineau had probably harboured a grudge against the author of *The Domestic Manners* ever since a New York publisher had advised her, concerning her own forthcoming book on America: 'Well! then you might Trollopize a bit, and so make a readable book.'[3]

However, Fanny was fully aware that her politics might horrify the more liberal-minded among her acquaintances. Mary Russell Mitford reassured her that 'my political prejudices are by no means shocked at your dislike of Republicanism. I was always a very aristo-cratic Whig & since these reforming days am well-nigh become a staunch Tory, for pretty nearly the same reason that converted you: a dislike of mobs in action.' The Garnetts, on the other hand, remained true to their radical American upbringing and were harsh in their criticisms of the book. 'I can well imagine,' Fanny replied to Julia's objections, how sweet and fondly cherished your recollections are of your New Jersey farm – your society, the very best in New York, and your manner of living, exactly what pleased yourself and your family – without coming (or knowing) much about the country you were in – It would give me great pain to differ from you, dearest, on any point in which I believed that your mature judgement was against me – but I feel so very certain that the same course would produce the same effects on your mind as on mine, that I only smile at your enthusiasm for a country that you do not know, and think how quickly you would change your opinions, were you to see what I have seen.

On hearing of Fanny's hard-won financial success with the book, Harriet, with characteristic arrogance, remarked to her sister, 'I wish she could have made money without the sacrifice of principle.' (Within a year, however, when confronted in Paris by a particularly brash American couple, the Fishers, and their 'two handsome vulgar girls', Harriet was forced to admit: 'Mrs Trollope is right – all Americans are vulgar – *sans exception*.')[4]

In America Mrs Trollope's provocative tone ensured that everyone was talking about – and buying – her book. The English traveller E. T. Coke, residing in New York when the first American edition appeared in the summer of 1832, wrote:

the commotion it created amongst the good citizens is truly inconceivable. The Tariff and Bank Bill were alike forgotten, and the tug of war was hard, whether the 'Domestic Manners,' or the cholera, which burst upon them simultaneously, should be the more engrossing topic of conversation. At every corner of the street, at the door of every petty retailer of information for the people, a large placard met the eye with, 'For sale here, with plates, Domestic Manners of the Americans, by Mrs Trollope.' At every table d'hôte, on board of every steam-boat, in every stage-coach, and in all societies, the first question was, 'Have you read Mrs Trollope?'[5]

Fanny had remarked in *The Domestic Manners* that 'other nations have been called thin-skinned, but the citizens of the Union have, apparently, no skins at all'. The book's author was caricatured in print and pictures: wax figures of Mrs Trollope appeared in the form of a goblin; she was portrayed as an ugly harridan talking to a black devil in D. C. Johnston's *Trollopiana: Scraps for the Year 1833* and satirized in the poem *The Trollopiad* by 'Nil Admirari, Esq' (1837). One American reviewer commented on the 'curious coincidence of her name' and suggested that it was, in fact, a '*soubriquet* bestowed upon her, for the purpose of expressing, with the greatest brevity possible, the precise idea that was entertained of her character'. Washington Irving claimed that it was 'all an admirable fabrication got up in London by someone who has never visited America'. The *New York Mirror* declared that her name had become a 'by-word in taverns and in the pit of the theatres, which, we doubt not, pleases her vastly ... Spitters and chewers, look to it; and ye indolent beings, who lounge on two chairs with your feet on the mantel-piece, remember Mr Herview's [*sic*] sketches, and be no more guilty of a *Trollope!*' (In fact, one American commentator confessed that 'this best abused writer on America was a beneficent, practical reformer', especially in the theatres, and Henry Wadsworth Longfellow remarked that he would forgive Mrs Trollope everything if *The Domestic Manners* helped to put a stop to spitting.)[6]

Fanny's critics on both sides of the Atlantic, however begrudgingly, gave her credit for a lively and witty style, but they doubted her method and judgement ('Mrs Trollope describes better than she thinks'). And they all, to a man, thought her unladylike and 'vulgar' for she 'saw many things which no refined Englishwoman would have seen, or seeing would have understood – still less have written and published'. Fanny was not immune to these criticisms. Although she admits her disillusionment with Frances Wright and confesses that, regarding her two years in Cincinnati, 'the only regret was that we had ever entered it; for we had wasted health, time, and money there', she was clearly concerned not to invite any scandal or ridicule, and to this end *The Domestic Manners* is a very carefully constructed work. Fanny makes no mention of her various money-making schemes in Cincinnati. The Bazaar is never named, though she does refer

cryptically to 'our Cincinnati speculation' and 'domestic embarrassments'. Furthermore, although she discusses the utopian community
at New Harmony, she does not mention that her son Henry had been
an inmate. She refers to Hervieu only once, describing him as
'our friend Mr H., who had accompanied Miss Wright to America'.
Fanny's silence in these matters is understandable, given the
ad hominem abuse she was subjected to. As far as the critics were
concerned, the sanguine Basil Hall who had had his share of abuse
in the press, advised Fanny to 'borrow a little of my philosophy &
accept all such things as compliments to your talents, & testimonies
to your truth'.[7]

However, the charge of 'sour grapes' made against her must have
hit a nerve. 'She sets off for America,' *The Literary Gazette* states,
'expecting to find it a complete Utopia. Of course these expectations
– like all air-castles, of which imagination, not reason, is the architect
– are disappointed; and then off flies the castle-builder to the other
extreme and can see no advantages, and make no allowances.'[8] But
the criticism holds no merit. It was precisely her disillusioning
experiences in Nashoba and Cincinnati which revealed to her the
reality behind the 'American Dream' and that most fundamental of
American principles, the 'pursuit of happiness'.

Fanny's book, with its insights and, above all, humour, became the
touchstone against which all subsequent accounts of that country
were tested. A visitor to Charles Dickens's house, on the eve of his
departure for the United States in 1841, found the writer's study
stacked with travel books on America, including Mrs Trollope's. More
than thirty years later Anthony followed in his mother's footsteps to
America. On his tour of the western states, including Ohio, he
discovered not only the Bazaar but also his mother's reputation intact.
A citizen of Rolla, Missouri, declared, when he had ascertained that
Anthony was Mrs Trollope's son, 'Then, sir, you are an accession to
Rolla.'* But Anthony had never forgiven his mother for abandoning
that insecure boy of twelve, and in his autobiography he set down a
harsh judgement on *The Domestic Manners*, the only thing she

* Anthony recounts this story in his own travel book on the United States, *North
America*, published in 1862.

managed to rescue from the wreck of her American dreams. 'No observer was certainly less qualified to judge of the prospects or even the happiness of a young people,' he wrote. 'No one could have been worse adapted by nature for the task of learning whether a nation was in a way to thrive. Whatever she saw she judged, as most women do, from her own standing-point.'

But perhaps the last word should go to Mark Twain, who knew the Mississippi and its environs so well. He carried a copy of *The Domestic Manners of the Americans* with him up the river, and his marginal notes show that he thought Mrs Trollope's 'snapshots' of American society were true to life:

She lived three years in this civilization of ours; in the body of it – not on the surface of it, as was the case with most of the foreign tourists of her day. She knew her subject well, and she set it forth fairly and squarely, without any weak ifs and ands and buts . . . She did not gild us; and neither did she whitewash us . . . It was for this sort of photography that poor candid Mrs Trollope was so handsomely cursed and reviled by this nation. Yet she was merely telling the truth, and this indignant nation knew it. She was painting a state of things which did not disappear at once. It lasted to well along in my youth, and I remember it.[9]

Fanny certainly did not scorn celebrity, but within a month she had tired of the empty flattery and false smiles. 'I never felt less in good humour with people in my life than I have done since I have been so be-puffed and be-praised,' she wrote to Mary Russell Mitford on 23 April 1832. Nowhere was she more popular than in high Tory circles, but she quickly became disillusioned: 'their apathy and despair provoke me beyond expression. If we are to be lost, it will be the fault of this party, who,' as she told one of these peers of the realm, 'appear to me to do nothing but lie on their sophas, and groan.' What mattered most to Fanny was neither the fame nor the politics, but the money. She had agreed on half profits with the publisher Whittaker, but this meant that she did not see a penny until the first issue of 1,250 copies had been sold. And she had to trust the publisher to make a fair rendering of costs *versus* income. This was not an ideal arrangement for, as Fanny wrote to Miss Mitford before the book came out, 'as we have been losing money on both sides of the Atlantic, a little money *in esse* would have been more agreeable than the hopes he gives *in posse*'.[10] Nevertheless, by the end of 1832 Fanny had received some £600 from Whittaker, and she promptly began repaying her debts. To Hervieu, in gratitude for all his help and financial assistance, she gave half the proceeds from the second edition of *The Domestic Manners*, that is £100. After Hervieu, she no doubt felt most in debt to the Harrow tradesmen 'who had hazarded the fruits of their time and industry by trusting to the honour of her family, and furnished them with the means of daily existence from believing in their honesty' (*Charles Chesterfield*). First on the list were those who had supplied her with all the coal and candles which she had used in her room over the last winter.

There was enough money left over to fulfil Fanny's greatest wish: 'to get back to my dear Julian Hill', as she confided to Julia. 'It will *I hope* be vacant at Michaelmas and I think that with my little gains, and steady economy we may be able to get on there again very well.' By the beginning of October, the Trollopes were reinstated at Julian Hill. 'The return of my mother,' Tom later recalled, 'and the success of her book, produced a change in the condition and circumstances of affairs at home which resembled the transformation scene in a pantomine that takes place at the advent of the good fairy.' Fanny paid for 'half a year's rent and taxes . . . in advance', bought 'a good bed, pillows, bolsters, sopha, and a chest of drawers' and was saving to purchase a cow and some malt for brewing. Fanny once more hosted her at-homes, produced theatricals, and devised charades for her family, friends and neighbours. Her little sketch entitled, 'Meeting of the Friends of Mutation', which includes the lines: 'For tories I care not a fig/My only terror is a whig,' probably dates from this period.[11] Fanny no doubt discovered that Tom, Henry and Anthony, aged twenty-two, twenty-one and seventeen, respectively, had developed that faculty common to most young men as well as mice, 'of finding their way in all directions when there is a chance of getting any thing to nibble, and who may be seen at the most crowded parties contesting with the domestics the shortest passages, and most direct access to that goal of all their wishes, the region of *pâte-gras* and champagne' (*Hargrave*).

Fanny would have savoured these hours of happiness and relaxation, reunited with her family and safely reinstated at her 'pretty cottage'. Her novel *One Fault* begins 'on a fine evening' in the year 1832. The whole of the Worthington family 'were luxuriating in the shade of a walnut-tree upon the lawn. A table with wine and fruit was in the midst of them; and though they had done with it, they still kept in possession of the spot, too comfortable or too lazy to remove. The group formed a pretty picture.' Two of the children, aged seventeen and twenty, are playing chess at one corner of the table, Mr Worthington is reading a newspaper, half asleep, Mrs Worthington 'appeared assiduously knitting, but chatted to them all in turn'. In a corner of the garden a Wykehamist friend of young Charles Worthington is playing 'a desperate game of romps' with the Newfoundland, Neptune, the name of the Trollopes' family dog.

As she luxuriated on the lawn, Fanny's thoughts might well have turned to Frances Wright, who only five years earlier, and probably on that very spot, had waxed lyrical about America and her plans for Nashoba. In *One Fault* Fanny recalls the two women with whom her fate had been so inextricably linked, Frances Wright and her sister Camilla, in her depiction of Mrs Worthington's two spinster sisters. The elder, Miss Christina, confident, outspoken, somewhat masculine and 'half-cracked', spends her time, like Frances, advocating women's rights and writing her great work 'on the powers of the female mind'. The younger, Miss Lucy, is sweet-tempered, soft-spoken and domestic, preferring needlework to politics, though she always listens to Christina 'with silent admiration', even if she does not understand, as was often the case with Camilla.

Fanny had kept track of the Wright sisters' movements while she was still in America. Within a year of Fanny's departure from Nashoba, Miss Wright had to acknowledge that her experiment had failed. Once she had secured asylum for the Nashoba slaves in the independent black republic of Haiti, the undeterred reformer set off on a lecture tour of America, making herself 'unpleasantly conspicuous'. Mrs Trollope heard her when she came to Cincinnati and again in Philadelphia, where the reformer was surrounded, rather incongruously, 'by a body guard of Quaker ladies' (*The Domestic Manners*). When the backwoods utopia was disbanded, Camilla and her husband went their separate ways: Camilla to nearby Memphis to give birth to a son, whom she named Francis.

Fanny had always been especially fond of Camilla. As far back as 1824, she had described Camilla as 'young, lovely – most attractive in manner – most estimable in mind, most amiable in nature. I would have had her the heroine of her own tale'. But Fanny astutely perceived that Camilla '*could* have no happiness distinct from her glorious sister. She lives in her light, and would droop, would perish, were she withdrawn from it.' Camilla and her child spent a month with the Trollopes in Cincinnati, and Fanny was pleased to see that the little boy had given Camilla a new interest in life. She wrote to Julia that she thought Camilla 'more sinned against than sinning – and that she still deserves all the fond affection that it is so impossible to withhold from her. I trust, dearest Julia and Harriet, that you are not separated from her forever. I am mistaken if she does not look with affection and regret towards Europe, and the dear beings she has left there.'[12]

But, within a year both Camilla and her child were dead. After her seven-month-old son's death, the broken-hearted Camilla decided to return to Europe with Frances. Despite Fanny's pleas on her behalf, she was ostracized by her friends back home. For all their radical talk, the Garnett sisters were unwilling to run the risk of being tainted by the scandal of Camilla's liaison with Whitby. They could only suggest that she should go to live with her uncle in Scotland and keep house for him: it would simply 'not do' for her to visit Julia in Hanover or the Garnetts in Paris. Camilla soon fell ill and died at Bordeaux 'in lodgings quite alone', abandoned by her sister, or so Fanny Trollope was told. 'Dear Camilla! she deserved a different fate,' she wrote on her return to Harrow. As for Frances Wright, Harriet remarked, 'old friendships I think she has forgotten, – old scenes have vanished from her mind'.[13] She married a Frenchman, much older than herself, had a child, and continued to travel and lecture. Ironically, Frances Wright's last resting-place was to be in Cincinnati, Ohio. Her headstone reads: 'I have wedded the cause of human improvement, staked on it my fortune, my reputation, and my life.'

Just after her return to England, Fanny had written to Julia that 'my friends all declare themselves delighted at my return – but if I can give no more parties – I shall not long count many friends. This I should care nothing about, could I see my dear boys placed in situations where their talents and good conduct might enable them to gain their bread.'[14] By this time, Tom had been at Oxford for two years, but it had been by no means plain sailing. When it became clear that a place at New College was not going to materialize, his father had enrolled Tom at St Alban Hall for no other reason than that its principal, Dr Whately, was a Liberal. The halls were considered a notch down from the colleges, 'a refuge for the destitute', Tom recalled. Whately proved a very strict Liberal, and he insisted that students return on the appointed day from the holidays. When Tom returned a day late, through no desire of his own but at his father's insistence, Whately ordered the young man to pay a fine to the servants. Thomas Anthony contested the principal's ruling and, according to Tom, 'the case attracted a good deal of attention in the university at the time' – none of which did the young man's Oxford reputation any good.

In the end Tom was forced to leave St Alban Hall and eventually found a place at the academically inferior Magdalen Hall, now Hertford College. Whately had found no fault with Tom in this matter, and was happy to give the young man a good reference. He clearly stated to Tom that his leaving St Alban Hall 'was entirely unconnected with any complaint against yourself'. 'I had cherished hopes of your eventually doing credit to yourself & my Hall; & I have no reason to think that, but for circumstances over which you had no control, you might not have continued there with perfect satisfaction to all parties.'[15] Whately had come across that fatal defect in his father's character which Tom later described in his memoirs: 'simple assent to his utterances of an argumentative nature did not satisfy him, he *would* be argued with', and these arguments led to 'scenes of painful violence'. The young Anthony also came up against his father's violent temper, for 'in passion he knew not what he did, and he has knocked me down with the great folio Bible which he always used' (*An Autobiography*).

At this stage in her sons' lives, a university degree seems to have been just as important to Fanny as it was to her husband. When Tom mooted the idea of writing a travel book on Germany while still a student at Oxford, his mother advised him to stick to his studies: 'a good degree will aid you at first setting out, beyond anything else whatever'. Much to Fanny's sorrow, Henry had to give up his chance of a university education at Caius College, Cambridge, after a very short time, owing to *'deficiente crumenâ'* (deficient funds), according to Tom. His next chosen profession was the law, which his father had wanted him to go into from the very first. However, Thomas Anthony was still loath to give Henry, or any of his sons, sufficient spending money. The defiant Henry 'deeply resented what he thought to be injustice, and the result were scenes of the most painful kind between father and son; scenes,' remarked Fanny's daughter-in-law, 'where the mother was called in by Henry to mediate between them, and became herself so shaken and agitated as to be obliged sometimes to have recourse to a dose of laudanum to procure a night's rest'.[16]

Anthony, still living at home and walking to Harrow every day, would have been privy to many of these fights. 'I wonder whether any one will read these pages who has never known anything of the bitterness of a family quarrel,' he wrote in *The Last Chronicle of Barset.* Perhaps after one of these dreadful interviews with Henry, Anthony caught his father sitting down in his study, his arms crossed and his eyes fixed on the ceiling, wondering, 'Why was it that, for him, such a world of misery had been prepared? What wrong had he done, of what imprudence had he been guilty, that, at every turn of life, something should occur so grievous as to make him think himself the most wretched of men?' (*The Duke's Children*). Thus Anthony portrays the Duke of Omnium after an unpleasant meeting with the headstrong young Frank Tregear. 'A more loving father there was not in England,' Anthony says of the duke, 'but nature had made him so undemonstrative that as yet they had hardly known his love. In all their joys and in all their troubles, in all their desires and all their disappointments, they had ever gone to their mother. She had been conversant with everything about them, from the boys' bills and the girls' gloves to the innermost turn in the heart and the disposition of each.'

Yet, despite the harrowing scenes between Thomas Anthony and his sons, Fanny could write with some satisfaction – and relief – to her friend Julia in the winter of 1831 that her family were well cared for and had every promise for the future: 'Cecilia is at Offham,' Sussex, visiting her aunt Penelope Partington, Thomas Anthony's sister, 'where they seem to be very kind to her – Tom at Oxford – Henry with a Barrister in London. Anthony at Harrow (where he just got a prize*) and Emily as usual about 24 inches from my elbow'. One of the reasons behind Fanny's optimism was that, perhaps inspired by his wife's energy and application, Thomas Anthony had begun his own literary project, an ecclesiastical encyclopedia. 'It was his ambition,' Anthony recalls in his autobiography, 'to describe all ecclesiastical terms, including the denominations of every fraternity of monks and every convent of nuns, with all their orders and subdivisions.' Fanny had, like Josiah Crawley's wife Mary, dreaded that her husband 'should sit idle over the fire and do nothing'. 'During these long hours, in which he would sit speechless, doing nothing, he was telling himself from minute to minute that of all God's creatures he was the most heavily afflicted, and was revelling in the sense of the injustice done to him' (*The Last Chronicle of Barset*). 'I cannot express my delight at his having found an occupation,' Fanny wrote to her son Tom. 'He really seems quite another being; – and so am I too, in consequence.' She elsewhere describes herself and her husband as 'a very industrious pair of quill-drivers'.[17]

During this same period Thomas Anthony had even roused himself to apply for a London magistracy, a paid post, through the influence of his uncle Adolphus Meetkerke. Melbourne, Home Secretary in Lord Grey's Whig government, agreed to meet Meetkerke and requested that Thomas Anthony write to him concerning the matter. The minister's reply was evidently ambiguous. 'The answer did not appear to me to be favourable,' Fanny confided to Tom. 'Your father, however, says that he *has no doubt* that Lord M. intended to intimate

---

* This was probably one of the essay prizes awarded weekly. Although Anthony claimed in his autobiography that he never won any of the prizes 'showered about' at Harrow, his schoolmate Lord Bessborough recalled that the headmaster, Dr Longley, told him 'Trollope writes better English than you do' (P. M. Thornton, *Harrow School and its Surroundings*, London, 1885, p. 250).

that he should have the office.' Fanny was right: Melbourne did not offer the London magistracy to her husband. Thomas Anthony's spirits, however, were no doubt lifted a short time later when the publisher John Murray told him that one of his readers had 'much approved' of the first instalment of his encyclopedia. Even so, the author probably left Murray's famous establishment in Albemarle Street with mixed feelings, for Murray seems to have spent most of their meeting talking about the soon-to-be-published *Domestic Manners.** 'By the bye,' Murray asked Trollope, 'who the devil *is* Mrs Trollope? Her book is the cleverest thing I ever read.' 'The lady is my wife.' 'Why did she not bring it to me? It will sell like wildfire! She ought to have brought it to me.' He then added, 'You must introduce me to her.' A few days later, when Thomas Anthony brought Fanny to Murray's drawing-room, he spoke to the publisher of nothing else but his own work, or so Fanny thought, else 'I should have got more conversation with him. He seemed very well inclined that way,' she wryly commented to Tom.[18]

With her husband thus occupied and her sons applying themselves to their studies, Fanny could turn her attention to her daughter Cecilia. By the time *The Domestic Manners* appeared in print, Cecilia had reached the age of sixteen, and Fanny took the opportunity of introducing her daughter into London society at the same time as her book. For part of the London season Fanny took lodgings in Thayer Street, off Manchester Square. Young Emily was sent to spend the Easter holiday with their Devon cousin Fanny Bent. Cecilia accompanied her mother through 'the whirl of engagements' and morning visits demanded by 'the mass of cards' round her chimney glass. She also acted as amanuensis for her mother, who was already working on a follow-up to *The Domestic Manners*. 'I have not given all my good Yankee stories to the public,' Fanny wrote to a friend, 'but in a short time another book of mine will appear, which though the personages are imaginary, will contain sundry sketches from the Life – the title will be "The Refugee in America." '[19]

The novel's rather melodramatic plot involves a young aristocrat

* Murray would have seen a proof copy in his capacity as publisher of *The Quarterly Review*.

fleeing to America in the company of an Englishman and his daughter to escape a trumped-up murder charge. The thriving town of Rochester, New York, its coarse and uncouth society, and Perfect Bliss, the utopia turned nightmare, are thinly disguised portraits of Cincinnati and Nashoba. Between the evening receptions and morning calls of the London season, Fanny could 'scarcely find an hour in each day to give to it', but she was determined not to deprive Cecilia of good society.[20] 'Is it that I have forgotten my favourite?' she asks regarding her young English heroine at the end of *The Refugee*, now safely returned to her native country. 'Far from it. But after such a banishment, I have a peculiar pleasure in leaving her to taste the enjoyment of one full unfettered season of English grace and splendour.' Possibly some hostesses thought there was 'an air of whimsical wilfulness to this determination of having her daughter always with her' (*The Blue Belles*).

Not surprisingly, Henry was easily distracted from his law studies by the charms of London society, and he often escorted his mother and sister to evening receptions. 'At the Miss Berrys' I had the honour and glory and so forth, of being introduced to the famous Countess of Morley,' he irreverently boasted to Tom. Henry as well as Tom seems to have had literary ambitions, at least of an amateur kind. In October 1832, coinciding with the Trollopes' return to Julian Hill, Henry became – probably self-appointed – editor of the latest family pastime, *The Magpie: A Weekly Magazine of Literature, Politics, Science, and Art*. Henry was by all accounts a 'Draconian' editor, and all the Trollopes, as well as their neighbour Mrs Grant and one of the Drury clan, contributed to the folio-sized scrapbook. Such was its popularity that Cecilia writes 'with grave indignation' to her brother at Oxford that 'she should not be surprised if *all Harrow became "Magpies" before his return!*' Even Mr Trollope submitted several long-winded and tortuously constructed items signed 'Your *intending* admirer and constant reader, Scrutator'. Fanny signed her light-hearted articles 'Grub Street', warning the editor '*never* to employ weary and hackneyed writers, who, if, by any unlikely chance, they should get hold of an idea, are certain to use it for the manufacture of three volumes post octavo, instead of presenting it in three lines to the *Magpie*'.*[21]

---

* Sadly, the folios of *The Magpie* have disappeared.

Henry's career was still of great concern to his mother. She desperately wanted to believe that, after all they had been through, the American experience had at least done Henry some good. 'I have no doubt,' Fanny confides to Julia, 'that Henry's character will have received a benefit which will last for ever, from the struggles, the disappointments, and the vexations he met with.' Elsewhere she confesses: 'Henry was far from steady, and I flatter myself that he is much more likely to become so, after all he has suffered.' With the profits from *The Domestic Manners*, Fanny writes to Mary Russell Mitford, 'My dear Henry ... is to be immediately entered at the [Middle] Temple', 'so *vive la plume!*'[22]

But Henry's great passion was certainly not the law, nor even literature, but geology, which was in the first half of the nineteenth century perhaps the most exciting of all the sciences. Among its devotees were Goethe and Wordsworth. In revealing the great age of the Earth, geologists were taking the first steps towards a theory of evolution, and their discoveries placed geology at the forefront of the growing conflict between science and religion. Henry almost certainly acquired his interest while in America: perhaps at New Harmony, presided over by William Maclure, the 'father of American geology', or at the Western Museum in Cincinnati, where valuable exhibits, made redundant by the popular wax figures, gathered dust in the basement. The notebook which Henry kept in America lists the items in his 'natural history' collection, including a 'Mammoth bone', three Indian axes and one arrow. His mother's friend and mentor, Basil Hall, had put Henry forward as a member of the Geological Society in May 1832. Henry made the acquaintance of the botanist Dawson Turner through Marianne Skerrett, his mother's old friend, and it was probably the presence of Adam Sedgwick at Cambridge, the most eminent geologist of his day, which had led Henry to go up to Cambridge rather than follow family tradition to Oxford.

From this time forward it appears that Henry was never to be seen without his geological hammer. In July 1832, just a month after entering the Middle Temple, Henry went on a largely geological tour of the West Country, literally dragging poor old Fanny Bent up and down the tors. His letters home are full of ebullience and *joie de vivre*:

The mines at Upton Pyne gratified me excessively. I got some good specimens of the black oxide from thence & hammer'd the rocks about to my hearts content – do you remember Hawkeye's boast that the crack of his rifle had been heard over the whole northwest America from the Alleghenies to the Rocky Mountains? My boast will be the clink of my hammer on every rock from Ottery & Exeter to the Land's End & the Lizard – de gustibus non est disputandum*... Oh my most venerable & much venerated she parent – oh much respected he parent – shades of my ancestors & most loved & loving contemporaries, what sights have my eyes this day beheld!! ... Oh mother how I longed for you as I gazed on all that passed beneath my feet ... What in the name of whatever deity geology is dear to – what am I to do with my specimens?

What Henry did was to send them to London in a hamper to be picked up and paid for by his father at Russell's Wagon Office – otherwise 'warehousage will have to be paid'. His mother's fame had preceded him on Dartmoor. In order to tour the ruins of Buckfast Abbey Henry was told to apply to a Captain White, RN: 'I hesitated – I was very dirty – *n'emporte* – I rang & sent in my name.' 'Ye gallant captain came out himself & not only shewed me ye ruin but asked me to dine, took me to his room where I washed & shaved & put on a coat & waistcoat of his!! To your fame oh illustrious mother do I owe this honour & dinner not to mention ruins – tea – conversation & cake.'[23]

In his letters Henry asks his mother to relay messages to his brother Tom and also to Hervieu. Hervieu was still made to feel an honorary member of the Trollope family by Fanny. His loyalty had saved her and her children from absolute want in a strange land, and she genuinely valued his talents as a book illustrator; as she later wrote, 'his strong points are correct drawing of the human figure, and the power of catching expression of feature and action'. She also believed that the Frenchman exerted a steadying influence on Henry, for he 'feels a gratitude to his benefactor which seems to soften his

* 'there's no arguing about taste'.

temper (ever much too haughty) and will ensure him a friend through life'.[24] Thus Hervieu continued to be a frequent guest at the Trollopes' house. He had even lived, at least for a time, with the family at Harrow Weald; he insisted that Fanny have his room to write in at night, while he made do with a smaller chamber.

One wonders if Hervieu's presence was wormwood to Thomas Anthony, for he could not but have heard – and read – the speculation and rumours concerning the artist and his wife in America. Perhaps like Robert Kennedy in *Phineas Finn*, Thomas Anthony 'had no strong wish to see again in his house the man respecting whom he had ventured to caution his wife; but he was thoughtful; and thinking over it all, he found it better to ask him there. No one must know that there was any reason why Phineas should not come to his house; especially as all the world knew that,' in Kennedy's case, the young Irishman had saved him from garrotting, while, in Thomas Anthony's, the Frenchman had safeguarded his wife and children (*Phineas Finn*).

Fanny was now the sole breadwinner in the family. Thomas Anthony had long given up his law practice; no money was to be made from the Harrow farm; and the £10 subscriptions for the *Encyclopaedia Ecclesiastica* which trickled in from old friends would have paid for paper and ink, but little more. Again with the help of Basil Hall's negotiating skills,* Fanny succeeded in selling the first edition of *The Refugee in America* to Whittaker for £400. On the day of publication he was to give her a bill, or promissory note, at six months – not unlike a post-dated cheque. The success of her first book made her much more nervous about the reception of her second: 'in short,' she confided to Tom, 'I am bepraised so violently that – I am afraid my poor little novel will disappoint everybody'.[25]

Her friends' advice did nothing to alleviate Fanny's apprehensions: 'the word of my Maecenas [Captain Hall], one from Miss Gabell in the same warning tone, and Miss Milman's laughing words, "You must not expect to make a thousand pounds *every* year!" have set me

---

* Basil Hall also encouraged Fanny to 'peruse & pilfer' his journals and his wife's letters for material on America with which to stock her novel (Hall to FT [1833]: Trollope Papers, special collections, UCLA Library).

thinking a little upon the uncertain nature of literary success. And I have therefore made up my mind to do without it.' 'Should my little fame expire directly, and no further returns reward my labours,' she confides to Tom, 'I shall burn my pen, and *immediately* seek a situation where I may earn something.' She even puts forward the idea of becoming a sort of head governess in a family 'of distinction', 'superintending masters and directing a course of study'. But, before it came to this, Fanny was determined to exhaust the possibilities of earning a literary income. She had written to Mary Russell Mitford for advice: 'What does one do to get business with the mags and annuals? Does one say, as at playing écarté, "I propose," or must one wait to be asked? Remember, dear, that I have five children.' The dramatist and essayist's advice had been to write novels, 'by far the most profitable branch of the literary profession' – though not, as yet, the most respected.[26]

The first edition of *The Refugee in America*, comprising 1,250 copies, quickly sold out. Friends were lavish in their praise. The actor George Bartley, who had toured America with his wife in 1818 and provided Fanny with some amusing scenes for the novel, admitted 'it is very seldom that I can command time to attack three volumes'; but he read *The Refugee* with 'great pleasure' and thought it 'capital'.* *The Westminster Review* admired the innate talent with which Mrs Trollope 'exhibits the foibles and follies of some of the middle ranks of society which belong as much to this country as America'. But Fanny was distraught at criticism which came from an unexpected source, *The Quarterly Review*. The anonymous reviewer – not Basil Hall, as he himself quickly sought to reassure her – claimed that the book was 'absurd nonsense from beginning to end': 'nothing but the reputation of the authoress could induce us to throw away a line upon it'.[27] Nevertheless, she adhered to Basil Hall's philosophy concerning reviews and reviewers, and kept at her writing. She transformed one of the upstairs rooms at Julian Hill into another 'Sacred Den' – the

---

* According to Bartley, Fanny based one of her characters in *The Refugee* on a friend of his, one Colonel Smith. The American girl, Emily, with whom the young aristocrat falls in love, is drawn from Fanny's memory of Timothy Flint's daughter, Emeline, whom Fanny praises in *The Domestic Manners*, surrounded as she was 'by a society totally incapable of appreciating, or even of comprehending her'.

room resembled Lady Augusta's 'little boudoir', with 'three windows, each commanding a different and very lovely view', a 'little fireplace below one of the windows, which in the winter was closed by one large shutter'. 'A balcony, upon which the other two windows opened, ran round the whole turret.' 'This lone chamber was the birth-place and cradle, as well as the repository, of her thoughts' (*Tremordyn Cliff*).

Fanny, now established as a well-known author, may have undertaken her next composition for a bit of fun and relaxation as well as lucre. *The Mother's Manual; or Illustrations of Matrimonial Economy* (1833) is a satirical poem on the subject of matchmaking mothers and husband-hunting daughters. It was published anonymously, with only the author's initials at the end of the preface, in a slim volume with illustrations by Hervieu. Fanny had long been accustomed to writing such humorous verse for the enjoyment of friends and family; and as Fanny's own daughter, Cecilia, had officially entered the marriage market, there is a lot of good-humoured self-mockery in the piece. Even Hervieu's depiction of one of the zealous matrons is suspiciously like his portrait of Fanny Trollope, which was at that moment hanging in the Royal Academy. Reviewing this portrait, one art critic claimed that Hervieu had vinegar in his brush when painting the 'sarcastic Mrs Trollope'. The family took great delight in this remark, and Cecilia wrote to inform Tom at Oxford that 'Mamma now goes by the name, at home, of old Madam Vinegar!'[28]

Mary Russell Mitford had confessed to Fanny that, if she were to follow her own advice and embark on a novel, she would try 'to come as near as I can to Miss Austen, my idol'.*[29] *The Westminster Review* might have been describing Jane Austen when it wrote of Fanny's ability to exhibit 'the foibles and follies' of the respectable middle classes into which both women were born; but, in a later age 'whose taste can only be gratified with the highest seasoned food', according

---

* Mary Russell Mitford had worked out the plot for a novel, to be entitled *Atherton*, in as early as 1825, and began writing in 1836, but, 'such was her distaste for the work', it did not appear until 1854 (MRM to FT, 20 February 1836: Boston Public Library; Vera Watson, *Mary Russell Mitford*, London, 1949, p. 202).

to one contemporary periodical, Fanny had always to keep the circulating library in mind. To this end she made her next novel a gothic romance, that genre made so popular by Mrs Radcliffe's *Mysteries of Udolpho* (1794), which Fanny had read as a girl, perhaps while sitting with a view of the dramatic Avon Gorge near her home in Bristol. Jane Austen had satirized rather than imitated the Gothic novel in *Northanger Abbey*: 'I could not sit seriously down to write a serious romance under any other motive than to save my life,' she remarked. Fanny, however, had a decided taste for the romantic and she no doubt relished the chance to try her hand at the genre. Her comments regarding architecture might equally well apply to literature: 'I like the Gothic style *best*' (*Vienna and the Austrians*).

The Abbess includes all the elements of the genre, including a pregnant novice threatened with live burial and merciless nuns, whom Fanny refers to as 'the four holy gossips'. Although set in the sixteenth century, the problems of the Count d'Albano are remarkably like those of Thomas Anthony Trollope. The count, a weak, proud, obstinate and ultimately broken man, finds himself and his estate financially embarrassed, with his rents 'spent three months before they are due'. His outburst before his household priest, 'Where are your benevolences, and your fees, and your candles to come from?' might have been Thomas Anthony confessing to his sons, 'Where are your pocket-money, and your books, and your waistcoats to come from?' Nor was the count any better at dealing with his children than Thomas Anthony: 'Like all other embarrassed people who hit upon an expedient promising relief', the count had persuaded himself that 'all his difficulties would vanish' if only his daughter would pursue the career which he had chosen for her – in this case, that of a nun.

One misfortune follows another, most crucially the death of his young son, until the count's mind was no longer 'capable of containing above one idea at a time', usually the degree to which he had been wronged. Indeed, 'his character, naturally feeble and fretful, now became so querulous as seriously to affect his health'; 'sometimes he would burst into a fit of uncontrollable rage'. The women of the tale, the count's daughter and his sister (both closet Protestants), are resilient and resourceful. The sister, the abbess of the title, is so formidable that her brother's priest 'would at any time have preferred taking his chance in a personal encounter with the prince of darkness, to having any direct intercourse with the Abbess'. According to *The Spectator*, Fanny had indeed accomplished what she had set out to do with *The Abbess*: 'the taste of the circulating library is remarkably well hit; there is no doubt but that it will extremely well suit the wants of the ladies who have been long pining for a genuine bit of romance, such as they used to be supplied with in the days of their youth – those "deep" times when Mrs Radcliffe made them hide their heads under the bed-clothes, and converted every sound into a warning and every sight into a ghost'.[30]

Fanny's original plan had been, after *The Domestic Manners* had come out and *The Refugee* gone to press, to visit Julia Pertz in Hanover, where she might 'be a few months very quiet, and very happy – where my children could be taking lessons, and I could be writing at *very* little expense'. Fanny had in mind another book of travels. She felt comfortable with the genre, and it was one which ideally suited her skills of observation. However, in the summer of 1832 Germany was 'a country visited by the cholera, and threatened by war', Fanny remarked to Julia. Not only in England, but across Europe, there was demand for political reform. Fanny's old friend, General Lafayette, with other like-minded radicals, had masterminded the revolt of July 1830 which overthrew the Bourbon Charles X and put a 'bourgeois' constitutional monarch, Louis Philippe, on the French throne. The revolt was an inspiration to German liberals, including Heinrich Heine and the other poets of the 'Young Germany' movement, who joined forces with the press to stoke the spirit of revolution which was taking hold on the Continent. The rulers of Saxony, Brunswick and Hesse-Cassel were all forced to abdicate, and in Hanover political agitation eventually secured a constitution in 1833. However, it was the cholera, not revolution, that struck real fear in men's hearts. There were reports of outbreaks in London and Edinburgh; the Trollopes' intrepid friend Captain Kater fled with his family to France to escape the rumoured epidemic. Fanny doubted whether they were any safer on the other side of the Channel: 'The Katers still stay trembling at Boulogne – Oh what a mock philosopher!'[31]

The following spring of 1833 Fanny returned to her idea for a travel book: 'The crossing the channel and leaving my dear cottage (so lately recovered) will not be exactly what I should best like – but *poverty* is the greatest despot existing,' she had confessed to Julia that February. There were inevitable delays. An influenza epidemic swept through Harrow, and the whole Trollope family succumbed to it, as well as to the apothecary's remedies. Leeches were applied, fourteen to Henry; Anthony bled until he fainted; Cecilia became hysterical from weakness; and Hervieu, after imbibing 'sundry powerful draughts', was found wandering in the fields, delirious.[32] At long last, on the first of June, exactly a week after the publication of *The Abbess*, which Whittaker had brought out on the same terms as *The Refugee*, Fanny, her son Henry and the loyal Hervieu started for Ostend. The itinerary was to include a trip down the Rhine, a visit to Julia and her family in Hanover, where Thomas Anthony was to join them, and then the scenic route back to England.

The next four months were full of incident, the first occurring before they had even left Ostend. There they were the guests of the English consul Mr Fauche and his wife Mary, a girlhood friend of Fanny whose father, Mr Tomkisson, had been a well-known pianoforte manufacturer. Mrs Fauche had organized some amateur theatricals, no doubt knowing Fanny's fondness for them. The play chosen was Goldsmith's *She Stoops to Conquer*: Henry, rather appropriately, played Tony Lumpkin and Hervieu, Diggory. While fighting a duel in the English burlesque which followed, *Bombastes Furioso*, Henry – who must have played Bombastes with his usual high spirits – managed to receive a deep wound in his thigh. He could not walk for ten days, and he received a stream of visitors, including 'his young adversary, whose constant attention showed a very amiable degree of regret for the unlucky accident' (*Belgium and Western Germany*). Henry left Ostend on crutches.

Fanny, Hervieu and her son, once fully recovered, made truly intrepid travellers. Henry, no doubt, acted like young Charles Worthington in *One Fault* on a Continental tour with his sister and her true love: 'Never, certainly, was there a happier trio; for if Charles entered with less enthusiasm than his companions into the study of art, he atoned for it by the zeal with which he acted as their truffle dog in seeking out whatever was best worth seeing in nature.' In this same passage, Fanny describes her mode of sightseeing: 'The hours devoted to painting and to sculpture were passed much in the same routine that others followed, who were engaged in the same pursuit; but their rides and walks were arranged on a plan entirely their own. Instead of contenting themselves with the *"points de vue superbes"* immortalized in the guidebooks, their custom was to turn aside as soon as these had been enjoyed, to ransack the hills and dales, the ins and outs of all the various mountain regions through which they passed.' Thus Fanny sat astride donkeys stumbling along narrow mountain passes (once, in a dreadful gale, she was even 'tied, and pinned' to the animal); she scrambled up and down mountainsides, braving thorns and brambles; she spent the night in a mountain hut amidst a terrible storm; and she explored ruins by crawling on all-fours through a breach in the wall or down a narrow passage. Dealing with the locals could be just as hazardous as the mountainous terrain. At Welmich 'a villainous innkeeper' attacked their party with a knife, claiming that he had not been paid enough.

Fanny and her party also ventured into 'civilization' from time to time, and it is here that her gift of looking at even the most familiar scenes with a fresh eye fully reveals itself. Comparing the baths at Baden and Wiesbaden, she concludes that Baden was the more fashionable, Wiesbaden the more medicinal, for at Baden the patients showed no want of health, whereas at Wiesbaden from seven-thirty to nine o'clock in the morning the promenade 'is filled with the most uncomfortable-looking set of ladies and gentlemen that I remember to have seen', all imbibing the 'nauseous and steaming potion' on offer. At Baden Fanny was horrified but at the same time fascinated by the lure of the gaming tables, and she evokes the almost ghoulish atmosphere: 'What can equal in dullness the whining, languid rep-etition of the croupier's cry, "Faites votre jeu, messieurs. Le jeu est fait . . . le jeu est fait . . . Trois . . . Quatre . . . Le rouge perd, le couleur gagne." And yet again the weary sound begins – "Faites votre jeu, messieurs . . ." '

On a visit to Waterloo Fanny does not give a potted history of the battle, nor does she comment on the pathos of the scene; rather, she describes the local men and women who surround her carriage, offering their services as guides and peddling war memorabilia: imperial eagles, bullets and brass buttons.* Fanny meant her book to be a practical guide, and so she travelled as other middle-class English people might travel. However, on one occasion Fanny took advantage of her new-found fame and waited upon Elizabeth, Land-gravine of Hesse-Homburg, George III's daughter, at her residence outside Frankfurt. She describes the princess's mainly English library, with books everywhere; in one room even the 'space below the hangings is lined with a wainscoting of books'. Fanny added to the princess's overflowing collection by presenting her with a copy of *The Mother's Manual*.†

As Fanny admits in *Belgium and Western Germany*, 'I sometimes withdrew my eyes from the landscape to look at my neighbours', that is the English abroad, and here she is perhaps at her best. On a boat trip up the Rhine, Fanny left off 'from the labour of twisting my neck this way and that' to spot the castles which dotted the shore, 'and ventured to give some portion of my attention to the scene on board', where there was 'a good deal of *genteel* comedy' among the English tourists. A young man read passionately from a 'pocket Byron' while his bride hid her frequent yawns in an embroidered handkerchief. Two young girls fought a race against time and each other to finish sketching 'the first turret of their castle, before it was half a mile behind them'. Fanny observed 'bustling young men' 'twisting about, guide-book in hand, and occasionally enjoying the landscape through an eye-glass'. One of them addressed a boatman with great linguistic skill: 'Woolen sie put cela avec the baggage?' Fanny even indulges in a little self-parody after she turns her eyes back to the shore. The most interesting castles, of course, 'came thicker and faster upon us as the hour of dinner approached: and, when we were actually seated

---

* When, in 1867, Tom Trollope visited Waterloo, the guide told him that 'he had accompanied a Madame Trollope more than thirty years ago, who was *une femme bien embêtante* [a very annoying woman], who asked him questions he could not answer, and was taking notes all the time'; the Americans on the tour, he added, did not like her (T. A. Trollope, *What I Remember*, II, p. 77).

† The copy presented by Fanny to Elizabeth, Landgravine of Hesse-Homburg, is now at Princeton University Library. Fanny later sent the royal princess a copy of *Belgium and Western Germany*.

at table, notice was given, by such as caught a passing glance through the windows, of such wondrous congregations of fortified towns, mouldering monasteries, and castled crags, that half the company started upon their feet, and the other half nearly choked themselves in the hope of getting their dinner dispatched before all the ruins were out of sight.'

But Fanny also had a more serious agenda than mere sightseeing. To 'discover the real state of political feeling in the countries through which we travelled,' Fanny wrote in *Belgium and Western Germany*, 'I threw myself in the way of what are called *liberal politics*'. Yet, she remarks, 'I never, except in one solitary instance, heard any sentiment or opinions expressed, in the slightest degree approaching to the mad licentiousness of doctrine, which is weekly and daily poured forth by the presses of England.'* One Frankfurt resident told her that the so-called revolution which the English papers went on about had terminated precisely three and a half hours after it had begun. Moreover, among the Germans, where 'the delicate and inoffensive lines of demarcation are sufficiently visible', there exists a 'graceful, easy benevolent sort of intercourse between all ranks' which England, 'divided against herself, as she now is', had lost. 'Woe betide those who would remove the sacred landmarks [i.e. traditions], that have served us so long and so well! Should they succeed, our best and wisest will forsake us,' 'while drooping commerce, expiring art, outraged religion, and polluted learning, shall each raise a dying voice, to thank the parricide patriots as they deserve'. Clearly, Fanny's experiences and observations of American society still coloured her political outlook. As she had earlier confessed to Julia Pertz, 'the effects of democracy as displayed throughout the [American] union sickened me of popular governments'.[33]

Early on Fanny nearly abandoned the tour when Cecilia wrote that Thomas Anthony had suffered, within a week of his wife's

---

* As always, Fanny solicited her children's help with research. She wrote to Julia and Georg Pertz that these mad doctrines appeared 'only in the innumerable penny and halfpenny publications which are addressed to the lower orders'. 'My sons, however, have found out many of the obscure nooks where these poisons are vended, and have brought us home both blasphemy and treason in terrible abundance' (17 November 1833: Garnett–Pertz Papers).

departure, an 'apoplectic' seizure of some sort. However, successive letters reassured Fanny of his recovery, and husband and wife met up in Hanover at the house of Dr Pertz and Julia as planned. The 'fatal winds of the first of September' had followed Thomas Anthony to Germany, and from this point onwards the trip, and consequently Fanny's narration, becomes less enjoyable – no doubt the result of Thomas Anthony's moody presence as much as the continued bad weather.

The journey back to England was not uneventful, mainly owing to the mysteries of border controls. Travelling by diligence to Minden, the party had, unbeknown to them, 'quitted the territory of King William, and entered that of Duke somebody, I know not who', wrote Fanny to Julia. 'Our trunks were abandoned to the will and pleasure of sundry officials.' The worst of it was, the 'tobacco-phobic' Fanny remarked to Julia, they had to wait for three hours in a horrid smoke-filled room. On the last leg of their journey home, Hervieu fell victim to a political dispute between the Dutch and the Belgians. At the Dutch town of Anaheim the travellers were made to surrender their passports overnight. Hervieu was told that, as his passport was Belgian, he 'should forthwith quit the Dutch territory'. To make a long story short, after persistent inquiries Henry discovered that his friend Hervieu would have to take a very roundabout route back to England in order to avoid the Dutch border controls. 'Poor Hervieu, who not only had no change of linen with him but very little money', had to rely on the kindness of an Englishman likewise inconvenienced in order to get back safely to England.

On her return to Julian Hill at the end of September, Fanny's time was commandeered by her family: 'my children have *liberally* held my hands – and would let me do nothing but talk'.[34] But she soon applied herself to the task of assembling her travel notes into book form and finding a new publisher, for she was fully aware that the money earned from her previous books was 'oozing fast'. Fanny's relations with Whittaker had not been good for some time, and she was greatly distressed to discover that he had printed a second edition of *The Refugee* without her knowledge. She was loath for Whittaker to publish her most recent travel book and, remembering Murray's enthusiasm for *The Domestic Manners*, she approached the 'autocrat of Albemarle Street', as she calls him. He offered half profits on the book, which did not suit Fanny, for she needed 'payment in ready money on account of Tom's taking his degree next month at Oxford – at which time all arrears are paid' to the college. In desperation, she went back to Whittaker who offered her £200 for 1,000 copies and £50 for every 500 printed thereafter. This was basically half what she had received for her previous two books, and so she retraced her steps to Albemarle Street. After all, she wrote to Mrs Bartley, 'John the Great is – John the Great.'[35]

But Tom's college bills were nothing compared to the financial crisis which was looming at Julian Hill. Over the Christmas period, while Fanny was working hard on her German volumes, the bailiff Quilton came to the house asking to see Mr Trollope. He found him in bed with one of his migraines, and saw Mrs Trollope instead. He asked her to tell her husband that his credit was no longer any good and he must settle his rent arrears without further delay. Quilton confided to Northwick a few days later concerning Trollope's affairs, 'he don't appear to me to have but very little Dead or alive', in the way of stock, 'and how he is to pay the second Bill & the Rent of the last half year I cannot imagine'. All this apparently came as a great shock to Fanny. As she later wrote to Julia, if only 'Mr Trollope had been more open with us all – We had no idea that', by this time, 'a year's rent of the *pernicious* farm which for twenty years has been so losing a concern for him, was due to Lord Northwick – *I* could have paid this at almost any other period since my first publications – but now it was impossible – my last summer's tour was very costly and my five children's private expenses as well as my own have swallowed the rest of what remained from furnishing Julian Hill.'[36]

Thomas Anthony had kept the true state of his financial affairs from his wife and family. 'Like all other discreet men of business,' Fanny wryly notes of Mr Holmwood in *Fashionable Life*, 'he was not, nor ever had been, in the habit of talking to the ladies of his family concerning his financial affairs, either private or commercial.' Thomas Anthony had merely sat alone in his study and penned a bitter letter to Northwick six weeks before Christmas, laying out 'the deplorable state to which my unfortunate engagement with your Lordship has reduced me – this now, my Lord, 20 years since that engagement was first entered into'. 'I have given up almost all society,' he laments, '& the education of my children has been neglected.'[37] Fanny, no doubt naïvely, believed that her husband would have discussed such important matters with his family; but she learned all too quickly 'the difference which exists in a household where the parents make a secret of all things of important interest, and where they do not'. 'Without this easy, natural, spontaneous confidence, the family union is like a rope of sand, that will fall to pieces and disappear at the first touch of anything that can attract and draw off its loose and unbounded particles' (*The Vicar of Wrexhill*).

It became clear to all concerned that the Trollopes could not remain at Julian Hill, but it was Fanny, not Thomas Anthony, who prepared for their departure. 'They have been sorely tried,' Fanny remarks of Edward and Lucy Bligh in *Jonathan Jefferson Whitlaw*, 'and, as I believe often happens, the woman has shown more passive courage than the man.' Early in the new year she called a family conference to discuss their future. If Thomas Anthony was to avoid arrest for debt, they would have to leave the country. Fanny had always considered as an option settling on the Continent, at least for a year or two, and even looked forward to it. The cost of living was markedly lower across the Channel, and many European cities had sizeable British expatriate communities. Bruges, which she and Henry had so lately visited, was decided upon as their next home. No doubt, 'the decision brought relief, as decision always does' (*Charles Chesterfield*). However, she did not have much time before the bailiffs swooped on Julian Hill. She sent Tom to collect Cecilia who had been visiting her aunt Die Trollope and some old family friends, the Dymokes, of Scrivelsby in Lincolnshire. Her immediate concern was to smuggle Thomas Anthony out of the country to escape debtors' prison. Fanny was perhaps counting on the element of surprise, for her husband had been confined to bed with migraine and the bailiffs no doubt thought he was too ill to travel. Anthony was summoned early on the morning of 18 April, just a few days before his nineteenth birthday, to drive his father to London. It was not until they had started that Thomas Anthony told his son to take him to the docks as he was bound for Ostend. The plan was to seek temporary refuge with the English consul there until Mrs Fauche could find a suitable dwelling for the Trollope family in Bruges, but 'it was not within his nature to be communicative,' Anthony observed of his father, 'and to the last he never told me why he was going to Ostend' (*An Autobiography*).

Anthony returned to an almost comic scene at Julian Hill. Thomas Anthony had told a somewhat surprised Quilton that he was going to Cheltenham for his health, but the bailiff was suspicious, especially at 'finding the Tubs, Barrells and many other things moving by divers persons with impunity'. Quilton eventually learned the truth from Colonel Grant and immediately issued a warrant of seizure. Fanny knew this to be her cue – perhaps a lesson learned through bitter experience in Cincinnati only four years before – to begin packing a 'certain number of pretty-pretties which were dear to her heart'. One such precious memento was the geometry book which her father had bequeathed to his grandson, Arthur.* Under the noses of Quilton's men, who had by this time arrived at the house, Cecilia and Emily passed the treasures through a gap in the hedge to the safety of their loyal neighbours, the Grants. The Grant girls and Anthony were also commandeered for the operation (*An Autobiography*). 'Oh ladies, who have drawing-rooms in which the things are pretty, good, and dear to you, think of what it would be to have two bailiffs rummaging among them with pen and ink-horn, making a catalogue preparatory to a sheriff's auction,' wrote Anthony in *Framley Parsonage*.

Fanny too drew upon this scene from her life when describing the Dowlings' fall from grace in *Michael Armstrong*. In the parlour, the bailiff's men stand about, some sticking slips of paper inscribed 'Lot No. —' on various articles collected there for the purpose. 'Others, with black canvas aprons and paper caps, were coming and going with no very apparent purpose; while another set, with cold meat and beer-flagons before them, sat round a small table in a corner, laughing at some good joke.' Fanny then describes Dowling's wife

---

* This volume (now privately owned) is inscribed by Fanny: 'Left to Arthur William Milton, by his grandfather the Revd William Milton. Arthur survived his grandfather only 10 days, dying July 22d 1824.' The book eventually went to Anthony and has his bookplate.

wrapping her 'most precious articles' in cotton wool and cramming them in a large basket which she covers with 'articles of female attire', all 'very cleverly calculated to make the whole pass under the general description of wearing-apparel, which the courtesy of the law permits to be removed by all persons in the unfortunate situation of her ladyship'. A few trinkets, either smaller or more precious than the rest, she thrusts into her pocket or up her sleeve. Mr Dowling even flees his creditors in just the same way as Thomas Anthony, for he too had been bedridden and considered too ill to move by the bailiff.

Fanny and her children finally surrendered the house to Northwick's men and took shelter under the Grants' roof. She had already managed to save most of the furniture through the clever ploy of 'selling' it to Colonel Grant. However, Quilton was not a fool and reckoned that Mrs Trollope and 'Coln. Grant had Robbed your lordship sufficiently by so clandestinely taking away to his House that portion of furniture that should have come to the Hammer.' The bailiff showed no mercy; Fanny had to scrape together £12 to buy back the remaining household items. Nonetheless, Northwick seems to have developed a grudging admiration for her resourcefulness, for he asked that his agents reimburse Fanny at least in part.*

As was inevitable, before the day was over the Trollopes' misfortunes had been published all over Harrow by 'the butcher, or the baker, or some other of those indispensable functionaries who know all things concerning those who live, move, and have their being, by means of their ministering ambulations, and who fail not to make all they know to circulate as freely as they do themselves' (*The Vicar of Wrexhill*). Fanny had always loved her 'pretty cottage': her two daughters had been born in the house, and she counted her neighbours among her closest friends. Now, Mrs Trollope prepared to leave for ever the place which she had called home for nearly twenty years. But on the eve of their departure she heard something that was more

---

* Fanny Trollope apparently had a secret admirer in Lord Northwick: at least three copies of her novels, *Michael Armstrong, Charles Chesterfield,* and *The Widow Married,* survive with Baron Northwick's bookplate (in the possession of Richard Mullen, Bernard Quaritch Ltd and Princeton University Library respectively.)

disturbing to her even than recent events. Anthony and the girls would have to go on ahead without her; she could not leave England for a few weeks yet.

CHAPTER NINE

Travels and Travellers

In the autumn of 1833, following his summer travels on the Continent, Henry had endeavoured to contribute to the family coffers by taking on a pupil for a few weeks in Fulham. Henry Milton, who resided in Fulham, may have recommended his nephew to a neighbour. In any case, Henry took a small lodging near his uncle and Cecilia stayed at the Miltons' house to look after her brother. Later in his novels Anthony was not very complimentary about Fulham: he thought it a rather dull place, full of 'cocknified, pretentious, and unalluring' villas with names to match (*Ralph the Heir*). On Henry's return to Harrow it was clear to all that he was not well. It was to be a 'cold and biting spring', and the Trollopes suffered much. 'I have never had so much sickness in my family as this year,' Fanny wrote to Julia in March 1834. 'For about ten days we were very seriously alarmed for Anthony – and since that, more seriously still for my poor Henry who has been and yet is, very ill. He is grown pale and thin beyond what you can imagine and has a cough that tears him to pieces. But our medical man assures me that *as yet* he perceives no danger, and that if he will not leave the house till the east winds are over, and warm weather settled in, he thinks he will recover the attack upon his lungs.'[1] The danger which Fanny could not bring herself to name was consumption, or tuberculosis, 'the white plague' of the nineteenth century which took thousands of lives every year in Britain and, like its medieval counterpart, did not discriminate between rich and poor. Fanny's reticence is understandable, for when she heard the doctor express concern about Henry's lungs, she could not help but think of his younger brother Arthur, whom the disease had killed ten years before.

It was only after Fanny had packed her family's trunks and sent them on board the boat bound for the Continent that Henry's prognosis changed. The Harrow doctor was no longer optimistic: he warned Fanny that the damp Belgium air could be fatal to Henry. This must have been a heavy blow, but Fanny had no leisure to dwell on events. Once Anthony had, with Hervieu's help, retrieved his mother's and Henry's cases from on board ship, she sent him ahead with his sister Cecilia to Ostend to join their father at the Fauches' residence. Meanwhile, Fanny travelled with Henry at great expense by coach to Dawlish, on the Devon coast south of Exeter, where her cousin had a modest seaside residence. Fanny Bent had always been ready to help her namesake in a crisis, and this proved no exception. Fanny left Henry in Miss Bent's capable hands, and returned once more to her sanctuary at the Grants. For several weeks Fanny left Tom in total ignorance of events at Harrow so as not to worry him during his Oxford finals. The Trollopes' friends, neighbours and relations showed themselves extremely loyal and supportive: the Grants, 'Pendulum' Kater, Basil Hall, the Gabells, Lady Dyer, the Freelings and the Misses Skerrett. No doubt 'but for the grace of God' was a phrase which crossed their minds. The Revd Henry Trollope and his wife Die lent Fanny £100. Both Lady Milman and, no doubt to Fanny's dismay, the evangelical Revd Cunningham offered Emily and Cecilia a home at Harrow.

On 17 May 1834, a month after the bailiffs had invaded Julian Hill, Fanny boarded the packet for Calais accompanied by Emily and with a heavy heart, for she later wrote Tom concerning their affairs at Harrow: 'Nothing, surely, of equal importance was ever left in such a manner (unless it were the bazaar at Cincinnati).' She had not even had time to sign the agreement with John Murray for the publication of *Belgium and Western Germany*. She left that, and the correction of the proofs, in the hands of her brother, Henry Milton. After her anxious journey to Devon she could only look forward with dread to the certain 'harass and fatigue of preparing a new home with such

little means of making it comfortable'.[2] 'Nothing,' Fanny observes in
Fashionable Life,

> is so utterly subduing to the spirit as the state in which an
> unknown, though certain suffering is before us –
>
> When forward, though we cannot see,
> We guess, and fear!

Fanny and Emily would have boarded ship at Tower Bridge, as
this was cheaper than the Dover route. Even in the midst of such
unhappiness, Fanny could not help but draw some amusement from
remarks she overheard as they disembarked at Calais for the night.
' "What a dreadful smell!" said the uninitiated stranger enveloping
his nose in his pocket-handkerchief. "It is the smell of the continent,
sir," replied the man of experience. And so it was,' Fanny recalled a
year later (*Paris and the Parisians*).

   With Mrs Fauche's help the Trollopes rented a house in Bruges,
the Château d'Hondt, just outside the southern gate, Smeerden Port,
in the hamlet of St Baess. It was one of the large, roomy, 'uncompro-
misingly ugly' suburban villas being built in the French 'château'
style at the time. 'There is an idle vacuity in the first hours passed
in a new residence under such circumstances, by no means favourable
to the subduing of melancholy thoughts,' Fanny later reflected in
One Fault. Yet, 'as the days and the weeks roll over us', she wrote in
a poignant letter to Colonel Grant,

> we begin to get filled into the places that fate and fortune have
> been pleased to choose for us, and so blessedly flexible is the –
> fancy, spirit, imagination – or whatever I should call that part
> of us which best endures change, that we each of us have already
> learned to fix ourselves in some selected corner of our different
> rooms, and believe ourselves at home. The old desks have found
> new tables to rest upon, and the few favorite volumes that could
> not leave us are made to fill their narrow limits in orderly rows
> that seem to say – 'here we are to dwell together' – All this is
> very well – I am quite satisfied with our house and have almost

learned to think the square garden, with its labyrinth walks through overgrown shrubs, a very pretty *bocage* – It has in truth some features that I should love any where – it is full of roses and nightingales, and the beautiful acacia trees bloom as freely as in America – All this prettiness I look down upon from the little room I have chosen to replace the one you have not yet forgotten with its balcony for the summer, and snug chimney corner for a winter *cause* – and if I cannot like it as well, it is not because I see windmills in the distance, instead of Westminster Abbey, but because the roof of your dwelling is not in sight. *Indeed, indeed* it is here that the change pinches most – The charming sound of some of your dear voices on the lawn, to refresh my spirits when weary of writing was more precious than all the undulations of the landscape between Harrow and London.

'But,' Fanny continues, 'you must not think for all this that I pass the hours in sadness and repining – or that I have leisure, like Jaques, to be "melancholy and gentlemanlike" – on the contrary I am almost as active and busy as when my Helps ran away from me in America, and have not yet found one moment's time to think of Mr Whittaker,* and the thousand pages I have promised him in January – The house is very large, and in order to *make believe* that it is furnished ingenuity is obliged to do the work of money and I am plotting and planning from morning to night how to make one table and two chairs do the work of a dozen.'[3]

As ever, Fanny was able to work miracles, and the Château d'Hondt became a gathering place for Belgians and Englishmen alike – 'the unvariable result of my mother's presence,' Tom later remarked, 'which drew what was pleasant around her as surely as a magnet draws iron'.[4] Fanny had been taken with Bruges, a beautifully preserved medieval walled town which sits like a gem on the surrounding northern plain. It was a peaceful place, with its narrow streets, picturesque canals, and the market hall's ancient carillon ringing out

---

* Fanny had recently begun her third novel, *Tremordyn Cliff,* which was eventually published, however, not by Whittaker but by Richard Bentley.

'sweet old tunes over the great square basking sleepily in the sunshine', as Tom remembers it. Fanny had also liked what she saw of Bruges society when she visited a year earlier. She had noted in *Belgium and Western Germany* that 'evening parties are frequent, and very agreeable, though not splendid or ostentatious in any way'. She, Henry and Hervieu had passed a pleasant evening at the house of a M. Moke, singing, playing witty word games in French and laughing 'till we were weary'.* The name 'Mrs Trollope' would have been well-known on the Continent, for *The Domestic Manners of the Americans* had been translated into French, German and Dutch. Soon after her arrival at the Château d'Hondt a rumour went about that an American captain had met Mrs Trollope on the public promenade at Ostend and insulted her. The truth, as always, was much less exciting: a Belgian with poor English had simply misunderstood the captain's request that the famous Mrs Trollope be pointed out to him.

Fanny's fame grew when *Belgium and Western Germany* was published in 1834, not only in London by John Murray† but also in Brussels by Adolphe Wahlen, printer to the Belgian court. Mary Fauche informed Fanny that the Belgian king Leopold had read it 'with great pleasure'. Fanny wryly remarked to Tom that Leopold was simply relieved that she had not launched too 'violent and vituperative' an attack on him and the recent 'popular' revolution against Holland, further fallout from the July revolt of 1830 which had put him on the throne. Whether Wahlen would have published it if the king had not been pleased is an interesting question. Authors such as Mrs Trollope meant big business for English bookshops on the Continent, catering to the many ruined British families who went abroad every year as well as those who were simply doing the Grand Tour. Publishers such as Baudry and Galignani in Paris as well as Wahlen in Brussels also printed books in translation. 'No work

---

* Mrs Garnett, who visited the Trollopes in Bruges in 1835, called it 'the dullest place I ever saw' (MG to JGP, 18 July 1835: Garnett–Pertz Papers).

† Fanny regretfully noted in *Belgium and Western Germany* that 'the sketches by Mr Hervieu, so frequently alluded to in the following pages, were intended to accompany this publication, but the expense of engraving them in the style they deserved was found so great, that the idea was abandoned'.

which was popular in England ever escaped being reprinted on the Continent,' Fanny observed in *Paris and the Parisians*. 'Though this is done solely as a sort of piratical speculation, for the purpose of inducing all the travelling English to purchase new books for four francs here, instead of giving thirty shillings for them at home.' As with the American publication of British works, the author received no remuneration for these Continental editions.

Tom found the English expatriate community in Belgium 'a queer and not very edifying society', especially as the married couples 'seemed to be continually dancing the figure of *chassée-croisez*' (that is, changing partners). There was Mrs Mackintosh, whose daughter insisted on bathing in the sea two or three times a day and who, it was believed, died as a consequence of her folly; Captain Smithett, a 'remarkably handsome man, and the very *beau-idéal* of a sailor', who was 'an immense favourite with all the little Ostend world – with the female part of it, especially' as was his channel ferry, the *Arrow*, which regularly crossed to Dover (where he kept his wife); Colonel Dickson, who was very particular about his dinners, and on one occasion came rushing in to his guests 'with his coat sleeves drawn up to his elbows, horror and despair in his mien, as he cried, "Great heaven! the cook has cut the fins off the turbot!" ' There were even old friends: the name Drury had become notorious amongst Harrow tradesmen, for the Revd Mark Drury, who had been too corpulent to climb Harrow Hill, and his son the Revd William Drury had also had to flee their Harrow creditors. In Anthony Trollope's novel, *Mr Scarborough's Family*, the snobbish wife of the British minister in Brussels complains about English people 'who had come to live there as a place at which education for their children would be cheaper than at home'. She did not see why she 'should be expected to entertain all the second-class world of London'.

The native Belgians who fraternized with the English community were, if anything, an even stranger lot. A 'silly little banker's wife' adapted and passed on verses sent her by a youthful admirer to 'quite other swains', including Captain Smithett. Count Melfort was a '*ci-devant* Don Quixote sort of a looking man, with a young and buxom wife who boasted some strain of I forget what noble English blood'. 'As is the case with many Belgians,' Anthony remarks of

Monsieur Grascour in *Mr Scarborough's Family*, 'he would have been taken as an Englishman were his own country not known. He had dressed himself in English mirrors, living mostly with the English. He spoke English so well that he would only be known as a foreigner by the correctness of his language.'

In Fanny's later novel, *The Robertses on their Travels*, Mrs Roberts reckons that her family can pass as 'fashionable people' on the Continent for £700 a year as she has heard that 'one pound on the continent will go as far as five in England'. But when they arrived at the Château d'Hondt, the Trollopes only guaranteed income was considerably less. It was only in early 1834, after her interview with Quilton, that Fanny had realized for the first time the extent of her husband's debts. She immediately set about trying to salvage what she could. With the help of her brother, Henry Milton, she pored over the Harrow farm accounts as well as those for the other properties in which her husband had invested. 'From this moment the confidence between the brother and sister was perfect,' Fanny wrote in *Tremordyn Cliff*, the novel which she had begun shortly before leaving Julian Hill. 'Every circumstance known to Miss Murray was canvassed between them, with a common stock of interest in the affair, and of judgement as to the manner in which it should be conducted.' At the very least, Fanny believed she had her marriage settlement to fall back on: 'that portion of the matrimonial arrangements which is seldom or never brought as a matter of consultation before the intended bride' (*One Fault*). Strictly speaking, a wife could not hold property independently of her husband. However, a good lawyer could find ways around this, the most important of which was a marriage settlement carefully drafted so as to protect the money which a woman brought to her marriage. Thomas Anthony had meant to be generous. 'In consideration of the fortune' which Fanny originally brought to the marriage (£1,200 in stock), Thomas Anthony had settled £6,000, which at the time was tied up in London property, on his wife and any children they might have.

But, as Fanny and her brother went over the various documents, a nightmare began to unfold before their eyes. First came the realization that two of Fanny's trustees, her stepmother's relation, Thomas Partington, and a William Taunton of Lincoln's Inn, had not signed the settlement. In any case, it had never been registered in the Court of Chancery. What is more, Thomas Anthony had for some time been borrowing money against the security of property which formed part of the marriage settlement, property which, had the document been valid, would legally no longer have been his. The matter was further complicated by the fact that some of the title-deeds were now in the hands of Thomas Anthony's creditors, including 'a person who showed a considerable disposition to detain them'.

Henry Milton, with the help of his solicitor, 'a great deal of trouble and some diplomacy',[5] recovered what title-deeds he could and managed to buy Fanny an annuity of £250. The only fee Henry's attorney would accept was a copy of *The Domestic Manners of the Americans*. Thomas Anthony did his best to cooperate in these matters and, no doubt with a heavy heart, agreed to surrender management of their finances to his wife. More importantly, from this time forward any money which Fanny made by her writing was to be held in her name, not that of her husband, thus ensuring that Thomas Anthony's creditors in England could not touch it.*

Fanny put on a brave face before her friends and family. 'My settlement (oh! what a blessed thing is a settlement) affords an income sufficient to support us in perfect comfort here,' she wrote to Julia Pertz, 'and if in addition to this, I continue to write we shall be much richer than we have ever been – even now, I feel a thousand times more at my ease than I have done for years. Mr Trollope permits me to receive our little revenue – every thing is paid *before* it is consumed.' To Tom, who was worried about his degree examinations, she urged:

Keep up your spirits, dearest Tom, and do not anticipate dis-appointment. We are, in truth, arrived at the *corner* I have so often talked about, and if we can but turn it, things must be better with us than we have seen them for years. £250 in a cheap country, with my own management, and the hope of

---

* At least one man tried to obtain money which Thomas Anthony owed him by 'interfering with engagements' existing between his wife and John Murray. In a letter to the publisher Trollope was adamant that his creditors should not touch his wife's hard-earned money (TAnT to Murray, 20 August 1834: John Murray Archives).

gaining more by my own means, yours, and Henry's, cannot be called a dreary prospect. Courage! And you will do well. You cannot suppose that the generality of those who have taken degrees are your superiors. I am sure they are not. Courage! And we will make a tour together yet.[6]

But, despite her optimism, her novels make it clear that Fanny deeply regretted not having had more control over her own finances early in her marriage. Her great heroine, the Widow Barnaby, who had been left well provided for by her first husband, was not to make the same mistake as Fanny when she married the cunning Major Allen. The major's 'notions of a well-regulated family economy might have led him to prefer taking his lady's income under his own immediate and separate control'. However, his not-so-tender bride insists that all that was hers should remain so, and he eventually yields, contenting himself 'with knowing that all household expenses, of every kind whatever, including of course his own dress and little personal appointments, were defrayed regularly' (*The Widow Married*). 'What is marrying to a woman,' the wily heroine Sophia Martin asks herself, 'but just giving up her money, if she has got any?' (*The Ward of Thorpe Combe*).

The question in everyone's mind must have been, how could Thomas Anthony, who was after all a Chancery barrister, have been so negligent in regard to the marriage settlement? His son Anthony tried to answer this question in his novels. In *Ralph the Heir* the barrister Sir Thomas Underwood, although honourable and upright, 'was a man so weak that he could allow himself to shun from day to day his daily duty, – and to do this so constantly as to make up out of various omissions, small in themselves, a vast aggregate of misconduct'. But the possibility must have crossed everyone's mind, had Thomas Anthony's sanity left him? Perhaps Fanny's husband, like the Revd Josiah Crawley in the matter of the missing cheque, came to doubt his own innocence. 'The truth is, that there are times when I am not – sane. I am not a thief – not before God; but I am – mad at times' (*The Last Chronicle of Barset*). Crawley feared the madhouse more than he feared prison. Thomas Anthony may well have shared this fear, for he had only recently rescued an old friend who had been wrongly committed to a private madhouse in Salisbury.* However, although Crawley could be 'morose, sometimes almost to insanity', 'the intellect of the man was as clear as running water in all things not pertaining to his daily life and its difficulties. He could be logical with a vengeance.' 'It was simply his memory that would play him tricks, – and his memory as to the things which at the moment were not important to him', or did not seem to need his immediate attention, in the barrister's case. Thomas Anthony's migraines – not to mention the 'remedy', the mercury-based calomel – might easily have led to lapses in concentration if not also memory.

In her own more limited exploration of her husband's character, Fanny does not dwell on the question of guilt or insanity, but on personal degradation. Thomas Anthony must have found it difficult to face his wife and, certainly, to maintain any sense of dignity in her presence. 'Before his preserver,' Fanny writes in *Hargrave*, 'his spirit was bent to the very earth; and though he well knew that she had saved him, his gratitude bore no proportion to the suffering produced by the conscious degradation into which he had fallen.' In hiding the true state of his affairs for so long, Thomas Anthony must have lied to his wife, Lord Northwick and others. Like Wentworth in *One Fault*, he had fallen as low as a man in his position could fall. He 'had not so perseveringly studied all the theory of the science that makes a gentleman, without knowing that lying makes no part of it; yet at that moment his heart told him that not only then was he guilty of the mean, vulgar, pitiful vice, but that he was habitually driven to practise it by the difficulties into which his unchecked violence was perpetually plunging him'. In a marriage, 'without the firmest esteem and the most undoubting confidence on both sides, it was impossible for either party to hope for happiness, or even to flatter themselves that they should be capable of doing their duty' (*The Blue Belles of England*).

What was probably the final blow to Thomas Anthony's pride occurred just at the time he was preparing to flee from his creditors

---

* According to F. E. Trollope, this Mr Smith spent a few days at Julian Hill with the Trollopes and charmed the family before he went to live with his devoted sisters.

in England. At the end of 1833 that rapacious collector of Ohio real estate, Nicholas Longworth, filed a complaint against the joint stock company of the Cincinnati Bazaar, of which Thomas Anthony was a member: Longworth, who held the mortgage on the property, was owed $1,612.97 interest. The building, overlooking the Ohio River, was appraised at $7,000 but went for only $4,667, two thirds of its value, at auction in February 1834. Longworth was the lucky buyer. Like the naïve Henry Bligh in Fanny's American novel *Jonathan Jefferson Whitlaw,* Thomas Anthony's 'ignorance of business had led him to conceive that the six thousand dollars he had placed in the bank was all he risked; but his name was in the firm, and house, lands, stock, and furniture, were all seized and sold by auction, towards clearing the large demands of the creditors'. Everything Thomas Anthony had set out to do in his lifetime had crumbled to dust in his hands: he must have felt himself, like the Revd Josiah Crawley, to be cursed. Yet, for all the abuse heaped on that building, the memoirs of many a Cincinnati resident for the next fifty years record pleasant evenings spent at the Bazaar attending a dance or concert, until its demolition in 1881.[7] Perhaps the greatest irony of all is that, only six months after the Trollopes left Cincinnati, in November 1830, the Bazaar was the venue for a ball held in honour of Fanny's friend Lafayette and the French Revolution.*

By July 1834 the doctors decreed that the Dawlish air had done Henry some good. Eager to join his family in Bruges, the invalid prepared to travel to the Continent via London. Always practical, Fanny asked that Henry bring with him a supply of old brown Windsor soap and six pounds of wax ends – not spermaceti – discarded by the wealthy London clubs and houses. These items were very bad and very dear in the Bruges markets. The plan was that Tom was to accompany his brother to Ostend. However, having left Oxford and gone down to London with a dismal third-class degree, Tom felt that he could not afford to neglect the first of many 'irremediably

---

* When Hervieu's interior murals were whitewashed, Harriet Beecher Stowe's uncle wrote to the *Cincinnati Gazette* condemning such 'vandalism'. Harriet's preacher father, Lyman Beecher Stowe, had moved to the wicked region of Cincinnati in 1832 to fight the battle for America's soul against the Irish Catholic and German 'infidel' immigrants (F. Wilson, *Crusader in Crinoline*, Philadelphia, 1941, p. 104).

stupid or idle' pupils which he took on for ten shillings an hour. After seeing Henry off at the dock, Tom noted in his diary that he was looking *desperately* ill'. He feared that, 'owing to his youth and strength' – all the Trollope boys had inherited their father's muscular frame – 'Henry's struggle with the dread disease may be long and painful'.

Fanny, too, must have been shocked at Henry's appearance when she met him in Ostend, especially after enduring the Channel crossing, which could last as long as thirteen hours in rough weather. Over the next few months Fanny stumbled from hope to despair and back again. 'I want you to give all your attention to a plan wherein lies nearly all my hopes for [Henry's] recovery,' she wrote to Tom. 'We have heard the most extraordinary account of the recovery of desperate cases, by a voyage to the West Indies. And my heart – as well as his own, poor fellow, – is now fixed on him going with *you* to Jamaica.' Fanny was sure that Bishop Lipscomb of Jamaica, an old family friend and near contemporary of Thomas Anthony at Winchester and New College, would receive them 'with all kindness'. 'The *means* for this,' Fanny continues, 'must come from Murray. His letter tells me that half the impression [of *Belgium and Western Germany*] is sold, and that *as soon* as the whole is disposed of, he will let me draw on him. My hopes and fears for this, make me sick at heart. Yet I do, and still trust that I shall not be doomed to see this precious hope pass away from me.'[8]

Murray was well aware of the Trollopes' situation, and he effectively advanced Fanny her share of the half profits for *Belgium and Western Germany*, amounting to £210 for the first edition of 1,250 copies, within three months of its publication in July 1834. John Murray, junior, paid the Trollopes a visit at the Château d'Hondt that August, clutching the latest *Quarterly Review*, with a favourable article on Fanny's book by Captain Frederick Marryat, and talking 'confidentially' of a second edition. 'He took coffee with us,' Fanny wrote, 'and gave us a delightful quantity of literary gossip, all fresh from the mint.' What Fanny did not know was that *The Quarterly Review*'s editor, John Murray, senior, had rejected Marryat's first, scathing review of *Belgium and Western Germany* on compassionate grounds. 'My dear John,' the captain replied to the autocrat of Albemarle Street, '*Poor Henry* shall go out to Jamaica, that is, I will not prevent him by any remarks upon Mrs Trollope's work – I will put my conscience in my pocket and the present Review into the fire and will concoct another.'[9]

Tom made the necessary inquiries and discovered that the cost of a single passage to Jamaica was £46; the purchase of two such fares was, he knew, beyond his mother's means. Fanny revised her plans accordingly: 'After many consultations, and collecting the best information I can get on the subject,' she writes to Tom at the end of July, 'we are led to think that sailing about from port to port in the Mediterranean, and passing the winter months on its shores, would be better for Henry than the West Indies. And he himself greatly prefers the idea of it. Let me know what your feelings are respecting accompanying him.' 'Now that I believe Henry's only hope of life hangs on the change of climate, you may guess with what anxiety I look for every indication that may give me a hope of finding the means of giving it him.' 'My mind,' she continues, 'is in no good state for composition, but I do my best. Henry is, I think, a *little* better. His cough is not so bad as I had expected; but his weakness is very great.'

Fanny's writing now took on a greater urgency than ever before. She returned to *Tremordyn Cliff*, the novel which she had left off on 'Friday 18th April, – on which day we turned our backs for ever upon Julian Hill'. The plot involves the illness and untimely death of the heroine's young husband. Fanny also asked Tom, who acted for all intents and purposes as her literary agent in London, 'to learn if possible how the sale goes on' for *Belgium and Western Germany*. 'It is dreadful to think that dear Henry's *life* may perhaps depend upon it!' By the middle of August a Belgian physician took pity on Fanny and gently dissuaded her from sending Henry abroad. 'I need not dwell upon the feelings produced by Dr B.'s letter,' Fanny informed Tom. 'Yet I feel that he is right. Henry bears the disappointment better than I could have expected, – but yet it is one.'

The local doctors had led her to expect the worst, but Henry, 'with the hopefulness peculiar to his malady', had 'no shadow of a doubt of his own recovery'. When he heard that Lady Dyer had refused to accept Fanny's offer to pay back a previous loan, Henry leapt upon the chance to visit London. She wrote almost apologetically to Tom that 'anything which relieved the tedium of the poor fellow's lingering complaint, would be a blessing'. Leaving her husband and son Anthony behind, Fanny travelled to London with Henry and Emily, whose health was also giving cause for concern. Tom had found them gloomy lodgings at 22 Northumberland Street (now Luxborough Street) off the Marylebone Road, 'opposite to the deadest part of the dead wall of the Marylebone Workhouse' (*Phineas Redux*). The respected London physician, Dr Edwin Harrison of Lisson Grove, whom Fanny's old friend Marianne Skerrett had recommended, paid a house call to the Trollopes in this seedy street. Afterwards Fanny took a long walk with Tom in nearby Regent's Park and told him that there was 'no hope' for his brother. Dr Harrison thought that Henry should not be told the truth concerning his condition. 'If it were possible to guard him from every powerful emotion, whether of sorrow or joy – from all fatigue of mind and body, and from every inclemency both of climate and season – he might live for years, my lady. But at his age we find it almost impossible to obtain this,' so the doctor tells the wife of the young lord in *Tremordyn Cliff.*

Henry was an extremely exigent and irritable patient. He demanded his mother's attention during all his waking hours, and when she was not reading to him, she was rehearsing all the different schemes to restore his health, from Mediterranean cruises to a new elixir. Henry dictated to his mother what must have been a heart-breaking letter to both her and Dr Harrison, who had insisted on waiving his fee: 'For the last few days he has expectorated much less than usual, and complains of great oppression and pain on his chest, as he thinks, in consequence. He also wished me to mention that every thing he eats causes him great pain as soon as it reaches the stomach, so as almost to make him dread taking any nourishment. Is there any thing that you can suggest likely to relieve these painful symptoms? Emily is certainly better,' Fanny adds, 'though not yet quite as I could wish.'[10] Most painful of all, recalls Tom, was when a family friend offered Henry free passage to Madeira, 'and my poor mother had the inexpressibly sad and difficult task of quashing them all without allowing her patient to suspect the real reason of their being given up'.* On 26 September Tom saw his brother, sister and mother off at Tower Bridge, bound for Ostend. He wrote in his diary, 'Poor Henry! Have I seen him for the last time?' What might he have said in farewell to the little brother who had been his constant companion and co-conspirator throughout the early, happy years in Keppel Street and Winchester?

Back in Bruges, with the help of two female servants, Fanny waited upon Henry throughout the day, snatching moments to write when her patient dropped off to sleep. 'Sometimes he lies in bed very late, and then I scribble away; but when he gets up,' Fanny writes to Tom, 'it is over for the day.' 'I sit alone with him from four o'clock – his dinner hour – till nine. This makes a long, long evening. For some time I did not even go downstairs to tea; but now I do, which is a great relief, though it lasts but for a few minutes.' The days no doubt 'passed away in the sort of shapeless way that days are apt to do, when there are invalids in a house whose indisposition is grave enough to prevent their coming downstairs' (*The Three Cousins*). 'The doctor's vials and the ink-bottle held equal places in my mother's rooms,' Anthony recalled: 'I have written many novels under many circumstances, but I doubt much whether I could write one when my whole heart was by the bedside of a dying son. Her power of dividing herself into two parts, and keeping her intellect by itself clear from the world, and fit for the duty it had to do, I never saw equalled' (*An Autobiography*). Most of *Tremordyn Cliff* was written in the small hours of the morning with the help of either coffee or green tea and laudanum. The laudanum may also have relieved the pain from an acute attack of rheumatism in the shoulders which Fanny suffered soon after her return from London. Not surprisingly, laudanum looms large in the novel: Lord Tremordyn is given hot bran sprinkled with laudanum for stomach pains (as, probably, was Henry),

---

* Frederic Chopin, also struck down by tuberculosis, wrote from his Mediterranean villa in Mallorca: 'I have been sick as a dog the last two weeks; I caught cold in spite of 18 degrees C. of heat, roses, oranges, palms, figs and three most famous doctors on the island. One sniffed at what I spat up, the second tapped where I spat it from, the third poked about and listened how I spat it. One said I had died, the second that I am dying, the third that I shall die' (quoted in M. F. Perutz, 'The White Plague', *The New York Review of Books* (26 May 1994), p. 35).

and a bottle of laudanum always stands on his sister Lady Augusta's toilette, which she takes either as a stimulant or in sufficient quantity to ensure sleep. She, 'however, was too careful of her health to use it habitually'.*

With two consumptive patients in the house, Fanny knew enough to send Cecilia back to England to stay with her brother in Fulham and to try and keep Emily away from Henry; but how to do this without admitting to her son that he was dying? Fanny explains to Tom that Emily 'comes up for half an hour after [Henry] has taken his tea, and stays while I read aloud two chapters in the Bible. This was *his* request. I place her on the side of the fire next me, and at a good distance from his place.' To alleviate the tedium of the sickroom 'Henry has taken to *carpentering*, and has bought various tools,' Fanny continues in her letter. 'It is astonishing to see the steadiness and firmness with which he hammers. I think, on the whole, he has suffered less of late.'[11] Henry's sudden burst of energy may have given Fanny a glimmer of hope. 'There are still moments,' she writes, 'when I think it *possible* he may recover. But my fears predominate. My life is too sad, and the calls upon me too incessant, to let me write much.' Fanny had learned that 'there is often a degree of steady courage found in despair which is wanting as long as hope remains to dally with us, and cheat us of our wisdom' (*A Romance of Vienna*). This is an observation which she returns to again and again in her novels.

Two days before Christmas, in the year 1834, Fanny tells Tom: 'It is over. My poor Henry breathed his last about nine o'clock this morning.' In *Tremordyn Cliff* Fanny describes the awful moment when Lord Tremordyn is found dead from a fatal haemorrhage similar to one a consumptive might suffer: 'The bed was steeped in blood, which had flowed, even to the floor – but now had ceased to flow.' 'Life was quite extinct, and even the inexperienced eyes of his poor wife, who had never looked on death before, could not mistake the fearful glare, the rigid stiffness, the awful strangeness that was left, where she had ever seen the soft, sweet smile.' Lord Tremordyn,

---

* In her first novel, *The Refugee in America*, Fanny wrote that 'laudanum placed beside a patient, will make him sleep, by removing his fear of lying awake'.

born in the same year as Henry, 1811, died at the age of twenty; Henry was twenty-three years old. Lady Tremordyn is certain that her husband's family 'will not let him lie in a foreign land'. Fanny had no choice but to bury Henry in Bruges.

Fanny wrote to John Murray a month later: 'My poor boy had suffered so long and so hopelessly, that his death was at last almost a blessing – but when the agony of watching these sufferings is forgotten, the memory of what he was when in health will come the more heavily.'[12] She had effectively devoted nearly ten years of her life, since his leaving Winchester in 1826, to Henry. His colourful character pervades *Belgium and Western Germany*, with descriptions of him acting as travel agent, gossiping with the locals and engaging in learned conversations with distinguished geologists. Fanny refers to Henry as 'our man of science', and on several occasions she copies out a note from his journal to give the reader a technical description of the area's geology. She also offers some charming vignettes of the three travellers, scrambling around rocks and waterfalls: 'Mr H[ervieu], having spied out some spot, which he thought more beautiful still, to sketch from, set off in that direction. My son mounted up, hammer in hand, to the summit of the rocky heights above our head. And I turned back, to scribble in my note-book.' None of her other children were to feature so largely in her travel books.

One feels that the lonely young Anthony may have resented the attention and affection which Henry received. The single-minded – and, one feels, misguided – devotion of mothers like Lady Mason in *Orley Farm* and Lady Carbury in *The Way We Live Now* to their sons is reminiscent of the sacrifices made by Fanny on Henry's behalf. Lady Mason had defied her husband for the sake of the honest but self-willed Lucius. As for Lady Carbury, 'her literary life, and her literary successes ... were after all but adjuncts to that real inner life of hers of which the absorbing interest was her son', Felix. Profligate though he was, Felix remained 'the darling of her heart' over and above her more trustworthy daughter. Perhaps Fanny was owning up to her failings as a mother when, in *The Robertses on their Travels* (1846), she describes in no very flattering terms the relationship between a no-good son and his fawning mother which anticipates that of Lady Carbury and Felix by thirty years: 'It would scarcely be doing justice to the character of Mrs Roberts to say that she was afraid of anything; but if her courage ever threatened to forsake her under any circumstances, it was when she thought that anything was likely to happen which might by possibility vex, embarrass, irritate, or in any way annoy her son. The idea of seeing him look either cross, or melancholy, was more than she could bear.'

Nevertheless, in a later novel, *Uncle Walter* (1852), in which she describes the fate of the two young Harrington boys, one of whom is a diligent classical scholar, the other a voracious reader of *Robinson Crusoe*, Fanny sought to give Henry's life an alternative, happy ending. Just when Walter Harrington's father despairs of his son ever succeeding in life, the young man is given the chance to travel to the new world (in this case, Australia) in order to 'find his own path in the world, in a manner that should be more congenial to his nature than the learned career in which he had so signally failed'. Walter makes his fortune, becomes a respected figure in the natural sciences, and returns to England as a handsome, healthy, very kind and very wise old man – the hero of Fanny's tale.

Anthony, too, felt compelled to speculate on what his brother's life would have been had he lived, but his version has a very different outcome. His short story, 'The Spotted Dog' (1870), opens with a job request addressed to a literary editor by the forty-year-old Julius Mackenzie, destitute and down on his luck:

I was educated at—, and was afterwards a scholar of— College, Cambridge. I left the university without a degree, in consequence of a quarrel with the college tutor. I was rusticated, and not allowed to return. After that I became for a while a student for the Chancery Bar. I then lived for some years in Paris, and I understand and speak French as though it were my own language. For all purposes of literature I am equally conversant with German.

He is also a poet. This could have been Henry's *curriculum vitae* forty years earlier. Like Henry, Mackenzie had been something of a romantic rebel; he too had worked 'in a dark corner of that suicidal old court' in Lincoln's Inn (Henry had been at Middle Temple), but

219

had quarrelled with his family. Despite the advantages of birth and education, Mackenzie's proud and temperamental character seems to thwart all attempts to make a success of his life. Married to a woman below his station who is a drunkard, he has been driven to write for the penny dreadfuls to feed his four children. Out of pity, the editor engages Mackenzie to index a learned Greek manuscript. Work progresses well, but in the end Mackenzie cannot escape his degradation, and he takes his own life. He had earlier confessed to his employer: 'My life, of course, has been a mistake. Indeed, to live at all, – is it not a folly?' Perhaps Anthony felt deep in his heart that it was better for Henry to have died young than to have lived a life of failure and disappointment.*

As both Tom and Anthony note in their memoirs, their mother had the remarkable ability to pick herself up after such a tragedy. Fanny herself describes such a woman in *Tremordyn Cliff,* Mrs Maxwell, after the death of the young lord, her daughter's husband: 'sorrow was a visitor who could never remain a moment longer in the heart of Mrs Maxwell than till she could find some knight errant of the family of Hope, who would help her to thrust him out again'. Fanny knew well the various stages of grief. After the initial shock, she writes somewhat wryly, there is the mourning dress, 'a business which, as she continually repeated to herself and her maid, was the most melancholy and heart-breaking in the world, but which was sure, nevertheless, of producing one good effect, namely, that of altogether turning her thoughts from the horrid images which filled them, to the considerably less excruciating occupation furnished by experiments and consultations as to what forms and fabrics amidst the comprehensive livery of woe would best accord her person' (*Charles Chesterfield*). Eventually, Fanny observes in *The Vicar of Wrexhill,* 'like all other periods of human life, whether marked by sorrow or by joy', Mr Mowbray's death 'passed away with as even and justly-measured a pace as if no event distinguished it from its fellow

* Anthony had had the sad task of informing the Geological Society, of which Henry had been a member, that his brother was dead. This is the earliest surviving letter from Anthony's pen; it is dated the 'General Post Office, Secretary's Office, 13th February 1835'. My thanks to John Thackeray, archivist of the Geological Society.

days; and then, by slow but sure degrees, the little trifling ordinary routine of daily circumstance came with its invisible and unnoticed magic, to efface, or at least to weaken, feelings which seemed to have been impressed by the stamp of burning iron in their souls'.

And then, of course, Fanny had her husband and four other children to think about. In Bruges Anthony felt himself to be 'an idle, desolate hanger-on, that most hopeless of human beings, a hobbledehoy of nineteen, without any idea of a career, or a profession, or a trade. As well as I can remember I was fairly happy, for there were pretty girls at Bruges with whom I could fancy that I was in love.' But, 'now and again,' he recalls, 'there would arise a feeling that it was hard upon my mother that she should have to do so much for us, that we should idle while she was forced to work so constantly' (*Autobiography*). When he first left Harrow, Anthony had tried and failed to gain various scholarships to Cambridge and Oxford. After Tom's third-class degree and Anthony's failure Fanny came to believe that a university education was not all it was cracked up to be: 'little distinction could be gained by the assumption of a title which was never used in society, and to which he conceived every Englishman to be eligible who could just read and write a little' (*Michael Armstrong*).

Rather extraordinarily, while in Bruges the ungainly Anthony was offered a commission in an Austrian cavalry regiment, but first he had to learn French and German, which studies he undertook while working as a 'classical usher' at the school which the Revd William Drury had established in Brussels – a task to which he was ill-suited. Fortunately, the Trollopes' plight had not been forgotten by their friends in England. Mrs Clayton Freeling, a friend from Fanny's girlhood days, begged her father-in-law, Sir Francis Freeling, then Secretary of the Post Office, to offer the young Anthony a post paying £90 per annum.* This all happened in October 1834, when Henry's condition was deemed hopeless. Nevertheless, Fanny was able to take great joy in Anthony's good fortune: 'I am happier in receiving this news than I thought anything just now could make me.' Anthony proceeded to London and shared Tom's lodgings in a 'queer' sort of

---

* Like Fanny Trollope, Sir Francis Freeling was from Bristol, and it was in this city that he began his Post Office career.

house with its own courtyard which belonged to a tailor and his mother in Little Marlborough Street, off Regent Street. Fanny wrote apologetically to William Drury, explaining why Anthony had left Belgium so abruptly.[13] Tom helped Anthony meet the Post Office's minimum requirements in penmanship, and the two brothers usually spent Sundays with the Grants at Harrow, walking back to London the next morning. The mother of one of Tom's pupils complained that he arrived at her house in Belgrave Square on Mondays 'in a very dusty condition'.

When the two brothers learned of Henry's death at the end of December 1834, Anthony found that he could not leave his clerkship at the Post Office, having only started two months earlier. Tom hastened to cross the Channel with Cecilia straightaway, but they arrived too late for Henry's funeral. Fanny Bent paid the Trollopes an extended visit in Bruges to comfort her cousin when she heard the sad news. As it was her first visit to the Continent, Tom escorted her on a sightseeing tour of Belgium, leading her to the top of every tower, just as Henry had dragged her up the Devonshire tors two years previously. In the spring of 1835 Tom at long last was offered a proper job, teaching at King Edward's Grammar School in Birmingham with a salary of £200 per annum. He recalls crossing to Dover with his good friend Captain Smithett on the *Arrow*, 'the only other passengers being a maniac and a corpse', to await his election by the governors of the school.

With her two sons apparently provided for and the second edition of *Belgium and Western Germany* selling well, Fanny could look forward to her next project. Since the previous summer, she had had in mind 'to scribble a little gossip on the present queer state of society in Paris', as she remarked to John Murray in July 1834.[14] Fanny had always loved Paris, whatever its politics, and she badly needed 'a change of scene – that much vaunted remedy for sorrow' (*Hargrave*). However, Emily's delicate state as well as her husband's declining health continued to be of concern, and another reason for visiting Paris was to consult a Dr Mojon, who had been specially recommended. Mrs Trollope and her rather motley entourage, including not only her husband and two daughters, but also the indefatigable Fanny Bent, Auguste Hervieu as illustrator and Tom (whose appointment to the Birmingham grammar school had been frustratingly delayed), established themselves in an apartment on the rue de Provence in early April 1835.

Tremordyn Cliff was to have been published by Whittaker. However, Fanny had managed to secure a better deal from Richard Bentley, and the Trollopes' stay in Paris was largely financed by Bentley's bills for the novel. Unlike Murray, Bentley did not like the half-profits system; to help his business's cash flow, he preferred to issue one or more promissory notes to the author, often spread out at four, six and nine month intervals from delivery of the manuscript. To compensate for the unpredictability of the book's sales, Bentley wrote in an escalation clause to Fanny's contract: he had agreed to pay £250 for an edition of 1,000 copies, plus an additional £100 if sales reached 950, another £100 for the sale of 450 in a second printing, and a final £100 if 700 copies of the second printing sold. (However, if sales were going slowly, the publisher might stop promoting a book to save paying out any more money.) Fanny probably cashed the first bill for £250 in advance, no doubt at a considerable discount, to use as travelling money. Two weeks later Bentley promised to pay Fanny £500 for the completed manuscript of *Paris and the Parisians* (for a first edition of 2,000 copies). On hearing these favourable terms, one friend remarked 'Mrs Trollope is *coining* money literally.'[15]

Fanny had last visited Paris for Julia Garnett's wedding in the autumn of 1827. Since then, Fanny wrote in *Paris and the Parisians*, 'I have journeyed half round the globe; but nothing I have met in all my wanderings has sufficed to damp the pleasure with which I enter again this gay, bright, noisy, restless city – this city of the living, as beyond all others it may be justly called.' Tom, who was making his first visit to Paris, was not so enamoured. He thought Thomas Carlyle's translation of the city's Roman name *Lutetia Parisiorum* as 'Mudtown of the Parisians' very apt.* Even his mother had to admit that the townspeople's habit of tossing their filth on to the streets (for lack of proper sewers) was shocking. 'Happy indeed is it for the humble pedestrian if his eye and nose alone suffer from these

---

* The Latin word for mud is *lutum*.

ejectments; happy, indeed, if he comes not in contact with them, as they make their unceremonious exit from the window or door: *"Quel bonheur!"* is the exclamation if he escapes.' Nor did Paris benefit from the recent British invention of macadamized roads, which greatly reduced the clatter of hooves and carriage wheels.

In 1827 Charles X, brother of the beheaded Bourbon Louis XVI, had worn the French crown. Eight years later the 'citizen-king' Louis Philippe was on the throne and Paris was a hive of political activity – so much so that a crowd gathering to watch an escaped canary might be mistaken for the revolutionary *'mouvement'* which was daily expected. Fanny immediately realized that to give a coherent narrative of events was next to impossible. Instead, she took the advice offered by John Murray, which was to present her book as a series of letters to an anonymous friend back in England, 'describing occurrences as they arise, and scenery as it presents itself to your *first* impressions'.[16] Thus, in *Paris and the Parisians* Fanny proceeds at a comfortable, 'idle, ambling pace', as she herself calls it, sticking to 'my old habit of noting in my journal all things, great and small, in which I took an interest'. Yet she does not shy away from political topics. 'We all declare ourselves sick of politics, and a woman's letters, at least, ought if possible to be free from the wearily pervading subject: but,' Fanny astutely observes, 'the describing a human being, and omitting to mention the heart and the brain, would not leave the analysis more defective, than painting the Parisians at this moment without permitting their politics to appear in the picture.'*

Despite the conservative outlook she had acquired in America, Fanny was too well aware of her own ignorance of French politics, and at the same time too amused by it all, not to take a detached and objective view. 'I learnt much of which I was – in common, I suspect, with many others – very profoundly ignorant. I found good where I looked for mischief – strength where I anticipated weakness,' she admits in her preface. Thus, Fanny learned of two very good reasons for maintaining the status quo in France: *'Louis-Philippe est roi,* PARCEQU'*il est Bourbon*' and *'Louis-Philippe est roi,* QUOIQU'*il est*

---

* Political intrigue abounds in Fanny's 'detective novel', *Hargrave* (1843), set in the Paris of 1834–5.

Bourbon.'* 'These two parties of the *Parceques* and the *Quoiques*, in fact, form the great bulwarks of King Philippe's throne' and 'in truth, form between them the genuine *juste-milieu* on which the present government is balanced'.

Fanny describes a picturesque scene in the Tuilieries Gardens. She and her party take 'possession of half a dozen chairs under the trees' to watch the three rival factions – the *doctrinaires* (or *juste-milieu*) who supported Louis Philippe, the royalists who sought a return to Bourbon rule, and the republicans who wanted no king at all – enjoying 'in common the delicious privileges of cool shade, fresh air, and the idle luxury of an *al fresco* newspaper' – but not just any paper. The *doctrinaire* browses through *Le Reformateur*; the royalist peruses *La France*; and the republican pores over *Le Journal des Débats*. The Trollopes themselves would have been reading *Galignani's Messenger*, the *Herald Tribune* of the nineteenth century, for its 'well-digested mass of all the news of Europe' (*Hargrave*).† Napoleon remained the national hero, 'the most popular tyrant that ever lived'. Outside the Ecole Polytechnique on a Sunday the promenade swarmed with 'young Napoleons', aided and abetted by their tailors. Even Fanny admits a sneaking admiration for the man, 'though the name of Napoleon brings with it reminiscences which call up many hostile feelings'.

Fanny spent her evenings visiting the famous Paris *salons*, where 'French talk was very like champagne', all fizz and no substance. Mrs Garnett wrote to her daughter Julia that Mrs Trollope was 'altogether the Lion of Paris'; indeed, at one soirée Fanny was greeted at the door by her hostess with the cry, 'Chère dame! I have collected *une société délicieuse* for you this evening.' Each hostess tended to gather round them particular types, whether military men, philosophers, royalists, 'foreigners of the philosophic revolutionary class', or

---

* 'Louis Philippe is king BECAUSE he is a Bourbon' and 'Louis Philippe is king ALTHOUGH he is a Bourbon.'
† Louis Philippe had been exiled in America while Fanny was there. On a later visit to Paris (in 1840), when she was presented to Louis Philippe in the Tuileries, 'the King asked me, with a look of something like fun, if I should like to go back to America. *I longed to return the question to him!*' (F. E. Trollope, *Frances Trollope*, I, p. 312).

musicians, to name but a few. But Fanny's personal favourite would have been *les soirées antithèstiques*, where there was a little of everything. The *salon* of the eccentric Mary Clarke, fifteen years Fanny's junior, was just such a 'mixed bag'. An Englishwoman raised in Paris, Miss Clarke was a neighbour of the ancient Madame Juliette Récamier, the great beauty of her day and friend of Madame de Staël. Madame Récamier had boasted the most distinguished *salon* in Paris after the Restoration, and Mary Clarke came to share her duties as hostess in a small apartment up three flights of ill-lit stairs above the nuns of the Abbaye-aux-Bois, situated on the Left Bank.* Madame Récamier, a ghostly figure always dressed in white, persuaded her old admirer, the even more ancient Chateaubriand, to read from his *Mémoires d'Outretombe* for Mrs Trollope and her daughters.[17]

During the Paris season Fanny also attended soirées hosted by 'Madame' Benjamin Constant, wife of the philosopher, whom she had met on her previous visit to Paris, and the Princess Belgiojoso, an Italian exile in Paris devoted to the cause of her country's independence. Their guests included Fanny's old friends, the Garnetts and General Pepe,† as well as celebrities such as the Abbé de Lamennais, a prophet of the later Christian Democratic movement, who was known by his enemies as 'Robespierre in a surplice', Franz Liszt, who played the whole score of Mozart's *Don Giovanni* with the princess on two pianos before fainting, and the scandalous Georges Sand. In Fanny's novels one moral stands out above all else: 'Judge not, that ye be not judged', and she practised what she preached: 'The private history of an author ought never to mix itself with a judgement of

---

* Harriet Garnett had written to Julia Pertz in 1831 that Miss Clarke 'is as queer as ever. She has given up her soirées and only now receives *men* of an evening – women are not admitted' (14 December 1831: Garnett–Pertz Papers). Mary Clarke was known to take notes on the behaviour of her guests: 'took no trouble to make himself agreeable', 'grumpy, shan't ask her in a hurry again', 'went away too soon; very rude of him'. See M.C.M. Simpson, *Letters and Recollections of Julius and Mary Mohl*, London, 1885.

† In 1833 Harriet Garnett had written to her sister Julia that if Mrs Trollope came to Paris 'the Lafayettes I am sure would not take any notice of her' owing to her conservative views (24 June 1833: Garnett–Pertz Papers). Whether or not this was true, Lafayette was dead by the time Fanny made it to Paris.

his works. Of that of Georges Sand, I know but little; but divining it from the only source that the public has any right to examine, – namely her writings, – I should be disposed to believe that her story is the old one of affection either ill requited, or in some way or other unfortunate' (*Paris and the Parisians*).* Fanny also met the young William Makepeace Thackeray, though she did not know it. She had organized a '*dîner sur l'herbe*' for twenty people outside Rousseau's house at Montmorency. The last of a series of disasters occurred when 'one of the gentlemen had been thrown from his horse and taken up for dead'. The 'wounded cavalier' was none other than the twenty-four-year-old Thackeray, who was at the time an art student in Paris, and the accident left a permanent scar on his nose.

It had not yet been six months since Fanny had stood beside Henry's grave outside Bruges, and certain passages in *Paris and the Parisians* make it clear that his death was never far from her mind. Witnessing the open display of grief shown by the French on a visit to the fashionable cemetery of Père Lachaise, Fanny confesses: 'This manner of lamenting in public seems so strange to us! How would it be for a shy English mother, who sobs inwardly and hides the aching sorrow in her heart's core.' Elsewhere in the book Fanny pays tribute to her cousin Fanny Bent, who had taken Henry into her home and nursed him, when she defends the unmarried woman and her role in society. 'It has been my chance,' Fanny comments, 'to have found my dearest and most constant friends among single women. Of all the Helenas and Hermias that before marriage have sat upon one cushion, warbling of one song, even for years together, how few are there who are not severed by marriage! Kind feelings may be retained, and correspondence (lazily enough) kept up; but to whom is it that the anxious mother, watching beside the sick couch of her child, turns for sympathy and consolation? – certainly not to the occupied and perhaps distant wedded confidante of her youthful days, but to her maiden sister or her maiden friend.'

---

* In 1850 a Parisian friend wrote to Fanny: 'I rarely see Pepe, who lives closeted with Georges Sand, who is helping him to write an appendix to his memoirs!' (F. E. Trollope, *Frances Trollope*, II, p. 183).

The Trollopes returned to Bruges in June, shortly before the end of the Paris season. Fanny set about transforming her Parisian notes into a two-volume manuscript for Bentley, while Thomas Anthony returned to his 'monks and nuns', as his son Anthony called them. Hervieu was also in Bruges, working on the lithographs not only for *Paris and the Parisians* but also for the *Encyclopaedia Ecclesiastica*. Tom wrote of his father during this period: 'I have seen few things of the kind with more of pathos in it than his persevering attempt to render his labour of some value by compiling' his ecclesiastical dictionary. 'It was a pathetic thing to see him in his room at the Château d'Hondt, ill, suffering, striving with the absolutely miserable, ridiculously insufficient means he had been able with much difficulty to collect, to carry on his work.' Tom believed that, in watching his wife work so hard, 'a painful but not ignoble feeling urged my poor father to live at least equally laborious days, even though his labour was profitless'. Thomas Anthony tried to draw some sort of comfort from his work. He writes in the preface to the *Encyclopaedia Ecclesiastica*:

> In whatever situation, indeed, of life we may be placed, upon whatever pursuits or undertaking we may be employed, it seems to be the intention of Providence that we shall have many difficulties to encounter . . . The mine must be dug before it will yield its treasure, the ground must be duly prepared before the husbandman can reap the harvest, and the acquisition of all knowledge is the fruit of labour and study.

Only one volume was ever published, A–F, the last entry being 'Funeral Rites'.*

As Thomas Anthony's condition worsened, Fanny's progress on her book slowed. The invalid was attended by an old army doctor who served under Napoleon, Dr Herbout. He had given no indication to Fanny that her husband's life was in danger, and so, when Thomas Anthony died on 23 October 1835, it came as a great blow to her.

---

* *An Encyclopaedia Ecclesiastica; or a Complete History of the Church*, vol. I, London, 1834.

Only the day before she had entrusted the first volume of *Paris and the Parisians* to a friend bound for London, Major Molyneux Williams, who had promised to deliver it to Bentley. What thoughts went through Fanny's mind as she sat beside her husband's deathbed? Did she feel the absence of 'natural sorrow, that was in itself terrible'? So it was with Clara Meddows on the death of her dissolute father in *Charles Chesterfield*. 'She felt that it would have been a blessing to her, could she have wept the gentle tears of affection.' In typically blunt fashion, Mrs Garnett wrote to her daughter when she heard the news, 'Mr Trollope's death will be a great relief to all his family',[18] and perhaps relief together with renewed confidence in the future were the overriding emotions with which Fanny was left after the initial shock. Certainly, this was the case with the unhappily married Lady Sarah de Morley in *Father Eustace* (1847) when her husband died:

> Some people, perhaps, may think that this sort of exceeding happiness, upon the loss of a husband who had never positively ill-used her, was by no means commendable; and probably there are but few women true-hearted enough, even when *tête-à-tête* with their own consciences, to acknowledge to themselves as frankly as Lady Sarah de Morley did, how very glad she was that the period of her wifehood was over.

Fanny drew several different portraits of Thomas Anthony in her fiction: the passionless, distant Mr de Morley in *Father Eustace*; the unyielding Marmaduke Wentworth in *One Fault*; the elder Lord Tremordyn in *Tremordyn Cliff,* the 'victim of disappointed hope and mortified ambition', who treats his wife with 'hourly fretfulness, the daily increasing coldness, the frequent harshness, and even violence, of a husband'; the tyrannical Mr Rixley in *The Young Heiress,* whose wife had 'learnt to welcome his departure from home with as keen a feeling of joy as happier wives welcome a husband's return'; and the selfish Count d'Albano in *The Abbess,* whose 'proud step changed for a fretful shuffle' of an old man. Tom also recalled his father in his portrait of the irritable barrister, Bentham Linacre, in *The Garstangs of Garstang Grange*. But it was

Anthony who was obsessed with the memory of his father. 'I sometimes look back,' he wrote in his autobiography, 'meditating for hours together, on his adverse fate. He was a man, finely educated, of great parts, with immense capacity for work, physically strong very much beyond the average of men'; he had no vices and was 'born to fair fortunes'. 'But everything went wrong with him. The touch of his hand seemed to create failure. He embarked in one hopeless enterprise after another, spending on each all the money he could at the time command. But the worse curse to him of all was a temper so irritable that even those he loved the best could not endure it. We were all estranged from him, and yet I believed he would have given his heart's blood for any of us. His life as I knew it was one long tragedy.'

The Parisian physician Dr Mojon had taken Thomas Anthony to be a man of eighty; in fact, he was just sixty-two years of age at his death. Anthony's novels are full of disappointed men, both minor and major characters, with stooped posture and a shuffling gait, who look twenty years older than their age. Such are Louis Trevelyan in *He Knew He Was Right*, Robert Kennedy and Lord Brentford in *Phineas Redux*, the Marquis of Stapledean, Arthur Wilkinson's patron, in *The Bertrams*, and even the Duke of Omnium in *The Duke's Children*. After Glencora's death the duke 'acquired a habit of stooping which, when he was not excited, gave him an appearance of age', and 'now it was so much exaggerated that he who was not yet fifty might have been taken to be over sixty'. But perhaps the portrait which most resembles Anthony's father at the very end of his life is that of the Revd Josiah Crawley in *The Last Chronicle of Barset*, as he sits 'recalling all the facts of his life, his education, which had been costly, and, as regarded knowledge, successful'; 'the short, sweet days of his early love, in which he had devoted himself again, – thinking nothing of self, but everything of [his wife]; his diligent working'; 'the success of other men who had been his compeers, and, as he too often told himself, intellectually his inferiors; then of his children, who had been carried off from his love to the churchyard'; 'and then of his children still living, who loved their mother so much better than they loved him. And he would recall all the circumstances of his poverty, – how he had been driven to accept alms, to fly from creditors, to hide himself, to see his chairs and tables seized' before his neighbours' eyes.

Thomas Anthony had died intestate. The Prerogative Court of Canterbury authorized one of his creditors, George Barnes, to seize the few 'goods and chattels' ('sworn under fifty pounds') which arrived back in England.[19] He was buried next to Henry in the cemetery a mile outside St Catherine's Gate. Tom composed the simple Latin inscription, adding a phrase in Greek at the bottom which translates 'in a foreign land'. Tom revisited the graves towards the end of his life and gazed at the Château d'Hondt 'in which so many hours of vivid pleasure and of crushing sorrow had been passed'. 'Was it,' he writes in his memoirs, 'could it be absolutely I, who within those very walls had done so many things, thought so many thoughts, felt so much love, laughed so many laughs, and shed so many tears?' The house no longer exists, but the two sombre memorials, a headstone for the father and an Ionic column for the son, still stand side by side in the Protestant section near the main cemetery gate – a small, dark corner set well apart from the ornate Catholic monuments which emanate from the central cross.

'Without meaning to be in the slightest degree uncivil to the lords of the creation, I certainly think that the demise of a husband may occasionally be felt rather a relief than as an affliction by his widow,' Fanny writes in *The Young Countess*. Fear of debtors' prison no longer kept them in Bruges, and Fanny was determined not to become one of the multitude of English bankrupts abroad who

> had sunk, and slunk, and dwindled away, becoming absorbed, as it were, into more or less width of space, and more or less length of time, till every familiar eye had ceased to follow them, while they were finally suffered to evaporate and vanish away, like so many pins, which everybody knows must be somewhere, but concerning whose disappearance from the light of day nobody thinks it worthwhile to inquire. Respecting this class – a much more numerous one than most of us are aware – Mrs Roberts knew little, and cared less . . . Yet there are enough of such to fill many a stirring volume; but they could not well be divided off into romances, for all the third volumes would be

wanting. They would rarely have any very striking catastrophe; ending for the most part in a cold, hopeless, helpless, cheerless blank (*The Robertses on their Travels*).

Fanny began to make plans to return home with her family.

CHAPTER TEN

A Romance of Vienna

Fanny Trollope's first object was to do what she could for the seventeen-year-old Emily. Leaving behind Tom and Cecilia at the Château d'Hondt to make a start on the packing, she travelled once more to London with Emily to consult Dr Harrison in Lisson Grove. Fanny had hoped that a journey to Italy might restore her youngest daughter's health, but the doctor thought that she should remain in England until the spring. Her letters to Tom and Cecilia over the next weeks are painful to read. 'I much wish I could come to help you in getting through all the business you will have to perform previous to bidding a final adieu to Belgium, but this is quite imposs-ible. [Emily] has by no means recovered from the cold and fatigue of her journey hither.' 'She is very weak, and eats hardly anything. I am *miserably* anxious, but struggle to keep up my spirits, as I must set to work again directly.' A few days later she writes: 'My fears are all directed to one point, – the health of my dear Emily. If she is *very* ill, I much misdoubt my power of writing.' And the situation only got worse. At the end of November Fanny tells her children: 'I am very very greatly alarmed about my Emily. She has lost strength rapidly, she eats nothing, her cough is decidedly worse than it has ever been. My *anxiety is dreadful*, – and the more so because I dare not show it. But this is a theme I must not dwell on – for all our sakes.'[1]

Fanny had returned to the same lodgings in Northumberland Street, opposite the Marylebone Workhouse, which Tom had found for his mother on her last visit to Dr Harrison with Henry and Emily. Anthony was living there now. Fanny was above all anxious to keep Cecilia away from Emily, just as she had tried, in vain, to protect Emily from Henry. The Trollopes' good Harrow friend, Lady Milman, invited Cecilia to stay with her at her house in Pinner. Fanny's next undertaking was to find a residence outside London, near enough so that Anthony and other family and friends could easily visit, but far from the city's smoke and grime. She found the perfect house in Monken Hadley, a village situated along the Great North Road, twelve miles from London. However, the owner, Mr Hervey (by coincidence, a friend of the Garnetts) informed her that the property would not be available to rent until early in the new year.

It must have been a melancholy and lonely Christmas that year, 1835. Tom was still in Bruges, and there was only Fanny, with the help of her maid, Mrs Cox, to nurse the dying girl, for by this time the mother realized there was 'no hope of her recovery'.* Being stuck in Anthony's dingy rooms in Northumberland Street would have only made matters worse. 'A family group placed in lodgings of which the females greatly disapprove, but which, being chosen by the male, must be endured, seldom manifest any striking symptoms of hilarity' (*The Widow Married*). Anthony is more specific: 'Lodgings in London are always gloomy. Gloomy colours wear better than bright ones for curtains and carpets, and the keepers of lodgings in London seem to think that a certain dinginess of appearance is respectable.' 'The big drawing-room and two bedrooms' which the squire of Allington took for his niece Lily Dale in Sackville Street 'were all that was proper, and were as brown, and as gloomy, and as ill-suited for the comforts of ordinary life as though they had been prepared for two prisoners' (*The Last Chronicle of Barset*). Hervieu might have shared their Christmas dinner, for he lived around the corner at 15 Nottingham Street.

At long last, Fanny, Emily and Mrs Cox made the journey to Monken Hadley with their few possessions. The village has changed little over the years. The roomy and attractive flat-fronted brick

* As Mr John MacGregor, who had visited Fanny in London, told Harriet Garnett (HG to JGP, 19 December 1835: Garnett–Pertz Papers).

house still faces on to the village green and lies within a hundred yards of the church. An ancient wisteria frames the drawing-room doors, which open out on to the spacious garden. The first acquaintance they made in Monken Hadley would have been the local physician, Dr Hammond. 'Nothing more rapidly lays the foundation of kindness, and not unfrequently of friendship, than the assiduous attention of a skilful physician to a dearly loved [one],' Fanny had written the year before in *Tremordyn Cliff*: 'His visits were frequent, and always most welcome so that by the end of six weeks, he felt himself, and was considered by them, as an esteemed and intimate acquaintance.' Like Katie Woodward in Anthony's *The Three Clerks*, Emily must have 'lived beneath a stethoscope, and bore all their pokings and tappings with exquisite patience. She herself believed she was dying.' Emily 'was never irritable, never exacting about engrossing her mother's society, as Henry had been', Frances Eleanor Trollope later remarked. She understood that her mother needed time alone to write. The child's patience and forbearance probably only made the situation all the more heartbreaking for her mother.

Anthony allowed Katie Woodward to live. He did not have the same power over Emily. On 12 February 1836, just a few weeks after her eighteenth birthday, she died. Anthony had the sad task of writing to Tom, who was still in Bruges: 'It is all over! Poor Emily breathed her last this morning. She died without any pain, and without a struggle. Her little strength had been gradually declining, and her breath left her without the slightest convulsion, or making any change in her features or face. Were it not for the ashy colour, I should think she was sleeping. I never saw anything more beautifully placid and composed.' 'It is much better that it is now,' Anthony continued, 'than that her life should have been prolonged only to undergo the agonies which Henry suffered. Cecilia was at Pinner when it happened, and she has not heard of it yet. I shall go for her tomorrow. You went to the same house to fetch her when Henry died.'[2]

For the third time in just over a year Fanny went through the rituals of death and bereavement. In *The Bertrams*, much of which takes place in Monken Hadley, Anthony recalls the scene in the house on the day of old Mr Bertram's funeral. Upstairs the undertakers are sealing the coffin, while in the dining-room below Bertram's nephew, business manager and doctor stand with their backs to the fire. 'Very few words passed between them, but they were not in their nature peculiarly lugubrious. And then there was a scuffling heard on the stairs – a subdued, decent undertaker's scuffling – as some hour or two before had been heard the muffled click of a hammer. Feet scuffled down the stairs, outside the dining-room door, and along the passage. And then the door was opened, and in a low decent undertaker's voice, red-nosed, sombre, well-fed Mr Mortmain told them that they were ready.' Earlier in the novel, when the Hadley church bells ring out for Caroline Waddington's wedding, the author interrupts the narrative: 'I know full well the chime with which they toll when the soul is ushered to its last long rest. I have stood in that green churchyard when earth has been laid to earth, ashes to ashes, dust to dust – the ashes and the dust that was loved so well.' Emily's grave lies beside the church, on the east side of the chancel door.

As the youngest child, Emily had been 'the pet of all the family', and her death had a profound effect on everyone. Even fifty years after the event, Tom retained a clear picture of Emily in his mind. 'She was a very bright *espiègle** child, full of fun and high spirits', with 'flowing flaxen curls and wide china-blue eyes'. She loved to gaze up at the sky, and wondered why those around her did not enjoy the cloudscapes as much as she did. As for his mother's grief, 'her youngest child had ever been to my mother as the apple of her eye, and her loss was . . . a crushing blow'. Fanny, indeed, seems to have been stricken by her loss. For the first few days she was incapable of reading the letters of condolence, let alone replying to them. During this time Anthony stayed with his mother in Hadley, taking care of the necessary correspondence and probably overseeing most of the funeral arrangements. Fanny then returned with Cecilia to Pinner to stay with Lady Milman for a few days.[3]

The widow Mrs Richards in *The Vicar of Wrexhill*, like Fanny herself, was small in stature but not in fortitude. Mrs Richards was 'at least six inches shorter than either of [her daughters], and aspired to nothing in the world but to make her . . . children happy'. 'All the

* 'mischievous'.

courage of which I have ever given proof,' the widow declares, 'has been inspired, strengthened, and set in action by my children, – by my love for them, and their love for me.' Fanny's first concern was for her surviving daughter, Cecilia. The Garnetts invited her for an extended stay in Paris, which Fanny gratefully accepted. Cecilia and Emily, like Tom and Henry, had always done everything together as children, and it must have been heartbreaking for her not to have had the chance to say goodbye to her little sister. 'She has suffered much lately,' Fanny wrote of Cecilia, 'and though *not ill* would I think derive great benefit from change of air and scene.' Fanny then had to exert herself to find not only the money for Cecilia's passage to Paris but also a travelling companion, for neither of her sons was available. Fanny sent off letters to the Murrays and other friends, and after several weeks suitable arrangements were made.*

The need to make money by her writing was as important as ever. Anthony was the only one of her three surviving children in employment, and yet he still managed to be always in debt. These were Anthony's 'hobbledehoy' days, when he flirted with the barmaids who served him his supper, played écarté with the other Post Office clerks, wandered across the Home Counties with his Harrow and Winchester school chums, John Merivale and Walter Awdry, fellow members of the 'Tramp Society', had certain dealings with a money-lender from Mecklenburgh Square, and always managed to turn up late to his office.* Anthony confessed that at this time his mother 'paid much for me, paid all that I asked her to pay, and all that she could find out that I owed. But who in such a condition ever tells all and makes a clean breast of it?' (*An Autobiography*). Thus, everyone in the family was relieved when Anthony reported to Tom at the beginning of 1836 that *Paris and the Parisians* was selling well. 'Mamma will, I feel confident, have a second thousand of the Paris. No work of hers was ever abused so much – or sold so fast – or

---

* He was threatened with dismissal for his tardiness, and Mrs Clayton Freeling 'with tears in her eyes, besought me to think of my mother' (*An Autobiography*). Many of Anthony's 'hobbledehoy' exploits are recounted in *The Three Clerks* and *The Small House at Allington*.

praised in the periodicals so little – especially by her own party.' One Tory reviewer accused Mrs Trollope of accepting a bribe from Louis Philippe's government to commend the citizen king in her book, contrary to her own convictions. Yet, for all the public abuse, she received many private tributes from friends, including Sir Francis Freeling in a letter to Anthony. 'But what is much more to the purpose than this,' she wrote to Tom, 'the book sells well.'*[5]

The fifty-seven-year-old Fanny considered herself first and foremost a travel writer and, more importantly, she could command a higher price for her travel books than her novels. Yet she found herself in a difficult dilemma, as she admitted to Richard Bentley. 'I am aware that though my novels are read my reputation must chiefly be sustained by travelling, and I love the occupation well enough to look forward with hope and pleasure to future occasions.' 'But the truth is, that however well the public may like my travelling memoranda, the expenses incurred in collecting them are much too heavy to render the employment profitable, or even prudent – The publishing some work of imagination, written in the retirement of my quiet home, in the interval between my costly ramblings, is the only method by which I can enable myself to undertake them.' Novels, however, were not considered to be a very respectable literary endeavour, though attitudes were beginning to change. In 1833 *The Athenaeum* published a spirited defence of the novel: 'A traveller may lie and we cannot find him out . . . but the novel writer must stick to the truth, or he sinks into neglect and oblivion.' 'Novel writing has been considered by many as a low pursuit,' the periodical continued a few weeks later; yet 'a writer of a great big book of travels, half lies and nine-tenths nonsense, has the arrogance to look down with contempt upon a mere novel writer; but where has a traveller half the exercise for skill and philosophy that a novel writer has?'[6]

Nevertheless, Fanny thought she might be able to find some other, more respected, means to employ her pen than novel writing. In

* While in Paris Fanny had agreed to help a Mr Cohen to translate *Paris and the Parisians* into French. 'I hope by this means to let the good people of Paris have my opinions such as they really are – an object not always attained by reading a translation' (FT to Bentley, 22 May 1835: Taylor Collection).

December 1835, a little more than a month after her husband's death, Fanny had written to Bentley from Anthony's lodgings in Northumberland Street with the idea of a monthly periodical, satirizing the politics of the day. The magazine would be heavily illustrated by one artist, none other than Auguste Hervieu, thereby 'bringing his pencil into notice'. She would contribute the text, 'a Hogarth style of caricature'.[7] Tom and Anthony clearly never understood their mother's continued loyalty to the eccentric and temperamental Frenchman, whom they jokingly called 'Heirview' – presumably because they thought he was sponging off their mother's growing reputation. However, neither Tom nor Anthony had lived through that dreadful time in America when she and her children would literally have starved if it had not been for Hervieu's kindness. What was more, Fanny sincerely believed, perhaps rightly, that she owed some of her success to Hervieu's etchings, in particular, those accompanying *The Domestic Manners of the Americans* and *Paris and the Parisians*. But there was another reason. Hervieu had been Henry's closest friend and companion, not only in America but also on their travels in Belgium and Germany, and for Fanny the Frenchman was a precious link to the past and to her dead son.

Bentley probably told Fanny that he did not see the need for yet another periodical competing in an already crowded market. However, after seeing Hervieu's portfolio, with many of the drawings dating from America, the publisher suggested that the artist and Mrs Trollope collaborate on a volume of sketches to be called 'Scenes on the Mississippi'. This was no doubt an attempt on Bentley's part to rival a similar collaboration, entitled *Sketches by Boz*, between the young journalist Charles Dickens and the more widely known illustrator, George Cruikshank. Fanny was happy to draw on her still vivid recollections of the Mississippi and its environs, but she preferred to write a continuous narrative on a subject she had long felt passionately about, slavery. Bentley agreed, and in December 1835 offered Fanny £350 for one edition (1,500 copies) of *The Life and Adventures of Jonathan Jefferson Whitlaw; or Scenes from the Mississippi*; if more editions were forthcoming, Fanny would, as usual, be duly remunerated. The twenty-three-year-old Dickens was thrilled to receive from his publisher a single payment of £100 for the copyright of the

Sketches, his first book; he would not see another penny from the publisher.*

Fanny's aversion to slavery had become even stronger after her return from the United States, as attitudes grew more and more polarized not only in America but also in Europe. Only a few weeks after Mrs Trollope's departure in 1831 Nat Turner's slave rebellion had struck fear into Southerners' hearts; in 1833 the American position became even more isolated following the abolition of slavery throughout the British Empire. The years 1825 to 1838 represented the height of activism against slavery in Britain, especially amongst women; a large network of ladies' associations across the country urged households to boycott slave-grown sugar, rum and tea. Fanny's contribution to the cause was to be, in fact, the first anti-slavery novel, *Jonathan Jefferson Whitlaw,* dedicated 'To those States of the American Union in which slavery has been abolished, or never permitted'. It was published in April 1836, more than fifteen years before Harriet Beecher Stowe's *Uncle Tom's Cabin.*† Fanny's wicked overseer, Whitlaw, and the slave couple longing to escape to freedom, Caesar and Phoebe, are clearly prototypes for Stowe's Simon Legree and George and Eliza.

When the story begins, the 'hero' (Fanny uses the term ironically) Jonathan Jefferson Whitlaw is just a small boy living on the Mississippi near Natchez, Louisiana, about 200 miles up river from New Orleans. The Whitlaws are a poor white family who live in the malarial swamps at the Mississippi's edge and survive by gathering firewood to supply passing steamboats. Fanny had described such a scene in *The Domestic Manners of the Americans.* We see the clever young Jonathan being slowly corrupted by a society which worships the dollar and champions slavery, until he grows into a 'tall handsome youth, with a quick restless eye which rarely met that of the person

* Fanny signed this agreement on 26 December 1835, the day after that miserable Christmas in Northumberland Street (BL, Add MS 46612, f. 201). *Sketches by Boz* appeared in February 1836, Fanny's novel *Jonathan Jefferson Whitlaw* in April of that year.

† Richard Hildreth's *The White Slave; or Memoirs of Archy Moore* also appeared in 1836, six months after *Jonathan Jefferson Whitlaw,* which was reissued in 1857 as *The Lynch Law* to capitalize on the popularity of *Uncle Tom's Cabin* (1852).

he conversed with'. In contrast to the 'hero' of the tale is the gentle Frederick Steinmark, an impoverished German who, with his English wife and children, has immigrated to Louisiana and successfully runs a farm without slave labour. Whitlaw has nothing but contempt for them: 'nobody that was anybody would ever think of getting along without a slave. It was plain that ... the Steinmarks were nothing but a set of beggarly hard-working foreigners, that did not know what it was to live like gentlemen and Americans.'

Fanny's depiction of the horrors of the slave system is both frank and convincing. One of the most powerful scenes in the book, illustrated by Hervieu, takes place in the Natchez dry goods store, where several gentlemen are lounging about: 'One sat astride the counter; a second had climbed to a third tier of woollen cloths set edgeways, apparently with no other object than to place his heels upon a shelf immediately above the door of entrance, so that by a judicious position of his head he was enabled to peep between his knees at every person who entered; the third sat deep sunk in an empty cask; while the fourth balanced himself on one leg out of four of a stool so placed as to permit his hitching his heels on the bar from which the shop-scales ... were suspended over the counter.' One of Fanny's chief protagonists, Edward Bligh, witnesses the men's cruel taunting of a young slave boy who is on an errand for his master; 'drops of agony stood on Edward's brow', but he could do nothing for the boy without betraying his abolitionist sympathies and thus exposing his friends to danger. Elsewhere, Fanny reflects the concern of female abolitionists in Britain for the protection of female slaves against the sexual abuse and exploitation of white men – and she does so in no uncertain terms. Although the word does not actually appear in print, there can be no question in the reader's mind that the overseer Whitlaw attempts to rape the slave girl, Phoebe.

Fanny's main purpose, however, was to expose the hypocrisy of the lynch law, whereby self-appointed courts without legal authority carried out summary justice. In the slave-owning states the law was directed especially against unmanageable blacks.* Fanny gives a

* The originator of the lynch law was Captain William Lynch of Virginia. The first such self-created judicial tribunal took place in Virginia in 1776.

vivid account of a lynching. At one point in the story a white mob approaches the Steinmarks' farm 'with gallows and effigies'. 'It must be observed,' Fanny states, 'that on all occasions when Lynch-law is administered, the real instigators never appear. It passes for the work of passion – a sense of injury – or overwrought enthusiasm on the part of the people; but never as the concerted project of a set of men, who, finding the laws incapable of giving authority as uncompromising as they wish to the iniquitous system which they are determined to pursue, though their country should fall to pieces in the struggle, have devised this appalling means to work their will.' Its adherents claimed that such a 'law' upheld 'the public good, and love of justice, and respect for our glorious constitution, and veneration for the memory of the immortal Washington – and the ever-to-be venerated Jefferson, both of whom approved the institution of slavery, and practised it greatly to their own comfort and advantage'.

Fanny also sought to undermine the other, less extreme arguments in favour of slavery held by otherwise decent-minded folk. She portrays a white woman who found 'all intercourse with [slaves] in some degree painful and degrading. She firmly believed that this marked and hitherto most unhappy race were the descendants of Cain, and her feelings towards them were the result of both superstitious abhorrence and wounded compassion.' 'Her deeply religious spirit was shocked to feel a sort of impious misdoubting of the justice of Heaven, as [the slaves'] degraded and terrible position was developed before her. From this most painful and guilty thought she was relieved by the persuasion which soon took possession of her mind, that this dreadful spectacle was the result of the immutable command of God.' As is evident in *The Domestic Manners*, Fanny had no patience with this 'biblical' view; nor did she have time for the widespread notion that although 'like all other human institutions, [slavery] may be liable to abuse, yet still that it is upon the whole an arrangement which admits of much mutual benefit to the parties'.

Fanny's stance is simple and uncompromising: 'the soul of a black man is like the soul of a white one'. Black or white, people share the same hopes, dreams and fears. Thus she describes Edward Bligh's sister Lucy and the slave Phoebe walking side by side: 'The white and the black girl had each a sorrow at her heart.' When a black mother runs into the woods to escape the sight of her child suffering at the hands of the overseer, Fanny remarks: 'She might have carried with her an anguish the bitterness of which no mother blessed with the power of protecting her offspring can conceive.' So must Fanny herself have felt when keeping vigil by the side of first Arthur, then Henry and finally Emily. To appreciate just how clear-sighted and 'modern' Fanny's views were, one has to realize that most female abolitionists of the period spoke of the black woman not as an equal but as a 'daughter'; they distanced 'themselves from the objects of their benevolence as from their domestic servants'.[8] Fanny insisted that 'the union of the States would never be securely cemented till they were all governed by equal laws, and till every human being who drew breath upon their soil might lift his voice to heaven and say, "I am an American, and therefore I am free." '

At the end of March, six weeks after Emily's death and a month before the publication of *Jonathan Jefferson Whitlaw*, Fanny was thinking ahead to another European excursion and travel book. She was always making plans, which meant she was forever changing them. Thus, she vacillated between a winter season in Vienna and a tour of Italy, long a dream of hers. In the end, she decided to do both, but only if funds were immediately forthcoming. On 28 March 1836 Fanny confessed to her publisher Bentley: 'When I began my literary career I was very strongly recommended not to part with my copy-rights,' but circumstances had changed. 'I will not trouble you by talking of private embarrassments which press me at this moment,' she continued; 'I am told that there is nothing which I have hitherto published which might not still be turned to profit by being reduced to a cheaper and more popular form – but to render this a desirable speculation to the publisher, he should himself be the owner of the copyrights.'

A month later, on the same day she wrote her preface to *Jonathan Jefferson Whitlaw* (27 April 1836), Fanny signed away the copyright for it (£350) as well as for three future books: *The Vicar of Wrexhill* (£400), *Vienna and the Austrians* (£500) and *A Visit to Italy* (£550). She also threw in the copyright for *Paris and the Parisians* for good measure.* Fanny no doubt felt that she had no other choice at the time. However, Fanny does not allow her Widow Barnaby to make the same mistake when discussing the terms for her own work on slavery with a Philadelphia publisher: 'I confess to you that the idea of parting with the copyright of a work which I have *reason* to believe will be very profitable, does startle me. I cannot but indeed consider it equivalent to parting with several thousand dollars' (*The Barnabys in America*).†[9]

When she made this agreement, Fanny was already hard at work on *The Vicar of Wrexhill.* She had not much time before she planned to set off for the Continent, and so she returned to her favourite theme, evangelicalism, about which she could write with conviction and also with relative ease. Fanny's purpose in creating the Revd William John Cartwright, vicar of Wrexhill, was, as *The Westminster Review*'s critic appreciated, to represent 'an Evangelical parson not certainly as all or even the majority of that body actually *are*, but as one of them *might* be, and may probably somewhat resemble'. The broad outline of the story was apparently based on the ordeal which her friend Henrietta Skerrett had suffered at the hands of an evangelical minister.[10] But God is in the details, and memories of her old Harrow neighbour, the Revd John William Cunningham, his mannerisms and habits, as well as her confrontations with him, no doubt provided Fanny with much of her material. The story unfolds as the unctuous Cartwright woos the recently widowed Mrs Mowbray and wins over her daughter, Fanny, with 'holy caresses' and 'the kiss of peace' behind a shrub in the garden. The young Charles Mowbray does not approve of the vicar's cant: 'I deplore . . . the grievously

---

* In another agreement with Bentley made the same day, Fanny also proposes an extraordinary four-volume work to be entitled *The Temporal History of the Pope*. Perhaps Fanny thought she would, possibly with her sons' help, make use of her husband's notes on ecclesiastical history. This proposal was cancelled by mutual consent two years later, in 1838 (BL, Add MS 46612, ff. 137−9).

† Coleridge thought 'the most prudent mode is to sell copyright . . . for the most that *the trade* will offer. By few only can a large remuneration be expected; but fifty pounds and ease of mind are of more real advantage to a literary man than the *chance* of five hundred with the *certainty* of insult and degrading anxieties' (Robert L. Patten, *Charles Dickens and His Publishers*, Oxford, 1978, p. 22).

schismatic inroad into our national church which these self-chosen apostles have made. But as one objection against them, though perhaps not the heaviest, is the contempt which their absurd puritanical ordinances have often brought upon serious things, I cannot but think that ridicule is a fair weapon to lash them withal.' His tactic to win back his newly 'pious' sister is by 'laughing at her rather than making a martyr of her'.

This is also Fanny Trollope's method of attack, for *The Vicar of Wrexhill* is a marvellous satire. Revd Cartwright transforms a little girl into a 'Methodist monkey; her card-boxes, into branch missionary fund contribution cases; her footstools, into praying cushions; and her sofa, into a pulpit and pew'. When the village hears that Mrs Richards has barred the vicar from her door, she is 'refused bread by a converted baker; beer, by an elected brewer; and soap and candles, by the pious, painstaking, prayerful servant of the Lord, Richard White, the tallow-chandler'. And there is the 'Serious Fun-Fair' (in aid of sending a converted Jew, one Mr Isaacs, to do missionary work in Africa), during which 'civil war' breaks out amongst the pious young ladies over who should man the best stalls. Fanny points out, however, that this was common to 'all fancy fairs, bazaars, and charity sales of every class and denomination whatever'. The story ends happily ever after. The Revd Cartwright, exposed for what he is, flees Wrexhill and 'a whole flight of evangelicals followed their incomparable vicar, till the pretty village of Wrexhill once more became happy and gay, and the memory of their serious epidemic rendered the inhabitants the most orderly, peaceable, and orthodox population in the whole country'.*

Fanny delivered the manuscript to Bentley in July 1836, just before setting off for the Continent. It must have been difficult for her to stay in the house at Monken Hadley after Emily's death, with her

---

* Fanny is possibly paying tribute to her other Harrow friends, the Grants, with her depiction of the Mowbrays' kindly if eccentric neighbours, Sir Gilbert and Lady Harrington. When Charles Mowbray and his other sister Helen despair over their new stepfather, they walk over to the Harringtons' house where Sir Gilbert, an old military man declares: 'Just let me know all that is going on in the garrison, and if I don't counter-plot them, I am a Dutchman.' Perhaps Colonel Grant had planned a similar campaign to outwit the Harrow bailiffs.

maid Mrs Cox as her only companion for much of the time. The plan was for Fanny, together with Tom, an Oxford friend of his with the Wildean name of Bunbury, Mrs Cox and the faithful Hervieu, to set off for Paris, pick up Cecilia who was still with the Garnetts and then proceed to Vienna. From her brother's house in 'Little Chelsea' (called Heckfield Lodge after their father's old vicarage), Fanny requested that Bentley deliver the bill which he owed her, 'for I have not only to get it discounted' at a loss, 'but afterwards turned into travelling money'.[11] As she prepared to depart – as a tourist rather than a bankrupt this time – Fanny must have truly appreciated her widow's cap, which Mrs Longueville 'was wont when in playful vein to call "the cap of liberty" '. 'Women always do so much better when they are left quite to themselves!' (*Charles Chesterfield*).

On 21 July 1836 the Trollope party assembled at Anthony's Northumberland Street lodgings before taking the night mail coach to Dover, from where they crossed the Channel *en route* to Paris. 'Once more, my dear friend, we are on the wing, or rather on the wheel . . . There certainly is in the blood of our race a very decided propensity to locomotion; for though we all cordially love our home, our English home, and have even, after comparing it with other resting-places, declared without a dissentient voice that none can equal it, yet the sight of a map as we sit in our chimney-corner sets us all madding again, and through each successive winter night our lengthening talk goes on of mountains and valleys yet unseen, the fever becoming stronger as the season advances, till just when our own garden is full of flowers . . . off we are again.' So Fanny begins *Vienna and the Austrians*, written, like its predecessor, in epistolary form. The Trollopes spent only a few nights in Paris, during which time the critical Mrs Garnett observed that 'Mrs Trollope is grown very fat.'[12]

En route Fanny, in her inimitable fashion, took all the 'road-side deviations' possible: 'Besides the gratification derived from their positive beauty, one always feels a sort of triumph, as if one had *stolen a march* upon all other travellers, by seeing more than was put down in the road-book.' As they travelled through Stuttgart, Tübingen, Augsburg, Salzburg, Munich and Ratisbon, Fanny braved steep slippery slopes and dark dank caverns, not to mention damp bed sheets and, on the Konigsee, 'a chapel to which pious pilgrims often repair, and a gasthaus to which no one should ever repair at all, if they can possibly avoid it'. Fanny tried the mineral baths at Cannstadt which she thought 'very refreshing' though the water looked 'extremely like dirty soap-suds ... defying the most accurate eye to discover what adventures it may have met with since first its uncrystal-like stream welled forth from its native font'. So as not to miss the mountain scenery of the Tyrol, Tom, Hervieu and Mr Bunbury 'clung about the outside of the vehicle, like squirrels fondly hanging upon the outside of their cage'. 'For more than half this day's journey they quitted it altogether, preferring the liberty of running *ça et là*', and Cecilia and Fanny soon joined them.

Mrs Cox, who seems to have stayed inside the carriage, probably thought her fifty-seven-year-old mistress mad for, according to Frances Eleanor Trollope, 'she was far more intolerant of the rough side of things than the rest of the party'.[13] She was also more xenophobic. At an inn along the Danube river Mrs Cox, to her horror, discovered a loose plank in the floor beneath her bed. On the good authority of some gothic tale or other which she had read once, she insisted it was the custom of the country for innkeepers to murder their guests in their beds and dump the bodies in the river through just such a trap door. Mrs Cox refused to accept that, if her body were dropped through the floor beneath her bed, she would land in the kitchen, not the river. However, she was half right about the innkeeper. The next morning, as they were setting off from the inn, Tom, Hervieu and Mr Bunbury were seized by the proprietor and his friends, and threatened with an axe until they met his demands for more money.

After a week travelling on a very uncomfortable cargo barge along the Danube, the party arrived at their final destination, Vienna. It was then mid-September, and the 'season' had not yet begun. Watching for 'society' to flock back to the city from their summer retreats, Fanny felt as though she had arrived at the theatre early and was left 'waiting for the curtains to draw up'. In the meantime, the party settled into apartments in the Höhen Markt, which comprised seven poorly furnished rooms with tiny beds and a small kitchen, at £100 for the season. Better, cheaper accommodation was to be found in the suburbs, or 'faubourgs', but, as Tom recalls, 'nobody who was anybody would have dreamed of living on the outside of the sacred barrier of the wall', only three miles long, which encompassed the tiny, and no doubt claustrophobic, metropolis.

Fanny had chosen Austria as the subject for her next travel book for the simple reason that the country was 'terra incognita to England'. An Austrian told Fanny that, a few years before, *The Edinburgh Review* had spoken of Prague as the capital of Hungary. When he asked the editor 'to restore to Bohemia her much-loved capital', the latter replied that it was the *Review*'s 'principle never to contradict themselves, and therefore [he] must beg to decline'. To an English person, Vienna indeed seemed like another world: its coffee-houses and markets were teeming with Hungarian gypsies, Bohemian wagoners, caftaned Jews from Galicia, and 'wild-looking figures from Transylvania', as well as Slavonians and Croats – all in exotic costume. Poor Hervieu was overwhelmed by the wealth of material for his pencil. 'It was not a little amusing,' Fanny remarked, 'to watch [Hervieu] chasing her [a bizarrely costumed old woman] round and round the market, while she was bargaining for a goose at one place, eggs at another, and cabbage at a third, till at length he fairly booked her.'

By October the season had begun, and 'whatever was the "Open Sesame" my mother possessed,' Tom remarks, 'the fact was that all doors were open to her'. Appropriately, the first 'Open Sesame' she uttered got Fanny and her party into a reception given by the Turkish sultan's representative in Vienna. The English guests were very impressed with the Turkish attendants wrapped in colourful veils until they were told that at such state galas 'it was the custom for the foreign legations to assist each other by the loan of attendants, and that upon the present occasion the Pope's Nuncio had obligingly furnished a considerable number'. Cecilia thought 'His Mussulman Excellency', with whom she conversed in French, 'great fun': 'he never uses any verbs, but he gets on very well without them'. He did, however, have a large stock of profanities, as Cecilia later discovered when she reminded the warm-blooded Turk one cold March evening that snow still lay on the ground. 'Neige! Cré nom! Neige, mois de mars? Diable, Diable! Pas joli. Diable!'[14]

Once Fanny had passed the 'introductory Rubicon', as she calls it, she then had to negotiate the incredibly rigid and complex society in which she found herself. There was, of course, *la société boursière*, the bankers and financiers, who between them kept Viennese society afloat but who were wholly excluded from the *beau monde*. However, above the *beau monde* there was yet another, more élite group who called themselves *la crème*, or if they were feeling particularly smug, *la crème de la crème*.* 'There is nothing very extraordinary or out of the natural course of things,' Fanny comments, 'in this wish to form a clique, or tribe, or clan, apart' and even their 'foolish little cabalistic vagaries' do no real harm. But she thought their rules of exclusion absurd. A member of the self-appointed *crème* would not think of dancing with anyone not of *la crème*: 'Young ladies, indeed, had better learn who's who, before they dance in a cotillon.' Fanny also warns the unanointed not to get too close to *la crème*, especially the ladies, at a social gathering for 'an almost preternatural exaltation of the voice into a sharp shrill scream in addressing each other, is the great external symbol of the clique'.

Fanny Trollope's personable, clever, but unconventional ways must have seemed like a breath of fresh air to the Viennese, smothered as they were in cream. In her subsequent novel, *A Romance of Vienna*, Fanny is probably recalling her own experience when she describes the good-humoured elderly Irishwoman, Mrs Palmer, who has taken up residence in that exotic city.† 'She was kindly, frankly, and hospitably received by the whole circle that forms "the society" par excellence of Vienna (a kindness, frankness, and hospitality, by the way, that can only be duly appreciated by those who have witnessed it).' She became 'a privileged person among the *haute volée* of Vienna; and might go, come, wear, say, or do whatever pleased her, with less risk of encountering blame or cavil of any kind'. Fanny was constantly stepping across the social boundaries, discussing literature with a Jewish widow and her daughter (the only cultural conversation to

---

* The *OED* mistakenly claims that this now familiar expression was first used of the Austrians by the actress and author Fanny Kemble in 1848. It is probable that, like 'go the whole hog', *'crème de la crème'* was introduced into idiomatic English by Fanny Trollope.

† Mrs Palmer is also, like Fanny, 'an active, fearless, enterprising traveller'.

be had in Vienna, according to Tom), taking coffee with a wealthy financier and then describing both these encounters to the *beau monde*, whose curiosity about the 'lower orders' was insatiable.

Certainly Princess Metternich found the unpretentious English-woman with a gift for gentle sarcasm particularly refreshing. Prince Metternich's third wife, Melanie, was a beautiful young woman whom many thought proud and haughty, but whom Fanny found intelligent, with a little 'piquante sauciness of manner'. The princess was devoted to her husband, but she was clearly bored with the society around her. The Trollopes were invited to numerous receptions at the Metter-nichs' residence; they also dined *en famille* with the aristocratic couple and were welcomed on Christmas day to watch the children distribute the 'pretty toys, bijous, and bon-bons' which hung on the Christmas tree.* The princess even condescended to sit for a portrait by Hervieu – on the condition that Fanny be with her during the sittings. 'J'ai le plaisir,' she later wrote to the English matron, 'de vous connaître telle que vous êtes, bonne, simple, bienveillante, et loin de tout ce que effroie et éloigné des reputations littéraires.'✝ Fanny's own portrait of her husband, Prince Metternich, however, is disappointing. Like Lafayette before him, she clearly worshipped the elderly statesman, the chief architect of the Congress of Vienna (1815). But, as *The Spectator* would rightly observe, 'honey is less pungent than gall, especially when produced from the *apis Trollopiana*'.‡[15]

Happily, the *Apis Trollopiana* was back on form when describing Vienna's Carnival season which brought in the new year of 1837. 'The balls are incessant,' Fanny wrote to Julia Pertz, 'the dinner parties hardly less so, and a visit or two in the interval is very necessary to guard against accumulating access [excess] of incivility.'[16] She notes in *Vienna and The Austrians* that during Carnival the city 'is in truth just now suffering severely from an access of waltzes', Strauss

---

* The tradition of the Christmas tree was not known in England until Prince Albert introduced it later in the nineteenth century. The scene which Fanny describes is like something out of Tchaikovsky's *Nutcracker*.

✝ 'I am fortunate to know you as you really are: good-natured, unpretentious, generous, and far from being frightening or aloof as your critics made you out to be.'

‡ 'Trollopian bee'.

waltzes. 'A pretty waltz, well played, has great charms; and till now I have always fancied that I had rather an over-weening liking for this species of composition; but I am now fain to confess that I am weary of it.' Fanny longed to hear Mozart once more. The dinners were no less excessive. 'There is one much-prized delicacy to be considered as indispensable', *pâté de foie gras*. 'Out of twenty-one dinner-tables I have missed it but at two; and as, moreover, no ball-supper is considered as perfect without it, the number of invalided geese must be greater than it is agreeable to think of.'

By early spring, Fanny was ready to quit Vienna. Just before Christmas Tom had, after more than a year, been summoned from his travels to take up his teaching post in Birmingham and Mr Bunbury returned home with him. The 'dissipation' of the Carnival season had taken its toll on both Cecilia and Fanny. Even more serious, Mrs Cox had begun to take on airs. She had been an interesting, if unreliable, source of information for Fanny from her 'conversations' with the German cook – the cook spoke no English and Mrs Cox spoke no German. However, Fanny wrote to Tom in Birmingham, 'you never saw anything more ludicrous than the general elegance of her manners since she has made the acquaintance of a set of fine English servants here'. 'She dined with a party of these exquisites the other day, and told us on her return that she had drunk four glasses of champagne; and that one *lady* who sat next her, declared she should like to drink three bottles!' Still under the influence of the champagne, she admitted that she suggested to one of the footmen, 'an uncommonly clever' chap, that he should write his own book of travels.[17]

In the end, they stayed on in Vienna until the late spring of 1837. 'My residence here has proved greatly more expensive than I anticipated,' Fanny had written to Bentley in February, 'so that in truth I cannot start upon my return till my funds are replenished.' She asked Bentley for an advance of £100, which he was to direct to her son Anthony, whom she had authorized to receive payment.*[18]

---

* Fanny also wrote to John Murray asking if there was any money forthcoming from the second edition of *Belgium and Western Germany* (3 December 1836: John Murray Archives.)

Fanny, Cecilia and Mrs Cox were finally able to start for England at the end of May. In her last entry, written *en route* from Rotterdam, Fanny is already looking forward to getting among 'my Hadley roses, which I left in full bloom, and hope to find in full bloom' (*Vienna and the Austrians*).

Fanny returned to her roses and worked hard to dispel the sad memories of Emily's death, which must have still lingered about the place. 'The scheme on which all her thoughts had fixed themselves ever since the full consciousness of her liberty had succeeded to the agitation of her unexpected widowhood, was the collecting round her a circle of amiable, intellectual, and accomplished people' (*The Young Countess*). Soon Hadley became 'a centre of social enjoyment and attraction for all, especially the young', Tom recalls. 'Our society consisted mainly of friends staying in the house, or of flying visitors from London. As usual, too, my mother soon gathered around her a knot of nice girls, who made the house bright. For herself she seemed always ready to take part in all the fun and amusement that was going; and was the first to plan dances, and charades, and picnics, and theatricals on a small and unpretending scale.' Fanny had always liked to have around her 'a coterie of pretty looking, well-dressed young ladies', and she no doubt felt Cecilia needed the companionship. They, for their part, showed that sort of enthusiasm for Mrs Trollope 'with which girls are sure to attach themselves to such female friends as, having qualities and talents to attract, are some years their senior, and seem willing to meet them on terms of mental equality' (*The Blue Belles of England*). Not surprisingly, Anthony was one of those frequent visitors from London, for 'at Hadley there were pretty girls with whom he could flirt'. 'There is,' he noted, 'or was, a pretty woodland lane, running from the back of Hadley Church, through the last remnants of what was once Enfield Chase. How many lovers' feet have crushed the leaves that used to lie in autumn along that pretty lane' (*The Bertrams*).

Fanny got in Marsala and others wines from London and Oxford merchants. She borrowed tables, benches and garden chairs for some outdoor extravaganza from her neighbour Mrs Green. This lady, the doctor Mr Hammond's sister, was married to Joseph Henry Green,

Samuel Taylor Coleridge's literary executor.* Her other great friends in Hadley besides Dr Hammond and the Greens were the Revd R. W. Thackeray, the young William Makepeace Thackeray's relative, and his family. Visitors included Hervieu, of course, Fanny's brother, Henry Milton, who came with the latest issue of Dickens's *The Pickwick Papers* in his pocket, Harrow friends, including the Grants and Sir William and Lady Milman, various West Country friends, Marianne and Henrietta Skerrett from London, Fanny's publishers, John Murray and Richard Bentley, Mary Fauche from Ostend, and Mary Clarke who, having temporarily abandoned her Paris salon, Fanny reported to Julia Pertz, 'continued to amuse us all exceedingly'. Fanny also invited Captain 'Pendulum' Kater's two sons down from Cambridge. Poor old Kater had died of a stroke in 1835, after having suffered for some time from hypochondria. However, Fanny's affection for the father did not transfer itself to the sons: the elder of the two 'is reckoned *very* agreeable – and I will not deny it – yet – I think him very superficial and *tant soit peu Humbug*',✝ the younger 'is the most perfect personification of Dullness I ever remember to have met'.[19]

One guest who might have set Cecilia's heart a flutter was the dashing Baron, Charles Hugel, who had just returned from a six-year tour of India, Australia, Van Diemen's Island and other exotic realms when the Trollopes were in Vienna. According to Frances Eleanor Trollope, Cecilia had taken 'a romantic, girlish interest' in the baron after hearing that he 'had been desperately in love with the beautiful Melanie Metternich before her marriage, and that when she accepted the Prince he set off in despair for the uttermost parts of India'. Perhaps it came as a shock to the twenty-year-old Cecilia when she discovered that the baron had not come to Hadley in search of love. Cecilia is rather a difficult person to make out. On a visit to Bruges in the summer of 1835 Mrs Garnett had thought her 'a fine handsome girl, but a little disposed to idleness and something of a fine lady – too much so, I fear'.[20] But one feels that Cecilia was a sensitive and

---

* Samuel Taylor Coleridge had died in 1834. One wonders if Joseph Green and Fanny discussed the poet's Bristol days.
✝ 'a little bit of a Humbug'.

shy young woman, for she had a kind, sympathetic ear.* Certainly, the tragedies of the last few years, the deaths of her father, brother and sister, had taken their toll on her.

Cecilia began to find consolation in the tenets of Tractarianism, known also as Puseyism or the Oxford Movement. Its leaders, John Keble, Edward Pusey and John Henry Newman, all Fellows of Oriel College, Oxford, sought to rediscover the spirituality of Anglicanism, most notably through the restoration of the ornate Church architecture, and the rituals which went with it, which had been stripped away in the seventeenth century. They also emphasized the Church of England's social obligations, particularly in the growing city slums. Tom was at Oxford in 1833 when Keble preached the sermon which effectively launched the movement, and he may have brought one or two of their *Tracts for the Times* home to Julian Hill to satisfy his family's curiosity. 'In those days,' Anthony remarks, looking back to this period, 'the Tracts were new, and read by everybody, and what has since been called Puseyism was in its robust infancy' (*The Bertrams*). In 1843 Tom wrote to a Parisian friend, 'all the world here are taking part on one side or the other in the great Puseyite controversy – with the exception of a few lookers-on at the fight like myself'. It was 'filling every man's – (and woman's, worse luck) mind and mouth', he added, perhaps thinking of his sister.

Anthony's mother undoubtedly belonged to the same church as Mrs Grantley in *Barchester Towers*: 'the high and dry church, the High Church as it was some fifty years since, before tracts were written and young clergymen took upon themselves the highly meritorious duty of cleaning churches' (*Barchester Towers*). But she was not as openly dismissive of High Anglicanism as Tom was, and she evidently tried hard to fathom Cecilia's faith. In *Hargrave*, published in 1843 at the height of the Oxford Movement, Fanny makes an odd little digression: 'If I believe in any earthly means of improving the moral and social condition of man, while in his mortal state, it is in the influence of a pious and pains-taking

---

* Fanny once told Tom to 'make Cecilia your confidante' (undated fragment: Trollope Family Papers, Special Collections, UCLA Library).

Anglo-Catholic priesthood,' but, like everything else, it is open to abuse. In the summer of 1837, when Cecilia was nearly twenty-one, Fanny no doubt began to feel the first glimmer of concern for her daughter's future. She would never have wanted Cecilia to suffer the fate of a governess, to have to learn 'to exchange the deep-felt realities of her own individual existence, for a succession of domestic connections, all alike foreign to her blood and her heart, yet all alike demanding as lively and demonstrative an interest, as if indeed each successive set, formed her only family, and her only care' (*Tremordyn Cliff*). But would the increasingly pious Cecilia be open to love and marriage?

It must have been a relief, and something of a surprise, when Cecilia returned the affections of Anthony's fellow clerk at the Post Office, John Tilley. Fanny later confessed to the Garnetts that she did not think Cecilia 'could have attached herself so strongly to any person'. 'Let no old gentlemen, nor old ladies either,' Fanny warns in *The Attractive Man* (1846), 'take it into their venerable heads that they can comprehend the young workings of the tender passion in their offsprings' hearts!' One can imagine that Tom and Anthony might have been hopeless at recognizing when Cecilia and Mr Tilley needed to be left alone to share a tender moment. 'Nobody thought it necessary to have letters to write in some particular part of the mansion where the lovers were not; neither did any one discover upon finding themselves *en tiers* with them, that they had left gloves, pocket-handkerchief, or smelling-bottle elsewhere' (*The Blue Belles of England*). Their mother would no doubt have devised ways to get her sons out of the room.

But, notwithstanding all the summer outings and winter festivities which Fanny organized, 'she was at her table at four in the morning, and had finished her work before the world had begun to be aroused' (*An Autobiography*). In the late summer of 1837 she set to work on a strange book, entitled *A Romance of Vienna*, a sort of gothic novel inspired by her fascination with the city, from its Jewish synagogues to *la crème de la crème*. Meanwhile, on 4 July 1837, only a month after her return to Hadley, Fanny had completed the manuscript of *Vienna and the Austrians*. Once again,

Fanny found that travel writing just did not pay. The book was to sell well (*The Literary Gazette* thought Hervieu's engravings 'excellent accessories to Mrs Trollope's letterpress'), but her sojourn in Vienna had cost her £700, for which she received £500 from the book and no more, for Bentley now owned the copyright.

Nevertheless, Fanny was determined to make Christmas 1837 a happy occasion: it was to be the first Yuletide holiday with all the family together, without the spectres of death or illness around them, since Julian Hill in 1833. Yet, she wrote to Tom almost apologetically, 'don't think me extravagant for this. I have worked so hard, that I think I may try to give my children a merry Christmas with a safe conscience.'[21] 'The Christmas-day passed as Christmas-days generally do, with more mirth in the kitchen than in the parlour, but a good deal of eating in both' (*The Ward of Thorpe Combe*). Fanny's New Year's resolution for 1838, she wrote to Bentley, was 'to remain in England and, as I hope, to put my time to better profit'. When she had invited Bentley to dine at Hadley the previous August, he had made some offhand remark about her idea, first mooted nearly two years earlier, of a monthly periodical. It was enough, however, to reawaken in Fanny 'all these speculations, and moreover set me upon discovering what friends I had who would be likely to help me' in such a literary enterprise, to be called *The Literary Museum and New Political Register.*[22]

Fanny had more than enough friends who would have been thrilled to contribute to a monthly magazine. Since the publication of *The Domestic Manners of the Americans* she had been inundated with manuscripts and letters from old and new friends alike, asking her to recommend them to a publisher. And Fanny usually obliged. She thanked Mr Horness for his 'admirable sermon, and his graceful and touching drama'; she wrote to Bentley on behalf of her Belgian acquaintance with the 'buxom' wife, Count Melfort, and also the unknown Mr S. Gnorowski, 'a distinguished Polish officer and political refugee'. She contacted all three of her publishers, Whittaker, Murray and Bentley, in an effort to help the literary career of Harriet Garnett, who grew increasingly envious of Fanny's success and income over the years, but to no avail.* Fanny also thought she could rely on more experienced and well-established authors, in particular, Mary Russell Mitford. Fanny had earlier been frustrated in her attempt to review, at the author's request, Miss Mitford's *Our Village* for Murray's *Quarterly Review*. She discovered to her dismay that women did not write for the *Quarterly*.[23]

Fanny also envisaged that *The Literary Museum* would be a family affair. Tom and Anthony, who had each acted as researcher, courier and literary agent for their mother, had both expressed a wish to follow in her footsteps as a writer. More than two years earlier, soon after Anthony began at the Post Office, Fanny had petitioned John Murray to help her youngest son 'find employment either by correcting the press, or in some other occupation of the kind', which he could do in the evenings. Anthony himself then applied to Richard Bentley, hoping to contribute, as he put it, 'lucubrations of my own in any of the numerous periodical magazines &c which come out in such swarms'.[24] But neither Murray nor Bentley had need of his services. In his autobiography Anthony claims that during this unhappy period in London he 'knew very few friends who would receive me into their houses'. 'Can it be that any mother really expects her son to sit alone evening after evening in a dingy room drinking bad tea, and reading good books?' (*The Small House at Allington*). This is unfair. Anthony received invitations from London friends and family to dine out and to meet other young men who were beginning to make a literary reputation for themselves, such as the poet Henry Taylor and John Forster, literary advisor to the publisher Chapman & Hall and Dickens's great friend. But he was too unhappy and dissatisfied to take them up, preferring instead to pursue his literary interests alone, planning his *magnum opus*, a history of literature,

---

* Harriet attempted two novels, *The Jersey Laurel*, set in America, and *The Italian Exile*, and numerous translations of German and French works into English; only one of these, a translation, found its way into print – at Harriet's own expense. In an effort to boost her career, Fanny printed one of Harriet's poems, a tribute to Chateaubriand, in *Paris and the Parisians*. Henry Milton had even sent *The Jersey Laurel* to his old publisher, Longman. In a letter to Julia, Fanny laments Harriet's want of occupation and her '*tristesse*' (2 August 1838: Garnett–Pertz Papers).

setting down his erudite views in 'a commonplace book' and building castles in the air.

Tom, five years Anthony's senior, had been longing for a literary career ever since his mother's first book was published, in 1832, when he proposed writing a book on Germany – a bad idea which Fanny had quickly squashed. Five years later Tom was no nearer his ambition. During the school holidays of 1837 he had spent six weeks travelling in Normandy to gather material for a series of articles on the province, which he intended to submit to the editor of *The Literary Museum and Political Register* – his mother. Anthony's fellow Wykehamist and 'Tramp', Walter Awdry, accompanied him. For Tom as well as for his brother, a lot was riding on the magazine's success. A middle-aged Anthony Trollope looked back on his family's project in his short story, 'The Panjandrum', which he contributed to the journal he was then editing, *St Paul's Magazine*, in 1870. 'It is now just thirty years ago since we determined to establish the "Panjandrum" Magazine.' 'We were all heart,' Anthony writes of the would-be contributors, including Mrs St Quinten, a lady devoted to 'literary pursuits'. 'I do not think,' Anthony remarks, 'that we dreamed of making fortunes; though no doubt there might be present to the mind of each of us an idea that an opening to the profession of literature might be obtained through the pages of the "Panjandrum."' Like the Trollopes, the group aspired to write 'short political essays which should be terse, argumentative, and convincing, and at the same time full of wit and frolic'.

Fanny was optimistic that Bentley would publish *The Literary Museum and Political Register*. Her confidence as an author had greatly increased since the successes of *Paris and the Parisians* and *Jonathan Jefferson Whitlaw*. The enthusiastic reception which she had encountered in Vienna and the compliments she had received from those who had read the proofs of *The Vicar of Wrexhill* had also boosted her morale. She now thought that her name as editor would do much to promote the '*decidedly strong saucy* conservative publication', which was to expose 'to ridicule and contempt what is worthy of it'. When *The Vicar of Wrexhill* appeared in September 1837, Fanny's reputation as a satirist was secured. The book created a minor sensation. Tory politicians used the book as ammunition against the Liberal government's proposed legislation to restructure and reform the Church, declaring on one occasion that a particular clause was 'worthy of the Vicar of Wrexhill himself'. Many readers did not think she had gone far enough (one such urged her to continue to employ her pen in 'this holy cause').[25]

However, there were rumblings from the critics that such satire was unfit material for a lady; 1837 was the year that the young Queen Victoria took the throne, and Fanny Trollope's sharp satirical wit, the result of her Georgian upbringing, was increasingly seen as 'coarse' and 'vulgar'. In its review of *The Vicar of Wrexhill, The Athenaeum* observed that Mrs Trollope 'scents out moral deformities with a sort of professional eagerness, and applies herself to their exposure, regardless of the uncleanness into which her task may lead her'. *The Times* worried that 'NO moralist (and above all, no woman moralist) can use such weapons as these without injuring herself far more than her adversary.' Thackeray, by this time fully recovered from Mrs Trollope's picnic of two years previously, expressed the true Victorian's view: Mrs Trollope 'had much better have remained at home, pudding-making or stocking-making, than have meddled with matters which she understands so ill'.*[26] Bentley obviously felt that women, though they might be authors, should not aspire to be editors. *The Literary Museum and Political Register* never got off the ground. Nor did *The Panjandrum* in Anthony's story: the group part company 'under the walls of Marylebone Workhouse'.

Tom, meanwhile, found himself 'engaged in the perpetual, and somewhat hopeless, task of endeavouring to manufacture silk purses out of sows' ears', that is, to turn the adolescent sons of Birmingham tradesmen into classical scholars. Tom had the same complaint as Anthony, for he had no company in the evenings but his book, teapot and pipe at Mrs Clements's lodgings. Yet he did not feel virtuous,

---

* The young poet Elizabeth Barrett wrote to her friend, Mary Russell Mitford, after she had read *The Vicar of Wrexhill*: 'What a lamentable book – & to be written by a woman . . . And I just remember that you call her "your accomplished friend!" – Ah! But she can't be a *friend* of yours in the real strict sense. Mrs Trollope can't be Miss Mitford's friend!' (29 September [1837]: *Letters of E. B. Browning to M. R. Mitford*, I, p. 47).

merely lonely and frustrated.* By September of 1837 Tom 'had almost made up [his] mind to quit Birmingham', or so Fanny feared, to cultivate a writing career alongside hers. She had encouraged both Tom and Anthony to follow their literary pursuits after hours, but she was worried sick that one or both of them might give up a decent salary.† Fanny knew she would be left to pick up the bill – and there was Cecilia still to think of. She was happy to urge Bentley to publish her son's tour of Normandy but, at the same time, she felt obliged to warn Tom: 'Recollect my dearest Tom before you throw to the dogs an independence of £200 per annum: *what* it is that you look for from me.'

I am fifty-eight years old, my dear Tom. And although, when I am well and in good spirits, I talk of what I may yet do, I cannot conceal from you or from myself, that my doings are nearly over . . . Think you that my work is not dull too? Think you that at my age, when the strength fails and the spirits flag, I can go on forever writing with pleasure? . . . You know what heavy, uphill work I have hitherto had; and may pretty well guess what the effect on me would be, of sanctioning your throwing up a certain maintenance, before I have cleared myself from the claims that still hang upon me.[27]

Over the next few months, while smoking a pipe over the teapot

---

* It was probably at this time that Tom addressed a poem, describing his loneliness and boredom, to an old Oxford friend (MS in Trollope Family Papers, Special Collections, UCLA Library). The last stanza reads:

> But the clock on the stairs has struck ten,
>   And my landlady's hanging her head.
> For in this distant country men
>   At ten think of going to bed.
> There's tobacco in every shop,
>   And a pipe on't, (encouraging thought)
> For a while the blue-devils may stop,
>   And reconcile me to my lot.

† Fanny also worried about her sons' meals. In one letter she consoles Tom on his miserable pork dinner, adding 'poor Tony is marvellously unlucky in his feeds' (27 September 1837: Parrish Collection).

in his Birmingham lodgings, the twenty-seven-year-old Tom plotted to leave King Edward's Grammar School without being a burden to his mother. At one point he thought of returning to Oxford to be ordained; Fanny intended to consult their old Harrow friend, the Revd Henry Drury, on the matter. As a priest Tom could pursue his own interests while tending his flock, as his grandfather had done, or, even better, take up a fellowship at Oxford, which would leave him with even more free time. Tom also continued to submit ideas and manuscripts to various publishers, but he only met with discouragement. Fanny consoled him by reminding Tom of her own literary failures – the rejected manuscripts, and those returned unopened – before the success of *The Domestic Manners*.[28]

Cecilia's announcement of her engagement to John Tilley in the spring of 1838 changed everything. Fanny was delighted for Cecilia; she would also have breathed a sigh of relief that she no longer had a daughter financially dependent upon her. But at the same time the thought must have struck her that she now faced the future alone. 'After much consultation and very many walks together round the little quiet garden at Hadley,' Tom later recalled, 'it was decided between us that I should send in my resignation of the Birmingham mastership, defer all alternative steps in the direction of any other life career, and devote myself, for the present at least, to become [my mother's] companion and squire.' Even before Cecilia's engagement and Tom's decision, Fanny had planned to leave Hadley and find a house in London for herself and Anthony. She knew that her youngest son was unhappy, and that he often did not have enough money to pay his long-suffering landlady. What was more, 'four hours out of every day,' she wrote Julia Pertz in January 1838, 'is too much for Anthony to pass in, or on, a coach, which is what he now does – and moreover I find the necessity of seeing London people, whether for business or pleasure, recurs too frequently for convenience or economy.' 'I love my pretty cottage here much and we have fallen into one or two cordial village intimacies that I shall regret to lose', but Fanny was looking forward to being 'among clever literary people' in the metropolis. On the eve of her departure, Fanny's neighbour, Joseph Henry Green, wrote some lines in her honour which show just how much she had enlivened the little village of

Hadley. Sadly, Coleridge's talent had not rubbed off on his literary executor, but the sentiment is there.

To Mrs Trollope
Once more we gather in thy social hall,
To feel what memory will in vain recall:
We mourn, tho' mingling smiles with our farewell,
The joy of which thy presence was the spell.
Our verdant hill no longer tempts thy stay,
To haunts more bless'd the Muses lead the way.[29]

CHAPTER ELEVEN

The Life and Adventures
of a Clever Woman

Before moving back to London, Fanny, Tom and Cecilia spent a few weeks that July at Dover, taking the sea air and visiting a Bristol cousin who had married the rector of St Mary's, Dover, the Revd Mr Maule. Perhaps Tom took a leaf out of his brother's book and indulged in some harmless flirtations on the pier, enjoying 'the waving outlines of the delicately draped ladies beside him, each clinging to him, and enveloping him with their floating scarves and veils, like colours clinging round a flag-staff in a breeze'. Dover became the setting for one of Fanny's best novels, *The Lottery of Marriage* (1849), in which she describes the casual goings-on amongst the 'gauche riche' and impoverished aristocrats who flock there in the summer. 'Great licence is given to invitations at a watering-place. A yachting-party, either given or postponed, which must depend more upon the caprices of the weather than on anything else, may both cause and excuse this.'

But the city beckoned. In August the Trollopes, including Anthony, set up house at 20 York Street, Portman Square. Perhaps, like the impoverished mother and daughter in *The Lottery of Marriage*, Fanny and Cecilia travelled with a chest full of 'stage props', an Indian screen, small Persian carpets, muslin curtains, squares of crimson satin and lace, embroidered cushions, footstools, a few richly bound volumes, smelling-bottles, ivory and tortoiseshell knick-knacks, all put to the same use: 'decorating and concealing' the invariably ghastly

263

decor of rented accommodation. After only half a day's work 'the effect produced upon the respective landlord and landladies, upon first entering their own domains afterwards, was ... a feeling of remorse for having let such beautiful rooms so shamefully cheap'.

Through her many London friends, including her publisher Richard Bentley and the actress Mrs Bartley, Fanny did indeed find herself 'among clever literary people'. Her reputation had preceded her. Anna Drury, the daughter of Fanny's old Harrow and Brussels friend, William Drury, tells the story of a luncheon party where the poet Samuel Rogers turned to the old lady next to him and declared, 'They told me Mrs Trollope was to be here. She has written a great deal of rubbish, hasn't she?' 'Well,' Fanny immediately retorted, for she was the old lady in question, 'she has made it answer!' 'It was too good a story to keep to herself,' Anna Drury recalled, 'and she told it to us in the drawing-room with great glee. But Mr Rogers was so annoyed when he found what he had done, that he very soon took his departure.'[1]

Other introductions were more successful. Fanny became close friends with 'Highways and Byways' Grattan and Judge Haliburton – one Irish, the other from Nova Scotia – both good company and full of fun. Thomas Haliburton, whom Fanny met through their publisher Richard Bentley, was a Supreme Court judge back home and author of the popular 'Sam Slick' series, recounting the adventures of a shrewd Yankee clock maker. Like his books, Tom recalls, Haliburton had to be 'taken in rather small doses'. The large, burly red-faced man was also an inveterate tobacco chewer, and tried his hardest to introduce Tom to the habit, probably just to tease Fanny, whose opinion on the matter was well-known. Although Bentley wined and dined Haliburton in London, the author received no remuneration (except for an engraved silver plate) from the publisher who had effectively pirated the original American edition of *Sam Slick*. Perhaps Fanny told the judge about the silver plate which her father had begrudgingly received from the city of Bristol. Fanny had much in common with the very Irish Colley Grattan, author of *Highways and Byways, or Tales of the Roadside*, for he too had fled to the Continent to escape his debts, ending up in Brussels at about the same time the Trollopes were in Bruges. He urged Tom to try his hand at a novel: 'Fiction, me boy, fiction and passion are what readers want!'

Grattan and Haliburton, both outsiders and both given to moodiness, clearly found Fanny a good friend and listener. 'My spirits are not the same, and when alone I suffer a good deal of depression,' Haliburton confided to Fanny in 1843 when he was back in England. 'Please God, on one or other of the days you have mentioned, I shall have the pleasure to shake you by the hand, and assure you of the attachment, of yours always, Thos. Haliburton.' Writing to Fanny from Boston, Massachusetts, where he was made British consul, Grattan finds comfort in the notion that he has ' "troops of friends" – you being one of the troopers – no matter how few others there may be'. Fanny always returned her friends' affection. She remarked to Julia Pertz of the Grattans: 'They are a very charming family and I miss their society greatly – They passed last winter in London, and we were much together spite of our differing politics.'[2]

Another London literary acquaintance was Charles Dickens. Fanny had first met Dickens in March 1838 at one of Mrs Bartley's soirées, where he asked to be presented to the famous Mrs Trollope. Fanny was no doubt curious to meet Dickens, the author of *The Pickwick Papers* and *Oliver Twist*, which was then appearing before the public in monthly instalments. Dickens was also the editor of *Bentley's Miscellany*, launched only a year after Bentley had turned down Fanny's *Literary Museum and New Political Register*. Mrs Trollope was on Bentley's list of contributors to the *Miscellany* – all names which Dickens thought 'excellent'.* In Mrs Bartley's drawing-room that spring she saw standing before her a young man of twenty-six, a year younger than Henry would have been had he lived. 'I had a good deal of talk with him,' she told Tom. 'He is extremely lively and intelligent, has the appearance of being *very* young, and although called excessively shy, seemed not at all averse from conversation.'[3]

Despite the lunch parties, dinner parties, soirées and house guests,

---

* Fanny still had not given up the idea of her own periodical. Two months later, in May 1838, she offered to submit a sketch of the sort of journal she imagined to John Murray. Murray showed no interest (FT to Murray, 30 May 1838: John Murray Archives).

Fanny carried on with her rigorous writing schedule. One visitor, the young Anna Drury, recalls 'an unlimited allowance of books by day, and, as I shared her room, a most delightful talk at night until one next morning!' They discussed Anna's 'youthful aspirations and plans for possible stories' and Fanny gave her the wisdom of her own experience. However, as she had to be back at her writing-desk between four and five o'clock the next morning, Mrs Trollope told Anna that she could not stay up that late again. In August 1838, soon after moving into York Street, she had agreed with Bentley to write a new preface and notes for a fifth edition of *The Domestic Manners*, for which she would receive £50. It was to be published in a cheap one-volume version, part of 'Bentley's Standard Library of Popular Modern Literature'.* By the end of 1838, on 26 December, her next book appeared in print: 'the redoubtable widow Barnaby', 'conjured up – a jovial New Year's guest – by the busy wand of Mrs Trollope', as *The Athenaeum* remarked. Fanny had first mentioned the Widow Barnaby to Bentley the previous Christmas: 'I have a character that will give occasion I hope for some comic situations, from efforts and pretensions resulting from vanity, a vulgar desire for fashionable homily.'⁴ After the success of *The Vicar of Wrexhill*, Fanny could command £600 for *The Widow Barnaby*. It was to be Fanny's best-loved and most enduring novel.

Bentley had evidently wanted the new creation to be a broad comic sketch of a *parvenue*, or 'upstart', who pushes her way into society. However, Fanny had in mind something equally comical but slightly more subtle. 'I am by no means certain that such a character comes *correctly* under the denomination of a *parvenue*,' she explained to Bentley.⁵ In fact, Martha Barnaby, née Compton, has a background very similar to Fanny herself and to her many readers from the growing middle class. Martha's father was a clergyman from an old, respected Devonshire family; her mother was the daughter of a tallow chandler. The story opens in the West Country in about the year 1813, with the Napoleonic Wars still raging on the Continent. The

---

* Fanny had eventually succeeded in wresting the copyright for *The Domestic Manners* from Whittaker. The new preface and notes highlight and strengthen Fanny's opposition to slavery.

seventeen-year-old Martha, 'tall, dark-eyed, fresh-coloured, bold-spirited', and her younger sister Sophy, with light hair, grey eyes and delicate complexion, spend their time flirting with the handsome, red-coated officers of the local militia. Sophy elopes with a lieutenant and soon dies, leaving behind a little girl, Agnes. But, as for Martha, the officers marched into town, whispered sweet nothings in her ear and then marched right out again. Finally, having reached the tender age of thirty, she does the sensible thing and marries an older man with money who adores her.

Yet, this is only the beginning of the story, for by chapter ten Martha's husband, Mr Barnaby, is dead. 'This event produced an entire and even violent change in her prospects and manner of life.' 'It is from this epoch that the narrative promised by the title of "Widow Barnaby" actually commences, the foregoing pages being only a necessary prologue to the appearance of my heroine in that character.' The rest of the book follows the widow, 'fair, fat and forty',* 'feathered, rouged, [and] ringleted' on her travels around southern England and through the complex strata of English society: from the shops of Exeter to the assembly rooms and wealthy merchants' houses of Clifton (the scene of Fanny Trollope's girlhood), and from the pump rooms of Cheltenham to London drawing-rooms. The vulgar Martha's one overriding ambition is to be accepted into fashionable society wherever she goes. 'Mrs Barnaby never quoted Shakespeare, or she would probably have added here, – "Why, then the world's mine oyster, which I with *wit* will open." '

Martha Barnaby is a female rogue, yet the reader cannot help cheering her on in her struggle to make something of herself without the advantage of youth and on a limited income. 'We hear much of the beautiful freshness of hope in young hearts just about to make their first trial of the joys of life; but it is quite a mistake to suppose

---

* In *Hargrave* (1843), a Frenchwoman 'remembered an anecdote of George the Fourth [and one of his mistresses,] which had led to a phrase, now passed into a proverb, always pleasantly recalled by beauties of a certain age. "Faat, farre, and forté." ' 'Fat, fair and forty were all the toasts of the young men' is a line from John O'Keeffe's *Irish Minnie*. In *The Lottery of Marriage* (1849) Fanny adapts the expression yet again when describing Mrs Codrington: 'fat, fair, and not near forty'.

that any such feeling can equal the fearless, confident, triumphant mastery and command of future enjoyment, which dilates the heart, in the case of such an outcoming widow as Mrs Barnaby.' In her search for a second husband she might cut a ridiculous figure, but she is no fool. 'Mrs Barnaby was not altogether so short-sighted as by-standers might suppose . . . and not the best-behaved and most discreet dowager that ever lived, was more firmly determined to take care of herself, and make a good bargain, *if she married again* than our flighty, flirty Widow Barnaby' (*The Widow Barnaby*). In creating Mrs Barnaby, Fanny had the pleasure of throwing the critics' favourite word for her, 'vulgar', back in their faces. And they loved it. *The Times*, which had often felt compelled 'to cry out against the errors and literary crimes of Mrs Trollope', waved the white flag. 'Pardon, sweet Barnaby, that we should have spoken ill of your brethren; henceforth your name shall be a signal of truce to us – a teaspoonful of oil to allay and spread smoothly over a whole ocean of critical anger.' 'The Widow Barnaby is such a heroine as never before figured in a romance,' *The Times* critic continues. 'Her vulgarity is sublime. Imaginary personage though she be, everybody who has read her memoirs must have a real interest in her.' The 'amiably disagreeable', 'delightfully disgusting' Widow Barnaby, 'such a jovial, handsome, hideous, ogling, bustling monster of a woman as maid, wife, and widow, was never, as we can recollect, before brought upon the scene'.[6]

The Widow Barnaby was an original, and as such she delighted her readers. However, the book is also a self-conscious pastiche of other well-known novels. Fanny conjures up the archetypal cad of Jane Austen's fiction: the fifteen-year-old Sophy Compton is carried off by a red-coated officer, as was the young Lydia Bennet in *Pride and Prejudice* – the man's name is Willoughby, the same name which Jane Austen gives to the scoundrel who steals Marianne Dashwood's affections in *Sense and Sensibility* (like *The Widow Barnaby*, set partly in Devonshire). Fanny also gives a nod to Dickens's *Pickwick Papers* when Martha Barnaby sets her sights on the eligible Lord Mucklebury. Intentions are misconstrued and, like Mrs Bardell, Samuel Pickwick's landlady, Mrs Barnaby decides to sue Lord Mucklebury for breach of promise. However, her attorney 'soon perceived that there was nothing in these highly-scented, but diminutive *feuilles volantes*' – which Lord Mucklebury dubs the 'Barnaby Papers' – 'at all likely to produce any effect on a jury approaching to that elicited by the evidence of the learned and celebrated Sergeant Buzfuz on an occasion somewhat similar' – that is, the famous action of Bardell *v.* Pickwick. Both Pickwick and Mrs Barnaby end up in debtors' prison, at the Fleet.

Fanny might well have conceived of her own 'picaresque' novel while listening to her brother Henry reading aloud from the latest issue of *The Pickwick Papers* at Hadley. She certainly believed in the salutary effects of comedy, which enables us to 'laugh ourselves into health again' (*Paris and the Parisians*). However, she did not appreciate Dickens's humour as much as others did, in particular, her brother Henry, who swore that each new number 'out-Pickwicked Pickwick'. 'I doubt,' she had written to Mary Russell Mitford in August 1837, 'if I have so much fun in me as heretofore, for I do not laugh at "Boz" half so perseveringly as most others do, and as I will not put this obtusity down to my want of capacity, I must attribute it to my age. You, my dear friend, who are . . . some half score of years or more my junior, can judge of these popular pleasantries more fairly, and I really wish you would tell me, if you go on number after number sharing the ecstasy that causes thirty thousand of the "Pickwick Papers" to be sold monthly.'[7] Nevertheless, Fanny did appreciate Dickens's success with the very recent innovation of publishing original novels in parts. (Only classic stories, such as *The Pilgrim's Progess*, had previously appeared in this way.)

Fanny saw that serialization, whether in separate monthly numbers or in magazines, would allow the author to have several books on the go, increasing his or her output and, more importantly, income. Moreover, the publisher normally paid for each issue or chapter as it arrived on his desk, thus easing the perennial problem of writers, cash flow. Fanny was to publish seven novels in serialized form, including one which was itself breaking new ground. Between May 1839 and June 1840 Henry Colburn published *The Widow Married; a Sequel to the Widow Barnaby* in *The New Monthly Magazine*, a periodical with a circulation of about 5,000 which aimed to provide middle-brow entertainment. The reading public had never before been presented with such a thing as a sequel. The character of the Widow Barnaby was her inspiration. 'With all her faults, and she has *some*,' Fanny later remarked, 'I love her dearly: I owe her many mirthful moments, and the deeper pleasure still of believing that she has brought mirthful moments to others also.'[8] Fanny also loved the widow's popularity and the revenue it brought her.

The widow has remarried twice by the opening of the sequel, and, although she is a lot fatter and no less vulgar, especially when 'preparing her three chins, and her thick articulation of dignified words' for posh visitors, she has also grown more astute. She and her husband, the bogus Major Allen, agree to 'carry on the war upon the same principle, setting our wits to work, one and all, to save money when nobody is looking at us, and to spend it in good style when they are, [so that] we may go on making an excellent appearance, and with no danger of getting into a scrape neither'. She also passed on an important lesson to her equally vulgar daughter, Patty: 'I do sometimes think . . . that great abilities, thorough real cleverness I mean, is a better fortune for a girl, that is supposing she is tolerably well-looking, than almost any money in the world.' *The Widow Married* is not simply 'more of the same'. Rather, it mimics real life: characters from the first book have grown older and moved on. The orphaned niece Agnes is married with children and only sees her aunt Barnaby now and again; Agnes's father, the wayward Lieutenant Willoughby, of whom we only caught a glimpse in the first novel, returns from his self-imposed exile in Jamaica an older and wiser man.

This sequel to the adventures of Martha Barnaby was still only in Fanny's mind when the Trollopes celebrated Christmas and New Year in 1838–9. The holiday was very much a family occasion, especially as Cecilia's wedding day, 11 February 1839, was fast approaching. Besides her children and their 'jovial New Year's guest' (the Widow Barnaby in her first incarnation), Fanny did invite one other, probably her future son-in-law, John Tilley, or perhaps the faithful Hervieu who found himself alone at Christmas. 'Will you come and share our roast beef and plum pudding?' Fanny wrote. 'We are literally to wait upon ourselves during the evening – but you shall have tea and coffee and cold chicken and punch at ten o'clock.'[9]

Cecilia's wedding, despite its being February, was a joyous, though evidently small, affair. It took place at the nearby church of St Mary's, Bryanston Square, and the Trollopes' old Harrow neighbours, Mary and Kate Grant, were bridesmaids. Presumably Tom or Cecilia's uncle Henry gave the bride away.

The congregation no doubt started to feel the midwinter chill during the probably rather lengthy homily of the presiding vicar *cum* bibliophile, the Revd Thomas Frognall Dibdin. He was a close friend of Harry Drury, and the Trollopes enjoyed his company whenever he called in for a chat at 20 York Street. Once Dibdin 'fell tooth and nail upon the Oxford Tracts men, and told us of a Mr Wackerbarth, a curate in Essex, a Cambridge man, who, he says, elevates the host, crosses himself, and advocates burning of heretics'. One hopes that Cecilia was not this fanatical. Although amusing enough in a drawing-room, Dibdin was diabolical in the pulpit. Tom recorded in his diary that one Sunday afternoon Dibdin preached 'with much gesticulation, emphasis, and grimace the most utterly trashy sermon I ever heard'. An old lady who overheard Tom remarked: 'Well, it is a very old story, young gentleman, and it is mighty difficult to find anything new to say about it!'[10] Anthony would have a similar sermon in mind when he lamented: 'No one but a preaching clergyman has, in these realms, the power of compelling an audience to sit silent, and be tormented. No one but a preaching clergyman can revel in platitudes, truisms, and untruisms, and yet receive, as his undisputed privilege, the same respectful demeanour as though words of impassioned eloquence, or persuasive logic, fell from his lips' (*Barchester Towers*).

After the bride and groom had departed the wedding breakfast, Fanny together with Tom and Anthony accompanied the two bridesmaids home to Hayes, a village just outside London where Colonel Grant and his family were then living. The next day the fifty-nine-year-old Fanny returned to London aboard the Great Western Railway. 'Her first journey on a railroad,' Fanny wrote of Mrs Morrison in *The Three Cousins*, 'caused a paroxysm of rapture that exhaled itself in sketching a network of railways over the earth and under the sea.' Ten days later, on 20 February 1839, she was on board the mail train heading north. Thirteen hours and one new engine later, she and

Tom – and presumably Hervieu as illustrator – arrived at Manchester and its factories to research her next book, *The Life and Adventures of Michael Armstrong.*

From the 1830s onwards industrialized England had been engaged in continual, but very slow and tortuous, efforts at reform, especially among the poor of the parish and the women and children of the factories – with good and bad results. Evidence was gathered and presented to government committees; influential journals, such as *The Quarterly Review*, published hard-hitting articles; both learned and inflammatory pamphlets were printed and distributed. Fiction, too, played its part. Harriet Martineau showed herself an advocate of social reform in her collections of stories, *Illustrations of Political Economy* (1832–4) and *Poor Law and Paupers Illustrated* (1833). Dickens entered the fray with *Oliver Twist* (1837–8), a condemnation of the Poor Law of 1834, which had transferred the care of the poor from the local parish community to centralized government workhouses. Fanny had already written two reforming novels: one against slavery, *Jonathan Jefferson Whitlaw* (1836), the other against the excesses of evangelicalism, *The Vicar of Wrexhill* (1837). Like Dickens, she had a journalist's nose for a good story. Tom recalls that his mother, having taken 'a great interest in the then hoped-for factory legislation, and in Lord Shaftesbury's efforts in that direction, determined to write a novel on the subject with the hope of doing something towards attracting the public mind to the question, and to visit Lancashire for the purpose of obtaining accurate information and local details.'

Lord Shaftesbury (then Lord Ashley), who was the leading advocate of factory reform in Parliament, took Mrs Trollope's interest in the matter seriously. 'We carried with us,' Tom continues, 'a number of introductions from Lord Shaftesbury to a rather strange assortment of persons, whom his lordship had found useful both as collectors of trustworthy information, and energetic agitators in favour of legislation.' There was one Reuben Bullock in Macclesfield and the radical bookseller John Doherty, an Irish Roman Catholic, in Manchester. Fanny and Tom invited Doherty to dine at their hotel one evening, 'but it was, I remember, with much difficulty that we persuaded him to do so, and when at table his excitement in talking was so great and continuous that he could eat next to nothing'. There was also a Mr Oastler, 'the Danton of the movement', six feet tall and the 'very *beau-idéal* of a mob orator', as well as the serious Revd Mr Bell, who introduced Fanny to the enlightened factory owners, Wood and Walker. Lord Ashley told Fanny: 'They will show you the secrets of the place, as they showed them to me.' Tom and his mother toured the factory floors, visited the slums and drove out to 'a miserable little chapel, filled to suffocation' with workers eager to hear the zealous Revd J. R. Stephens preach on the evils of the factory system. These were the strangest of bedfellows for the short, rather plump matron; even her association with Lord Ashley was odd for, although he was a Tory and an old Harrovian, he was also an evangelical churchman.

The story of *Michael Armstrong* begins with the chance meeting between a young factory boy, Michael Armstrong, and a Manchester heiress, Mary Brotherton. Michael's personal story of poverty and abuse sets Miss Brotherton on a moral journey to learn the truth about working conditions in the cotton mills. Her father, while he was alive, 'like most others of his craft, was not in the habit of indulging his family by exhibiting to them the secret arcana of that hideous mystery by which the delicate forms of young children are made to mix and mingle with the machinery, from whence flows the manufacturer's wealth'. Mary sees for herself young children amongst 'the whirling spindles urging the little slaves who waited on them to movements as unceasing as their own', surrounded by 'the scents that reek around, from oil, tainted water, and human filth'. She visits the slum of Ashleigh where Michael lives with his dying mother, 'the most deplorable hole in the parish', with its 'long, closely-packed double row of miserable dwellings, crowded to excess', 'crawling infants, half-starved cats, mangy curs' and 'an odour, which seemed compounded of a multitude of villainous smells, all reeking together into one'. All around the slum 'forests of tall bare chimneys, belching eternal clouds of smoke, rear their unsightly shafts towards the sky, in lieu of verdant air-refreshing trees'. 'The black tint of loathsome factory seems to rest upon every object near it. The walls are black, the fences are black, the window-panes (where there are any) are all veiled in black.'

Mary Brotherton's journey was, in fact, the author's own. Like Fanny, she pays a visit to the Revd Mr Bull (a thinly disguised Revd Mr Bell), an advocate of the Ten Hour Bill to limit children's working hours. Fanny even includes real people in the novel: through Revd Bull, Mary meets the exemplary mill owners, Wood and Walker. Like Fanny, 'on the question of negro slavery she had from the very earliest infancy heard a great deal'. Her father had been an abolitionist, drinking 'Mr Wilberforce's health after dinner when he had company at his table' and lamenting the fate of 'the sable sons of Africa, all uttered comfortably from a soft arm-chair, while digestion was gently going on, and his well-fed person in a state of the most perfect enjoyment'. But, 'concerning the nature of the labour performed in the factories by whose chimney her pleasant park was surrounded – the age, sex, or condition of the labourers – the proportion of their daily existence devoted to toil . . . of all this Mary Brotherton was as ignorant as the sleek lap-dog that dozed upon her hearth-rug'.

Mary must confront and acknowledge the hypocrisy of her father; for Fanny, it was the hypocrisy of a nation. Perhaps when faced with the wretched conditions in the slums Fanny, like her heroine, was at first inclined to blame the poor themselves for their wretched plight. Perhaps she, like her heroine, for a brief instant drew comfort from the thought '(as [had] multitudes of amiable-minded ladies and gentlemen besides), that it was perfectly impossible such horrors could exist on the glorious soil of Britain, unless indeed, as in the case before her, the unhappy drunkenness of the father plunged his helpless family into a degree of poverty'. But 'out of the mouths of very babes and sucklings' – Mary only has to hear the testimony of one child to realize that she has been deceiving herself. 'Mother said he took to it [i.e. drink], as most of the others do in all the mills, on account of hating to come home so, when we young ones comes in from work. I have heard mother say that father cried when I, that was the biggest, com'd home first beaten and bruised with the strap and billy-roller.' As in her anti-slavery novel, Fanny identifies a parent's inability to protect a child as the greatest horror, and ultimate expression, of powerlessness in society. There is no doubt that Fanny herself had felt this same impotence in the face of illness and, to some extent, poverty. Both Fanny and her heroine Mary Brotherton now knew that there could be no excuse for such horrors on British soil. 'How comes it that ALL the people – the only phrases I have heard upon the subject were very comprehensive – how comes it . . . that ALL the people, young and old, who work in the factories are classed as ignorant and depraved? . . . If thousands of human beings in a Christian country are stigmatized as wicked, because their destiny has placed them in a peculiar employment, that employment ought to be swept for ever and for ever from the land, though the wealth that flowed from it outweighed the treasures of Mexico.'

In her story 'A Manchester Strike' (1834), the young reformer Harriet Martineau advances the precept which was already a commonplace of nineteenth-century social thought, that the poor must help themselves. Mrs Trollope, on the other hand, understood that these men, women, and especially the children, were simply not in a position to do so. The naturally pragmatic and optimistic Fanny had confidence in the possibility of reform, if only enough pressure could be put on the government to eradicate the evils of child labour and sixteen-hour working days. She aimed not merely to stir up indignation in her readers, but to spur them to action: 'Let none dare to say this picture is exaggerated, till he has taken the trouble to ascertain by his own personal investigation that it is so. It is a very fearful crime in a country where public opinion has been proved (as in the African Slave Trade) to be omnipotent, for any individual to sit down with a shadow of doubt respecting such statements in his mind. If they be true, let each in his own little circle, raise his voice against the horrors detailed by them, AND THESE HORRORS WILL BE REMEDIED' (*Michael Armstrong*).[11]

This was the first novel which Fanny produced in serial form. It came out in twelve separate monthly numbers, from March 1839 to February 1840. She alternated her exposé of the factory system, vividly illustrated by Hervieu, with the merry adventures of *The Widow Married*, which was appearing simultaneously in *The New Monthly Magazine*. The publisher Henry Colburn thought it worth his while to pay Fanny £800 each for *The Widow Married* and *Michael*

*Armstrong.** Illustrated monthly numbers, costing only one shilling, could mean a very large circulation for *Michael Armstrong*, especially with the aggressive advertising for which Colburn was famous. He announced in *The Examiner* (3 February 1839) that *The Life and Adventures of Michael Armstrong, the Factory Boy* was to be 'printed and embellished uniformly with "Pickwick Papers," "Nicholas Nickleby," &c.' – neither of which was published by Colburn. Dickens was understandably annoyed. 'The whole affair of Mrs Trollope is a "do,"' he wrote to a friend. 'If Mrs Trollope were even to adopt Ticholas Tickleby as being a better-sounding name than Michael Armstrong, I don't think it would cost me a wink of sleep, or impair my appetite in the smallest degree.'[12]

Dickens had, in fact, visited the Manchester cotton mills in November 1838, three months before Fanny's trip north, to see for himself the factory conditions which Lord Ashley had brought to public notice and possibly to find some new material for *Nicholas Nickleby*, which had begun to appear in monthly parts the previous April. He had also hoped that Lord Ashley would provide him with introductions to his friends in the north, but it is not known if he obliged the young author. In any case, after viewing working conditions in the mills, Dickens vowed to 'strike the heaviest blow in my power for those unfortunate creatures, but whether I shall do so in the "Nickleby," or wait some other opportunity, I have not yet decided'. Dickens modelled his enlightened factory owners, the Cheeryble brothers, on the Grants, whom he had met in Manchester, but the appearance of *Michael Armstrong* almost certainly stopped Dickens from focusing on the cotton mills of the north in *Nicholas Nickleby*. He would not return to the subject until *Hard Times* in 1854. He declared that the market for one shilling numbers was not big enough for both *Michael Armstrong* and *Nicholas Nickleby*, but he was confident that he would win the circulation war, for his novel had already been running for

* In June 1839 Fanny was able to send her son Anthony to Colburn to collect a cheque for the sixth number of *Michael Armstrong* and the fourth number of *The Widow Married*. Anthony's unpunctuality was obviously still a problem: she tells Colburn 'in order to permit his getting to his office at the usual time it will be necessary for him to call rather before ten' (FT to Colburn, 17 June 1839: Misc. Papers, MSS & Archives, New York Public Library).

nearly a year when *Michael Armstrong* came along in March 1839. 'I will express no further opinion of Mrs Trollope, than that I think *Mr* Trollope must have been an old dog and chosen his wife from the same species.'*[13]

Dickens obviously had difficulty coming to terms with the fact that his principal rival was a woman, and one, moreover, who was old enough to be his mother. Fanny was an immensely popular author who, like Dickens, was at home with both broad comedy and the 'social novel'; and she shared with Dickens the physical stamina and facility with her pen required to keep two books going simultaneously in monthly issues (she was the only female novelist at the time to do so). And, brilliant as Dickens was, Fanny excelled him in one thing: her female characters are strong and vibrant women, of all ages, who think and act for themselves. Dickens's literary repertoire included only two types of women: young insipid angels and old drunken harridans. Fanny's characters, even the male ones, were mentioned in the same breath as those of Dickens: 'What things these are,' Mary Russell Mitford wrote, 'the Jack Sheppards, and Squeers, and Oliver Twists, and Michael Armstrongs – All the worse because of their power to move men's souls.'†[14]

Michael Armstrong certainly made a powerful impact on the critics. *The Athenaeum* suggested that, 'among an ignorant and excited population to which her shilling numbers are but too accessible', Mrs Trollope's novel was 'scattering firebrands among the people' and 'setting fire to the four quarters of the kingdom'; 'the most probably immediate effect of her pennings and her pencillings will be the burning of factories'. *The Bolton Free Press*, whose readers in the industrial town just outside Manchester would be in the firing line, declared 'the author of *Michael Armstrong* deserves as richly to have

---

* Just before the storm broke, in January 1839, Fanny tried to get Dickens round for dinner at York Street – perhaps to discuss her proposed journey to Manchester – but he apparently never made it (Dickens to FT [30 January 1839]: Dickens, *Letters*, I, p. 490; see also his letter to her [6 January 1839]: ibid., VII, p. 797).

† Jack Sheppard, raised in a workhouse to become one of the most infamous of the eighteenth-century highwaymen, was the subject of a novel by W. H. Ainsworth (1839); Squeers is, of course, the evil headmaster of Dotheboys Hall in *Nicholas Nickleby* (1838–9).

eighteen months in Chester Gaol as any that are now there for using violent language against the "monster cotton mills." '* *The New Monthly Magazine* declared:

> It is a great mistake, and a still greater injustice, to suppose that Mrs Trollope offers *The Factory Boy* as anything like a pendant to the admirable works of Mr Dickens, which have appeared under a similar form. The great and leading characteristic of those works, is humour – broad even to caricature . . . But *The Factory Boy* had a deeper design, and aims at the accomplishment of that design by other, still more rare and estimable means. It is evidently intended to be a deep, moral satire, having a serious, and even a solemn purpose to accomplish, and good alone as the ultimate end; every step of the path being made irresistibly attractive by the inexhaustible amusement that is scattered over it.[15]

This last opinion was not, however, a bona fide review but rather a bit of 'puffery' on the wily Colburn's part, for he both owned *The New Monthly Magazine* and published *Michael Armstrong*. Despite Colburn's best efforts, Dickens was right about the circulation war. *Nicholas Nickleby* had got there first and, although there are some very amusing scenes, *Michael Armstrong* was perhaps a little too earnest. Fanny wrote: 'The "Widow" continues to be in great favour. But between ourselves, I don't think any one cares much for "Michael Armstrong" – except the Chartists. A new kind of patron for me!'[16]

The year 1839 was an extraordinarily productive one for Fanny. Not only did she keep up the monthly instalments of *Michael Armstrong* and *The Widow Married* for Colburn, but she also wrote a novel for Bentley, *One Fault*. It is almost impossible to say how she managed it, although Tom's services as travel and literary agent, research assistant and, no doubt, editor must have been invaluable. 'If I had

---

* In 1839 the Revd J. R. Stephens, whose meeting Fanny attended outside Manchester, had been sentenced to eighteen months imprisonment for using seditious and inflammatory language.

not found out that *time* was so very precious a commodity I think I should set off today either to pay a visit to Mrs Milton at Chelsea – or to you at Whitehall,' she wrote her brother Henry in March. 'But it must not be – Colburn was here last night – and Tom settled with him (for I escaped the job by *retiring* to dress for a party).' She ends her note with the cry, 'to work, to work, to work'. She apparently cut down on her morning visits but not the evening parties – nor on her travels. At some point in the early summer Cecilia wrote to her mother with the news, very obliquely worded, that she was expecting her first child. 'I have made my husband promise dearest darling mother to frank this letter to you without reading it . . . I scarcely know how to put "in black and white" as Hervieu calls it the communication I wish to make.' Cecilia confessed that she cried and cried: 'I fear I am only too happy for it seems impossible that I should remain perfectly happy for a great while and now there is no single circumstance I could complain of if I sought for one. Much as I loved my own dear John before I was married and happy as I fancied I should be as his wife I had not conceived that I should be so completely happy for I did not know that I should love him infinitely more than ever.'[17] Fanny immediately made plans – as soon as she had recovered from the serious throat infection which confined her to bed for several weeks – to visit Cecilia in Penrith, on the edge of the Cumbrian hills, where her husband was surveyor of the Post Office's northern district.

While in Penrith, from the end of July to the end of September 1839, Fanny and Tom took the opportunity to call upon the *literati* of the neighbouring Lake District. The author Captain Thomas Hamilton had long ago thrown aside his unhappy first impression of Fanny at Niagara Falls. He had been very kind to Cecilia when she first moved to Cumbria, and he took Fanny and Tom sailing on Lake Windermere. The day did not turn out quite as the Captain had hoped, for there was a sudden change in the weather and the three of them returned 'in the condition of drowned rats'. Fanny was later to use this incident in her novel *The Laurringtons* (1844), set in the Lake District. It was apparently Hamilton who introduced Fanny and Tom to his neighbour, Wordsworth.[18] Tom was not impressed with the sixty-nine-year-old poet when they visited him at Grasmere.

'The evening, I think I may say the entire evening, was occupied by a monologue addressed by the poet to my mother, who was of course extremely well pleased to listen to it.' Throughout it all Wordsworth continued to look down 'with a green shade over his eyes even though it was twilight'. Tom decided that it was all a 'performance . . . got up to order, and repeated without much modification as often as lion-hunters, duly authorized for the sport in those localities, might call upon him for it'. Apparently John Tilley, as Post Office surveyor, and Wordsworth, who received £400 a year as distributor of stamps for Westmorland, were often at loggerheads over best practice. The Trollopes also saw much of Herbert Hill, Robert Southey's son-in-law and an old schoolfriend of Tom, who was living in nearby Rydal.*

Fanny thoroughly enjoyed her stay in Penrith, not least because she saw that Cecilia and her husband were very happily married. To Julia Pertz she described her son-in-law as 'a very admirable person, and all the minor matters of income, house, and so forth are quite as I could wish, so that I feel that *that* part of my business on earth has been very well accomplished. Nothing can be prettier than her residence. Her windows look out upon the pretty lake mountains, which though on no very large scale, are beautiful in no ordinary degree from the boldness of outline, and the great variety of picturesque combination which they display.'[19] It was here, with this view before her and in the pleasant atmosphere of her daughter's home, that Fanny tried to come to terms with the disintegration of her own marriage in the largely autobiographical novel *One Fault*. Perhaps Fanny had, like her heroine Isabella, 'pondered deeply on the mysterious web' in which she had been entangled, and on 'the airy nothings' that had made her 'so unspeakably wretched in the midst of seeming happiness' in her marriage. In the early years Fanny had been as happy as Cecilia with her husband. Thomas Anthony was in many respects an admirable man, but she had come to realize that 'probity,

* Fanny had written to John Murray, asking for an introduction to Southey, but there is no record of their meeting (FT to Murray, 24 July [1839]: John Murray Archives). Perhaps it is just as well, for Southey is reputed to have returned a packet of Charlotte Brontë's poems with the comment: 'literature cannot be the business of a woman's life, and it ought not to be'.

liberality, temperance, observant piety, may all exist with a sour temper'. 'Many a human being has been hung in chains whose justly punished deeds have not caused one hundredth part the pain to his fellow men which a cross temperament is sure to give' (*One Fault*).

Fanny returned to London in the late autumn where she completed *Michael Armstrong* and *One Fault* before setting off for Paris in early December 1839.* Her trip to the French capital, she explains to Julia Pertz, 'is a promise of long standing to Anthony, whose official duties prevent his sharing the travelling delights of his errant family, and who on this occasion will be permitted to be with us for a few weeks – a couple of months we hope – which will give him, perhaps the only opportunity he may have of seeing la belle ville'.[20] Fanny and Anthony travelled to Paris via Boulogne in order to spend some time with Harriet Garnett and her mother, who had recently moved to the port town owing to increasingly straitened circumstances. (Tom had gone ahead to tour Germany before rendezvousing with his family in Paris.) Harriet wrote to her sister Julia regarding Mrs Trollope: 'I never saw her looking better, thinner, and I think with less colour – her manners gentler & better, and as kind as possible.' In Paris Fanny, together with Anthony and Tom, once more haunted the salon of Miss Mary Clarke and Madame Récamier, attended the English ambassador's receptions and enjoyed the musical soirées of Princess Belgiojoso. Fanny was not quite sure how she would be received by the Italian patriots in Paris following her trip to Austria, where she had so openly consorted with the enemy, for the Austrian Empire still occupied the Italian states of Lombardy and Venetia. With a sigh of relief Fanny wrote to Cecilia that Pepe 'seems quite to have forgiven me, dear soul, for all my *Austrian* sins'. Despite her admiration of the Austrians and especially Metternich, she remained sympathetic to the cause of Italian independence. She asked a London publisher (probably Murray or Bentley) to review the general's work

---

* Colburn also published *Michael Armstrong* in a three-volume edition in December 1839, although the parts continued to come out until February 1840. Bentley published *One Fault* in three volumes in 1840. *The Widow Married* continued to appear in Colburn's *New Monthly Magazine* until June 1840.

on Italy: 'However much I may differ from you on some political questions,' Fanny remarked, 'the state of – "Sad and sunken Italy" is not one of them.'*[21]

'Mrs Trollope is more than ever the fashion in Paris,' Mrs Garnett wrote to her daughter Julia on 8 March 1840. 'Not a fine ball or a soirée at any Ambassador's that her name is not mentioned in the papers.' 'She is the most indefatigable person at sixty-six' – in fact, she was two days short of sixty-one – 'I ever heard of. She brings out novels in succession and makes doubtless a fine income.' Fanny herself wrote to Julia: 'I might truly say that I have never had a single hour disengaged after my first week here. I look back upon it all as if I had been in a mill whirling round and round with unceasing velocity – and truly sometimes I have felt somewhat giddy.' And to Cecilia she confided: 'Three parties a night, sometimes too beginning with a dinner, is too much to bear – I go to bed almost when it is time to get up – and of *work*, I do very little indeed. But all this will I trust be amended speedily.' And if all this were not enough, Fanny had the end of the world *and* the birth of her first grandchild to worry about. She wrote to her daughter in Penrith in January 1840: 'The comet that is to eat us up on the 6th *has been seen*. If the predictions prove true, this letter will be so scorched before it reaches Penrith, that you will be unable to read it. However, as you will yourself be a cinder, it will not so much signify!' Nevertheless, in reponse to the news that Cecilia had given birth to a baby girl, she thought it worth adding that 'her being named Frances Trollope, is of all my honours and glories, the one I like best'. The Garnetts put a typically cynical gloss on the situation, remarking that Cecilia is 'very proud & fond of her baby, tho' she never liked other people's babies or children'. The young mother 'preferred her mother's coming to the christening instead of the birth, & Mrs Trollope was nothing loth to exchange the gaieties of Paris for a sick room'.[22]

In Paris Fanny met Lady Rosina Bulwer, the estranged wife of the

---

* One Italian patriot, Count Gonfaloniere, told Fanny that when he was imprisoned by the Austrians for thirteen years, Metternich wanted to furnish the count with books from his own library to pass the time, but the emperor replied that 'the object of imprisonment was not amusement' (F. E. Trollope, *Frances Trollope*, I, p. 313).

author Sir Edward Bulwer (later Sir Edward Bulwer-Lytton). Fanny did not yet consider herself either too old or too famous to make new friends and lend them her support when it was called for. Bulwer's father, an army man, had bullied his wife, and the pattern repeated itself when his son Edward married, against his mother's wishes, Miss Rosina Doyle Wheeler, an Anglo-Irish beauty whose own parents lived apart. After enduring her husband's infidelities and violent temper, Lady Bulwer obtained a legal separation in 1836. Two years later Bulwer took their two children from Rosina, and when Fanny Trollope met her in 1839 she was living, lonely and embittered, in the rue de Rivoli, Paris. That year Rosina published her first novel, *Cheveley, or the Man of Honour*, in which the villain is clearly a portrait of her husband. Lady Bulwer was very handsome, intelligent and, above all, passionate. She could also amuse with her withering comments about people. She called her publisher Colburn an 'embodied shiver' which, Tom comments in his memoirs, 'will bring a smile to the lips of those . . . who remember the little man'. (Dickens called him a 'sneaking vagabond'.) Rosina once wrote to Fanny: 'I hear Lady S— has committed another novel, called *The Three Peers*, no doubt *l'un pire que l'autre!*'* She also had a penchant for melodrama and was always pleading poverty. (On their separation Bulwer made an allowance of £400 a year to his wife.) Tom tells of one occasion when, having complained for days of feeling unwell, she turned on Fanny with tears in her eyes when the latter suggested she see a doctor: 'How *can* you tell me to do any such thing, when you know that I have not a guinea for the purpose?' At that moment in walked a servant announcing that the tradesman wanted payment for the little silver spurs and ornamented silver collar which Lady Bulwer had ordered for the 'ceremonial knighting of her little dog Taffy!'[23]

Rosina, although more than twenty years her junior, had much in common with Fanny. They both wrote to supplement a modest income, and they shared a publisher in Colburn. Fanny could no doubt sympathize with Rosina's unhappy marriage. Only a few months before Fanny had written in *One Fault* that the wife is 'the

* 'worse than the other'.

principal victim' of a man's abuse. 'Father, mother, brothers, sisters, nay, even children, if the torment become intolerable, find resolution to struggle for, and pitying friends to aid in the separation necessary to their tranquillity ... But if a wife tries this, she is disgraced ... may be robbed of her children, if she have any, and can be but scantily and cautiously supported by her friends, let her conduct have been ever so blameless.'* Unfortunately for Lady Bulwer, whatever her conduct before the separation, her outrageous behaviour afterwards exasperated all her friends and lost her most people's sympathy. Even when in March 1840 she successfully prosecuted her husband's agents for breaking into her apartments and stealing papers, few stood by her. Fanny, however, remained by her side throughout the trial. Back in England the *Morning Post* reported that Mrs Trollope had entered the courtroom with Lady Bulwer and 'appeared to watch the proceedings with great anxiety'.[24] The vindictive Bulwer (Rosina always referred to him as 'the reptile') retaliated by stopping all correspondence between Rosina and her children.†

---

* Fanny may have had in mind the infamous case of Caroline Norton, who left her violent husband in the mid 1830s and was denied access to her children. Fanny would have known her, for she contributed a piece, 'The Lake of Canandaigua', to *The English Annual* of 1835, which was edited by Mrs Norton. Mary Fauche, Fanny's girlhood friend who had hosted the Trollopes in Ostend, had also recently separated from her husband. To counteract damaging reports which Mr Fauche had been circulating about his wife, Fanny declared that he was a 'heartless, dissipated man, who treated his wife in a shameful manner, neglected his children, and squandered his money' (quoted by JGP to Minna Meyer, 23 July 1845: Garnett–Pertz Papers; see also FT to Mary Fauche, 12 February 1841: Parrish Collection). Fanny suggests to Lady Bulwer that she visit Mrs Fauche at Heidelberg (FT to Lady Bulwer, 9 July 1840: quoted in Louisa Devey, *The Life of Rosina, Lady Lytton*, London, 1887, p. 202).

† Children were considered the 'property' of the father. The Infant Custody Act of 1839, largely a result of Caroline Norton's campaigning, conceded that children under seven should be able to spend time with their mother, if she was deemed fit. Lady Bulwer was not so deemed.

The eccentric Mary Clarke also took Rosina's side, urging her not to move to Italy, as she planned, but to stay in Paris. Miss Clarke brandished 'Queen Caroline at me as a warning as to what may be said of me if I go to Italy!' (Lady Bulwer to FT, 20 July 1840: Trollope Family Papers, Special Collections, UCLA Library). Caroline, the estranged wife of George IV, was accused of taking a lover during her exile in Italy.

Even Fanny found Rosina trying, especially when she caused embarrassing scenes in front of Sir Henry Bulwer, her brother-in-law, who was then first secretary to the British legation in Paris and a good friend of the Trollopes. Fanny confided to Cecilia:

> My interesting difficulties respecting Lady Bulwer and her brother-in-law increase greatly. All jesting apart, it is exceedingly embarrassing. He is decidedly one of the most agreeable, animated, conversable people in existence; and she is one of the most ill-used and pitiable. I believe her character to be perfectly irreproachable. But she is not as quiet as I would wish her to be, in her grief; and were it not that the enforced absence of her children excuses any violence of sorrow, I should say that she compromised her dignity by her lamentations. As it is, however, I do pity her heartily, and most certainly shall not close my doors against her until I have reason to change my opinion of her.[25]

Lady Bulwer dedicated her second novel, *The Budget of the Bubble Family* (1840), to Mrs Trollope. She had intended to use the dedication as yet another opportunity to vent her spleen against 'the reptile', but Fanny counselled her: 'Do not *for the world* allude to the Bulwer race. Stand before the public clear of them, dear friend. *Your literary reputation requires it.*' 'You have a great many things to thank God for. – That you have been *sorely tried* is true – but you have that within you that *ought* to enable you to rise unscathed from it all. Now do not shake your head, and say "foolish old woman!" – but be good, and mind what I say to you, and I shall live yet to see all the world admire you as much as I do.' Lady Bulwer took Fanny's advice. In the final version of the dedication she pays tribute to her friend Mrs Trollope, not because of either her fame or her talent – 'indeed I have almost forgotten that you have talents, so merged have my affection and admiration been for qualities in the possession of which you are, alas! almost unique' – but because of her 'unflinching integrity', 'courage', 'honesty and justice'. The author has others to thank as well, 'and for their timid silence . . . I do not even blame them'. Fanny had been neither timid nor silent in Lady Bulwer's defence.[26]

Anthony had made his way back from Paris to London in March 1840 to resume his Post Office duties. Within a month or so, aged twenty-five, he had fallen dangerously ill with a strange respiratory disease. Fanny had been planning to travel to Penrith in June to attend her granddaughter's christening, but everything had to be postponed. She returned to London at the end of May to nurse Anthony at his new lodgings in Wyndham Street, in the Bryanston Square area and not far from York Street. It had been only three years since Emily's death, and Fanny felt she must expect the worst. She wrote to Lady Bulwer:

> Oh! how your kind warm heart would pity me could you witness the anxious misery I am enduring! My poor darling lies in a state that defies the views of his physicians as effectually as it puzzles my ignorance. It is asthma from which he chiefly suffers now; but they say this can only be a symptom, and not the disease. He is frightfully reduced in size and strength; sure am I that could you see him, you would not find even a distant resemblance to the being who, exactly three months ago, left us in all the pride of youth, health, and strength. Day by day I lose hope, and so, I am quite sure, do his physicians; we have had three consultations, but nothing prescribed relieves him, nor has any light been thrown on the nature of his complaint.

In another letter Fanny confides to her friend that 'Anthony goes on decidedly improving, but so slowly as to make every morning's inquiry one of fear and trembling'.[27]

Two of Anthony's visitors during his illness were the Okey sisters, who were about thirteen and fourteen years of age. The Trollopes knew them through Dr John Elliotson, a man then in his late thirties who had treated Fanny's throat infection the previous year. Fanny had first met Elliotson at Colley Grattan's house. Elliotson was a respected clinical doctor (he was the first to use a stethoscope), but his special interest in the nervous system had led him into the more 'philosophical' side of medicine. He adhered to Anton Mesmer's theory that the human nervous system was charged with 'animal' magnetism

– so-called because of its association with the soul or *anima* – which could be harnessed by a trained practitioner. This was the idea behind 'mesmerism', otherwise known as hypnotism. Animal magnetism became quite a fad, and Elliotson counted among his friends and followers most of literary London: Dickens, Harriet Martineau and Thackeray, to name but a few. The medical establishment became alarmed, however, when Elliotson began to practise mesmerism in University College Hospital. The Okey sisters, who suffered from convulsions, were two of his most responsive patients and they took to going around the hospital wards declaring they could see a ghostly figure, whom they called Jack, at the bedside of certain patients, who soon thereafter died. Mesmerism was shading into spiritualism. The medical journal, *The Lancet*, claimed that the sisters had already achieved notoriety in a London Pentecostal church for 'speaking in tongues'. In 1838 Elliotson was dismissed from the hospital and the prestigious Chair of Medicine at University College, London. He took the Okeys into his own home for observation and maintained a thriving private practice.[28]

Fanny was no doubt impressed by Elliotson when she first met him at Grattan's house, and she was curious about mesmerism. However, her interest almost immediately turned to alarm when she astutely perceived that Jane and Elizabeth Okey were being exploited.* From Paris Fanny had written to her old friend Mrs Grant, who also had concerns for the girls' welfare, reiterating her fears that Elliotson's enthusiasm for his 'science' was leading him to continue experiments which were potentially harmful to the girls and, worse, cut them off from their friends and family. By the time of Anthony's illness Fanny had lost all her respect for, and no doubt faith in, Dr Elliotson, and she did not ask for his medical advice concerning Anthony. Elizabeth Barrett, whose brother knew Elliotson, described Fanny as 'an investigator' rather than a believer

---

* Tom had also met the famous French mesmerist, Baron Dupotet, through the Trollopes' impressionable friend, Henrietta Skerrett. Tom always had a keen interest in these occult sciences, but the mesmerists eventually lost interest in him, for he could not be got into a trance. He was told that he was a 'bad subject'.

in mesmerism. 'Mesmerism, as connected with electricity, and the Witch of Endor',*Fanny comments wryly in *The Three Cousins* (1847). Fanny had the Okey girls to visit that summer in order to get them away from the clutches of their 'keeper' Elliotson as much as possible. (Tom comments that they travelled to Wyndham Street on the omnibus, where they used to spot 'Jack' sitting beside certain passengers.) Practical as always, Fanny thought the girls should concentrate on their needlework, which they did very well, rather than their 'prophetic powers'; and then they 'might gain a living, if friends would come forward to set them going'. Nevertheless, Jane and Elizabeth offered their kind friend the encouraging news that they saw 'Jack' beside Anthony, 'but only up to the knee'.†[29]

Anthony's illness, or certainly the severity of it, might well have been brought on by depression. 'I hated the office. I hated my work. More than all I hated my idleness. I had often told myself since I left school that the only career in life within my reach was that of an author, and the only mode of authorship open to me that of a writer of novels,' Anthony later wrote in his autobiography. 'I had resolved very early that in that shape must the attempt be made. But the months and years ran on, and no attempt was made. And yet no day was passed without thoughts of attempting, and a mental acknowledgement of the disgrace of postponing it. What reader will not understand the agony of remorse produced by such a condition of mind?'

He could 'build castles in the air' but nothing more tangible. Seeing his mother and brother getting on with their writing careers must have made it all worse. Tom had been sending off 'articles on all sorts of subjects – reviews, sketches of travel, biographical notices, fragments from the byways of history, and the like, to all kinds of periodical publications', and in 1840, the year of Anthony's illness, Tom's first book saw the light of day: *A Summer in Brittany*, edited – as the title-page declares in large letters – 'by Frances

---

* I Samuel xxviii.

† According to Tom, the daughter of one of the sisters was later employed as a maid by Anthony and his wife Rose at Waltham Cross.

Trollope'.* This was another example of Colburn's aggressive advertising, for Fanny had originally turned down the £50 which the publisher offered her to appear as editor.[30] Tom received £300 together with a commission from Colburn for another book, this time on western France. After a favourable review in *The Times* John Murray told him, 'There! So *you* have waked this morning to find yourself famous!' Tom was in seventh heaven: a season in Paris was certainly 'better than teaching Latin to the youth of Birmingham', and he was being paid for what he loved best, travel. 'I was a born rambler,' he later declared. Even Anthony's uncle, Henry Milton, had a book published in this same year, appropriately named *Rivalry*, for like *The Widow Barnaby* it takes place in the West Country at the height of the Napoleonic Wars.†

Anthony's mother was at the height of her career. In this same year, 1840, the critic for *John Bull* noted Mrs Trollope's 'power and indefatigability' and called her 'certainly the most fertile of all writers, having during the year published – how many novels it is scarcely possible to say'. Fanny had two novels on the go beside Anthony's sickbed that summer. The first, *The Ward of Thorpe Combe*, is the story of a greedy, power-hungry orphan girl who tries to ingratiate herself into the last will and testament of her rich uncle and the heart of his aristocratic neighbour. Bentley paid her £650 for the copyright.[31] The second book, *Charles Chesterfield; or the Adventures of a Youth of Genius*, which began to appear in Colburn's *New Monthly Magazine* that July (*The Widow Married* had finished in June), is no less than the story of her son Anthony. Of all her children, Fanny had spent the least time with Anthony. In her efforts over the years,

---

* Bentley had proposed to churn out yet another American volume with sketches by Hervieu and the text by Tom, based on his own journals and his mother's notebooks. Happily, this did not materialize (TAT to Bentley, 16 September 1838: Taylor Collection).

† Henry Milton must have cringed when he read one critic's comment that *Rivalry* was 'of Mrs Trollope's school', though it lacked 'the breadth and vigour' of her humour and caricature (*New Monthly Magazine*, 59 (1840) pp. 136–7.) Henry was one of Fanny's sternest critics. Regarding *Hargrave*(1843), for example, he suggested that she should 'lay it aside and write another' (F. E. Trollope, *Frances Trollope*, I, p. 323).

first to recoup her husband's losses and settle the exigeant Henry in America, then to maintain the family by her writing, even while nursing two dying children, Fanny was unable to give her youngest son the attention he needed or wanted. Nevertheless, Tom recalls that Anthony was the 'Benjamin' of the family. It was a struggle to get inside Anthony's young mind, for by his own admission he was extremely shy and self-conscious. Yet his mother probably knew him better than he knew himself at this period in his life.

Charles Chesterfield, which she began to write at Anthony's bedside, is the story of a young man thirsting for literary fame. The young Charles inherits a substantial sum and leaves his parents' farm for the metropolis to join the ranks of the London literati. The occupation of writing 'had indeed become so habitual, and so fascinating to him, that the idea of every other had long grown distasteful'. 'Despite the boy's quiet and even submissive manners ... there was a vein of latent ambition within him.' 'Many were the hours spent by him in solitary musings upon the possibility of his rising, by the strength of his own genius, above the humble and obscure position in which nature had placed him.' He longed for 'fame, renown, applause – applause, renown, and fame such as he had heard tell of'. Sir Walter Scott, Lord Byron, these were the sort of people 'whose exertions he determined to emulate, and whose fame in his heart of hearts he hoped to equal'. 'Yet common sense had not so utterly forsaken him as not to leave a vague consciousness that to all others, save his inspired self alone, the hopes he was feeding on would seem absurd. He carefully enclosed them therefore in the most secret cells of his heart, and like a miser gloating over his unsunned treasure, or a lover taking stolen glances at the portrait of one beloved in mystery, his emotions were all stronger for being unwitnessed and unshared.'

'The only individual of the party who had the slightest notion of what was really working within him,' Fanny wrote, 'was his mother', who 'doted on this gifted child of her old age'. 'Of all those who sat in judgement on the symptoms he betrayed, she alone had any sympathy with the feeling in which they originated. Mrs Chesterfield was, in truth, as vain of the intellectual talents of her younger son as he could be himself.' Charles, like Anthony, wanders about the London parks, 'building all sorts of castles, possible and impossible,

16 & 17. Tom Trollope, aged twenty-two, above, and seventeen-year-old Anthony, below, by Auguste Hervieu, 1832. When *The Domestic Manners* appeared, Tom was at Oxford and Anthony was still at Harrow. Both sons dreamed of following in their mother's footsteps and taking up a literary career.

18. Portrait of Colonel James Grant by William Salter, 1840. Of the Trollopes' life at Julian Hill, Anthony wrote that 'a great element of happiness was added to us all in the affectionate and life-enduring friendship of the family of our close neighbour, Colonel Grant'.

19. The graves of Henry and Thomas Anthony Trollope in the cemetery at Bruges. The two sombre memorials, a headstone for the father and an Ionic column for the son, still stand side by side in the Protestant section near the main gate – a small, dark corner set well apart from the ornate Catholic monuments.

20. 'A Store at Natchez', Hervieu's illustration for *Jonathan Jefferson Whitlaw*, 1836.
A powerful scene in Fanny's anti-slavery novel in which one of the white men lounging
around the dry goods store kicks the coins out of the hand of the little black slave who has
come on an errand for his master, while the onlookers 'burst into a shout of laughter'.

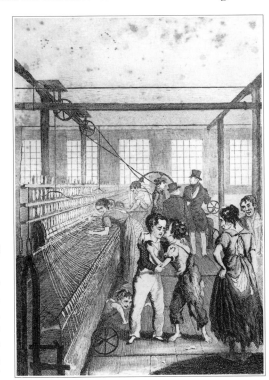

21. 'Love Conquered Fear',
Hervieu's illustration for *Michael
Armstrong*, 1839. 'The dirty, ragged,
miserable crew were all in active
performance of their various tasks;
the overlookers, strap in hand, on
the alert; the whirling spindles
urging the little slaves who
waited on them to movements
as unceasing as their own.'

22. 'A Composing Draught', illustration by 'Phiz' for *Charles Chesterfield*, 1841. 'Know you the great omnipotent, the one invincible, the hidden yet proclaimed, the ruler of the universal intellect, the ever-present, never-present WE?' Marchmont, the editor of *The Regenerator*, was said to be a caricature of Dickens's friend, John Forster.

23. 'Mrs Barnaby Commences Her Work on America', illustration by John Leech for *The Barnabys in America*, 1843. 'Mrs Allen Barnaby in turning over the first page of her book turned over a new page in her own history also … and she doubted not but that she should date from it the growth and the ripening of honour, profit and renown.'

24. Theodosia Garrow Trollope. Tom said of his first wife, a poet and journalist, 'she was all in all to me for seventeen years. She brought sweetness and light into my life and into my dwelling. She was the angel in the house, if ever human being was.'

25. The Villino Trollope, Piazza dell'Indipendenza, Florence. Tom and Theodosia, her father, Joseph Garrow, and Fanny Trollope inhabited separate floors, each one 'as large as a house in England', according to Elizabeth Barrett Browning. The Villino Trollope became a fixture in the social life of the expatriate colony in Florence.

26. Fanny with her son Tom, Theodosia and their daughter Bice on the loggia, *c.* 1860. 'Here of a summer's night, burning no other light than the stars, and sipping iced lemonade, one of the specialities of the place, the intimates of Villino Trollope sit and talk of Italy's future, the last *mot* from Paris, and the last allocution at Rome.'

27. Tom Trollope and his brother Anthony in the early 1860s. Anthony wrote beneath this photograph, which he sent to a relation: 'Here you have my brother and self. You will perceive that my brother is pitching into me. He always did.'

28. Tom Trollope and his second wife, Frances, in or after 1866. Frances was the sister of Dickens's mistress, Nelly Ternan. Dickens wrote to Tom on his marriage: 'I little thought what an important master of the ceremonies I was when I first gave your present wife an introduction to your mother.'

29. Fanny Trollope, about eighty years old. In her last letter to Anthony, Fanny remarked, 'You ask me to write – I and my pen have been so long divorced that I hardly know how to set about it – But you ask me to write and therefore write I will – though I have no news to tell you more fresh than that I love you dearly.'

30. The graves, with matching headstones, of Fanny Trollope, on the right, and Theodosia, on the left, in the English Cemetery, Florence. Around them lie the other members of the Anglo–Florentine community, including Theodosia's father, Joseph Garrow, Elizabeth Barrett Browning, Walter Savage Landor and Hiram Powers.

in the air'. Neither young man had very admirable personal habits. Like Anthony, Charles tends to be 'indolent': 'putting things in good order [was] by no means one of his accomplishments'. Perhaps Fanny saw that sometimes Anthony loathed even the sight of a book, creating as it did 'a painful emotion of envy towards the author, *for it was printed!*' Certainly this was the case with Charles when his manuscripts are sent back unopened. Fanny, too, had experienced that same feeling of rejection before the publication of *The Domestic Manners of the Americans.* There is a wonderful moment when a certain publisher, after receiving a pretentious, confused letter from Charles – much like the one Anthony had sent Bentley concerning his 'lucubrations' – replies: 'The only part of your dispatch intelligible to me is that wherein you inquire about my cat. She is very well, I thank you.'

There would have been much for Anthony to laugh at in *Charles Chesterfield*, particularly the portrayal of *The Regenerator*'s editor, Marchmont. Charles first sees Marchmont, dressed in the 'Vandyck style', with long hair and open collar, leaning against the chimney-piece at a literary salon, 'silently reconnoitring the company by a pair of glasses which were suspended round his neck, though looking the while as if he scarcely thought it worth his trouble to do so'. 'Know you the great omnipotent, the one invincible, the hidden yet proclaimed, the ruler of the universal intellect, the ever-present, never-present W E?' the editor asks an awe-struck Charles. According to Elizabeth Barrett, Marchmont is a caricature of John Forster, Dickens's great friend, who at the age of twenty-eight was the 'literary and dramatic critic' for *The Examiner*. 'Between Mrs Trollope & . . . Lady Bulwer, poor Mr Forster is done to no gentle death.' (Lady Bulwer had portrayed him as the 'lick-dust' Fuzboz.)[32]

However, Anthony would not have appreciated the ending of *Charles Chesterfield.* The aspiring author bravely acknowledges defeat, marries his childhood sweetheart and becomes a country parson. Whatever Fanny really thought of Anthony's future, she no doubt hoped that he would realize, as did Charles, that his worth as a person was not tied to his success as an author. 'You have almost removed the bitterness of my disappointment,' Charles says to a friend, 'by showing that you did not care the less about me for it – and that makes me hope that they won't despise me for it at home, either.'

Anthony remembered his mother's advice at the time to be: 'We Trollopes are far too much given to pen and ink as it is, without your turning scribbler when you might do something better. Harrow and Winchester will stand you in good stead at the Post Office; make St Martins-le-Grand the instrument that will open the oyster of the world. Imitate my particular industry as much as you like, only do not let the publishers break your heart by treating its products as their playthings.'[33] Whether or not these were her exact words, it is clear that Fanny knew how sensitive Anthony was to criticism and failure, and she did not want him to be disappointed.

While still writing *Charles Chesterfield*, Fanny conceived of a second satire on the London literary scene, *The Blue Belles of England*, and the two together make suitable book-ends. If anything, *The Blue Belles*, which began to appear in *The Metropolitan Magazine* in January 1841, is even more cutting. Mrs Sherbourne, the unprincipled female author in *Charles Chesterfield*, gave Fanny the idea. She offers to sell her memoirs to Marchmont. 'Few of your profession, or mine either,' she tells him, 'are ignorant of the fact that biting personal anecdotes are the most marketable of all literary commodities; and when they are skilfully given, with just enough of concealment to produce the effect of mystery, and yet with sufficient clearness not quite to elude the curiosity they provoke, the demand is, I believe, as certain as that for green peas during the last days of May, or for partridges during the month of September.' And this is just the effect which *The Blue Belles of England*, a tale of a country girl amidst the London 'blue belles' – literary figures and their hangers-on – had on Elizabeth Barrett. She writes to the author's friend, Mary Russell Mitford, 'have you read the "Blue Belles"? Do – It is very clever – and besides I want you to send me the little key which belongs to the personalities.'

Miss Mitford did not seem to be privy to a key and could only 'guess at Mrs Trollope's people',* but she reckoned that amongst those caricatured are the Scottish playwright and poetess Joanna Baillie, the painter Bradley Edwin Landseer, Charles Dickens, copying

---

* Frances Eleanor Trollope says that Fanny Trollope wrote the names of the originals whom she caricatures in the margins of her own copy of *The Blue Belles*. Its whereabouts are unknown.

down the droll expressions of his coachman, and the Italian scholar and uncle of the Misses Skerretts, Thomas James Mathias, who Miss Mitford claims never knew a word of Italian. Fanny also took her revenge on several prominent literary figures, including the poet Samuel Rogers, who had made the remark about her writing 'a great deal of rubbish', and James Fenimore Cooper, who had apparently refused to meet her on her last visit to Paris, declaring 'No woman on earth is worth talking to – nor is any one worth looking at after fifteen.'* Most interesting of all, according to Mary Russell Mitford, some of the phrases from the mouth of the social-climbing Mrs Hartley were those which she had often heard Fanny herself use: for example, 'dear friend', 'Do you understand me?' and 'Sons are expensive, dear friend.' Elizabeth Barrett thanked her for the '*Key*'. 'I used it with the eagerness of Blue Beard's wife – & am satisfied, thank you, to the uttermost of the curiosity of my malice – or the malice of my curiosity . . . whichever it should be philosophically.'[34]

Since the previous winter in Paris Fanny had been hoping to go on her long-awaited tour of Italy; she and Lady Bulwer (along with Madame Récamier and Chateaubriand) had even made arrangements to meet in Venice. However, she confessed to her friend as she sat by Anthony's sickbed in early July 1840, 'at this moment I *dare not* think of pleasure; I *dare not* plan a future'. She was further put off her plans when a Paris friend described to her the general state of anarchy on the Continent: 'only last Monday, all diligences and omnibuses passing through the Quartier St Antoine were seized and overturned to make barricades by the mob; all business at the Bourse was stopped, the shops shut, and very general fear of a universal rising of the operatives throughout France seems to exist'.[35] But by the end of July Anthony was on the mend. He accompanied his mother to Cumbria to attend the postponed christening and to convalesce before

---

* Cooper had resented the success of *The Domestic Manners of the Americans*: 'in truth, the English reading public would greatly prefer reading abuse of us than any thing else. Mrs Trollope has made three times as much (I happen to know her receipts) by her travels than I can get for a novel' (J. F. Beard, ed., *The Letters and Journals of James Fenimore Cooper*, vol. 2, Cambridge, MA, 1960, p. 358).

his return to the Post Office. Cecilia asked Anthony to be godfather to Frances Trollope Tilley.

Fanny stayed on in Penrith through the winter. Within only a few months of her first confinement, Cecilia had become pregnant again, and Fanny was worried for her daughter's health.[36] She was there when their second child, Cecilia Isabel Tilley, came into the world in November 1840. The Tilleys' house was very isolated, and Fanny naturally felt that she wanted to be near her daughter. Her wanderlust – and her need to collect material for her books – was too strong to give up travelling altogether, but she thought she might make the Lake District her base. Fanny had found her life in London expensive. 'She had entertained a good deal, giving frequent "little dinners," ' Tom recalls. 'But dinners, however little, are apt in London to leave tradesmen's bills not altogether small in proportion to their littleness.' Fanny's offhand remark to Tom that 'potatoes have been quite exceptionally dear' in London became the family joke. Moreover, 'there was a certain unavowed feeling,' Tom wrote, 'that we had eaten up London, and should enjoy a move to new pastures'. Certainly, the London literary establishment must have felt they were being eaten alive as the monthly instalments of *Charles Chesterfield* and *The Blue Belles* relentlessly appeared over the course of 1841.

Except for her two extended sojourns in America and Bruges, Fanny had lived in and around London (including Harrow and Hadley) since the age of twenty-four. The decision to abandon London altogether was a momentous one. At the same time she was also leaving behind something else which had been very important to her in the past, her collaboration with Auguste Hervieu. She had known Hervieu for nearly fifteen years. He had accompanied the Trollopes on all their travels – Cincinnati, Paris, Bruges, Vienna – and he had been a loyal friend to them in both good and bad times. He had become the family artist, illustrating not only seven of Fanny's books but also her husband's ecclesiastical encyclopaedia and Tom's first two travel books. Richard Bentley had been content to use Hervieu; but the astute Henry Colburn knew that the illustrator could be as important to the success of a book as its author. He clearly felt that Hervieu's name, which was still relatively unknown, was dragging Fanny down. If their nickname for the artist, 'Heirview', is anything to go by, Tom and Anthony must have thought so too. So, Colburn employed other artists, including Charles Dickens's best-known collaborators, John Leech and Hablot Knight Browne ('Phiz'), to illustrate Fanny's books.*

Relations between Fanny and the excitable Hervieu must have become strained, and it was clear that she could no longer prop up Hervieu's career as she had been doing. In 1839 Anthony had sent Tom £50 travelling expenses for Brittany: 'I trust you get on well in your tour, & your book. Give my love to Heirview.'† This is the last we hear of Hervieu in the family correspondence until 1866, when Anthony writes to an unknown correspondent: 'Hervieu still lives, & is I think in London. But I never see him.' He married a Swiss girl in 1842 and continued to exhibit paintings, including portraits of his old Harrow acquaintances, Colonel Grant and his wife, at the Royal Academy throughout the 1850s.[37]

Back in Cumbria, Fanny had hoped to buy a house near Cecilia which belonged to a Mr de Whelpdale, but there was a problem with title-deeds. In the autumn of 1840, near the time of little Cecilia's birth, she bought a plot of land, within half a mile of the Tilleys, 'in a very beautiful situation overlooking the ruins of Brougham Castle and the confluence of the Eden with the Lowther', as Tom describes it. She well knew from her experiences with Julians (Harrow) and the Cincinnati Bazaar the risk of escalating costs inherent in construction, but she was now a successful author who could count on between £600 and £800 per book. She also had seemingly endless energy. Fanny, therefore, set about 'building myself a nest wherein I may be near Cecilia and my grandchildren', as she wrote to her old friend Mary Russell Mitford. 'I believe there be wise folks, and perhaps you, dear Mary, will be among them, who hold me to be very much on

---

* Hervieu, together with R. W. Buss and T. Onwhyn, illustrated *Michael Armstrong* (1839–40); Buss, *The Widow Married* (1839–40); Browne ('Phiz'), *Charles Chesterfield* (1840–1); Leech, *The Barnabys in America* (1842–3) and *Jessie Phillips* (1842–3) – all published by Colburn.

† In this same letter, Anthony also writes that he does not think his fellow 'Tramp Society' member, Awdry, will join Tom again in France, 'as he says he shall have no money, but he is so uncertain and capricious that there is no guessing what he means to do'.

the windy side of reason in thus troubling my old age with building – but nothing in the shape of a comfortable residence was to be found within reach of Cecilia – and moreover, if I continue to make as pretty and comfortable thing as I hope to do, I have the satisfaction of knowing that it will not be buried with me, but may be a source of pleasure to those I love, after I am gone.'[38]

To finance her 'pretty nest', every day over the course of that autumn and winter found Fanny awake at her usual time of half-past four, putting the finishing touches to *The Ward of Thorpe Combe*, churning out *Charles Chesterfield* for Colburn's *New Monthly Magazine*, writing her Parisian detective novel, *Hargrave; or the Adventures of a Man of Fashion*, and beginning the monthly instalments of *The Blue Belles*. Colburn gave Fanny a terrible fright when he refused to accept her manuscript for *Hargrave* at the beginning of 1841, for she had already begun construction on the house. He was furious that she had undertaken to write *The Blue Belles* for a rival publication, *The Metropolitan Magazine*, to appear at the same time as *Charles Chesterfield*. The 'embodied shiver' threatened to go to court and publish all the particulars. The family lawyer, John Young, who was Thomas Anthony Trollope's first cousin on the Meetkerke side, assured Fanny that Colburn was legally obliged to honour his contract: he coughed up £625 for *Hargrave*.

By the following March of 1841, with the house well under way, money in the bank and less turmoil on the Continent, Fanny decided to fulfil her long-held dream to travel to Italy; Tom, who had been in France and Bavaria since December, was to meet up with her *en route*. 'Shall we really go to Italy?' she wrote to Tom. 'Is it possible after so many impediments? . . . I can be ready to leave this place by the first; but as that is All Fools' Day, let us say the *second* of April! God speed us on our way, dear Tom! Truly, if the journey gives us pleasure, we have not got it without pain.'[39] 'Italy was before them, with all her hoarded treasure of art, and all eternal splendour of her sun; and thither they repaired.' The time 'they passed in Italy, almost sufficed to make them forget that they had ever accounted themselves unhappy' (*Charles Chesterfield*).

That same year Anthony, too, had reason to consult the family lawyer, whom he later portrayed as Thomas Toogood, Mrs Crawley's 'good-humoured, cheery-looking' cousin who helps solve the mystery of the cheque despite Crawley's ingratitude (*The Last Chronicle of Barset*). Anthony was still unhappy, and with the whole family settled in Cumbria he no longer felt that he had any close ties to London – though he still had plenty of debts there. When in the summer an opportunity arose to take up the humble post of surveyor's clerk in the west of Ireland, he leapt at the chance to leave his London life behind him and, as he hoped, to start afresh. He asked no one's advice – his mother and brother were in Italy by this time – but, with 'pitying eyes', John Young agreed to loan him £200 for moving costs. Their respective journeys to Italy and Ireland would be the start of new chapters in the lives of both mother and son.

CHAPTER TWELVE

A Visit to Italy

On 2 April 1841 Fanny left Penrith to rendezvous with Tom in London, before crossing the Channel to Boulogne, where they saw the Garnetts; they then proceeded through Paris, Lyons, Chambery, across the Alps at Mont Cenis, and finally arrived in Turin. 'Turin, 13 April 1841. Sixty mortal hours!' remarks Fanny at the start of her book, *A Visit to Italy*. For three days and two nights Fanny and Tom had been trapped in a coupé with two 'unpleasant Frenchmen' – two *disgruntled* unpleasant Frenchmen because Fanny would not allow their huge hunting dog to complete the cosy party. Tom was by now, at thirty-one years of age, an experienced traveller, and his services meant that Fanny could dispense with 'that necessary but alarming race of men, called COURIERS'. Clara Holmwood, the heroine of *Fashionable Life*, 'had been repeatedly assured that all that was to be hoped for, from the very best among them, was a familiar knowledge of many languages, and of many roads; and that if she obtained, in addition, a civil manner, a tolerably good memory as to what hotels were to be resorted to, and what avoided, and the courage necessary to cock a pistol, in case her roving fancy led her to visit Greece or Spain, she might consider herself exceedingly fortunate, let the cheating principle be acted upon to any degree it might, short of positive swindling'.

In their usual style, the Trollopes strayed from the beaten path whenever and wherever they could. Outside Sestri Levante, on the Italian Riviera, their obliging driver suggested that Tom and his mother might like to get out and have a look at the view. But, 'having once set us loose he had the greatest possible trouble in catching us again, till at last, he seemed to give the matter up in despair, and sat down on the step of the carriage, looking as cross as his particularly agreeable features would permit him to do'. On one occasion Fanny braved the hospitality of the monastery at Vallombrosa in Tuscany, where 'the spiritual care of our hosts for us deemed it right and fitting that we should lie . . . if not in sackcloth . . . then in something that was harsher still'. 'A bed of thorns would have been quite as agreeable as the bed of sand (for such it seemed to be) which they had prepared for me.' But, on the whole, Fanny was pleased to find that her tastes coincided with the Italians, especially in the matter of facial hair. At Modena, south of Parma, she heard the story of an Englishman who had been told to leave the province within twenty-four hours owing to 'a rather flourishing pair of moustaches on the upper lip', for the Duke of Modena, like his father-in-law, the King of Sardinia, had an aversion to them. 'A sumptuary law in both countries, usually followed by summary execution of its shaving enactments, keep the populace for the most part, extremely clear and clean from this offence.'

Although she had never visited the country before, Fanny had long had a love affair with Italy, and Florence, in particular; it was, after all, the birthplace of her favourite poet, Dante. 'In approaching any place that has been during the long years the object of hopes and fears, of wishing and despair,' Fanny confessed, 'it is, I suppose, rational to be a little excited; though I know that some tempers take this sort of thing much more quietly than others, wisely enjoying whatever pleasure may chance to meet them, without any previous suffering from impatience, or any unreasonable ecstasy when it arrives.' But she had never been one of these: 'Perhaps I never felt this fever of anticipation more strongly than in approaching Florence . . . Though the coffee on which I had breakfasted had been as innocently free from all exhilarating qualities as the purest decoction of endive, my heart beat as I passed the last milestone before reaching the gates of Florence, as if I had taken a bowl of Parisian *café noir*.'

Happily for Fanny, the city lived up to her expectations, though she soon lost patience with the guidebooks which, when it came to art, contradicted each other as often as she contradicted them. Nor did Fanny have much sympathy with the nineteenth-century mania for restoration. Her views are surprisingly modern: 'I am no great friend to very bold picture cleaning; and retouching, under any circumstances, I hold to be a sin of presumption.' Her tour of the Uffizi Gallery was hampered not only by sparring guidebooks and the restricted opening hours but also by that other age-old complaint of the tourist, a lack of benches. 'I would,' she pleads, 'that some humane speculator on the causes of human joy and woe, would dedicate an eloquent little essay to the generous-hearted Grand Duke [of Tuscany] upon the different degrees of enjoyment arising from contemplation in a state of rest and in a state of unrest.' 'I do truly believe that the consequences of such an appeal would be the glorious acquisition of two or three dozen moveable seats, scattered throughout these enormous corridors.'

The sociable Fanny looked forward, perhaps, most of all to what awaited her at the end of a long, hot, gruelling day in the Uffizi: an evening drive to the Cascine, a park on the banks of the Arno just west of the city centre. 'The flowers you get there, and the lazy chit-chat, and the ice of Donay's afterwards, are all obtained and enjoyed with so trifling a demand upon our activity, that we still continue the system which seems throughout Florence to render them as necessary a part of the day's history, as getting out of bed in the morning.' In the Cascine conversation flies from carriage to carriage, as do the young men, 'making their wished-for perchings on the steps' (*A Visit to Italy*). The Irish author Charles Lever evocatively wrote that 'the Cascine is to the world of society what the Bourse is to the world of trade. It is the great centre of all news and intelligence, where markets and bargains of intercourse are transacted, and where the scene of past pleasure is revived, and the plans of future enjoyment are canvassed.' The wealthy set's 'equipages lie side by side, like great liners; while phaetons, like fast frigates, shoot swiftly by, and solitary dandies flit past in varieties of conveyance to which seacraft can offer no analogies'. 'Scandal holds here its festival . . . The witticism of Paris – the last duel at Berlin – who has fled from his creditors in England – who has run away from her husband in Naples.'*

* Charles Lever, *The Fortunes of Glencore*, London, 1857.

Fanny had no trouble infiltrating the expatriate communities of Florence and Rome, for she knew many of those, both English and American, who had at one time or another made Italy their home. In Florence she and Tom stayed with Lady Bulwer in her apartment at the Palazzo Passerini until they found their own lodgings. Lady Bulwer adored Tom, who had been acting as her literary agent: she addressed him in letters as 'Illustrissimo Signor Tommaso'.* An extraordinary reunion took place when Fanny was invited to meet a young American sculptor called Powers, who was fast gaining a reputation for himself. 'I felt not the slightest doubt,' wrote Fanny, 'that by going to his studio I should meet my old acquaintance', Hiram Powers, whom she had last known in Cincinnati as a 'lad who had seen nothing of any art'. It was Hiram Powers, then aged twenty-two, who had modelled the wax figures for Fanny's 'Infernal Regions', nearly fifteen years earlier. Powers, financed by his Ohio 'Maecenas', Nicholas Longworth, had worked in Washington, DC, before settling in Florence in 1837.✝ By 1841, when Fanny met him again, he was already considered the most gifted sculptor of his day.[1]

For part of that summer Fanny followed the flock of Englishmen who migrated from hot, dusty Florence to the Bagni di Lucca, set in the cool hills overlooking the Ligurian Sea to the west. Fanny loved Lucca for its shade and its freedom from both mosquitoes and the usual social conventions. Thus the English clubhouse, complete with

---

* Tom says that they stayed with Lady Bulwer in Florence in 1843, but he must be confusing his dates since she had moved to Geneva by then. Sadly, Lady Bulwer could not put aside her feelings of hatred for her husband. In 1858 she went so far as to denounce him to the crowd at Hertford on the day of his election to parliament; she was certified insane and placed under the care of a physician, but was released a few weeks later and returned to France.

✝ Fanny would no doubt have been amused to learn that Powers named one of his sons Longworth in honour of the same man who had bought up the Cincinnati Bazaar so cheaply in 1834. When in 1843 a copy of Powers's most famous sculpture, 'The Greek Slave', depicting Turks capturing a scantily clad Greek woman, was unveiled in Cincinnati, 'the matter was solemnly referred to a committee of clergymen who after due consideration gave the statue their approval' – although no one had asked for it (*Dictionary of American Biography*). This puts one in mind of the Cincinnati authorities' notorious prosecution of an exhibition in the 1980s featuring photographs by the American artist Robert Mapplethorpe.

billiard room, card room, ballroom, and supper room, was open to both men and women. At Lucca 'you may be at a ball three times a week, and occupied in riding parties, driving parties, dining parties, and pic-nic parties every day, and all day long . . . if you like; but, if you do not, you may be a hermit'. 'In our own case,' Fanny writes in *A Visit to Italy*, 'we seem to have mixed the two systems together; our early rising giving us ample opportunity for being solitary and sublime as we like, without losing any of the amusement offered by the society assembled here.' However, Tom and his mother did, at least on one occasion, overdo things. At the Duke's ball 'I was playing whist in the Duke of Lucca's drawing-room at half past three,' Fanny admits; 'but nevertheless at six I was with my three faithful companions actually on the road to Gallicano!' – all for a picnic.

The uninitiated at Lucca soon learned that homage was paid not only to the reigning duke, but also to the 'Queen of the Baths', one Mrs Stisted, a 'stout old lady, with large rubicund face and big blue eyes, surrounded by very abundant grey curls', who lived in Lucca all the year round with her 'long, lean, grey-faced, exceedingly mild, and perfectly gentlemanlike' husband. 'She was one of the queerest people my roving life has ever made me acquainted with,' Tom later recalled. She spoke of Lucca's seasonal guests as her subjects and would take drives in the evening to go out amongst them. Mrs Stisted also played or, rather, professed to play, the harp, and wore a surplice of free-flowing muslin at concerts which made her look like the proverbial King David. But 'the specialty of the performance', Tom commented, was that 'no sound whatever was heard to issue from the instrument!'[2]

Fanny found Rome much less hospitable than Florence. In the first place, there was the sheer filth, 'which in every . . . quarter of the city appears to struggle with magnificence, leaving it often doubtful which is the more distinguishing feature'. The drawing-room receptions, such as those given by Lord Adam, the former British minister in Greece, were very unsatisfactory affairs to Fanny's mind because of all the rigmarole and fuss that was made every time a cardinal came into or went out of the room. What was worse, protocol also determined that men and women should remain in separate reception rooms. Together with her forays into the best society, Fanny continued to throw herself wholeheartedly into the role of tourist, climbing to the roof of St Peter's in Rome, and in Venice, where Tom attended the 'Congress of Savans', a sort of forerunner of the modern international scientific conference, she went to the top of the campanile in the Piazza San Marco.

Tom and his mother had been in Italy nine months when they decided to cut their tour short and return to Penrith, for Cecilia had written to say that she was pregnant with her third child. They set off at the beginning of January 1842, the worst time of the year to try to cross the Alps, so that Fanny could be with Cecilia during her confinement. The journey over the pass at Mont Cenis on sledges in heavy snowfall 'to me was,' Tom recalls, 'a very acceptable experience, but to my mother was one which nothing could have induced her to face, save the determination not to fail her child at her need'. Cecilia gave birth to Anna Jane Tilley in February 1842.

Fanny's house, Carlton Hill, would not be finished until the summer, so she and Tom stayed with the Tilleys at Fell Side for the first six months of the year. Building work is always stressful, with the inevitable delays, occasional mishaps and constant financial worries. Matters were further complicated for Fanny by local legend and superstitious – and interfering – neighbours. Sir Charles Musgrave of Edenhall expressed his dismay when the Trollopes had the course of a spring altered slightly to improve the approach to the house. He declared, Tom later wrote, that 'we had moved . . . a holy well, and the consequence would surely be that we should never succeed in establishing ourselves in that spot'. Musgrave apparently had a lot to say about the Trollopes' new home. He thought, for example, that the house and grounds should be called 'St Michael's Mount', presumably as an act of appeasement to the local saint, for it was St Michael's well which had been disturbed. Fanny opted for the name Carlton Hill.

Musgrave, 'the *beau-idéal* of a country gentleman of the old school', was a popular landlord; his wife, Tom wrote, was particularly lady-like and elegant, and tried her hardest to adopt the local Cumbrian dialect, always pronouncing the word 'cow' as 'coo'. However, an invitation to dinner at Edenhall was not something to be taken lightly. A glass goblet, which had been in the Musgrave family since time immemorial, bore the legend: 'When this cup shall break or fall,/Farewell the luck of Edenhall.' Sir Charles insisted that his guests pass the goblet round the dinner table, otherwise the luck would not be tested properly. 'I remember to have dined at a house,' Anthony Trollope later wrote, 'the whole glory and fortune of which depended on the safety of a glass goblet' (*The Small House at Allington*). The American poet Henry Wadsworth Longfellow wrote some lines featuring the Musgrave goblet, entitled 'The Luck of Edenhall'. Sir Charles was horrified to discover that at the end of the poem the glass is broken. He invited Longfellow to dine only to berate the unsuspecting poet for 'transcending all permissible poetical licence'.

Once when the Trollopes dined at Edenhall Tom himself became the focus of his host's indignation. The young man had tried to sneak out of the dining-room, where the men had been left to their wine and walnuts, in order to join a very pretty girl who had retired with the rest of the female company to the drawing-room. Musgrave, alluding to Tom's recent excursions on the Continent, roared, 'Come back! we won't have any of your d—d forineering habits here! Come back and stick to your wine, or by the Lord I'll have the door locked.' Yet, despite (or perhaps because of) their eccentricities, the Trollopes became very fond of the Musgraves: 'I think they will be very pleasant neighbours,' Fanny wrote. 'I *get on* with them.'*[3]

Along with the other changes in her life, that of becoming a grandmother and settling down amidst the relative peace and quiet of Cumbria, Fanny saw an opportunity to claim a government pension, something which would afford her greater financial security and, perhaps, allow her a less gruelling writing schedule. Fanny had, of course, been seen as a vocal Tory supporter ever since the publication of *The Domestic Manners*. When the Conservatives, led by Sir Robert Peel, ousted Melbourne's Liberal government in 1841 she thought

---

* Lady Musgrave must have had some 'forineering habits', for she had spent time abroad. Fanny Trollope presented her with a copy of *A Visit to Italy*: 'Your long acquaintance with Italy my dear Lady Musgrave makes me hope that you may look over my notes with interest – Will you do me the pleasure of accepting the accompanying copy. Yours very truly, Frances Trollope' (Special Collections, University of Michigan Library).

that, at long last, there was a chance 'that my small income might be augmented by the aid which the government has of late years extended to authors who are in want of it'. Thus she wrote to the Earl of Lonsdale at Lowther Castle, one of her Cumbrian neighbours (and an old Harrovian) who, as newly appointed postmaster-general, had a seat in Peel's cabinet. 'I cannot at this moment help, for the first time, hoping that I shall no longer be considered as the blackest sheep in the flock, and that were my name mentioned to Sir Robert Peel by the influential voice of the Earl of Lonsdale I might succeed in obtaining what would so essentially add to the comfort of my declining age.' Lonsdale did indeed write to the prime minister, although his wording is rather cryptic: 'Mrs Trollope's Pretensions as an authoress are before the Public, you can best judge how far she is entitled to the Notice she attaches to it.' Peel politely replied that only limited funds were available for pensions each year and that these had all been allocated by Lord Melbourne before he left office.[4]

Fanny must have been disappointed, for without another source of income she was condemned to rising between four and five o'clock each morning to fill her quota of pages. On her return to Penrith in January 1842 she immediately set about revising her notes for *A Visit to Italy*, published in the same year. It was not a great success. Fanny had been too much in love with her subject and, as a consequence, the book is on the dull side. The critics longed for 'Mrs Trollope's more caustic manner'. 'Assuredly, Mrs Trollope cannot produce the effective etchings without *acids*; her subjects, to convey any notion of her artistic ability, must be *bitten* in.' 'The language of panegyric,' *The Athenaeum* continues, 'fits her pen badly.'[5]

A Visit to Italy was the last of Fanny's books to bear Richard Bentley's imprint. Bentley had published ten works by Mrs Trollope, including two of her most popular novels, *The Vicar of Wrexhill* and *The Widow Barnaby*. Only a few years earlier, in May 1838, Fanny had undertaken to write two books a year for Bentley, 'provided that the kind public continue to abuse and read me'. However, he did not give her the terms which she had originally asked for, £700 for the copyright of each book.[6] As a result, between 1838 and 1842, Bentley published only two works by Mrs Trollope, *One Fault* and *The Ward of Thorpe Combe*, in addition to those which she had contracted to write in 1836, *The Widow Barnaby* and *A Visit to Italy.** Henry Colburn, on the other hand, with his aggressive marketing, had been willing to pay high prices for Fanny's novels, and so, with a couple of exceptions, Fanny was to remain with him and his successors for the rest of her writing career.

Largely with a view to financing the last stages of construction on Carlton Hill, Fanny hit upon the idea of bringing together her best-loved character and her most popular travel book – *Widow Barnaby* meets *Domestic Manners of the Americans*. It was somehow fitting that Fanny should send her favourite heroine 'to a land which', as she tells her readers, 'all the world knows I cherish in my memory with peculiar delight'. *The Barnabys in America; or Adventures of the Widow Wedded* appeared in Colburn's *New Monthly Magazine* between April 1842 and September 1843, with illustrations by John Leech. The twenty-five-year-old Leech had already been contributing satirical cartoons to *Punch* for two years and, in the same year that *The Barnabys in America* was published in one volume (1843), he collaborated with Charles Dickens on *A Christmas Carol*. However, owing to a general depression in the book trade as well as to the fact that he was still annoyed with Fanny for taking *The Blue Belles* to a rival periodical, Colburn did not offer her particularly good terms for *The Barnabys in America*. As Frances Eleanor Trollope notes, 'she candidly told the publisher that she wanted money to pay for the building of the house' and that his offer of payment in monthly instalments would help with cash flow. Of the final agreement she wrote, 'I think it is a very bad one, my dear Tom; nevertheless I *accept*, – as the man said at Cincinnati when he was going to be hanged!' At about this time she asked that Tom be especially careful with money: 'If you were sixty-two years old, and had to get up at four o'clock every morning to work for it, you would not wonder at my saying this!'[7]

---

* Bentley, of course, owned the copyright of many of Fanny's books, including *The Domestic Manners of the Americans*, and he continued to reprint these in the series, 'Bentley's Standard Library of Popular Modern Literature'. Fanny contributed only one story to *Bentley's Miscellany*, 'The Patron King', a retelling of 'The Emperor's New Clothes'. It appeared, with an illustration by Hervieu, in November 1839 (after Dickens had given up the editorship), and was reissued in the collection of stories, *Tales from Bentley*, in 1859.

Several events had conspired to set Fanny thinking about her own American adventures: the building work she had undertaken in Cumbria together with her chance meeting with Hiram Powers in Florence no doubt brought back memories of Cincinnati, 'The Infernal Regions' and, most especially, the Bazaar. Moreover, Charles Dickens had gone on a much publicized tour of the United States in 1841 and published his *American Notes* the following year. He had studied the literature on America, including Mrs Trollope's *Domestic Manners*. The radical Dickens was determined to like the new, burgeoning democracy and to produce his own account, proving Mrs Trollope and others wrong. He wrote to Andrew Bell, author of *Men and Things in America*, 'I think you are rather hard on the Americans and that your dedication like Mrs Trolloppe's [sic] preface seems to denote a foregone conclusion.'[8]

Of course, like Basil Hall, Dickens was 'received in full drawing-room style' on his relatively brief tour of America but, as with both Hall and Mrs Trollope, the reality did not live up to the expectations. Dickens wrote to Fanny's old friend, the actor William Charles Macready: 'I *am* disappointed. This is not the Republic I came to see. This is not the Republic of my imagination.' 'I cannot change, my dear Macready – my secret opinion of this country; its follies, vices, grievous disappointments. I have said to Forster that I believe the heaviest blow ever dealt at Liberty's Head, will be dealt by this nation in the ultimate failure of its example to the Earth.' And Dickens came to the same conclusion as Fanny Trollope: if a radical were to come to the United States, he writes to Forster, unless a radical 'on principle, by reason and reflection, and from the sense of right', 'he would return home a Tory'. Dickens's hopes for America were, in their way, as great as Fanny Trollope's had been, and the disappointment was just as deeply felt. He confided to Forster from America: 'I think it impossible, utterly impossible, for any Englishman to live here, and be happy.'*[9]

When it was published, Dickens's *American Notes* was judged by

---

* In Boston, Dickens spent a pleasant day with Fanny Trollope's good friend, the British consul, Colley Grattan. Mrs Trollope's name may well have come up in the conversation.

the critics in terms of *The Domestic Manners.* One American journalist had been 'happy to see that the sycophants of Dickens . . . are to be well *Trollopized* before they escape his claws'. The *Morning Chronicle,* on the other hand, commended him because 'he never twaddles . . . but, which is better praise, he never *Trollopizes*'. On its publication, Fanny wrote Dickens a letter of congratulations from Penrith which has not survived, though Dickens's gracious reply of 16 December 1842 has:

> *My Dear Mrs Trollope,*
>
> Let me thank you most cordially for your kind note in reference to *my* Notes; which has given me true pleasure and gratification.
>
> As I never scrupled to say in America, so I can have no delicacy in saying to you, that allowing for the change you worked in many social features of American Society, and for the time that has passed since you wrote of the Country, I am convinced that there is no Writer who has so well and accurately (I need not add, so entertainingly) described it, in many of its aspects, as you have done, and this renders your praise the more valuable to me . . .
>
> Always believe me,
Faithfully Yours,
Charles Dickens[10]

When he wrote to Mrs Trollope, Dickens had recently begun work on his first novel since his return from the United States, *Martin Chuzzlewit,* to appear in monthly parts from the end of December 1842. Although he had some good material left over from his American tour, Dickens set the novel in London and rural England – perhaps he felt that America was not big enough for both Mrs Trollope's Barnaby, who had already been there a year, and his own hero, young Martin Chuzzlewit. However, *Martin Chuzzlewit* did not get off to a good start: its sales figures did not reach even half those of *Nicholas Nickleby.* Dickens had nothing to lose; so, in an effort to revive the book's sales while at the same time responding to his caustic transatlantic critics, Martin Chuzzlewit boarded ship bound for America in the June 1843 number. But this time Fanny had beaten her young rival to the post, and the fortunes of Dickens's novel never really revived.

The young Martin's experiences in America are not very different from those of Mme de Clairville, who had left France to join the community of Perfect Bliss on the banks of the Red River in Fanny's first novel, *The Refugee in America* (1832). Martin is swindled out of his money by the Eden Land Corporation, which sells him a miserable piece of swamp on the banks of the Mississippi, and nearly dies of fever. With *The Barnabys in America* Fanny Trollope turned the tables on her hosts: Martha Barnaby and her husband, the major, inflict some elaborate money-making scams on unsuspecting, but very deserving, Americans. After one such scheme Martha congratulates her partner on the 'jest played off to avenge, as it were, the numberless tricks which we hear of as practised against our countrymen . . . and in that light, my dearest major, it commands my warmest and most patriotic admiration'. The similarities between *Martin Chuzzlewit* and Mrs Trollope's American books did not go unnoticed. Fanny's old friend Marianne Skerrett, who had by this time been in Queen Victoria's household for six years, wrote to Fanny from Buckingham Palace: 'I have no doubt that "Martin Chuzzlewit" is even better than I can conceive, in the American part. I thought of you the moment I read it.'* No doubt many others did too.

Five years earlier Dickens might have made some rude remark about Mrs Trollope sending the Barnabys to America on the back of the publicity surrounding his American tour. However, Dickens's sojourn in the United States had been a sobering experience; he returned to Europe with a better understanding of Mrs Trollope and the reputation which had been thrust upon her as the author of *The Domestic Manners of the Americans*. His manners towards her became

---

* In this same letter of 15 July 1843 Marianne Skerrett paints a rather melancholy picture of her life in the palace, 'without a creature, of *my* companions, who knows anything of what I should like to talk of. It is only by a strong taste for all book things, and the possibility of sometimes indulging it, that I keep up (at least I hope I do) something of the auld lang syne' (F. E. Trollope, *Frances Trollope*, II, p. 23). A mutual friend writes to Julia Pertz that 'Marianne is a close prisoner at Court. She can hardly ever see any friend but her sister, and even her she can only receive, not visit' (Julia Smith to JGP, 2 July 1845: Garnett–Pertz Papers).

decidedly more gentle and respectful. In any case, by 1843 Dickens's reputation as a novelist was secure; there was no longer any reason to see the sixty-five-year-old Mrs Trollope as a threat. Dickens did not even flinch when Mrs Trollope brought out *Jessie Phillips; a Tale of the Present Day* in one-shilling monthly parts from December 1842 to November 1843, published by Colburn with engravings by John Leech. In *Jessie Phillips* Fanny's two main targets were the very same ones which Dickens had attacked in *Oliver Twist* (1837–8): the New Poor Law of 1834 and the abolition of the bastardy clause, which had allowed the mother of an illegitimate child to make claims on the father. A clear difference had emerged in the style and approach of these two authors, which they themselves no doubt appreciated. Dickens was pioneering the genre of the expansive 'social novel', in which a whole world is created against a backdrop of social themes; Fanny's method was more pointed and didactic – she was writing novels of protest with the explicit aim of spurring her readers to action.

At the opening of *Jessie Phillips*, the reader learns that the 'gay-looking, nicely whitewashed, flowery little village of Deepbrook' has been disfigured by the erection of that 'bare-faced monster', the Union Workhouse, and the 'pernicious modern system of CENTRALIZATION' which built it. Under the new law, as Fanny illustrates in the novel, the responsibility for the relief of the poor and destitute has been transferred from the individual parish to a board of guardians, representing a 'union' of parishes covering a large catchment area. No able-bodied man would receive assistance unless he entered a workhouse; these were intended to be 'uninviting places of wholesome restraint'. Thus many, including the aged and the young, were condemned to undergo the degradation of imprisonment without due consideration of their circumstances or character.

As in *Jonathan Jefferson Whitlaw* and *Michael Armstrong*, Fanny was once again speaking out against what she saw as the betrayal of our common humanity and our responsibility towards the innocents of society. In *Jessie Phillips* the Revd Remmington remarks to a supporter of the new law, 'though we have very decidedly the fear of the law before our eyes, we have the fear of the Gospel also. The law . . . seems to assume as a principle that the poor, who, as we are told, we have always with us, have no natural RIGHT to assistance from the rich.' 'But,' he continues, 'a good many of us think that the doctrine of the Gospel is at variance with it.' At this same dinner party, the usually conservative Mrs Buckhurst is no doubt speaking the author's mind when she declares: 'it would be very terrible to think that a measure which has brought increase of suffering to many a needy, hard-working man, should bring superfluous wealth to the idle rich'. The affluent lawyer, Mr Lewis, remarks: 'I never expected that I should live to see you turn Radical.' 'Live a little longer,' Mrs Buckhurst retorts, 'and you may chance to see the very staunchest old Tories among us turn Chartist.'

When Parliament introduced the New Poor Law it also abolished the old bastardy clause which had required that the fathers of illegitimate children be traced and made financially responsible for their offspring. Fanny thought it outrageous that 'the male part of the population' – 'being of the sex which makes the laws' – 'should be guarded, protected, sheltered, and insured from all the pains and penalties arising from the crime meditated'. She points out 'the obvious and horrible injustice of thus making one responsible for a fault committed by both'. In the novel Fanny allows her 'hapless heroine', Jessie Phillips, the pretty but innocent village seamstress, to be seduced by the unscrupulous son of the local squire, Frederick Dalton. When the local ladies discover that Jessie is pregnant, they cease to give her employment and she is condemned to the workhouse. 'It was in vain,' Fanny says of Jessie, 'that she repeated to herself, "I have deserved it all." The magdalen humility by which she strove to reconcile herself to offended Heaven was no longer genuine and sincere. She did not deserve the degradation to which she was now exposed, and she knew it.' Jessie escapes from the workhouse to ask Dalton to maintain the as yet unborn child. He refuses, as is his right by law, and eventually murders the child, though it is Jessie who is charged with the crime. Overcome by grief and despair, Jessie dies before learning of her acquittal.

The critics' reaction to *Jessie Phillips* was all too typical. *John Bull* remarked that 'Mrs Trollope has sinned grievously against good taste and decorum. The particular clause of the Act which she has selected for reprobation is the *bastardy clause* – not perhaps the very best subject for a female pen.'[11] Yet, *Jessie Phillips* made an important contribution to the debate concerning the bastardy law which had been raging in the House of Lords and elsewhere, and within a year of its publication the bastardy clause was back on the statute book.* In 1847 a government minister was made responsible for the Poor Law Board, which brought some improvements, though the system continued through to the First World War.

Soon after the first number of *Jessie Phillips* had appeared, Fanny turned to Charles Dickens for advice on a matter concerning its publication in America. She would have known of Dickens's campaign for international copyright; indeed, in America he had made himself very unpopular by his outspokenness on the subject. As matters then stood, British authors did not receive any compensation for American editions of their works (and vice versa, as in the case of Judge Haliburton). However, the American publishers had an informal 'trade courtesy' agreement which stipulated that the first publisher to announce that a particular British title was 'in press' secured the exclusive right to that work. To beat his rivals to the post, an American publisher sometimes thought it worth his while to pay a token sum to an especially popular British author, thereby securing advance proofs of a forthcoming book. Both Mrs Trollope and Charles Dickens had by this time been marked out as best-selling authors across the Atlantic, and Fanny had apparently been paid a small amount, probably about £50, to send advance proofs for each issue of *Jessie Phillips*. However, she clearly had the same problem as Dickens, who often had no 'advance' proofs to send since, as he told one American publisher, he 'only completed each Number a day or two before its publication'. Fanny received a rude and threatening letter from a Mr Marshall, the publisher's London agent, in January 1843, and she immediately wrote to Dickens for advice. Dickens sympathized with Mrs Trollope, for he had also received a letter from Mr Marshall. He suggested that she should follow his lead and

---

* Fanny Trollope replied with characteristic sarcasm to an unknown correspondent who had sent her pamphlets supporting the new Poor Law: 'Till some means have been discovered by which relief from labour shall be made unpalatable to the idle and profligate, without making parochial relief come in the shape of isolation and imprisonment to the aged and infirm, I remain, Sir, your obliged servant, Frances Trollope' (27 February 1843: Historical Society of Pennsylvania).

return unopened any further correspondence from this 'skulker under the Black Flag of Literature'.[12]

Fanny was able to write much of *The Barnabys in America* and *Jessie Phillips* in the sanctity of her own Cumbrian home, for by 23 July 1842 Carlton Hill was ready to receive its owners. The house was not unlike the Trollopes' first building venture, Julians at Harrow: squarely and solidly built, with three two-storey bays across the front rather than the one larger bowed window, and a commanding view of the countryside. Fanny and Tom held a small house-warming party and drank the toast *'Stet fortuna domus.'*** Over the remaining summer and winter months of 1842–3 the Trollopes' Exeter cousin Fanny Bent came to visit Carlton Hill, as did Anthony from Ireland. Fanny wrote to her friend Mary Russell Mitford: 'I venture to look forward to some bright future summer when you will come and see me, and my lakes, and my grand-children, and my son Tom, and my pretty cottage, and, though last, not least, your old acquaintance Wordsworth.'†[13] Fanny and her family took long walks, went on drives and called on neighbours together. In the late summer of 1842 Tom returned with Anthony to roam around Ireland; Anthony joined him when he could. This was probably the first occasion since those dark days at Harrow Weald that the brothers had spent any time alone together. Tom noticed that even after just a year in Ireland Anthony was 'already a very different man from what he had been in London'; 'the rejected of St Martin's-le-Grand was already a very valuable and capable officer'. No doubt Fanny and Cecilia thought so too.

---

* 'May this house have good fortune.' The rich, handsome wallpaper which Fanny had chosen for the drawing-room was still there nearly fifty years later, in 1891, when Tom revisited Carlton Hill. The then owner refused his wife's petitions to change the old-fashioned and worn paper: 'It was put there by Mrs Trollope, and there it shall stay, because she put it there' (F. E. Trollope, *Frances Trollope*, II, p. 42).

† In this same letter, Fanny consoles her friend on the death of her father. George Mitford was, in fact, an inveterate gambler and left his daughter with huge debts. An appeal was launched in *The Times* and the *Morning Chronicle*, and within a short time over £1,500 had been raised. Among her benefactors were Queen Victoria, Maria Edgeworth and Fanny Trollope, though she could ill afford it (Watson, *Mary Russell Mitford*, pp. 251–4).

Despite these happy family reunions, Fanny made up her mind to leave Carlton Hill before she had lived in the house for a year. There were many reasons – the weather, for one. Tom wrote in his memoirs that 'the sun yoked his horses too far from Penrith town'. Though, as he later confided to his nephew, Anthony's son Harry, this had merely been 'an amiable euphemism' which the family gave out. 'The truth is that we found our neighbours dull and stupid. You need not mention this to Tilley; – not that we found him or my dear sister or his house dull; – but the neighbours were all his friends.' Her daughter-in-law Frances Eleanor Trollope tactfully noted: 'The plums in the social pudding were too few and far between both in space and time; and, to state the case, not completely, but compendiously, she found the life dull.' Certainly Fanny would not have long been able to abide the 'sameness' of the 'rotary' dinner parties she describes in *The Laurringtons*,* published the year after she left Carlton Hill and set in the Lake District, where 'English gentlemen, before dinner, may generally be observed to keep together in groups, either on the hearth-rug, or round a book-table, or at a window, as time and place may permit; but they rarely, before revivifying themselves by this necessary refreshment, appear to have courage sufficient to enter into conversation with ladies'. Elizabeth Barrett put it best: 'the spirits of the hills conspired against her the first winter & almost slew her with a fog & drove her away to . . . where the Oreadocracy has gentler manners'.✝[14] The Trollopes' decision came as no surprise to Sir Charles Musgrave. As Tom wryly comments, the old squire 'knew perfectly well that it must be so, from the time that we so recklessly meddled with the holy well'.

On a more practical level, the big house proved expensive to run, especially in the cold winter months, and Fanny feared that she would no longer be able to afford to visit old friends and new places both

---

* *The Laurringtons* was Fanny's only novel to be published by Longman, her brother's old publishers, in 1844.

✝ An Oread, in Greek and Roman myth, is a mountain nymph. In this same letter of 1845 Elizabeth Barrett relates that Harriet Martineau had recently begun to build a house in the Lake District, at Ambleside, and was there converting Whately, Archbishop of Dublin and Tom Trollope's old principal at St Alban Hall, Oxford, to mesmerism.

in England and on the Continent. What was more, Cumbria proved a difficult and expensive place for Fanny's friends to get to, and she missed their society. She loved her grandchildren. 'I can now tell you *from experience* that grand children (before our eyes) are very dear things,' Fanny wrote to Mary Russell Mitford. To the Garnetts she boasted, as all grandmothers do, that 'the eldest child', her namesake, 'is the most beautiful she has ever seen'.[15] Nevertheless, both Fanny and Tom felt a great weight had been lifted when, in April 1843, 'we literally stood with no *impedimenta* of any sort save our trunks, and absolutely free to turn our faces in whatsoever direction we pleased'. They had the comfort of knowing that the house, on which they had lavished so much care and expense, would remain in the family, for Cecilia, John and their three children moved into Carlton Hill within a few months of Tom and Fanny's departure. Fanny's plan was to return every year or two to Cumbria to see Cecilia and the grandchildren.

Fanny spent the spring and summer of 1843 in the West Country, using Bastin's Hotel in Exmouth as a base from which to visit and receive her friends and family who were living in the area, including her sister Mary Clyde, Fanny Bent, the Gabell sisters, now residing in Clifton, Mrs Nutcombe Gould (Kate Grant of old), and Mary Russell Mitford. It was not until one day in June, when Tom and his mother were out walking on Exeter Northernhay, that they decided what their next port of call was to be. 'Dresden was talked of. Rome was considered. Paris was thought of. Venice was discussed,' Tom recalls. But, in the end they chose Florence, 'the paradise of exiles and the retreat of Pariahs', as Shelley wrote. In *A Visit to Italy* Fanny had written that the one drawback to living the year round in that country, the summer heat, 'is rarely an evil to me, and though I do not walk quite so much as I should like to do were the heat less, I enjoy the sunshine and the exquisite race of flowers'. Most important of all, it was one of the least expensive European capitals. Thus, on 1 September 1843 Tom and Fanny began to retrace their steps via Lyons across the Alps to Florence.

Their first home in Florence was the Casa Berti in the Via de' Malcontenti, on the east side of the church of Santa Croce; after a year and a half they moved to the Casa Olivieri in the Via del Giglio, the same house in which John Milton had lodged when in Florence two centuries earlier. Protocol required that an English person had to have been presented at Court back home before he or she could be received by another reigning sovereign. This regulation had prevented Mrs Trollope from entering certain circles in Austria, but not in Tuscany. The Grand Duke, whatever else he may have been (his subjects dubbed him 'Grand Ciuco', or Grand Ass), was not a snob, and virtually all the expatriates were presented at the Pitti Palace, including the Trollopes on 1 January 1844. As Tom remarked, 'the Duke was credibly reported to have said that he "kept the worst drawing-room in Europe" '. The table manners exhibited by the English at the duke's balls were certainly appalling. They 'would seize the plates of *bonbons* and empty the contents bodily into their coat pockets. The ladies would do the same with their pocket-handkerchiefs.' The Italians were even worse. 'I have seen large portions of fish, sauce and all, packed up in a newspaper, and deposited in a pocket' as well as whole fowls and hams, not to mention 'jelly carefully wrapped in an Italian countess's laced *mouchoir!*' 'I never saw an American pillaging the supper table,' Tom notes; 'though, I may add, that American ladies would accept any amount of *bonbons* from English blockade runners.'

The most riotous time of year occurred during Carnival. Fanny wrote to a friend back in staid old Protestant England: 'You would think us mad, all of you, sober people as you are, were I to tell you exactly how we have been passing the Carnival. We were not in bed until three o'clock in the morning during nearly the whole of it. And the crescendo movement with which it concluded gave us three costume balls, and three masked ditto, within eight days!' At the British minister Lord Holland's ball Fanny went as a Quakeress; Tom, as a court jester, formed part of a 'splendid feudal group' got up by one of the Englishmen.[16] The rest of the year could not be described as dull either. There were morning salons, dinners, whist parties, concerts, picnics and amateur theatricals.* Sheridan's *The*

---

* The Parrish Collection is full of short notes, to and from the Trollopes, issuing and replying to invitations in Florence. For example, on 5 March 1845 Fanny received an invitation from Cavaliere Buonarroti, a descendant of Michelangelo, to partake in an 'act of domestic religion' by celebrating the sculptor's birthday (Trollope Family Papers, Special Collections, UCLA Library).

Rivals was a great favourite in the Trollope household. In the first of many performances, Tom was miscast as Bob Acres. Eventually he finally found the perfect role, the warm-hearted but choleric old man, Sir Anthony Absolute, and this was to become Tom's stock part. His mother always 'brought the house down' as Mrs Malaprop, with her delivery of such classic 'Malapropisms' as 'headstrong as an allegory on the banks of the Nile'.* Their rendition of Matthew Locke's *Macbeth* even merited a column in *Galignani's Messenger*: 'An English lady of distinguished merit, Mrs Trollope, has had the idea of getting up in her house a performance of the chorus of the witches of *Macbeth*, composed half a century after the time of Shakespeare, by Locke.' The paper continues: 'She had a little stage fitted up in her drawing-room, and every care was taken to perform those traditional scenes with the greatest accuracy in regard to costume and everything else. A numerous party of English ladies and gentlemen sang the choruses, and acquitted themselves very well.' Fanny persuaded the famous Austrian contralto, Madame Sabatier (née Caroline Unger), who had recently retired, to play one of the principal witches.✝[17]

Fanny's crowded weekly Friday receptions, first at the Casa Berti, then at the Casa Olivieri, became a regular feature of the Florentine social scene. The reclusive Elizabeth Barrett Browning, who came to Florence in 1847 after her elopement with Robert Browning, spoke of Mrs Trollope's 'royal "drawingrooms" ' where the English do the usual 'work of routs & whist & double gossip'.[18] Friday was also the day when Mr Sloane gave his famous dinner parties. Mr Sloane was a wealthy Catholic to whom the church of Santa Croce owes its present elaborate marble facade. Tom reckoned that 'the principal object' of holding his dinners on a Friday night, a fast day according to the Catholic calendar, was to show 'how entirely the spirit and

---

* No doubt the scene in which Sir Anthony and Mrs Malaprop discuss circulating libraries was also a big hit: 'Madam, a circulating library in a town is an evergreen tree of diabolical knowledge. It blossoms through the year; and depend on it, Mrs Malaprop, that they who are so fond of handling the leaves will long for the fruit at last.'

✝ Caroline Unger had sung the contralto solo in the premier of Beethoven's *Missa Solemnis* in 1821.

intention of the Church in prescribing a fast could be made of none effect by a skilfully-managed observance of the letter of its law'. It was at one of these extravagant 'feasts' that Fanny met Frederick William Faber, who had been at Harrow with Anthony. At Oxford he came under John Henry Newman's spell and in 1845 converted to Catholicism. Faber told Mrs Trollope that at Harrow her old friend the Revd Mr Cunningham 'gave him his earliest religious thoughts, – but that he always had a sort of misgiving that he occasionally talked nonsense'.*

In the autumn of 1844 Charles Dickens and his wife arrived in Florence on his first tour of Italy and presented their cards at the Casa Berti. Fanny had, of course, seen and spoken to Dickens on more than one occasion, but Tom apparently had not. On meeting the thirty-three-year-old Dickens, two years his junior, Tom was 'at first disappointed, and disposed to imagine there must be some mistake! No! *that* is not the man who wrote *Pickwick*! What we saw was a dandified, pretty-boy-looking sort of figure, singularly young looking, I thought, with a slight flavour of the whipper-snapper genus of humanity.' 'His laugh,' Tom recalls, 'was brimful of enjoyment. There was a peculiar humorous protest in it when recounting or hearing anything specially absurd, as who should say "Pon my soul this is too ridiculous! This passes all bounds!" and bursting out afresh as though the sense of the ridiculous overwhelmed him like a tide, which carried all hearers away with it.' Fanny would have made both Dickens and his good-natured but rather awkward wife feel at home in a strange place.

Tom soon overcame his initial misgivings and became a close friend of Dickens: the two men saw each other in London and Florence, and Tom became a regular contributor to Dickens's *Household Words*. 'To the Italian Trollopes, as they may be called,' another friend wrote, 'Dickens was most partial.'[19] Fanny, in turn, seems to have been partial to Dickens; certainly, she was fond of making little references to his books in her own novels. In doing this, she was undoubtedly paying homage to the young man's talent; Fanny also probably

---

* Faber was appointed head of the Brompton Oratory in 1849 (then called the London Oratory).

intended it as a bit of fun – perhaps even a gentle dig – for she only alluded to those works of Dickens which have marked similarities with her own: *Pickwick Papers, Oliver Twist, Nicholas Nickleby* and *Martin Chuzzlewit.**

In the spring of 1844 Frances Eleanor Trollope remarks, 'the first tidings reached Casa Berti of the engagement of Mrs Trollope's son Anthony, to Miss Rose Heseltine'. Anthony had met Rose, the daughter of a Yorkshire bank manager, then in her early twenties, at Kingstown, Ireland, in 1842. The wedding was to take place on 11 June. In May Tom and Fanny travelled to Cumbria to stay with the Tilleys at Carlton Hill. Fanny may have hoped to attend Anthony's wedding; but by June Cecilia was in the early stages of her fourth pregnancy, and, with three children under the age of five, Fanny would have thought it best to stay with her daughter. Thus, the first time any one in Anthony's family laid eyes on his wife was when the newly-weds visited the Lake District later that summer. In his novel *The Claverings* Anthony appeals to those women who remember the first time they were taken to meet their husband's family: 'she will understand how anxious must have been that young lady', Harry Clavering's fiancée, 'when she encountered the whole Clavering family in the hall. She had been blown about by the wind, and her cloaks and shawls were heavy on her . . . and she felt herself to be as dowdy as she appeared among them. What would they think of her, and what would they think of Harry in that he had chosen such a one to be his wife?' Rose instantly took to Anthony's mother. 'Nothing,' Rose later told her sister-in-law,

> could have been kinder or more affectionate than the way she received me – kind, good, and loving, then and ever afterwards. No one who saw her at this date could suppose she was in her sixty-fourth year, so full was she of energy. There was no one more eager to suggest, and carry out the suggestions, as to mountain excursions, picnics, and so forth. And she was always

---

* These allusions to Dickens's novels appear in *The Widow Barnaby* (1839), *Charles Chesterfield* (1841), *Father Eustace* (1847), *The Three Cousins* (1847) and *The Life and Adventures of a Clever Woman* (1854).

the life and soul of the party with her cheerful conversation and her wit. She rose very early and made her own tea, the fire having been prepared over night – (on one occasion I remember her bringing me a cup of tea to my room, because she thought I had caught cold during a wet walk in the mountains) – then sat at her writing-table until the allotted task of so many pages was completed; and was usually on the lawn before the family breakfast-bell rang, having filled her basket with cuttings from the rose-bushes for the table and drawing-room decorations.

These warm feelings were mutual. Fanny still found it difficult to communicate with the reserved Anthony. As is clear from his conversations with his first biographer, T. H. S. Escott, Anthony seemed to take her well-meaning advice as implicit criticism. Perhaps Fanny felt that 'the peculiarity that was called shyness in him was much more owing to a habit which he had contracted of examining the minds of others, than to real propensity of thinking about himself, which latter propensity is in truth the real source of all the peculiarities of a genuinely shy man' (*The Lottery of Marriage*). Fanny soon discovered that she could talk and write to Rose as 'an affectionate friend and mother'; and she no doubt hoped that she could get closer to Anthony through Rose. Anthony's wife, her other daughter-in-law comments, 'was a source of heartfelt satisfaction to Frances Trollope, who was not long in recognizing the excellent influence of the young wife on her son's life in every way'.[20]

That same summer of 1844, when Anthony first introduced Rose to his family, he also confessed that he was writing a novel on an Irish theme, inspired by the sight of a ruined country house in County Leitrim. In August, after Anthony and Rose had returned to Ireland, Fanny wrote to her new daughter-in-law, 'I am very glad, dearest Rose, that the library subscription is paid, and I hope you carry with you to Banagher a good package, to comfort you in your retreat.' Apparently there had been some hopes of Anthony being based in Dublin; perhaps Fanny or John Tilley had petitioned the postmaster-general, their Cumbrian neighbour, the Earl of Lonsdale: 'I do not yet give up all hopes of Dublin for you,' she continues, 'but as yet we have nothing in the way of information on the subject. This delay is very vexacious and must be *very* vexacious to you – for suspense is always more tormenting than any certainty.' In all the confusion surrounding the wedding, Anthony must have mislaid his manuscript, for Fanny continues: 'I rejoice to hear that Anthony's M. S. is found, and I trust he will lose no *idle* time, but give all he can, without breaking in upon his professional labours, to finish it.'*[21]

Although Anthony had gained more confidence since his move to Ireland and his marriage to Rose, still the old insecurities persisted. By the next summer, when the whole family was once again gathered at Carlton Hill, Anthony brought with him the completed manuscript of *The Macdermots of Ballycloran.* He gave it to his mother, 'agreeing with her that it would be as well that she should not look at it before she gave it to a publisher. I knew,' Anthony continues in his autobiography, 'that she did not give me credit for the sort of cleverness necessary for such work. I could see in the faces and hear in the voices of those of my friends who were around me at the house in Cumberland, – my mother, my sister, my brother-in-law, – that they had not expected me to come out as one of the family authors.' This is unjust. Fanny had known of Anthony's literary ambitions since he was a teenager, and the previous summer she had encouraged Anthony – through Rose – to finish *The Macdermots.* What Anthony saw as indifference in his family's faces was probably a combination of sheer exhaustion and utter distraction, for there were now four screaming children to feed, wash, placate, amuse and dote on, Cecilia having given birth the previous December to her first boy, touchingly named Arthur.†

* A few weeks later, Fanny wrote to her 'dear daughter' Rose: 'Many thanks my dearest Rose for your letter – I don't know what the town of Banagher might think of you – but in my estimation you very decidedly *are* a heroine' (FT to Rose Trollope, 30 August 1844: Taylor Collection).
† Fanny received the announcement of Arthur's birth while having breakfast in the Casa Berti. She was in floods of joyful tears when her manservant, Luigi, came into the room. 'I wish you could have seen his terrified countenance,' she later wrote to John Tilley. 'When I explained to him, however, the cause of my queer condition, he seemed to think it reasonable enough; and uttered the words "Maschio? Bene!" as if (conceited he-thing!) he thought the ecstasy perfectly well accounted for.' The proud grandmother also addressed a note to 'Miss Frances Trollope Tilley' informing her that 'a night-cap and a shift for your doll, – which is all that I have had time to make' is on the way (F. E. Trollope, *Frances Trollope*, II, pp. 60–61).

What obviously bothered Anthony was that, as he later wrote, 'there were three or four in the field before me, and it seemed to be almost absurd that another should wish to add himself to the number'. His mother was, of course, continuing to churn out, on average, two novels a year. His uncle, Henry Milton, who visited Carlton Hill that same summer, had published a second novel in 1843, *Lady Cecilia Farrencourt*. Tom was for the most part publishing articles on historical themes, although he had an idea for a book on the Stuarts for John Murray's 'Home and Colonial Library' series. Even Cecilia had somehow found the time to write a novel – a very pious work, entitled *Chollerton*. Its author declares her allegiance from the very start when describing the pretty village of Chollerton and its fine old church, 'which only needed to be brought under the influence of the lately-revived good taste and right feeling of the age for its interior to elevate and soothe the heart of the worshipper within, as much as the external aspect of the time-honoured edifice gratified the taste of the passing lover of ecclesiastical architecture without'. In August 1843 Fanny had sent Cecilia's manuscript to John Murray. 'Of course I am no fair judge of it,' she told Murray, 'but there is, as it seems to me, so much of deep-felt quiet piety in it, and a tone of purity so perfectly unaffected and natural that I think it *not* quite undeserving your attention.' Fanny suggests that the publisher show it to his sister, 'as I believe the opinions, being what I call a little *cathedralist*, resemble in some degree her own'.[22] Murray was not tempted; her uncle Henry Milton's publisher, Ollivier, finally brought out *Chollerton*, 'by a lady', in 1846.

When in the summer of 1845 Fanny promised to find a publisher for Anthony's precious manuscript as well, she could see that the anxious young author did not want or need any criticism – constructive or otherwise. Perhaps they were both sensitive to the objection raised by *The Literary Gazette* when Tom's *Summer in Western France* came out in 1841. 'This "editing" has become a queer business,' the *Gazette* remarked, 'since even grown-up esquires and bachelors of arts cannot publish their own works without the superintendence of their mothers.' Anthony may also not have wanted his mother, at least at this stage, to see the parallels between the Macdermots' plight and the Trollopes' own history: a proud family who incur large debts in building a house, their efforts to maintain a certain social standing despite their poverty, their inevitable decline into squalor and despair, and the father's descent into madness. At one point Fanny wrote to Cecilia: 'I have seen Newby about Anthony's book. He, like *everybody* else, gives a most wretched account of the novel market. It is, I fear, but too true. He has offered to print the book at half profits – but declares that he has *no* hope that there will be anything above expenses. He says that he thinks it very cleverly written, but that *Irish* stories are *very* unpopular.'[23] Nevertheless, Anthony signed an agreement on 15 September 1845 with Thomas Newby for half profits; *The Macdermots of Ballycloran* appeared in 1847. However, his mother's literary fame continued to hang over Anthony like a dark cloud. In promoting *The Macdermots*, Newby omitted the author's christian name, allowing the public to believe that it was yet another book by the industrious Mrs Trollope.

The Macdermots of Ballycloran was not a universal success, and it certainly did not make any money. *The Athenaeum* suggested that Mr A. Trollope find another name, for he 'comes before the public with the disadvantage of *not being* the popular writer for whom careless readers might have mistaken him'. 'Seldom have we seen such slovenly writing,' *The Critic* remarked; 'whether Mr Trollope be boy or man, we know not; but we suspect, nay, for his own sake we hope, the former, and that he has perpetrated the publication of this juvenile essay without consulting his friends.' This must have been all the more painful set alongside a review of the rather silly anti-Jesuit tale Fanny published in the same year as *The Macdermots, Father Eustace. The Critic* opined: 'Everybody will abuse, and everybody will read it. Critics will condemn, but librarians will buy, and their customers will borrow.'[24]

Fanny continued to travel, always with a view to collecting material. In the summer of 1846, following her annual visit to Penrith, Fanny set off for Gräfenberg with a friend, Lady Sylvestre, her cousin Miss Hall and Tom as courier. Their intention was to try the famous Preissnitz's water cure, which consisted of douches, packing wet towels round the body, lots of water to drink and vigorous constitutionals. That dilettante Mrs Morrison in *The Three Cousins*, who dabbled in animal magnetism and homoeopathy, 'at last came to the conclusion that Preissnitz was the only physician who really knew how to set the human frame to rights when it went wrong'. Tom and Fanny wintered in Florence and in April 1847 set off once more for England to visit the Tilleys at Penrith. On this visit Fanny was particularly concerned for Cecilia's health, for she had given birth to her fifth child, Edith, the previous November. 'My dear Cecilia is, on the whole, better than I expected to find her,' she wrote to a friend, 'but the having four children younger than [seven] is not likely to contribute to the strength of a delicate woman. Her five children are however very nice little creatures, and all well both in mind and body – and this is some little consolation for their having come upon us so rapidly.'[25] In July Tom and his mother returned to the Continent to travel through Germany, where she and Tom met up with her old friend Colley Grattan, who was taking a break from his duties as British consul in Boston.

In the midst of their tour, Frances Eleanor Trollope writes, 'there arrived on the morning of the 2nd of August a letter from England which, for two persons, cast a shade over all the brightness. Mr Tilley wrote that the doctors had recommended – or, rather, had *ordered* – his wife to pass two years in Italy.' The word was apparently not mentioned, but understood well enough by everyone – Cecilia was showing early signs of consumption. Tom left within ten days in order to meet his sister at Ramsgate and escort her thence to Florence. But at Ramsgate he found a letter from John Tilley informing him that Cecilia was not up to the long and arduous land journey across France to Italy; she would proceed to Leghorn (modern-day Livorno, on the east coast of Italy) by steamer from Southampton. Tom retraced his steps back to the Continent and met Fanny at Lake Geneva, from where they proceeded together to Florence in order to prepare for Cecilia's arrival. On 30 September Fanny travelled the fifty miles to Livorno to meet Cecilia off the boat. 'The invalid was looking very pale and ill, and was evidently very weak; but the doctors,' so Frances Eleanor Trollope writes, 'had declared that "Mrs Tilley's lungs were not touched." ' Fanny had heard these words before, and they could not have been of much comfort.[26]

By October of that year, 1847, the 'homoeopathic' doctor (what his treatment was we do not know) attending Cecilia decided the winter climate in Florence would be too severe for his patient, and suggested Rome. Within a month the move had been accomplished, and the Trollopes took an apartment in the Via delle Quattro Fontane, near the church of Santa Maria Maggiore. With them as Fanny's guest was Miss Theodosia Garrow. The twenty-two-year-old Theodosia, petite and delicate, with masses of dark hair, grey eyes and an olive complexion, had an exotic background. Her paternal grandfather, a British officer in India, had married a high-caste Brahmin woman. Their son Joseph, Theodosia's father, was educated in England and, at twenty-five, married a Jewish widow twenty-three years his senior, with two children.* Mrs Garrow gave birth to Theodosia when she was in her fifties – some say fifty-nine. Theodosia grew up in Devon, showed great promise as a poet (the great Walter Savage Landor called her 'more intense than Sappho'), and in Torquay sat at the feet of Elizabeth Barrett Browning.

The Garrows moved to Florence in about 1844, and came to know the Trollopes there. Theodosia was extremely fond of her half-sister Harriet, 'neither specially clever nor specially pretty, but,' as Tom recalled, 'the most absolutely unselfish human being I ever knew, and one of the most loving hearts'. However, as Tom put it, Mrs Garrow 'was not, I think, an amiable woman', nor very bright. She was, moreover, jealous of Theodosia's close relationship with her father – so much so that, Tom states, 'I am afraid that Mrs Garrow did not love her second daughter at all.'† Theodosia was attracted to the maternal but clever Mrs Trollope, so different from her own mother, and the young poetess seems to have adopted the Trollopes as a second family. Theodosia had written to Fanny at Dr Preissnitz's institute the previous summer to tell her the good news that she would be spending the winter of 1846–7 in Florence after all:

You, who know what charms Florence has for me, can guess that I am not a little rejoiced at this change in our prospects. And I shall see you again before long, my kind friend! and though

---

* Joseph Garrow's grandfather had been the schoolmaster at Monken Hadley, where Fanny lived between 1836 and 1838.
† The Stebbinses conjecture that Theodosia was, in fact, Harriet's illegitimate daughter (L. P. and R. P. Stebbins, *The Trollopes: The Chronicle of a Writing Family*, London, 1947, p. 122).

it were ridiculous to fancy that you can look forward to this as
I do, yet I *know* you will be glad to see your poor puss again . . .
Few things could have given me so much pleasure as the receiving your charming *infinitesimal* letter. Like other homoeopathic
doses, it has more potent virtue in it, than the multifarious
scribbled sheets which testify rather to the patience of the reader
than the wit of the writer. And so you would have said, if you
had seen how heartily we all laughed at the image of your watery
world, so vividly conjured up before us. We are told of (but not
by) your son, that he is a walking advertisement of the powers
of the Great Water Wizard. May it be so! and may we meet you
both this winter![27]

Theodosia and the thirty-one-year-old Cecilia became very close
that winter of 1847–8 in Rome, although Tom states it was an odd
friendship 'in that they were as the poles asunder in opinions and
habits of thought'. Cecilia was as fervent a 'Puseyite' as ever, and her
religion 'made the greatest part, and indeed nearly the whole of her
life'. Theodosia, on the other hand, 'had no Church opinions at all,
High or Low', rather, poetry and art were her religion. Perhaps
Cecilia lent a sympathetic ear to Theodosia's family problems. Much
of their conversation, although he did not know it, probably centred
on Tom, for it must have become clear to everyone that winter that
Theodosia had grown equally fond of Tom, and the feeling was
mutual. Tom was fifteen years older than Theodosia, but at thirty-
seven he was still quite young looking, five feet ten inches tall, with
blond hair, blond eyebrows and lashes, grey eyes and an oval face.*
By the end of December 1847 the couple were engaged, to the delight
of everyone in the Trollope household, but not so in the Garrow
camp. Tom wrote in his diary at the time: 'We wrote to Garrow.
Much opposition, and very harsh letters in reply. Days of distress
and anxiety. Garrow fixed to come here [to Rome] on Thursday. Our
anxiety at agony point. He came, awfully savage. Terrible scenes!'[28]
Eventually, owing partly to Fanny's 'tact' and 'good sense' and partly

---

* These details appear on Tom's French passport, issued in 1846, among the
Trollope Family Papers, Special Collections, UCLA Library.

to Mrs Garrow's 'desire to get Theo out of the house', the engagement was back on. Theodosia returned to Florence with her father, and Tom followed a few weeks later.

This was a stressful time for Fanny. Not only did she have her daughter's health, her son's marriage and her own work to worry about, but cholera and revolt were also in the air. Throughout Europe 1848 was the Year of Revolutions – there were riots in Vienna and Berlin, revolution in Hungary and an abortive attempt at national unification in Germany. In France the people deposed Louis Philippe, established the Second Republic and elected Louis Napoleon President. In Italy the previous year Count Cavour had founded the newspaper *Il Risorgimento*, which gave its name to the movement for Italian independence and unification. In 1848 there was unrest across the peninsula, and the rulers of Naples, Tuscany and Piedmont were induced to grant constitutions (only the Piedmontese constitution lasted more than a few months). After five days of street fighting the Austrians were ejected from Milan, and in Rome the Pope was forced to flee in November 1848; the subsequent Roman Republic was defended by Giuseppe Garibaldi and survived until July 1849 when the French overthrew it. There seemed to be rioting, or the threat of rioting, in every Italian city.

However, despite the upheavals all around, Cecilia was Fanny's first concern. In January 1848 she wrote to Tom, by now back in Florence, 'I have had great numbers of new people calling on me. I wish they would keep away, for I *cannot*, at present, receive. Cecilia, I think, is pining for fresh air; but is still forbidden to stir out of doors. It is cold and raw.' Over the next few weeks she reports that 'Cecilia is much the same as when you left us – She looks very well, but is very weak'; 'I think Cecilia's gentle, even, nay often cheerful state of spirits, is quite wonderful. She is an admirable creature!' 'Cecilia behaves very well,' Harriet Garnett told her sister Julia, 'never expressing a regret at being separated from her beloved husband and children, but,' Fanny had confided to her friend, 'she sees it preys on her mind'.[29]

In February Tom returned to Rome to escort his sister and mother back to Florence; on their journey they passed a detachment of 'ragged', 'ruffianly, indeed blackguardly, looking' Roman volunteers *en route* to fight against the Austrians in Lombardy. Within a few days of their return Tom and Theodosia decided, at a day's notice, to get married. The very quiet ceremony took place at the British minister's chapel on 3 April 1848. The Trollopes' family and friends were all very happy for Tom. Henry Milton wrote to his nephew, 'If, my dear Tom, you make half as good a husband as you have been a son, your wife may think herself a fortunate woman.' The Garnetts echoed this view: 'He will I am sure make an excellent husband, for he has been and is a most devoted son.' Though Harriet could not resist adding, Tom 'has been in the best society at Florence, and his manners are much improved, – still I wonder that so distinguished a girl as Theodosia Garrow ... should have taken a fancy to him. I think the mother must be as great an attraction as the son, and to live with her may be a great inducement in the young lady's mind.' And there were others who thought it an odd match. Elizabeth Barrett Browning wrote to Mary Russell Mitford from Florence: 'Are you aware that Miss Garrow, praised by Landor, has married Mr Tom Trollope, praised, I believe, of horse-jockeys generally? He is said to be goodnatured – & they are to live with Mrs Trollope ... & Robert was sitting with Powers the sculptor, when a tribute of wedding cake arrived for the latter. It strikes me as a strange marriage.'*30

Back in Florence Cecilia's condition was rapidly deteriorating; all she wanted now was to return to England to be with her husband and five children. Fanny wrote to Tom and Theodosia, who were taking a honeymoon tour around Tuscany, 'I have been very, very anxious about my poor Cecilia. Her weakness is excessive. And it often seems to me impossible that she should endure the fatigue of

---

* The reference to 'horse-jockeys' reflects the feeling that Tom was a dilettante and not taken seriously as a writer. The fact that Walter Savage Landor had called Theodosia the new Sappho had always rankled with Elizabeth Barrett Browning: 'Theodosia Garrow I have seen face to face, once or twice. She is very clever – very accomplished, with talents and tastes of various kinds, a musician and linguist in most languages, and a writer of fluent graceful melodious verses ... but more intense than Sappho!' (EB to Robert Browning [20 November 1845]: P. Kelley and R. Hudson, eds., *The Brownings' Correspondence*, XI, Winfield, KS, 1993, pp. 182–3).

the voyage. But she will not listen to the idea of postponing the voyage.' On 3 May 1848 Fanny, Tom and Theodosia helped Cecilia on board ship at Livorno. Harriet Garnett, who was living in Brighton by this time, had heard that Cecilia was so weak on her return that 'she is carried from her bed to the sofa'. What was more, 'her husband met her in London, and had the sad task of telling her that her eldest child, Fanny, is said by the medical men to be in a deep decline. She has been confined to one room the whole winter, and like her mother grows every day weaker. Cecilia bore this calamity with great fortitude, and is quite aware of her own danger, and composed. How hard to leave a husband she is devotedly attached to, and four young children, without counting her poor little Fanny, who will perhaps go before her.'[31]

In the meantime, Fanny and her son and daughter-in-law retraced their steps to Florence, where rumours of an impending Austrian victory sent many of the English expatriates packing. The sixty-nine-year-old Fanny did not know what to fear most: a letter announcing her daughter's death or Austrian troops entering Tuscany. She needed a rest from her recent anxieties, both personal and political, and so, in the company of Tom and Theodosia, she set off for the Swiss Alps in the summer of 1848. However, they were unable to escape the alarming reports which were coming out of Italy, and at one point, in September, Fanny sent Tom to Florence to sell everything: they would spend the winter at Lake Geneva and then possibly return to England to live. Within a few days, Fanny had changed her mind, and she and Theodosia soon joined Tom back in Florence. Sometimes Fanny's impatience and frustration led her, as on this occasion, to act rashly. Twenty years earlier she had written to her son Tom from America: 'You know I can bear anything better than uncertainty. The apprehension of misfortune has often agitated me even to agony; but when once the misfortune was there, I have not been cowardly.'[32]

That moment arrived in the spring of 1849. Fanny received word from John Tilley that she had better come to England to see her daughter for the last time. In October 1848 the Tilleys had sold Carlton Hill and moved to London after John was appointed assistant secretary of the Post Office. Fanny travelled without stopping for fear of losing a day and finally, on 10 March – her seventieth birthday

– reached the Tilleys' door at 6 Allen Place, Kensington, 'without knowing whether [Cecilia] was alive or dead'. She wrote to Tom the next day:

> I arrived here last night, my dearest Tom, and had the unspeakable consolation of finding that my darling Cecilia had again rallied, and was able to converse with, and welcome me, as if in perfect health. Yet I am still told there is *no* hope! This dreadful sentence is pronounced with a degree of certainty that precludes my daring to doubt it; but there are moments when it is difficult to believe. She seemed delighted to see me, and her joy at our meeting again was almost equal to my own. For myself, I am better than I had hoped to be. The long and solitary journey was a dismal trial to my strength of all kinds. Thank God it is over, and that I am not too late![33]

Her publisher Henry Colburn paid her a visit in Kensington: 'He was prodigiously civil; told me I was a little behind my time' with her latest book, *The Old World and the New*. But, Fanny confides to Tom, 'to write more than a page at a time, is pretty nearly impossible. And even so, I scarcely know what I am writing.' Over the past five years, since her novel set in the Lake District, *The Laurringtons* (1844), Fanny had continued to supply Colburn with good circulating library fare: *Young Love* (1844), *The Attractive Man* (1846), *The Robertses on their Travels* (1846), *Travels and Travellers; a Series of Sketches* (1846), *Father Eustace* (1847), *The Three Cousins* (1847), *Town and Country* (1848), *The Young Countess* (1848) and *The Lottery of Marriage* (1849). Yet, even now, she felt driven to write on. Theodosia had no fortune of her own to bring to the marriage beyond £1,000, and the 'Italian Trollopes' depended in large part on Fanny's earnings. Despite Cecilia's state, which required 'constant, unremitting watchfulness both day and night', the anxious mother somehow found the time to write, just as she had done when Henry and then Emily were struck down by the same disease. Like Emily, Cecilia's 'patience, her trusting confidence in the fate that awaits her, and her tender thoughtfulness for every one, are more beautiful and more touching than I can describe. She has often talked of you and your dear wife, and always with the greatest affection.' In this same letter to Tom Fanny enclosed a note to Theodosia: 'It is the saddest scene that ever mother watched. Her poor dear devoted husband never leaves her side when not forced away by official duty. It is piteous to watch him hanging over her. Little Fanny is getting better, I hope. The other poor unconscious little things seem well.'

Finally, on 14 April 1849 Fanny wrote to Tom and his wife:

Your dear sister breathed her last at midnight on Tuesday the 10th of April. It was as though she had fallen asleep. But for a day or two previous, she had suffered sadly. Sweet soul! She longed – but never with impatience – for the moment of her release.

I have, as you well know, my dear Tom, suffered ere now, and very severely; but I almost think the last month has been the most suffering period of my existence. Tilley, poor fellow, has behaved admirably, but he cannot, with all his efforts, prevent my seeing what is passing within. Time, I doubt not, will do much for us both. But it is a tremendous shock that has fallen on us! . . . Though I feel that I am almost too old for a *rally*, I will do the best I can to get over it.

She adds that she has found the letters of condolence overwhelming: 'I really think that every friend and every relation you ever heard of in your life, has written to me', and they all demanded a reply. 'The dear children are too young to understand their loss; and, greatly weaned by the long banishment from their mother's room, which her extreme weakness rendered necessary, they feel less than I expected they would. But I ought to rejoice at this.'

Anthony had travelled to London to see Cecilia in February; he had taken Cecilia's youngest child, Edith, back with him to Ireland to ease the Tilley's burden. In reply to Rose's letter of sympathy Fanny wrote:

Your letter, my dearest Rose, gave me pleasure in every way – and thankful am I again to feel that I can take pleasure in anything! I have indeed suffered, more than I can express, more even than I expected.

I have great satisfaction in knowing that yourself and Theodosia – the only daughters now left me – have both known enough of my lost treasure, to value and cherish her memory – Theodosia passed a month with her at Rome – and so enough to make her fully comprehend why we all feel her loss so severely – And as for you, dearest Rose, you knew her in her last and happiest days – and I do truly believe you loved her as a sister – When we meet there will be as much pleasure as pain in talking of her – Sad as the scene was, I almost wish you could have witnessed her departure – She was like an angel falling asleep in happy certainty of awakening in Heaven – I am very *very* glad that my dear Anthony saw her on her death bed – The impression left on his mind, however painful at the moment of receiving it, will remain with him for ever more as consolation, than sorrow.

John Tilley is not a demonstrative man as Anthony knows – but his eyes filled with tears when he read your mention of his poor little Edith – God bless you for all your kindness to her, my dear daughter! We shall none of us ever forget it . . . Adieu dear Rose . . . The idea of my visit to you is rarely out of my head – Give our affectionate love to your dear husband and accept the same yourself from your loving mother,

Frances Trollope[34]

CHAPTER THIRTEEN

Charles Chesterfield;
or the Adventures of a Youth
of Genius

Fanny handed in the manuscript of her novel *The Old World and the New* to Colburn at his offices in Great Marlborough Street on 22 July 1849. The next day she and John Tilley travelled to Mallow, Co. Cork, to visit Anthony, Rose and their two sons, three-year-old Harry and Fred, who was nearly two, as well as Cecilia's little Edith, who was somewhere in between. Recent events and her seventy years had taken their toll on Fanny. Although she entered into everything that Rose and Anthony had planned, including long walks around the lakes of nearby Killarney and a private bagpipe concert, her mother-in-law sometimes showed signs of fretting, according to Rose:

> one day we put her on one of Bianconi's cars running to Glengariff, after much protest on her part against the ramshackle looking machine. Presently, however, after a few jerks, and a dozen 'Niver fear, yer honour!' from Mick the driver, she almost persuaded herself that she would rather travel through Ireland in that way than any other!
>
> Glengariff was not a success. She was tired with her journey; the tea was rubbish; the food detestable; the bedrooms pokey; turf fires disagreeable and so on. And now looking back on it all, I feel that she had ground for complaint; and I should vote it – nasty.

One cannot help feeling, as Anthony no doubt did, that Tom knew better how to handle his mother.

Nevertheless, Fanny managed to enter into local legend when, with her usual good humour, she bestowed a silver sixpence on an old man breaking stones below her window. The Trollopes' Irish groom related the story to all and sundry, and, in time-honoured fashion, the single sixpence had soon turned into a shilling every day for a month. When Fanny heard this, she remarked, 'Ah, that shows on what slight thread hangs the report of our good deeds – and our evil ones!' It was at this time that she acquired the Irish name, which all the family came to use, of 'the Mammy'. From Dorset, where she went to visit her sister Mary Clyde on her return from Ireland in August, Fanny wrote to the 'Irish Trollopes' that she missed the supplies of 'new-laid eggs, salmon curry, Irish potatoes (1849),* and bread and butter, together with a little honey and a little coffee and a little porter from the same green land', which Rose had laid on for her guests. 'God bless you both,' she ends her letter, 'and thank you a thousand times for the sweet welcome you gave me! Kiss the dear little group and tell them it comes from Grandmama – ever dearest Anthony and Rose, your affectionate mother, Frances Trollope.'[1] With her usual economy, Fanny was to use the Lakes of Killarney as the opening setting for her novel, *Second Love* (1851). In it she reflects on her attitude towards recent events:

There assuredly are some people, and it may be feared not a few, who deem it a sin if they too easily permit themselves to feel happy. Such phrases as the following, for instance, have often been uttered in my hearing, nor can I believe that I have been the only one so favoured: –

'Oh dear! I am sure we ought not to laugh so! Who knows what may be going to happen to us?'

'Really it is quite wrong, and unnatural for us to take pleasure in anything after all we have gone through so lately! It is quite enough to bring a judgement upon us!'

'Don't fix your heart so upon anything! It is like a defiance

---

* That is, potatoes from the first crop since the famine.

of Providence! I always tremble when I see people so happy, to think what may come after!'

And so on, with ungrateful moanings, more numerous, more long, and more dismal than I have patience to write. But Baron Rittesberg read the stars differently, and notwithstanding his loving and his constant nature, he did not believe that he was committing a sin by feeling gay and happy, although his wife he had so fondly loved had not died more than eighteen months before.

After her return from Ireland in August 1849, Fanny spent the autumn visiting friends and family in southern England and stayed for a time with her son-in-law in London to help care for Cecilia's children. She literally did not know where she was to live. Her furniture and other property had been stored in Florence, but, as Tom had noted in his diary the day before his mother left Italy the previous spring: 'Public matters here have gone on from bad to worse; and we quit Florence when it is becoming almost too hot to handle.'[2] With Cecilia's death, her last close tie to England had been severed. Fanny understood that John Tilley would have to get on with his life; apparently Cecilia's last wish, with which her husband complied, had been that he should marry her cousin, Mary Anne Partington.* The events of the past year, from her daughter's passing to the political turmoil on the Continent, as well as her concerns for the future, led Fanny to look back at her life and to reassess some of her actions and the convictions which lay behind them.

First Henry, then Emily and finally Cecilia – all three children whom Fanny had taken with her to America were now dead. The illness, poverty and rejection which she and her children had suffered there, together with her hatred of slavery and hypocrisy, had informed Fanny's criticisms of the fledgling democracy in *The Domestic Manners of the Americans*. But since its publication in 1832 Fanny had written about the injustices she had seen in her own country, in particular child labour and the iniquities of the new Poor Law. 'Live a little

---

* Cecilia had spent many holidays with the Partingtons at Offham, Sussex; Mary Anne's mother, Penelope, was Thomas Anthony Trollope's sister.

longer,' Mrs Buckhurst had said, 'and you may chance to see the very staunchest old Tories among us turn Chartist' (*Jessie Phillips*). Fanny did not turn Chartist, but in that tumultuous year of 1848, with revolution sweeping across the Old World, the great experiment of the New World began to look much more attractive to Fanny. In *The Old World and the New,* the novel which Fanny had struggled to write during Cecilia's last illness in the spring of 1849, an English family, the Stormonts and their cousin Katherine Smith, immigrate to the Ohio Valley to begin a new life; in the same year of 1848 their liberal-minded friend, Clementina Maitland, heads for Paris – 'really the only city in Europe that any intelligent being, enjoying the privilege of choice, would select as a residence'.

The forthright and independent Clementina is an exact portrait of Frances Wright, even down to her almost masculine features and 'tall, finely-formed figure'. Like Frances, Clementina has a gentle, timid sister, Sophy, whom she drags along with her to Paris. 'How different will be the scenes we shall have to paint!' Clementina writes to her friend, Mary Stormont, in Cincinnati: 'You, occupied in watching the young vagaries of an infant state of society, and I, contemplating the ingenious experiments of all sorts of philosophy in the old.'* Clementina's letters provide the novel's best comic moments. She revels in the excitement of revolutionary Paris until she and Sophy are nearly crushed to death in one of the barricades and are forced to flee for their lives. By contrast, the Stormonts, after much hard work and the investment of a considerable amount of capital, build a successful farm and become valued members of the Cincinnati community. Fanny was, of course, rewriting her own history; she was also making her peace with the New World. She

---

* One wonders if Fanny also had in mind the Garnetts and their friend Julia Smith, by this time all living in England. Miss Smith wrote to Julia Pertz, who was surrounded by cholera and revolution in Berlin: 'You who were born & bred under liberal institutions [New Jersey], who have long seen the people in possession of power, & using it on the whole well, why should you be in such an agony of fear when you see them about to gain possession of what surely *you* will not deny to be their just right, namely to enjoy a portion in their own government?' Julia Pertz retorted: 'You in your quiet peaceful happy English home have no idea what we have suffered here' (Heineman, *Restless Angels*, pp. 163–7).

had come to believe that America, with its equality of opportunity, could offer someone like the Stormonts' English servant Jack Parish, a penniless orphan (thus the name), possibilities of advancement undreamed of back home. An American girl tells her English friend, Katherine Smith, that despite its problems, 'I love my beautiful country, and I am proud of it. I feel that it is a country of strength and of promise. But I would that it were – that it were older, Katherine; for I do sometimes . . . indulge myself in the belief that our corners will wear off in time' (*The Old World and the New*).

Although Fanny was clearly wary of the socialist fervour in France, the Risorgimento in Italy was quite another matter. Since the early days of her marriage, when she welcomed Italian patriots such as Guglielmo Pepe and Ugo Foscolo to Keppel Street, Fanny had taken an interest in the struggle for Italian independence. Neither her disillusionment with American democracy nor even her admiration for one of Italy's main oppressors, Metternich's Austria, had altered her views. In *A Visit to Italy* (1841) Fanny declared her anger when 'I hear persons, who think themselves peculiarly clever, sneer at Italy as a country not competent to take care of herself, and absolutely requiring help of some invading hand or other to save her from falling.' For Fanny, Italy was a nation of great men.

From the time they made Italy their home, in 1843, Tom became an even more zealous advocate of the Italian cause. In 1846 the nationalist writer Massimo d'Azeglio asked Tom to persuade the British minister in Florence, Lord Holland, to issue passports to a group of refugees so that they could escape extradition by the Austrians. (Lord Holland laughed at the boldness of the request, but complied.) One visitor to Florence in 1847 remarked that Tom Trollope was 'very enthusiastic about Italian destinies, and very busy about a newspaper which is to be published', *The Tuscan Athenaeum*; its purpose was to inform the English-speaking world on matters relating to Italian independence. Theodosia was also involved in the enterprise. Harriet Garnett rejoiced to hear that Fanny was once again espousing a liberal cause: 'She is and always was a liberal at heart,' she declared to her sister Julia in September 1847.[3]

Still, the question remained, should Fanny return to Italy? In July 1849, while Fanny was in Ireland, Tom and Theodosia had been called to the Garrows' residence in Torquay, where Mrs Garrow was very ill. They remained there for several months, during which time Fanny did not see them. At the beginning of October, after Mrs Garrow's death, Fanny, who was herself recovering from bronchitis, wrote to Tom:

> My health and spirits have been shaken by all the sorrow I have gone through. And I confess to you that I feel my separation from you to be almost too painful under my present circumstances. For very nearly forty years, my dear son, you and I have lived together in more perfect harmony than is often found, I believe, in any connection in life. And now, when I so very greatly need the comfort and support of your society, I am deprived of it. I should be very unwilling to put you and your dear wife to any serious inconvenience, but I feel that your coming to me for a few weeks now [at 6 Allen Place,] might be *very* beneficial to me.[4]

They came to London, but still nothing was decided. Mr Garrow, now a widower, wanted his precious Theodosia to come live with him in Torquay. The medical profession helped to decide the Trollopes' fate. The London doctors recommended Italy to Fanny for her recurrent bronchitis; her physician in Torquay told the delicate Theodosia, who had not been well, that she must live in southern climes. For Fanny, as for Mary Brotherton in *Michael Armstrong* (1839–40), circumstances 'had rendered her own country less dear to her than it is to most others; she therefore not only determined to plant herself elsewhere, but to do so in such a manner as would enable her to make her new abode her home, in the best sense of the word, and this could only be done', she believed, by making 'it the home of others, also'.

Towards the end of 1849 it was clear that the Italians had utterly failed to liberate their country from either the French or the Austrians; but the fighting had stopped and Florence became once more 'the paradise of exiles and the retreat of Pariahs'. After many protestations, Mr Garrow agreed to live with his daughter, son-in-law and Mrs Trollope in Florence. It promised to be a very odd household. In

November Fanny travelled with the young couple across the Channel. While Tom and Theodosia proceeded to Florence to look for a house that would suit everyone – which would take some doing – Fanny remained at the Pyrenean mountain resort of Pau, writing rather melancholy letters to her son and daughter-in-law in between games of whist, a case of the mumps and painful visits from the dentist. Eagerly awaiting news from Florence, she wrote: 'The only excuse for my impatience is that I *am alone*: – a condition so very uncongenial to my nature, as to render me not only miserable, but most savagely cross! And so full of moral angles that everything seems to hit against me, jar me, and shake me!'[5]

Resources were pooled, and together with the substantial sum which her half-sister, Harriet Fisher, had left to Theodosia on her death from smallpox the previous winter, the Trollopes were finally able to find a very large three-storey house which was still under construction at the north-west corner of the Piazza Maria Antonia (now the Piazza dell'Indipendenza). Tom and Theodosia spent the spring fixing it up, and by the end of May 1850, to Fanny's great relief, it was ready for occupation. Fanny, Mr Garrow and the young couple were to inhabit separate floors, each one 'as large as a house in England', according to Elizabeth Barrett Browning. When Fanny realized that she was making better time than she had calculated on her journey from Pau to Florence, she wrote to Tom and Theodosia *en route*: 'Be not alarmed, my dear young ones, but I am coming down upon you by a forced march, and shall probably reach Florence much before you expect me.'[6]

The Villino Trollope, as it was called, quickly became a fixture in the social life of the expatriate colony in Florence. The beautiful young American, Kate Field, first visited the Villino Trollope in the autumn of 1860, when the middle-aged Anthony Trollope fell madly and innocently in love with her. Tom was an enthusiastic antiquarian and collector, and Kate Field described the house as being 'quaintly fascinating with its marble pillars, its grim men in armour, starting like sentinels from the walls, and its curiosities greeting you at every step'. The villa was overflowing with Florentine bridal chests, richly carved furniture, and thousands of rare books in the library.

Then in the spring, when the soft winds kiss the budding foliage and warm it into bloom, the beautiful terrace of Villino Trollope is transformed into a reception room. Opening upon a garden, with its lofty pillars, its tessellated marble floor, its walls inlaid with terracotta, basreliefs, inscriptions and coats of arms, with here and there a niche devoted to some antique Madonna, the terrace has all the charm of a *campo santo** without the chill of the grave upon it . . . And here of a summer's night, burning no other light than the stars, and sipping iced lemonade, one of the specialities of the place, the intimates of Villino Trollope sit and talk of Italy's future, the last *mot* from Paris, and the last allocution at Rome.

In reply to a cheerful letter from Fanny, Mary Russell Mitford states: 'You have well earned the happiness domestic & social which you enjoy, dear friend.' Anthony, too, sent his congratulations on the new abode: 'To be sure there are certain very palpable delights in being *expeditus*; – in living in other people's houses, being served by other people's servants, eating other men's roast and boiled, and have one's *gendarmerie* paid for by other men's taxes! But still there is a comfort, a solidity, a *nescio quid decori*,† in one's own armchair by one's own fireside, which after all I should not wish to want.' 'So,' Elizabeth Barrett Browning remarked, 'Mrs Trollope has built her nest in Florence, "for good," as people say.'[7]

As permanent residents of the city, the Trollopes could sit back and wryly observe the changing of the seasons in the Tuscan capital. In his first novel, *La Beata* (1861), Tom noted that

Florence was beginning to have more of winter than of summer in its composition. The season of emptiness, vacancy, and summer idleness was coming to an end; and Florence was expecting her usual immigration of winter guests . . . The annual flight of strangers are at the city gates, and Florence must gird up her

---

* 'consecrated ground' or cemetery. Kate Field was probably reminded of the Campo Santo in Pisa, a cloistered burial ground next to the cathedral.
† Best translated as 'je ne sais quoi'.

loins to the serious business of making her livelihood out of them. So the lodging houses are spruced up and painted; the shops get their stock of goods from London and Paris; the hotels put themselves on full war establishment; the artists give the last touches to the works they have been engaged on; and the picture-dealers and owners of 'galleries' set their wares in order . . . the anxious question has to be asked, 'Here for the winter, or going on to Rome?' For the position of fair Florence on the highway to the Eternal City is the cause of many a sad slip between the cup and the lip in these matters.

Once the political turmoil in Italy had abated, the English colony expanded rapidly to include the young diplomat Robert Lytton, Lady Rosina Bulwer's son, Frederick Tennyson, brother of the more famous Alfred, the writers Charles Lever, Walter Savage Landor, Isa Blagden, who like Theodosia had Indian blood, George Eliot and G. H. Lewes. Although they had lived in Florence since 1847, the Brownings had not yet met Mrs Trollope: the Trollopes had been in Rome and then England for much of that time, as had, of course, Mrs Browning's Torquay acquaintance, Theodosia. However, the main reason for their not meeting was Robert Browning, who had warned his wife, 'there is that coarse, vulgar Mrs Trollope – I do hope, Ba, if you don't want to give me the greatest pain, that you won't receive that vulgar pushing woman who is not fit to speak to you'.

Nevertheless, the meeting took place. 'The other day,' Mrs Browning wrote to a friend,

> Mrs Trollope and her daughter-in-law called on us, and it is settled that we are to know them; though Robert had made a sort of vow never to sit in the same room with the author of certain books against liberal institutions and Victor Hugo's poetry.* I had a longer battle to fight, on the matter of this vow, than any since my marriage, and had some scruples at last of taking advantage of the pure goodness which induced him to

---

* In *Paris and the Parisians* Fanny had remarked how dreadful she thought Hugo's writing was.

yield to my wishes; but I *did*, because I hate to seem ungracious and unkind to people; and human beings, besides, are better than their books, than their principles, and even than their everyday actions, sometimes.

Mrs Trollope 'was very agreeable, and kind and good-natured,' the reclusive poetess added, 'and we mean to be quite friends, and to lend each other books, and to forget one another's offences, in print or otherwise. Also, she admits us on her private days; for she has public days (dreadful to relate!), and is in the full flood and flow of Florentine society.' As far as politics was concerned, the feeling was mutual. Fanny wrote to her son Tom that Mrs Browning 'is very anti-Austrian, but *nevertheless* very charming! She is prepared for the acquaintance', no doubt through the intercession of their very dear mutual friend, Mary Russell Mitford.* To another friend Miss Mitford described Mrs Trollope as a 'most elegant and agreeable woman'; 'I have known her these fifty years; she must be turned of seventy, and is wonderful for energy of mind and body.'[8]

Those like Robert Browning who confused people with their politics or, even worse, with their reputation amongst literary critics, invariably assumed that Fanny Trollope would be 'coarse' and 'vulgar'. But they were nearly always pleasantly surprised when they met her. In October 1847, walking down the street in Florence, Tom ran into Dr Jeune, headmaster of King Edward's School in Birmingham where Tom had briefly taught. Jeune wrote to his daughter that he was 'received kindly' by Mrs Trollope. 'I am to dine there this evening, and she is to drive me to see a few things tomorrow. This will be agreeable, but what delights me most is her cordiality. She told me she was an old friend, though she had never seen me, and said, "Tom would have fretted if you had left Florence without seeing him."' The next day he adds, 'I dined with the Trollopes last night. I expected to find Mrs Trollope epigrammatic, – I found her clever, intelligent, and domestic.' When the newly appointed Poet

---

* It was Mary Russell Mitford who presented Elizabeth Barrett Browning with her cocker spaniel, Flush; Virginia Woolf was later to write a biography of the poetess through the eyes of her dog, entitled *Flush*.

Laureate, Alfred Lord Tennyson, visited his brother Frederick in Florence in 1851, Fanny Trollope called on them. Lord Tennyson's wife Emily remarked that she was 'a kind motherly sort of body & not at all coarse as one would expect from her works'.[9]

The Villino Trollope also welcomed other Americans as well as the young Kate Field. In 1859 Harriet Beecher Stowe, author of *Uncle Tom's Cabin* (1852), was a guest at the Trollopes' home, as was another American abolitionist, Bayard Taylor. No doubt Mrs Stowe, who had moved to Cincinnati in 1832, talked to Tom and Fanny about the city; perhaps she told them how the Bazaar had fared after their abrupt departure. 'That lady whose famous book on America is no gauge of her cordiality towards Americans,' so Bayard Taylor describes Fanny Trollope in his book *At Home and Abroad* (1860). 'Her book which, spiteful and caricaturesque as it was, did us no real harm,' he continues. 'We can afford now to be friendly towards a witty, cheerful and really warm-hearted woman – who having forgotten what she lost, remembers only what she admired among us.'*[10]

Anthony and Rose first visited Florence in April 1853. Rose later wrote that her mother-in-law 'took me about everywhere, and explained everything to me. And she made me happy by a present of an Italian silk dress. She also gave me a Roman mosaic brooch, which had been a present to her from Princess Metternich.' (Anthony has La Signora Madeline Vesey Neroni wear this same brooch, with 'a magnificent Cupid' in the centre, in *Barchester Towers*). Rose adds: 'there was nothing conventional about her, and yet she was perfectly free from the vice of affectation ... she was lavishly generous as regards money; full of impulse; not free from prejudice – but more often in *favour* of people than otherwise, – but once in her good books, she was certain to be true to you. She could say a sarcastic word, but never an ill-natured one.' Frances Eleanor Trollope, who knew the expatriate community in Florence as well as anyone, wrote that in Italy 'her social popularity was very great. And yet she was not a

---

* Not all Americans had forgiven Mrs Trollope. The American journalist Margaret Fuller spotted her in Rome in 1847 and wrote, in error, that the old woman was 'pensioned at the rate of two thousand pounds a year to trail her slime over the fruits of Italy . . . after having violated the virgin beauty of America' (*The New York Tribune*, quoted in Mullen, *Birds of Passage*, p. 128).

famous sayer of witty things; she had no reputation of former beauty, which often arouses an interest or curiosity; she did not trade upon an audacious self-assertion and disregard of other people's claims and feelings . . . she was not wealthy; and although she was a successful writer of books, she did not hold a pre-eminent position in literature. But she had admirably good sense, much genuine humour, great knowledge of the world, a quick appreciation of others' gifts, and, above all, a character of the most flawless sincerity, and a warmly affectionate heart.' Anna Drury said of Mrs Trollope, 'It has always seemed to me that those who only knew her through her novels did not half know her ability. To do that, it was needful to listen to her conversation.'[11]

Frances Eleanor Trollope, née Ternan, had first met 'the Italian Trollopes' in the autumn of 1858. Her youngest sister Ellen was at this time Charles Dickens's mistress, and the author paid for the twenty-three-year-old Frances Ternan to travel to Italy to study singing. Dickens equipped Frances with the mandatory letters of introduction, including one to Mrs Trollope. 'I have given her such letters as I think most likely to serve her,' Dickens wrote to Mrs Trollope, 'and I cannot resist the temptation I feel to add this to the List, because I know that she must naturally have a great desire to see you, and because I am not less sure that you will appreciate her.'[12] Fanny certainly would have been amused by the story of the young woman's birth aboard a paddle-steamer in Delaware Bay when her parents, both actors, were on an American tour. Perhaps her young guest told Fanny the latest news of her old friends William Charles Macready and George Bartley, whom the Ternans knew well.

In March 1853 Theodosia had given birth to a little girl, Beatrice. Bice, as she was called, was a very beautiful child, and Fanny's greatest pleasure was to hear her sing, which she did exceptionally well from a very early age. 'I remember on one occasion,' Frances Eleanor Trollope wrote of this period, 'the delight with which she listened to little Bice's voice carolling forth some Tuscan *stornello* in an adjoining room; and how she clasped her hands together as she listened, exclaiming softly, "Dear creature! Dear creature!" ' When Bice was not yet two, the proud grandmother boasted to Anthony of the little girl's 'musical propensities', as well as her dancing, artistic sensibilities and her linguistic skills. Tom added '!!!' in the margin next to these passages. Bice was inevitably spoiled by the Villino Trollope adults. In his memoirs Tom wrote of his wife Theodosia that, 'after the birth of her child, I came second in her heart. But I was not jealous of little Bice.'*

Theodosia had not, however, enjoyed her pregnancy. Fanny was very solicitous of her daughter-in-law's health at this time, and she continually urged Theodosia to join her at Bagni di Lucca during the hot summer months. 'Do you think it would be possible to persuade her to come here *bag and baggage?*' Fanny asked Tom on one of many occasions. Frances Eleanor Ternan remarks that Mrs Trollope 'writes constantly to her daughter-in-law, omitting no detail or suggestion that may be of value. She never manifests the least impatience with poor Theodosia's plaints and low spirits. She never lectures her; she never worries her. She is always kind, always tender.' Perhaps Theodosia, who by all accounts was somewhat lethargic, felt that Fanny's concern could be a little oppressive and her energy simply overwhelming. Fanny clearly tried to give her son and daughter-in-law the privacy they needed by often spending part of the summer at Lucca and part of the winter at Pau, but she still found it 'uncongenial' to be on her own.✝ From Lucca she writes to Tom: 'I really have taken the question whether to go or stay very often into consideration. But I always feel that if I walked in to the Villino saying, "I have come to take care of Theo," I should only be laughed at even by Bran [one of Tom's favourite dogs].'‡[13]

Besides the society at Lucca, Fanny particularly enjoyed the games

---

* Two years after the death of Theodosia (1865), a nasty rumour circulated among the English colony in Florence that Tom was not Beatrice's natural father. Tom's great friend, Isa Blagden, wrote to Robert Browning that it was all nonsense. Florence was not all sunshine and flowers (E. C. McAleer, *Dearest Isa: Robert Browning's Letters to Isabella Blagden*, Austin, TX, 1951 pp. 276–9).

✝ Anthony was to use Florence and Bagni di Lucca, which his mother knew so well, as locations for his novel *He Knew He Was Right.*

‡ John Tilley told Frances Eleanor Trollope that 'mothers-in-law are not popular. Mrs Trollope stayed with us for many months after our marriage, and never could any person have been more charming' (F. E. Trollope, *Frances Trollope*, II, pp. 287–8).

of whist. In the summer of 1850 she met the Irish author Charles Lever at the spa and joined his whist table every evening: 'Nothing can be more agreeable,' she writes to Tom. (Her contribution to the costs of the game were four new packs of cards which she asked Theodosia to bring from Florence.)* At the Villino Trollope, Rose Trollope noted, Fanny 'always had her own special whist-table'. Once, when Fanny was very ill, her Florentine doctor, who also happened to be 'an admirable whist player', proposed to bleed her. Lord Holland, however, sent over his own physician, who stopped the phlebotomy and prescribed that other great nineteenth-century remedy, port wine. Fanny's doctor was so offended by this that he refused to attend her regular Friday-night whist table. Tom later suspected that 'if she could have been consulted', his mother 'would have sided with phlebotomy and whist'. Another absentee from Fanny's special whist table was Charles Lever. Although Lever had been charm personified at Lucca, he apparently did everything he could to avoid her as a whist partner back in Florence for fear that he would end up caricatured in one of her stories.†[14]

This was rich coming from Lever, who confessed that his 'receptions are my studies. I find there my characters, and pick up a thousand things that are to me invaluable. You can't keep drawing wine off the cask perpetually, and putting nothing in, and this is my way of replenishing my brain when I have exhausted it.' Lever was not the only one who feared Fanny's sharp eyes and ready pen. Elizabeth Barrett Browning talks of Mrs Trollope's ' "public mornings" which we shrink from. She "receives" every Saturday morning in the most heterogeneous way possible. It must be amusing to anybody not overwhelmed by it, & people say that she snatches up "characters" for "her so many volumes a year" out of the diversities of masks

---

* During this same summer Fanny writes to Theodosia concerning the eccentric Mrs Stisted, self-appointed 'Queen of the Baths', 'Thus far I have fenced off Queen Zoe very well; – and I do not mean to give up this wholesome exercise!' (ibid., II, p. 209).

† Charles Lever had also charmed Elizabeth Barrett Browning at Lucca and then snubbed her in Florence. She remarked that he had apparently 'seen enough of us – he could put down in his private diary that we had neither claw nor tail' (EBB to MRM, November [1850]: *Letters of E. B. Browning to M. R. Mitford*, III, p. 314).

presented to her on these occasions.' Though she avoided these receptions *antithétiques*, the poetess still fell victim to Fanny's satiric pen: 'Mrs Browning in her shawl,/Which she wears at every ball,' sings the caricaturist Mr Richards in *The Life and Adventures of a Clever Woman* (1854).* The English community in Pau, where Fanny spent much of the winter, was equally afraid of her. As a teenager Sabine Baring-Gould met the 'good-humoured, clever, somewhat vulgar old lady. She took much notice of me.' 'The English residents,' however, 'were not a little shy of her, fearing lest she should take stock of them and use them up in one of her novels.' When confronted with their suspicions, Fanny replied: 'Of course I draw from life – but I always pulp my acquaintance before serving them up. You would never recognize a pig in a sausage.'[15]

Caricaturists such as Mr Richards find their way into several of Fanny's later novels, and each time she describes their methods she is, in fact, revealing her own. In *The Lottery of Marriage* (1849) Cassandra de Laurie is a gifted artist, but caricature 'was her talent, *par excellence*, it was her *forte*, and it was her delight also; and had it not been for her rare discretion in the use of it, she would probably have seen the world in general, and her acquaintance in particular, running away from her, as people always do run away from things that sting'. Cassandra always kept two volumes of her work: one of *bona fide* portraits, the other of the corresponding caricatures. Only a chosen few were 'permitted freely to turn the leaves of the volume that was decidedly the most precious in the eyes of the artist', the caricatures, 'while the other was open to all, with the most affable and confiding good nature imaginable'. Perhaps like Cassandra, Fanny made only a few select friends privy to the 'key' to her satires, such as that belonging to *The Blue Belles* which Elizabeth Barrett Browning had been so keen to get hold of. The general reading public, however, could enjoy her playful and good-natured references to well-known figures, such as the sculptor Hiram Powers and Charles Dickens.

Her critics continued to marvel at Mrs Trollope's industry. In as

---

* The character Mr Richards was based on a fashionable London portrait painter by that name (F. E. Trollope, *Frances Trollope*, II, pp. 246–7).

late as 1852, when Fanny was seventy-three, Colburn's *New Monthly Magazine* boasted: 'In vain have reviewers tried to keep up with her. A blue-stocking who travels in seven-leagued boots may well run critics and criticasters out of breath – *she* triumphantly ascending the hill Difficulty, as fresh as a daisy, while *they* wallow, and struggle, and give up the race (and almost the ghost) in the Slough of Despond. Pant and puff as they will to run her home, she is in a trice miles out of sight, over the hills and far away, and wondering what those sluggard lamenters are doing in the rear.' Her friends and neighbours also marvelled at her strength and energy. Elizabeth Barrett Browning wrote to Mary Russell Mitford in 1854: 'Here is your friend Mrs Trollope who ebbs & flows like the sea – has attacks affecting vital organs, and recovers, and takes long walks again and writes half a dozen more romances.'[16]

However, Fanny's extraordinary resilience had begun to wane. Within two years of Cecilia's death in 1849, four of her children had followed their mother into the grave – all stricken with the family curse, consumption: Cecilia Isabel, nine years of age, in April 1850, five-year-old Arthur a few weeks later (only days after his father's marriage to Mary Anne Partington), Anna Jane, aged eight, in August and, finally, her grandmother's namesake, eleven-year-old Frances, the following June, 1851. Only the baby, Edith, survived. If all this were not enough, in December 1851 Mary Anne, Fanny's niece, died a week after giving birth to a son, called Arthur after his half-brother.

During this same dreadful period, in January 1850, Fanny also lost her brother, Henry Milton. In the spring and summer of 1849 Fanny had made frequent visits to Brighton where the ailing Henry was taking the sea air. One of his last letters addressed to Fanny shows the affection – and sense of fun – which brother and sister shared. The doctor had put Henry on a strict diet, soup being expressly prohibited. Henry's wife apparently made a dreadful scene as the invalid gleefully tucked into a large bowl of the forbidden substance one evening at Fanny's lodgings in Brighton. (It is not hard to imagine that Henry was a difficult patient.) He later wrote to Fanny: 'You have almost made a sad widow of Henry's wife. However, I forgive you. But oh, that murderous soup! ... My dear Fanny, on that never-to-be-spoken-of-without-a-groan evening, the better to disguise your designs, you gave me some very nice, light-coloured, and very light-bodied white wine. Will you kindly tell me what it is called . . . ?' Despite the soup incident, Fanny clearly worried about her brother's health and was reluctant to leave the seaside resort. Henry reassures her at the end of his letter: 'God bless you, my dear Fanny. We will not talk of your now rapidly approaching departure. It is too melancholy a subject. But it is *quite* right that you should go. And the sooner the better. Your affectionate brother, H. M.'[17]

The cruel succession of these individual tragedies left Fanny with a certain sense of detachment from even her oldest friends. She was no longer able to mourn their passing as she once might have done. In 1852 Fanny's lifelong friend, Julia Garnett Pertz, died. Her grieving husband, Georg Pertz, wrote to Fanny: 'You my dear friend who knew her so intimately and possessed her love and gratitude like very few, under whose hospitable roof our loving hearts were united to each other for ever, you feel what a blessed life has been mine, and you will feel with my present bereavement.' He then asks if she could send any letters of Julia still in her possession or, perhaps, write down 'for me and our children' her memories of Julia and her sisters. In a short though heartfelt letter of condolence, Fanny remarks of Julia that 'some of my most cheerful and most happy hours have been passed in her dear society, and I shall remember her, and all her charming qualities till I cease to remember anything'. However, concerning Dr Pertz's sentimental request, she is curt, almost dismissive, pleading that, owing to her 'wandering habits', she has made it a policy never to save letters, 'neither is it in my power to comply with your wishes respecting memoranda of my dear lost friend – for I have never kept journal or notes of any passing events'.[18]

There were other signs that the years were overtaking Fanny. In 1855, when Anthony and his wife met Fanny and Tom in Venice for a holiday, Rose describes her seventy-six-year-old mother-in-law's reaction to being caught in a thunderstorm on their way back from the Murano. The gondola began to roll about unpleasantly in the swell, and Fanny's 'nerves gave way, and she fairly broke down with terror'. She was all right again in the evening, drinking coffee and eating ices while the Austrian band played in the Piazza San Marco, but it must have come as a bit of a shock to Anthony, who had not seen her for two years, that his mother, who had always shown such strength and vigour, had suddenly become an old woman.*[19]

Rose attributed 'the break-up in her mother-in-law's faculties and general health,' Frances Eleanor Trollope remarks, 'to the prejudicial effects of the excitement' of the séances which were all the rage both in London and Florence at this time. Fanny's old friend, Henrietta Skerrett, the same woman whose unpleasant experiences with an evangelical clergyman had formed the basis for *The Vicar of Wrexhill*, had taken Tom to his first séance some years back. On two visits to England in 1854 and 1855, Fanny attended séances led by the young Scottish-born American, Daniel Hume (also Home), at the home of John Rymer in Ealing, west of London. (The red-haired, blue-eyed Hume was said to be the son of the 10TH Earl of Home.) Prominent London literary figures, such as Sir Edward Bulwer-Lytton and the Brownings, made the trek to Ealing to witness tables levitating, lamps twirling, empty chairs rocking and spirits talking. Even Anthony accompanied his mother to Rymer's house on at least one occasion. The evening usually ended with Hume falling into a trance and uttering the words, 'when Daniel recovers give him some bottled porter'.[20]

Some people were openly sceptical from the start. In answer to an invitation by Fanny to join her at one of Mr Hume's 'events' in Ealing, Charles Dickens replied that he had 'not the least belief in the awful unseen World being available for evening parties at so much per night'. (He was, however, curious enough to send a pair of spies to a séance in 1852.) Fanny was willing to suspend disbelief. In December 1854 she told James Jackson Jarvis, who shared her interest, that she appreciated his attitude towards spiritualism, 'so equally removed from enthusiasm on one side, and incredulity on the

---

* Fanny was not the only member of the English colony at Florence who was getting on. Tom describes a visit he paid to the poet Walter Savage Landor, four years Fanny's senior, who was the model for the irascible and generous Lawrence Boythorn in Dickens's *Bleak House*. 'I remember him asking me after my mother . . . I told him that she was fairly well, was not suffering, but that she was becoming deaf. "Dead, is she?" he cried, for he heard me imperfectly. "I wish I was! I can't sleep." '

other . . . That so many thousands of educated and intelligent people should yield their belief to so bold a delusion as this must be, if there be no occult cause at work, is inconceivable.' Fanny, having witnessed the moment of death with each of her four children, felt that there was something yet to be explained. 'Children,' she wrote to Jarvis a few days later, 'at the moment of passing from this state to that which follows it will often (as I well know) speak with a degree of intelligence that strongly suggests the idea that there are moments when the two conditions *touch.* That the region next above us is occupied by the souls of men about to be made perfect, I have not the shadow of a doubt. The puzzling part of the present question is this . . . why do we get a dark and uncertain peep *now* at a stage of existence from which philosophy has so long been excluded? And I am inclined to say in reply, "be patient, and be watchful and we shall all know more anon." '[21] In an age when the best that medical science could offer seemed to be a choice between bleeding and port wine, this sort of thinking was understandable, especially in a woman who had lost so many loved ones.

Hume and Rymer followed the Trollopes to Florence in October 1855, and for a month the Villino Trollope became the gathering place for spirits and mortals alike – the latter category including Hiram Powers, the Brownings, of course, and Charles Lever, whose curiosity must have overcome his fear of Mrs Trollope. The spirits of Fanny's father, her mother and several of her children were summoned. 'Her imagination and romance,' Rose wrote, 'got the upper hand. The effect of these visits told upon her spirits.' Frances Eleanor Trollope was not so sure, for nowhere in the family correspondence or in Tom's journal did it state that Fanny was agitated or upset by these séances. Apparently Tom, who was equally if not more enthusiastic than his mother, had a tendency to badger the spirits with questions, and the unearthly visitors showed a distinct unease under his cross-examination. On one occasion Fanny seems to have lost patience when a table went hurtling towards the door, and cried 'Damn it, let it go!' Perhaps it was at about this time that Fanny's natural scepticism returned, for, according to another one-time believer, Elizabeth Barrett Browning, Mrs Trollope threw over Hume 'from some failure in his moral character in Florence . . . I have no doubt that the young man, who is weak and vain, and was exposed to gross flatteries from the various unwise coteries at Florence who took him up, deserves to be thrown over.'*[22]

If nothing else, Fanny certainly viewed these séances as a rich source of material for her novels. In *Fashionable Life; or Paris and London* (1856) she draws a thinly disguised – and not very complimentary – portrait of Hume in the character of the medium, Mr Wilson: 'He was a quiet young man, quiet in manner, apparently, both by temperament and by principle, and well it was for him that he should be so, for,' Fanny comments, 'the great majority of those whom curiosity led to witness the marvellous phenomenon . . . proclaimed him fraudulent.' 'This was certainly a painful ordeal for the transatlantic seer to go through; but he endured it all with a sort of passive philosophy' (*Fashionable Life*). Wilson's tools of the trade, according to Fanny, were a small round table covered by a carpet, a heavy lamp, paper, pencils and letters of the alphabet on pasteboard. To enable the spirit to communicate, the medium recited the alphabet until the ethereal guest identified the correct letter by a sharp rap on the table, whereupon it was written down and the whole process repeated as often as necessary. (By this means, Tom's detailed cross-examination of the spirits must, indeed, have been a painful experience for everyone present.) Fanny makes it clear that the most enthusiastic spiritualist in the novel, Mme de Charmont, is also the most susceptible, for she has recently lost her father and daughter.

Fashionable Life, published in 1856, was to be Fanny's last work. She was seventy-seven. She had written six travel books and thirty-five novels in twenty-four years; she published nearly half of them with Henry Colburn and, from 1853, his successors, Hurst and Blackett. She had retained her popularity to the end. In its review of *Fashionable Life, The Critic* deemed Mrs Trollope 'the *doyenne* of English authoresses'. Fanny's forte was broad satire, but she also succeeded in combining witty social commentary with strong and often melodramatic plots in which princes wander about the countryside disguised as peasants, wives are kidnapped and held captive by their husbands,

---

* Hume seems to have landed on his feet. He became all the rage at the Russian Court, and eventually married into the Russian aristocracy.

and young girls are seduced. In her novels Fanny explores marriage and the importance of marriage settlements; a social gathering in a country house is the scene for many an intrigue; and the watering holes of England bring together a whole menagerie of amusing characters. She astutely aimed to hit the somewhat lowbrow taste of the circulating library, and this, as *The Spectator* noted, she did 'remarkably well'.

Yet contemporary critics also appreciated Fanny's skills as an author and the accuracy of her outlook on society. The *Morning Post* spoke of 'Mrs Trollope's high reputation as a novelist' and called her 'one of the ablest fiction writers of the day'. One reviewer wrote that, as a satirist, she ranked alongside Thackeray. Fanny Trollope had succeeded in creating a fictional world all her own: 'Her people,' a contemporary wrote, 'talk as real men and women talk . . . Hence they make upon the mind and the memory the same impressions as are made by personages whom we have known. They do not pass away with the closing of the book, as is usual with the characters to whom we are introduced in ordinary novels, but they form a part of the crowd of recollections that continually recur in after life, and as vividly as any of the forms that memory cherishes.' 'Her own sex,' *John Bull* remarked of Fanny Trollope, 'she seems to have studied with profound attention.'[23]

Even Thackeray, who at one time thought that Mrs Trollope should stick to making puddings, later confessed: 'I do not care to read ladies' novels, except those of Mesdames Gore and Trollope.' Charles Dickens's young friend, Percy Fitzgerald, wrote: 'As a child I can recall the amazing popularity of Frances [Trollope]. In the forties she was the one and only "fashionable" story-teller to be read, and certainly her "Widow Barnaby" and other jovial tales gave great entertainment, and was the pattern for a whole school of such things.' (To name just one example, Sophia Martin, the unscrupulous, ambitious and conniving 'heroine' of *The Ward of Thorpe Combe* (1841) is almost certainly the model for Thackeray's Becky Sharpe in *Vanity Fair*, published six years later.) Of course, not everyone liked Fanny's books. In his critical symposium, *A New Spirit of the Age* (1844), R. H. Horne talks of Mrs Trollope's 'constitutional coarseness' and her 'vulgarity'. One of Horne's collaborators, Elizabeth Barrett Browning, was not Mrs Trollope's greatest admirer; however, she felt compelled to rebuke Horne: 'it really does strike me strongly that you & your critic do no manner of justice to Mrs Trollope, who is a very clever writer'. She is, Mrs Browning continues, 'very acute – absolute over laughter in matters of caricature on the coarse scale'. 'Certainly,' comments *The New Monthly Magazine*, 'no other author of the present day has been at once so much read, so much admired, and so much abused.'[24]

In 1855, the year before Fanny laid down her pen for the last time, Anthony's novel *The Warden* appeared. Following *The Macdermots of Ballycloran* in 1847, Anthony had published a second Irish novel with his mother's publisher, Henry Colburn, *The Kellys and the O'Kellys* (1848). It fared no better than the *Macdermots* and Colburn told Anthony that Irish novels were not popular; moreover, he added, 'it is impossible for me to give any encouragement to you to proceed in novel writing'.[25] Undeterred, the young author set his next two works, *La Vendée* and a play, *The Noble Jilt*, in eighteenth-century Europe. *The Macdermots of Ballycloran* had been unfavourably compared with his mother's books. It was almost as if Anthony dared not venture into the sphere of contemporary English manners, which he knew so well, because he feared further comparisons with Fanny's writing. Anthony showed *The Noble Jilt* to his mother's old friend, the actor-manager George Bartley. His very negative reaction, Anthony recalls in his autobiography, 'was a blow in the face!' Despite his reservations, Colburn did bring out *La Vendée* in 1850, but historical subjects were about as fashionable as Irish ones.* So, finally, for his next literary venture Anthony accepted his destiny and wrote *The Warden*, a novel set in the England of his day.

Fanny had seen Anthony struggle to become established as a novelist. When she read *The Warden* in 1855, she knew that he had achieved his ambition and created a style and a vein of gentle,

---

* At this same time Anthony submitted to John Murray a travel book on Ireland. The manuscript was returned unopened. Perhaps Murray did not think that Anthony would have the same skill of lively description as his mother; the great publisher is supposed to have remarked concerning the south-west of England, that it was 'a district not yet trollopised'. See S. Smiles, *A Publisher and his Friends: Memoir and Correspondence of the late John Murray*, 2 vols., London, 1891.

sometimes mocking, humour all his own. 'Of this,' Anthony recalls her saying, 'you owe nothing to me, and as yet I have observed nothing like it in others of your period.' Fanny, too, was adept at this sort of subtle wit, but she had preferred to rely upon broad satire to attract readers. Anthony's brother Tom had continued to write learned articles as well as a travel book, *Impressions of a Wanderer in Italy, Switzerland, France and Spain* (1850) and a historical tome, *The Girlhood of Catherine de Medici* (1856); Theodosia was by this time the Tuscan correspondent for *The Athenaeum*. But Fanny clearly perceived that it was Anthony who would continue what by now had become the family tradition of novel writing. In the summer of 1856 she wrote to Anthony:

Age eighty, (minus not quite three) thermometer eighty, (plus rather more than four) must be accepted as an excuse my very dear Anthony both by you and my highly valued correspondent [Harry] for not having acknowledged your very precious *packet* earlier. I am in truth grown most woefully idle, and, worse still, most woefully *lazy*, and this symptom is both new and disagreeable to *me*. But the degree of activity of which I have been wont to boast, and on which I have so often been complimented might have been accounted in my very best days as positive *idleness* when compared to what you manifest. Tom and I agree in thinking that you exceed in this respect any individual that we have ever known or heard of – and I am proud of being your mother – as well for this reason as for sundry others. I rejoice to think that you have considerably more than the third of a century to gallop through yet before reaching the age at which I first felt inclined to cry halta la!

Tom added at the bottom: 'My mother is pretty well, though weak, and it is impossible not to see that the last year has made a greater change in her than ever any one year did before. She does not suffer in any way but from inability to exert herself.'[26]

Perhaps Fanny no longer felt the need to exert herself. Her one and only reason for writing had been to provide for her family and to give her children a good start in the world. Looking around her, aged seventy-seven, she saw both her surviving sons happily married. Tom and Theodosia had the Villino Trollope and were able to produce an adequate income from their writing. Anthony had a good job at the Post Office; more importantly, he was now well on his way to becoming a successful author.

The publication of *The Warden*, which evokes the world of the English cathedral close, marks the moment when Anthony Trollope came into his inheritance, the Trollopian realm for which he would become famous but which was his mother's before him. As one critic noted, the English clergy, from the poor country curate to 'haughty, dictatorial, heartless Bishops and preferment-seeking Rectors', had been considered Fanny Trollope's province since the publication of *The Vicar of Wrexhill* in 1837.[27] She set the scene for one of her later novels, *Petticoat Government* (1850), in a cathedral town 'which we will distinguish by the name of Westhampton – chiefly because we know of no town so called'. Just five years later, Anthony tells his readers that *The Warden* takes place in a cathedral town, 'let us call it Barchester. Were we to name Wells or Salisbury, Exeter, Hereford, or Gloucester, it might be presumed that something personal was intended.' Anthony later claimed that, when he wrote *The Warden*, he had 'never lived in any cathedral city . . . never knew anything of any Close, and at that time had enjoyed no peculiar intimacy with any clergyman' (*An Autobiography*). This is somewhat disingenuous: he knew the clergy through his mother. Fanny's father had been a West Country clergyman; family holidays were often spent in the cathedral town of Exeter visiting her cousin; and her clashes with the evangelical Revd John Cunningham were famous throughout Harrow.

Barchester Towers, published in 1857, was Anthony's first real commercial success: it was the moment that he had been dreaming of for twenty-five years. It had been a year since Fanny Trollope's last novel had appeared; the critics, with very short memories, made no more comparisons between mother and son, yet Anthony continued to draw on his mother's fictional world. That world was filled not only with clergymen but also with strong-minded women. Some are high-spirited and warm-hearted like Kate Harrington in Fanny's *Uncle Walter* and Lady Mary Palliser in Anthony's *The Duke's Children*

– both determined to marry the men they love in the face of parental opposition. There are also haughty, ambitious and selfish women who have long since learned that they cannot afford to fall in love: such are Cassandra de Laurie in Fanny's *Lottery of Marriage* and Arabella Trefoil in Anthony's *American Senator*.

Most of these women have only their charms to rely on. The beautiful, capricious Mrs Morley in Fanny's *Blue Belles of England*, a woman with a tragic past and an only daughter, returns to her native England from Italy: her expression could flit from one of melancholy to playful mischief and she 'had the art of ever making a sort of throne of the seat she selected' to which men flocked in the hope of an intimate *tête-à-tête*. La Signora Madeline Vesey Neroni, said to have been crippled by her cruel Italian husband, returns to Barchester and employs this same strategy in *Barchester Towers*, draping herself on the sofa and monopolizing the attention of the men around her. When the grasping female novelist, Mrs Sherbourne, 'particularly dreaded a writer of biting paragraphs, she managed to get introduced to him ... and to calm the terrors of his pen,' Fanny explains in *Charles Chesterfield*, 'by that gentle tone of independent weakness'. Anthony's Lady Carbury in *The Way We Live Now* likewise charms editors and critics with hospitality and female wiles, pleading to one influential editor: 'I myself am so much in want of support for my own little efforts.'

Central to the plots of both authors are an alarming number of motherless heroines and interfering aunts, such as Martha Barnaby and her niece Agnes Willoughby in Fanny's most popular book, *The Widow Barnaby*. Martha's bumptious nature and amorous exploits reappear in the character of Arabella Greenow in Anthony's *Can You Forgive Her?*, where they provide light relief to the main story of the motherless Alice Vavasor's dithering. Mrs Greenow, like Martha Barnaby, marries late and well, and is widowed early. They both enjoy their newly acquired wealth by sporting luxurious widows' weeds, cambric handkerchiefs and crocodile tears while carrying on flirtations with bogus military men, much to the embarrassment of their nieces who are travelling with them. Despite the fact that they are in mourning, Arabella Greenow and Martha Barnaby both insist on putting down their names for the assembly rooms in the resort towns where they are staying – ostensibly so as not to deprive the young girls of society.*

As we have already seen, Anthony's books are often reminiscent of Fanny's because mother and son are drawing on experiences they shared and people they both knew. An unctuous evangelical clergyman, greedy for power and 'accustomed in the course of his ministry to win young ladies . . . by means of a little propitiatory love-making', courts a rich widow and, in doing so, divides her family. The Vicar of Wrexhill, like Anthony's Obadiah Slope in *Barchester Towers*, was based on the Trollopes' Harrow neighbour, the Revd John Cunningham. Their much-loved Devonshire cousin, Fanny Bent, was the inspiration for Fanny's Miss Elizabeth Compton in *The Widow Barnaby* and Miss Jemima Stanbury in *He Knew He Was Right*. Both are Devonshire-bred, old-fashioned and outspoken spinsters. Like Miss Compton, Miss Stanbury decides to take in her penniless niece. Fanny describes Aunt Betsy's thoughts as 'alternatively both sweet and bitter, sometimes cheering her with a vision of domestic happiness and endearment to soothe her declining age, and sometimes making her shudder as she had fancied her tranquil existence invaded and destroyed by the presence of one whom she might strive to love in vain'. These are Miss Stanbury's exact same musings thirty years later. Both mother and son explored the tragic figure of Thomas Anthony Trollope in their fiction. Like Fanny's *One Fault*, Anthony's *He Knew He Was Right* is the study of a husband's obsessive attempt to control his wife. 'To have three long volumes devoted to the development of one ingredient, and confined to the effects of the conduct of a husband upon a wife . . . is too much. The perpetual repetition of the same causes, with the same results, grows tiresome; and we feel that a tithe-part of them would have wrought more impressively than the whole.'[28] This criticism of *One Fault* would also be made against *He Knew He Was Right*.

The list of characters and plot lines which Anthony borrowed from his mother could go on and on. The plots of Fanny's *Mrs Mathews*

---

* The characters of Arabella Greenow and Alice Vavasor first appeared as Madame Brudo and Margaret de Wynter in Anthony's unpublished play, *The Noble Jilt*, written in 1850, only eleven years after the publication of *The Widow Barnaby*.

and Anthony's *Mr Scarborough's Family* both hang upon the terms and conditions of a will. A young penniless orphan, greedy, selfish and devious, connives to inherit a rich estate and runs away with the family diamonds: this describes both Sophia Martin in *The Ward of Thorpe Combe* and Lizzie Eustace in *The Eustace Diamonds*. A ruthless financier of dubious origins flaunts his wealth, is admitted to 'the best society', and thus attracts investors in a high-risk speculation; the bubble bursts, the investors are ruined and suicide follows. Monsieur Roche in *Fashionable Life* and Augustus Melmotte in *The Way We Live Now* are two such men. An old bachelor friend of the family, who is still considered handsome for his age and generally popular, though he has no intimate acquaintances, woos the young woman whom he has known since she was a baby merely to flatter his own vanity. The actions of both Mr Cuthbert in *Town and Country* and Colonel Osborne in *He Knew He Was Right* have dreadful consequences for the naïve and sheltered young heroines. In Fanny's *The Laurringtons* Charlotte Mastermann pushes her charming but unprincipled brother Frank to marry the wealthiest woman in the district. Charlotte Stanhope is no less scheming on behalf of her attractive but equally unscrupulous brother Bertie in *Barchester Towers*, urging him to propose to the unsuspecting widow, Eleanor Bold. Like Bertie, Frank's most remarkable feature were his eyes: 'they sparkled, they flashed, they laughed . . . yet sometimes there was a wicked spark of mischief in this mirth, that in the sharp-sighted might beget more fear than sympathy'.

A critic once said of Fanny Trollope's novels: 'She interests her readers because she is in earnest; what she says she means, and what she means she says.'[29] This is also true of Anthony's fiction. Both authors have a strong narrative voice, creating a certain rapport – even intimacy – with their readers. Just as Fanny interrupts her story to inform her readers on all sorts of matters, from the perfect number to have at a dinner party to the elusive nature of happiness, so Anthony gives his opinion on everything from women's fashions to liberal politics. Sometimes their opinions clash. Fanny often wrote on the delights of a picnic; Anthony – no doubt having been dragged along on too many family picnics – hated them and said so in his novels. Both novelists occasionally leave their characters in suspended animation. In *Fashionable Life*, when Henry Hamilton proposes to Caroline Holmwood, Fanny explains at some length the heroine's feelings on the matter before declaring: 'But I am leaving Henry Hamilton too long upon his knees.' So, Anthony apologizes for having 'kept the Greshamsbury tenantry waiting under the oak-trees by far too long' at Frank Gresham's twenty-first birthday party while he discussed the Gresham family background in *Dr Thorne*.

Anthony, like his mother before him, often subverts the concept of hero and heroine. Thus the scheming Sophia Martin and Lizzie Eustace are the declared heroines of *The Ward of Thorpe Combe* and *The Eustace Diamonds*, respectively. In *The Attractive Man* Fanny confesses to her readers: 'I scarcely know how it has happened, but I find, upon consideration, that I have reached this advanced stage of my labours, without having any heroine at all ... I find this deficiency of a heroine exceedingly inconvenient, as it greatly impedes the natural progress of the narrative, and obliges me to appear inconsistent myself, when, in point of fact, all the inconsistency is in my people.' Anthony finds himself in the exact same dilemma near the end of *Ralph the Heir*: 'The writer of this story feels that some apology is due to his readers for having endeavoured to entertain them so long with the adventures of one of whom it certainly cannot be said that he was fit to be delineated as a hero.'

Mother and son do not flinch from admitting to the difficulties of narration. Both find the task of ending a novel particularly troublesome. In *Charles Chesterfield* Fanny bemoans the fact that

> the kindest-hearted critic of them all invariably twits us with the incompetency and lameness of our conclusion. We have either become idle and neglected it, or tedious and over-laboured it. It is insipid or unnatural, over-strained or imbecile. It means nothing, or attempts too much ... I can only say that if some critic, who thoroughly knows his work, and has laboured on it till experience has made him perfect, will write the last fifty pages of a novel in the way they should be written, I, for one, will in future do my best to copy the example.

In the same vein Anthony laments at the end of *Barchester Towers*:

And who can apportion out and dovetail his incidents, dialogues, characters, and descriptive morsels, so as to fit them all exactly into 476 pages, without either compressing them unnaturally, or extending them artificially at the end of his labour? Do I not myself know that I am at this moment in want of a dozen pages, and that I am sick with cudgelling my brains to find them?

Finally, even some of the innovations which scholars have claimed for Anthony's fiction actually make their first appearance in Fanny's. Samuel Bozzle in *He Knew He Was Right* is not the original ex-policeman turned private detective; that distinction belongs to Mr Hannibal Burns in Fanny's very first novel, *The Refugee*, followed by the Maigret-like chief inspector, M. Collet in *Hargrave*. In one marvellous scene M. Collet and another man called Ruperto interrogate the prisoner and their eyes meet. 'There was at this moment something like a trial of skill between them, and each desired to see the effect which this remarkable alteration in the demeanour of the prisoner produced. The Italian smiled, and perhaps the Frenchman returned it; but if he did, the dignity of office prevented his permitting it to be visible, for his hand gravely enveloped the lower part of his face' before he uttered to the guard "Donnez le clef, mon ami!" ' Nor was Anthony the first English author to create a fictional series with the Barsetshire novels. That innovation, too, was his mother's: as we have seen, she had traced the history of the Widow Barnaby over the course of three books. Like the Barsetshire novels, the Barnaby series mimics reality: characters float in and out, they grow older, and sometimes wiser. However, when praised at a London literary dinner for this innovation in the English novel, Anthony did not take the opportunity to mention the precedent set by his mother.*[30]

An intellectual property lawyer, looking at the evidence, would undoubtedly conclude that there was a very strong prima facie

---

* From the 1830s the French author Honoré de Balzac reintroduced characters in his 'Comédie Humaine' series. The use of silly names, like Mr Quiverful and Farmer Cheeseacre, belongs exclusively to Anthony. However, Fanny was particularly fond of the expression 'omnium gatherum' and she uses it frequently in her novels – she even names a lecturer on female rights 'Mr Omnium' (*The Laurringtons*). The Duke of Omnium and Gatherum Castle belong, of course, to Anthony's Palliser novels.

case for plagiarism here. However, if we are to accuse Anthony of plagiarism, then we must also accuse his brother Tom of the same crime. When he eventually followed Colley Grattan's advice and turned to fiction, in 1861, Tom, like his mother and brother, created a strong narrative presence and used many of the same characters – usually those modelled on people the Trollopes knew, such as their Exeter cousin, Fanny Bent, and also their father. Tom even sets a series of three novels in the cathedral town of Sillchester and the surrounding county of Sillshire, a thinly disguised Exeter and Devon.* In turn, Tom willingly furnished both his mother and brother with the plots to *Petticoat Government* and *Doctor Thorne*, respectively. All of the Trollopes considered writing to be first and foremost a trade: Anthony famously compared himself to a shoemaker. Characters and plots were simply tools of that trade, to be shared freely between the various partners in the family firm of Trollope, Trollope and Trollope. (Fanny's habit of early hours apparently became company policy, for Tom and Anthony also rose between four and five in the morning in order to write before breakfast.) Fanny would not have minded the literary borrowings; when Anthony recycled one of her plots, she would have considered it thrift rather than theft. After all, such borrowings were evident enough in *The Warden*, yet she told Anthony that she was proud to be his mother. She was pleased that Anthony had taken on board the advice which she had once tried to give to Harriet Garnett. One must first know how to 'condescend to popular taste', Fanny had written to Julia Pertz concerning her sister; then 'the best feature in the business [of writing] is that this first struggle once past, the rest is easy – nothing more being required than just so much application to your pen as may suffice to produce the *quantity* you desire to *sell*. This is not very sublime but it is very true.'[31]

As Anthony gained more and more confidence, especially following his marriage to Rose and the birth of his sons, Harry (named after his brother) and Fred, in March 1846 and September 1847, respect-

---

* Tom's Sillshire novels, begun after Anthony was well into his Barsetshire novels, comprise *Lindisfarn Chase* (1864), *Artingale Castle* (1867) and *The Garstangs of Garstang Grange* (1869).

ively, his relations with his mother improved. He begins to write her gossipy letters about the children and new hats, signing himself, 'God bless you dearest mother, ever your own little boy, A. T.' Even before his success with *The Warden* and *Barchester Towers*, he is able to speak light-heartedly about his literary ambitions when he informs Fanny that, at the forthcoming Great Exhibition of 1851, 'I mean to exhibit four 3-vol. Novels – all failures! – which I look on as a great proof of industry at any rate.' Anthony had finally learned what his mother had known before him: not 'to mistake the absence of perfect happiness for the presence of misery' (*Petticoat Government*). Fanny's trip to England in 1855 had been her last; Anthony and Rose visited Florence again in 1857, when Rose found her mother-in-law 'much changed and broken, not caring for her afternoon drive, and indifferent to her rubber of whist'. By their next visit, in 1860, Fanny's short-term memory had begun to fail, though 'of the past she still remembered much, and still vividly'. Each afternoon she asked Tom 'to trot me out' round the beautiful garden; people continued to call at the Villino Trollope to converse with Tom and Theodosia while paying their respects to old Mrs Trollope. Her last surviving letter to Anthony, which probably dates from 1859, reads:

> *My Dear Anthony,*
>   You ask me to write – I and my pen have been so long divorced that I hardly know how to set about it – But you ask me to write and therefore write I will – though I have no news to tell you more fresh than that I love you dearly – I should like to see you again, but can hardly hope it! God bless you my dear dear Son!
>
> Your loving mother,
Frances Trollope[32]

Fanny did see Anthony twice more, in 1860 and 1863, though it is doubtful that she recognized him on his last visit for, as Tom wrote, 'during the last few years the bright lamp began to grow dim and gradually sink into the socket'. Soon after Anthony's departure, on 6 October 1863, Fanny Trollope died, aged eighty-four, peacefully in bed. Her last words were 'Poor Cecilia!' Tom, with some difficulty, complied with his mother's wish that a vein be opened in her arm to ensure that she was not buried alive. She was laid to rest, Tom states, in the 'beautiful little cemetery on which the Apennine looks down'. The English cemetery is now a traffic island in the Piazzale Donatello, but is otherwise much as it ever was. Around her lie the other members of the Anglo-Florentine community whom she knew so well: Theodosia's father, Joseph Garrow, who died in 1857, Elizabeth Barrett Browning, who passed away in 1861, Walter Savage Landor and her Cincinnati acquaintance, the sculptor Hiram Powers. On her gravestone the Latin inscription composed by Tom is still faintly visible. In translation it reads: 'Frances Trollope. Here lies what is mortal, but the remembrance of her divine spirit needs no marble.'

Twelve years later, in 1875, the sixty-year-old Anthony had begun to write his memoirs. As he looked back over his life, all the misery and resentment which he had felt throughout his childhood came once more to the surface. Reading *An Autobiography*, one catches a glimpse of the unhappy and reticent little boy whose 'mother was much from home or too busy to be bothered' and whose father 'was not exactly the man to exact confidences'. This is the same little boy whom Anthony sometimes described in his novels: 'A favourite sister may perhaps be told of the hard struggle and the bitter failure, but not a word is said to anyone else. His father, so thinks the boy, is angry at his failure; and even his mother's kisses will hardly be warmed by such a subject. We are too apt to think that if our children eat pudding and make a noise they require no sympathy' (*The Bertrams*). Fanny must have seen that Cecilia was that sympathetic younger sister who loved her older brother 'beyond all things, and knowing herself, all childish as she was, to be his only confidante and advisor' (*The Widow Married*).

In his autobiography one recognizes the boy who felt that he and his father had been abandoned by Fanny when she went off to America, taking his brother and two sisters with her. Again and again in his novels, Anthony tells his readers that 'a wife does not cease to love her husband because he gets into trouble. She does not turn against him because others have quarrelled with him. She does not separate her lot from his because he is in debt! Those are the times when a wife, a true wife, sticks closest to her husband, and strives the hardest to lighten the weight of his cares by the tenderness of her love!' (*Rachel Ray*). Perhaps Fanny had understood Anthony's feelings of abandonment: 'It would be,' she writes in *The Life and Adventures of a Clever Woman,* 'untrue to say that at the age of eighteen Zelah did not blame the conduct of her parents towards her' after they went abroad to escape debtors' prison, leaving her behind. 'She did blame it.' Fanny had also seen Anthony's anguish at their poverty: 'During all the pecuniary embarrassments which had immediately preceded and followed his father's death, he had always felt himself, poor boy, on the defensive with his fellow creatures' (*Petticoat Government*).

In portraying his mother, Anthony seems to have become once more that nineteen-year-old youth who went to the trouble of copying out all sixty-one stanzas of her poem on the burial of Byron's daughter Allegra, adding his own often harsh and, one might almost say, spiteful comments in the margins: 'these lines are bad', 'twaddle all this'; 'perspicuity of style is by no means one of the merits of this poem'.[33] This is the aspiring author, with the conceit of youth, whom Fanny portrays in *Charles Chesterfield; or the Adventures of a Youth of Genius.* In his autobiography Anthony criticizes his mother's politics: 'with her politics were always an affair of the heart, – as, indeed, were all her convictions. Of reasoning from causes, I think that she knew nothing.' He faults *The Domestic Manners of the Americans*: 'no observer was certainly ever less qualified to judge of the prospects or even the happiness of a young people. No one could have been worse adapted by nature for the task of learning whether a nation was in a way to thrive. Whatever she saw she judged, as most women do, from her own standing-point.' And last, but not least, he condemns her novels: 'she was neither clear-sighted nor accurate; and in her attempts to describe morals, manners, and even facts, was unable to avoid the pitfalls of exaggeration'.

Anthony did acknowledge and praise his mother's courage, *joie de vivre* and enormous capacity for work; nevertheless, Tom was horrified when he read what Anthony had written about her. He thought the fault lay in the fact that 'from the time that he became a clerk in the Post Office to her death, he and my mother were never together but as visitors during the limited period of a visit'. But there is clearly more than ignorance at work here. Throughout the whole of Anthony's writing career, Fanny's books were reprinted and reissued in cheap editions, appearing alongside his own in shops, circulating libraries and railway stations. Fairly early in his career, in 1859, the critics had praised him in almost the same terms as they had his mother before him: 'Mr Anthony Trollope is, in fact, the most fertile, the most popular, the most successful author – that is to say, of the circulating library sort.'[34] Fanny had been content with this. Her overriding aim had been to make enough money from her books to support herself and her children. Writing at great speed, often under enormous pressure, she perhaps never achieved her full potential as a novelist.

But Anthony sought more than success among the circulating libraries. He had the inner drive to fashion himself into a truly great writer. Moreover, he wanted to be recognized as such. In his memoirs, Anthony admits that he had always had 'before my eyes the charms of reputation' as well as a 'craving for love' and 'a wish to be liked by those around me'. He coveted, and eventually obtained, the accolades of his peers: membership of the Garrick Club, invitations to London literary dinners and even the editorship of a monthly periodical, *St Pauls.** To the aspiring man of letters his mother's reputation as a 'coarse' and 'vulgar' author must have been a continual embarrassment, and he used his autobiography as an opportunity to publicly distance himself from both her writing and her politics. Unsurprisingly, nowhere in his autobiography does Anthony even hint at the debt which he owed to Fanny's example. Anthony's criticisms seemed to have hit their mark, because from the time *An Autobiography* was published, in 1883, the year following Anthony's death, Mrs Trollope's novels suddenly ceased to be published. Anthony had, in effect, buried his mother's literary reputation.†

---

* In 1865 Trollope succeeded where his mother had failed when he helped to establish *The Fortnightly Review*. However, it was not successful.

† Fanny Trollope's most popular novel, *The Widow Barnaby*, last appeared in England in 1881; an American edition came out in [1885]. *Michael Armstrong* was reissued in London in 1888, to coincide with the labour unrest at the time. The Americans eventually reprinted *The Domestic Manners of the Americans* in [1894], and again in 1901, 1904, 1927, 1949, etc.

Although he does not mention it, Tom did not fare much better in Anthony's autobiography. While Anthony remarks that he and his brother 'have been fast friends' for forty years, in describing his school days at Winchester he claims that Tom 'was, of all my foes, the worst': 'as part of his daily exercise,' Anthony recalls, Tom 'thrashed me with a big stick'. Tom is today remembered by Anthony's biographers as a bully. Yet this is unfair. Tom was very clever, clever perhaps to the point of precociousness. Yet unlike the self-centred Anthony, he spent most of his life looking out for other people. He sat up with Anthony in their dingy London lodgings to help his brother with his penmanship the night before his second interview at the Post Office. He acted not only as his mother's literary agent, but also as Anthony's, and it was Tom's assertiveness with the publisher which gained Anthony his first literary income, £20, from *La Vendée*.

Fanny, in effect, supported Tom for nearly twenty years, but this was not without some personal sacrifices on his part. It must have been increasingly difficult to act as Fanny's courier and general companion, especially as she became more fretful with age. Although Fanny and Theodosia were genuinely fond of each other, Tom would have inevitably found it a strain dividing his time between his mother and his wife. His own writing career as an historian and novelist did not really begin until after Fanny had ceased to be active, in about 1859: before this date he had only published four out of an eventual total of thirty-five books. However, in his memoirs, written at the age of seventy-seven, he states that he had never regretted one moment of the life which he had chosen. 'During many years, and many, many journeyings, and more *tête-à-tête* walks, and yet more of *tête-à-tête* home hours,' Tom writes of himself and his mother, 'we were inseparable companions and friends'; until 'the time of my marriage, she was all in all to me!' Like Fanny, Tom had no pretensions as an author: he wrote novels – fifteen in all – to make money. They 'had no great, but a fair, share of success', he remarks in his memoirs. Those on Italian subjects, 'if I may be allowed to say so, are good'; 'those which I wrote on English subjects are unquestionably bad'. His real interest had always been Italian history, though the subject enjoyed a 'comparatively limited audience'. Tom had inherited his mother's good-humoured realism.

The contrasting relationships between Fanny and each of her two sons are reflected in Tom and Anthony's very different attitudes towards the other women in their lives. The Garnetts had said of the thirty-one-year-old Tom in 1841 that he 'is very like his father in manner, cross & contradictory'. (This may have been due in part to the fact that, like his father, he suffered from migraines until his early forties.) Tom may not have suffered fools gladly, but he treated everyone equally, including women. Anthony liked to flirt with kitchen maids. When as teenagers Tom and Anthony had walked the fourteen miles from Harrow Weald to Vauxhall Gardens, it was Anthony who danced all night while Tom preferred to watch the firework display. From his mother's example, Anthony knew that 'a woman can do things for which a man's strength would never be sufficient' (*Orley Farm*); nevertheless, he told his readers again and again that the best career for even the most strong-minded woman was marriage and motherhood. Anthony even advised the young and ambitious Kate Field to give up writing and 'go & marry a husband'.[35] He himself had married the very sensible but mousy and conventional Rose.

Tom, on the other hand, was somewhat shy with women who could not hold their own in an intellectual conversation. Thus, he was attracted to the clever and talented Theodosia. They helped each other in their writing and collaborated on a book which documented the events which eventually led to the proclamation of the Kingdom of Italy in 1861, *Tuscany in 1849 and 1859* (1859). In another work which he published this same year, entitled *A Decade of Italian Women*, Tom declares that 'the degree in which any social system has succeeded in ascertaining woman's proper position, and in putting her into it, will be a very accurate list of the progress it has made in civilization'. By this measure England had not yet reached 'the age of discretion'. 'The absolute *sine qua non*,' Tom asserts, for 'the advancement of a civilization', must be 'the solidarity, co-operation, and mutual influence of both the sexes'.

Tom says of himself that he was not 'clubbable' in the way that Anthony was. Tom did not have that same desperate need to belong as his brother; he possessed a quiet self-confidence which made him an easy person to be with. He was also, by all accounts, a more enjoyable companion at a dinner table. Whereas Anthony was 'as unhelpful and impatient an arguer as I ever met', recalls Alfred Austin, Tom shone in debate: Elizabeth Barrett Browning called him 'Aristides the Just' and, no doubt to Anthony's annoyance, the beautiful Kate Field agreed. G. H. Lewes wrote in his journal that his Florence neighbour Tom was 'a most loveable creature'. There was a competitive side to the relationship between the two brothers. Tom recalled that 'my brother and I used to compare notes as to which of us had written the most' – and the fastest. In 1864 Anthony had to concede, after Tom wrote a two-volume novel in twenty-four days (*Beppo the Conscript*), that 'he could not do the like to save his life and that of all those dearest to him'.*[36] With characteristic honesty, Tom remarks that the novel may have been 'trash', but at least the publisher liked it. He wrote of his little brother that 'work to him was a necessity and a satisfaction'; his 'insatiable ardour . . . (taking into consideration his very efficient discharge of his duties as Post Office surveyor) puts my industry into the shade'. At the same time, Anthony envied Tom's capacity to be idle, that is, relaxed.

In 1865, only two years after his mother's death, Tom lost his wife Theodosia. 'She brought sweetness and light into my life and into my dwelling,' Tom wrote fifteen years later. 'She was the angel in the house, if ever human being was.' The Villino Trollope 'was indeed left unto me desolate, and I thought that life and all its sweetness was over for me!' She too lies buried in the English cemetery a few feet from her mother-in-law: their two matching headstones face each other as if in conversation. Aged fifty-five, Tom sold the house – at a loss – and moved to a villa at Ricorboli, outside the Porta San Niccolò, south of the Arno. The following summer of 1866 Frances Ternan returned to Florence as the governess of twelve-year-old Bice.† Alfred Austin commented that Miss Ternan, 'though thoroughly feminine in every respect, had an almost masculine mind in the sphere of serious intellectual deliberations, in which, so different

---

* Tom wrote at such great speed to earn the money to take his then ailing wife Theodosia somewhere more conducive to her health.
† In 1880, the twenty-seven-year-old Bice married Charles Stuart-Wortley; tragically, she died soon after giving birth to a baby girl in the summer of 1881.

in that respect from his brother Anthony, Thomas Adolphus and I also greatly rejoiced'. Within a few months, Frances Ternan and Tom were engaged to be married: 'Yes, of course! I knew you would,' wrote Anthony. Robert Browning was pleased: 'I think him [Tom] affectionate, good, full of various talent, – all of which his wife will soon find out.'

Frances Ternan's first novel was at this time being serialized in Dickens's *All the Year Round,* and Tom was proud of her achievement. Dickens replied to Tom's announcement:

No friend that you have can be more truly attached than I am. I congratulate you with all my heart, and believe that your marriage will stand upon the list of happy ones. As to your wife's winning a reputation out of your house – if you care for that; it is not much as an addition to the delights of love and peace and a suitable companion for life – I have not the least doubt of her power to make herself famous.

I little thought what an important master of the ceremonies I was when I first gave your present wife an introduction to your mother. Bear me in mind then as an unconscious instrument of your having given your best affection to a worthy object.[37]

Tom and Frances continued to write novels and collaborated on several books, including *The Homes and Haunts of the Italian Poets* (1881). After some years as a correspondent in Rome, Tom and Frances moved back to England, to Budleigh Salterton in Devon. During a brief visit to Clifton, where his mother had spent her girlhood, Tom died at the age of eighty-two. He had said to his wife, 'Mind, where I fall let me lie. Make no fuss. Give no trouble.' And so, Frances writes to a friend, 'I left him on the slope of a pretty cemetery close to Bristol.' 'I lived with him,' she continued in the same letter, 'for six-and-twenty years in the most intimate communion possible between two human beings, and I can say after the most searching examination of the past, that I never detected in him one base, insincere, or ungenerous thought. Flaws and errors there must have been, because he was human. But of envy, hatred, malice, and all uncharitableness he was incapable.'[38]

After Tom's death Frances, then fifty-seven years old, lost interest in writing: her last published work was the biography of Tom's mother, whom she had known only briefly. Her sister, Nelly, helped her collect the necessary material. 'I cannot refrain from saying that, high as my respect for "the Mammy" (as we always spoke of her *en famille*) has been ever since I first heard or knew anything of her, it has been enormously increased by my perusal of these family papers,' Frances wrote to her publisher George Bentley in 1894. 'She was a splendid specimen of an English woman. Her courage, perseverance, energy, and unselfishness are amazing, and a really bright example to all who can appreciate them.'*[39]

But perhaps the most lasting tribute to Fanny Trollope's indomitable spirit is to be found, paradoxically, in the work of her son, Anthony. If it had not been for Fanny's courage and industry, the whole family might have sunk into destitution and poverty without a trace. Her example inspired Anthony to write, and it was only with her help that he was able to launch his literary career. In a word, without Fanny Trollope we would have no Barsetshire or Palliser novels, no *Orley Farm* or *The Way We Live Now*. Although in his memoirs Anthony could not bring himself to be as generous to his mother as perhaps he ought to have been, he honours her with the innumerable strong-willed and brave-hearted women who appear in his fiction. I like to think that one of Anthony's best-loved creations, Glencora Palliser, is a conscious and deliberate portrait of his mother. Untypically of his heroines, Glencora, like Fanny, is 'short in stature, and her happy round face lacked, perhaps, the highest grace of female beauty. But there was ever a smile upon it which it was very pleasant to look at; and the intense interest with which she would dance, and talk, and follow up every amusement that was offered her, was very charming' (*The Small House at Allington*). 'Many feared her and she was afraid of none,' Anthony wrote in *The Prime Minister*, 'and many also loved her – whom she also loved, for her nature was very

---

* Many of the family letters, including Tom's journal, were destroyed by Nelly's son, Geoffrey Wharton Robinson, when he discovered the truth behind his mother's relations with Charles Dickens. See Claire Tomalin, *The Invisible Woman: The Story of Nelly Ternan and Charles Dickens*, London, 1990.

affectionate. She was happy with her children, happy with her friends, in the enjoyment of perfect health, and capable of taking an exaggerated interest in anything that came uppermost for the moment.' In describing Glencora in *Can You Forgive Her?*, Anthony perhaps came closest to capturing his mother's essence: 'she was not softly delicate in all her ways; but in her disposition and temper she was altogether generous. I do not know that she was at all points a lady, but had Fate so willed it she would have been a thorough gentleman.'

NOTES

Frequently Cited Works and Manuscript Collections

Garnett–Pertz Papers (bMS Eng 1304.2), Houghton Library, Harvard University

Morris L. Parrish Collection, Department of Rare Books and Special Collections, Princeton University Library

Robert H. Taylor Collection, Department of Rare Books and Special Collections, Princeton University Library

Browning, Elizabeth Barrett, *The Letters of Elizabeth Barrett Browning to Mary Russell Mitford, 1836–1854*, 3 vols., Winfield, KS, 1983.

Dickens, Charles, *The Letters*, Pilgrim Edition, edited by M. House, K. Tillotson and G. Story, Oxford, 1965–   .

L'Estrange, A. G., ed., *The Friendships of Mary Russell Mitford as Recorded in Letters from her Literary Correspondence*, 2 vols., London, 1882.

Trollope, Anthony, *The Letters*, edited by N. J. Hall, Stanford, CA, 1983.

Trollope, Frances Eleanor, *Frances Trollope: Her Life and Literary Work from George III to Victoria*, 2 vols., London, 1895.

Trollope, Thomas Adolphus, *What I Remember*, 3 vols., London, 1887–9.

CHAPTER 1 *Days of the Regency*

1. Mrs George Mitford to Mary Russell Mitford, 14 November 1802: L'Estrange, *Friendships of M. R. Mitford*, I, pp. 7–8. For Jane Austen, see Deirdre Le Faye, *Jane Austen's Letters*, 3rd edn, Oxford, 1995.

2. T. A. Trollope, *What I Remember*, I, p. 18.

3. F. E. Trollope, *Frances Trollope*, I, p. 8.

4. Records exist in the Bristol Record Office for the Milton family, including John Milton's will (24 November 1777, with a codicil dated 1788). For William Milton's election to the living of Heckfield, see James Woodforde, *The Diary of a Country Parson*, 1758–1802, ed. J. Beresford, vol. 1, Oxford, 1924. There are various sources which can be used to trace William Milton's movements in the Bristol area. The most important are the baptismal records of his children: St Thomas's church, 29 March 1776; St Augustine's, 22 February 1778; St Michael's, 17 March 1779, 1 February 1781, 8 July 1782, 20 May 1784. Sketchley's *Bristol Directory* has also been extremely useful in tracing not only William Milton but his Bristol contemporaries as well; Milton's curacy in Almondsbury is recorded in Bishop Secker's *Diocese Book*. The Gresley family tree appears in J. Burnaby, *Study of English Apothecaries*, Medical History Supplement, Wellcome Institute, London, 1983.

5. F. E. Trollope, *Frances Trollope*, II, p. 286; [Timothy Flint,] 'Travellers in America', *Knickerbocker, or New York Monthly Magazine*, 2 (1833), pp. 286–8, 290–91.

6. Arthur Tindal Hart, *The Country Priest in English History*, London, 1959, p. 79.

7. A. F. Williams, 'Bristol Port Plans and Improvement Schemes of the Eighteenth-century', *Transactions of the Bristol and Gloucestershire Archaeological Society*, 81 (1962), pp. 138–88; R. A. Buchanan, 'The Construction of the Floating Harbour in Bristol: 1804–1809', ibid., 88 (1969) pp. 184–204; J. F. Nicholls and J. Taylor, *Bristol Past and Present, Civil and Modern History*, 3 vols., Bristol, 1882.

8. See Helen Reid, *A Chronicle of Clifton and Hotwells*, Bristol, 1992; Vincent Waite, *The Bristol Hotwell*, Bristol, 1960.

9. See Pamela Bright, *Dr Richard Bright (1789–1858)*, London, 1983.

10. Mary Russell Mitford, *Our Village*.

11. F. E. Trollope, *Frances Trollope*, II, p. 286.

12. L'Estrange, *Friendships of M. R. Mitford*, I, p. 239.

13. George Pitt, first Baron Rivers. See *Burke's Peerage*, quoting the R-L Register, 1781.

CHAPTER 2 *The Lottery of Marriage*

1. See Roy Porter, *London: A Social History*, London, 1994; John Summerson, *Georgian London*, London, 1970.

2. A. G. L'Estrange, ed., *The Life of Mary Russell Mitford*, 3 vols., London, 1870, II, p. 261; Arthur Lucas, *John Lucas: Portrait Painter 1828–1874*, London, 1910.

3. T. A. Trollope, *What I Remember*, I, p. 25.

4. The Revd Anthony Trollope's will is in the London Public Record Office, Prob. 11/1453.

5. The courtship letters between Fanny Milton and Thomas Anthony Trollope are part of the Taylor Collection.

6. The marriage settlement is in the Gloucester Record Office, D34/9/94.

CHAPTER 3 *The Mother's Manual*

1. These letters from the early years of the Trollopes' marriage are included with the courtship letters in the Taylor Collection.

2. These and other recollections of his childhood are taken from Tom's memoirs: T. A. Trollope, *What I Remember*, I, chaps. 1–4.

3. William Milton to Tom and Henry Trollope, 18 November 1823, and to the Trollopes, 27 November 1823: Taylor Collection.

4. F. E. Trollope, *Frances Trollope*, I, p. 63.

5. L'Estrange, *The Life of Mary Russell Mitford*, III, p. 241.

6. Recounted by John Herman Merivale in his diary, dated 11 February 1822: A. W. Merivale, ed., *Family Memorials*, Exeter, 1884.

7. TAnT to FT, 10 August 1810, and FT to TAnT, 12 August 1810: Taylor Collection.

8. Details of the Harrow farm are all to be found at the Greater London Record Office, Acc. 76.

9. FT to TAnT, [1813]: Taylor Collection. This is the same letter in which Fanny thanks her husband for his 'balsam'.

10. 12 February 1820: quoted in Helen Heineman, *Mrs Trollope: The Triumphant Feminine in the Nineteenth Century*, Athens, OH, 1979, p. 23. The original manuscript, belonging to the Vaughan Library, Harrow School, has been lost. My thanks to the Harrow School archivist, Alisdair Hawkyard.

11. FT to Colonel James Grant, 3 June [1834]: Parrish Collection.

12. F. E. Trollope, *Frances Trollope*, I, pp. 48, 89–90.

13. ibid., I, p. 55.

14. TAT to Mary Grant Christie, 3 October 1883: Parrish Collection.

15. F. E. Trollope, *Frances Trollope*, I, p. 140.

16. ibid., I, p. 92.

17. For this episode, see N. J. Hall, *Salmagundi: Byron, Allegra and the Trollope Family*, Pittsburgh, 1975.

18. This is amongst the Trollope Family Papers at the University of Illinois Library, Urbana-Champaign.

19. F. E. Trollope, *Frances Trollope*, I, pp. 288–9.

CHAPTER 4 *One Fault*

1. F. E. Trollope, *Frances Trollope*, I, pp. 77–8.

2. Revel Guest and Angela V. John, *Lady Charlotte: A Biography of the Nineteenth Century*, London, 1989, p. 6.

3. As in the previous chapter, these and other recollections of his childhood are taken from Tom's memoirs: T. A. Trollope, *What I Remember*, I, chaps. 1–4.

4. *The Gentleman's Magazine*, 84 (January 1814), p. 38; ibid., 88 (May 1818), pp. 406–7.

5. Merivale, *Family Memorials*, pp. 199–200. For the National Gallery, see F. E. Trollope, *Frances Trollope*, I, p. 58; A. Trollope, 'The National Gallery', *Saint James's Magazine*, 2 (September 1861).

6. See Frances Wright, *Course of Popular Lectures*, London, 1820.

7. John Garnett to Gen. Horatio Gates, 4 May 1796: Gates Collection, New York Historical Society.

8. Robina Craig Millar to HG and JG, 21 June 1820; FW to HG and JG, October 1821: Garnett–Pertz Papers. The information concerning John Garnett and his family is taken from Nicholls and Taylor, *Bristol Past and Present*, and Helen Heineman, *Restless Angels: The Friendship of Six Victorian Women*, Athens, OH, 1983.

9. FT to Jeremy Bentham, 25 December 1822: British Library, Add MS 33545, ff. 605–6; Robert Dale Owen to FW, 21 September 1827: Special Collections, Joseph Regenstein Library, University of Chicago; G. Pepe, *Memoirs*, 3 vols., London, 1846, III, p. 236.

10. Her journal is part of the Trollope Family Papers, University of Illinois Library, Urbana-Champaign.

11. S. T. Williams, ed., *The Journal of Washington Irving, 1823–24*, Cambridge, MA, 1931, p. 42.

12. P. N. Furbank, 'A Simple Facilitator', review of L. Kramer, *Lafayette in Two Worlds*, in *The New York Review of Books* (11 July 1996), pp. 50–52.

13. F. E. Trollope, *Frances Trollope*, I, p. 56.

14. The letter concerning Arthur's health exists only in a fragment among the Trollope Family Papers, Special Collections, UCLA Library. William Milton to Tom and Henry Trollope, 18 November 1823: Taylor Collection. William Milton's will is in the London Public Record Office, Prob. 11/1694.

15. FT to JG and MG, 6 August 1824: Garnett–Pertz Papers.

CHAPTER 5 *The Old World and the New*

1. FW to JG, 4 December 1825: Garnett–Pertz Papers.

2. For this episode, see Vera Watson, *Mary Russell Mitford*, London, 1949, pp. 165–84; L'Estrange, *Friendships of M. R. Mitford*, I, pp. 158–67.

3. FT to MRM, 10 June 1827: Parrish Collection; L'Estrange, *Friendships of M. R. Mitford*, I, pp. 167–9. Hervieu's letter to Tom is quoted in F. E. Trollope, *Frances Trollope*, I, p. 96; for Tom's childhood memories, see T. A. Trollope, *What I Remember*, I, chaps. 1–4. For Hervieu, see A. Graves, *The Royal Academy of Arts: A Complete Dictionary of Contributors . . . 1769–1904*, 4 vols., London, 1905; F. F. McDermott, 'Mrs Trollope's Illustrator: Auguste Hervieu in America (1827–1831)', *Extrait de la Gazette des Beaux-Arts* (March, 1958), pp. 169–90.

4. F. E. Trollope, *Frances Trollope*, I, pp. 43–4; Pepe, *Memoirs*, III, p. 270.

5. FT to JG, 17 May 1827: Garnett–Pertz Papers. Georg Pertz's memoirs are quoted in Heineman, *Restless Angels*, pp. 49–50.

6. G. F. Nott to FT, 20 February [1825]: Trollope Family Papers, Special Collections, UCLA Library. The correspondence between FT and TAT is quoted in F. E. Trollope, *Frances Trollope*, I, pp. 57–9, 82.

7. Quoted in Eric J. Evans, *Britain before the Reform Act: Politics and Society, 1815–1832*, London, 1989, p. 104.

8. For Thomas Anthony's attitude to his sons, and Henry in particular, see F. E. Trollope, *Frances Trollope*, I, pp. 75–7.

9. FT and TAnT to the Monods, 5 March 1827: Historical Society of Pennsylvania.

10. For Henry in Paris and at home for the holidays, see F. E. Trollope, *Frances Trollope*, I, pp. 83–8, 96–7.

11. FW to HG and JG, 30 October 1824: Garnett–Pertz Papers.

12. Robert Dale Owen to FW, 25 August 1827: quoted in Heineman, *Mrs Trollope*, p. 44.

13. This phrase is quoted by FT in *The Domestic Manners of the Americans*. For a general introduction to utopianism, see P. A. Neville-Sington and D. Sington, *Paradise Dreamed: How Utopian Thinkers Have Changed the Modern World*, London, 1993; for Frances Wright, see C. Morris Eckhardt, *Fanny Wright: Rebel in America*, Cambridge, MA, 1984.

14. FW to JG, 30 August 1827; FW to JGP, 26 December 1827; HG to JGP, 12 December 1827; HG to JGP, 21 October 1827; Lafayette to JG, 14 June 1827; Robina Craig Millar to HG and JG, 2 June 1827: Garnett–Pertz Papers.

15. FT to JG, 17 May 1827: Garnett–Pertz Papers. Carlyle, writing in 1819, is quoted in L. A. Ellis, *Frances Trollope's America: Four Novels*, New York, 1993, p. 133.

16. FT to JGP, 7 October 1827, FT to HG, 8 October [1827]: Garnett–Pertz Papers. For Tom's memories of Frances Wright, see T. A. Trollope, *What I Remember*, I, pp. 151–4.

17. FT to HG, 7 December 1828: Garnett–Pertz Papers.

18. FW to Mary Shelley, 15 September 1827; FW to HG, 20 March 1828; HG to JGP, 19 August 1828: Garnett–Pertz Papers.

19. FT to JG, 17 May 1827, and FT to HG, 8 October 1827: Garnett–Pertz Papers.

20. FT to HG, 7 December 1828: Garnett–Pertz Papers.

21. FW to HG, 20 March 1828; FW and FT to JGP, 26 December 1827: Garnett–Pertz Papers.

22. FT to HG, 8 October 1827: Garnett–Pertz Papers; see also Sophia Hay to JGP, 29 December 1827, in the same collection. FT's letter to TAT is in F. E. Trollope, *Frances Trollope*, I, p. 95.

23. HG to JGP, 13 November and 12 December 1827; FW and FT to JGP, 26 December 1827: Garnett–Pertz Papers.

CHAPTER 6 *The Refugee in America*

1. FT to HG, 7 December 1828: Garnett–Pertz Papers.

2. FT's comment about Frances Wright's dress, looks and manners appears in her rough draft of *The Domestic Manners of the Americans*, among the Trollope MSS at the Lilly Library, Indiana University. HG to JGP, 29 April 1828; FT to HG, 7 December 1828; HG to JGP, 3 May 1829: Garnett–Pertz Papers.

3. FT to HG, 7 December 1828, and FW to HG, 20 March 1828: Garnett–Pertz Papers. Hervieu's reaction is recorded in F. E. Trollope, *Frances Trollope*, I, p. 107.

4. Cited in A. J. G. Perkins and T. Wolfson, *Frances Wright, Free Enquirer: The Study of a Temperament*, New York, 1939, p. 190.

5. For Cincinnati, see Clara Longworth de Chambrun, *Cincinnati: Story of the Queen City*, New York, 1939; W. H. Venable, *Beginnings of Literary Culture in the Ohio Valley*, Cincinnati, 1891; R. C. Vitz, *The Queen City and the Arts: Cultural Life in Nineteenth-century Cincinnati*, Kent, OH, 1989.

6. F. E. Trollope, *Frances Trollope*, I, p. 111.

7. FT to MRM, 20 January 1829: L'Estrange, *Friendships of M.R. Mitford*, I, p. 191.

8. See Richard Mullen, 'Introduction', *Domestic Manners of the Americans*, Oxford, 1984, p. xvi; D. Smalley, 'Introduction', *Domestic Manners of the Americans*, New York, 1949, p. xxviii. For Tom's recollections of America, see T. A. Trollope, *What I Remember*, I, chaps. 7–8.

9. Venable, *Beginnings of Literary Culture*, p. 315. See also E. R. Kellog, 'Joseph Dorfeuille and the Western Museum', *Journal of the Cincinnati Society of Natural History*, 22 (April 1945), pp. 8–13.

10. The story of Henry's Falstaff is described in C. T. Greve, *Centennial History of Cincinnati and Representative Citizens*, 2 vols., Chicago, 1904, vol. I, part 2, p. 644. His poems are in a notebook, now part of the Trollope MSS, Lilly Library, Indiana University; see also, D. Smalley, 'Henry Trollope: Poems in America', *Nineteenth-century Fiction*, 4 (March 1950), p. 259.

11. Tom describes Dr Price and his family in *What I Remember*. Ophia D. Smith, 'Joseph Tosso, the Arkansaw Traveler', *Ohio State Archaeological and Historical Quarterly*, 56 (1947), pp. 25–6.

12. F. Marryat, *A Diary in America; with Remarks on its Institutions*, ed. S. Jackman, New York, 1962, p. 225.

13. [Flint,] 'Travelers in America', pp. 286–8, 290–92; Chambrun, *Cincinnati*, p. 145.

14. Both letters are quoted in F. E. Trollope, *Frances Trollope*, I, pp. 113–14.

15. ibid.

16. Trollope MSS, Lilly Library, Indiana University.

17. MG to JGP, 1 July 1828; FT to HG, 7 December 1828; MG and HG to JGP, 27 November 1827; HG to JGP, 12 December 1827; HG to JGP, 23 January 1828: Garnett–Pertz Papers.

18. HG to JGP, 30 March and 7 April 1828: Garnett–Pertz Papers.

19. F. E. Trollope, *Frances Trollope*, I, pp. 111–14. HG to JGP, 15 July 1828; Marianne Skerrett to JGP, 15 September 1828: Garnett–Pertz Papers.

20. FT to Charles Wilkes, 14 February 1828: Cincinnati Historical Society.

21. See Clay Lancaster, 'The Egyptian Hall and Mrs Trollope's Bazaar', *Magazine of Art*, 43 (1950), pp. 94–9; J. Morley, *Regency Design, 1790–1840*, London, 1993.

22. FT to JGP, 22 August 1831: Garnett–Pertz Papers.

23. FT to HG, 7 December 1828 and [27 April 1829]: Garnett–Pertz Papers. FT's comment about Henry's age is in a letter to MRM, 20 January 1829: L'Estrange, ed., *Friendships of M. R. Mitford*, I, p. 192.

24. FT to TAT: F. E. Trollope, *Frances Trollope*, I, pp. 128–9. FT to HG and JGP, [27 April 1829]: Garnett–Pertz Papers. The quotations from

the *Cincinnati Chronicle* and the details concerning the gas lights are to be found in Smalley, 'Introduction', pp. xli–v.

25. Flint, in his article 'Travelers in America', talks about the goods which Thomas Anthony sent out. For Fanny's explanation of events, see her letters to Tom in F. E. Trollope, *Frances Trollope*, and to JGP, 22 August 1831: Garnett–Pertz Papers.

26. ibid.

27. Joseph Cowell, *Thirty Years Passed among the Players in England and America*, New York, 1844, pp. 89–90.

28. W. C. Macready, *The Diaries of William Charles Macready, 1833–1851*, ed. William Toynbee, 2 vols., New York, 1912, I, p. 270.

29. Timothy Flint, *Western Monthly Review*, 3 (February 1830), pp. 440–47.

30. FT to HG, [27 April 1829]: Garnett–Pertz Papers. [Flint,] 'Travelers in America', p. 289; H. Martineau, *Retrospect of Western Travel*, 2 vols., London, 1838, II, p. 249; Marryat, *A Diary in America*, p. 225; C. Abbot, 'The Location and External Appearance of Mrs Trollope's Bazaar', *Journal of the Society of Architectural Historians*, 29 (1970), pp. 157–9.

31. FT to JGP, 22 August 1831; FT to HG, [27 April 1829]; HG to JGP, 11 April 1830: Garnett–Pertz Papers. F. E. Trollope, *Frances Trollope*, I, p. 128. [Flint,] 'Travelers in America'.

32. F. E. Trollope, *Frances Trollope*, I, pp. 118–20; Lafayette's letter is part of the collection of the Beinecke Library, Yale University.

33. FT to JGP, 12 March 1830 and 22 August 1831: Garnett–Pertz Papers.

CHAPTER 7 *The Domestic Manners of the Americans*

1. FT to JGP, 22 August 1831: Garnett–Pertz Papers. The document regarding the Cincinnati Bazaar, dated 13 March 1830, is in the Parrish Collection.

2. FT to JGP, 22 August 1831: Garnett–Pertz Papers. F. E. Trollope, *Frances Trollope*, I, pp. 125–9.

3. For this period, see T. A. Trollope, *What I Remember*, I, chap. 11.

4. This correspondence is in the Greater London Record Office, Acc. 76/

2277–86. For the economic situation of the period, see D. G. Wright, *Democracy and Reform 1815–1885*, London, 1976, and *The Victoria County History*, vol. 4 (Middlesex).

5. F. E. Trollope, *Frances Trollope*, I, p. 145. See William Gregory, *An Autobiography*, ed. Lady Gregory, London, 1894.

6. F. E. Trollope, *Frances Trollope*, I, p. 131.

7. MG to JGP, 20 November 1827: Garnett–Pertz Papers.

8. FT to JGP, 12 March 1830: Garnett–Pertz Papers.

9. FT to Charles Wilkes, 14 February 1828: Cincinnati Historical Society; FT to JGP, 12 March 1830: Garnett–Pertz Papers.

10. FT to TAT, 30 June 1828: F. E. Trollope, *Frances Trollope*, I, p. 115. FT to MRM, 20 January 1829: L'Estrange, *Friendships of M. R. Mitford*, I, p. 193. Fanny's notebooks and rough draft are among the Trollope MSS in the Lilly Library, Indiana University.

11. FT to Charles Wilkes, 18 June 1828: Parrish Collection. FT to TAT: F. E. Trollope, *Frances Trollope*, I, p. 131.

12. FT to MRM, 28 July 1830: L'Estrange, *Friendships of M. R. Mitford*, I, pp. 219–20; FT to JGP, 18 April 1831: Garnett–Pertz Papers.

13. FT to JGP, 22 August 1831; Anna Maria Stone to JGP, 30 May 1828; FT to JGP, 18 April 1831: Garnett–Pertz Papers.

14. FT to MRM, 29 May 1831: L'Estrange, *Friendships of M. R. Mitford*, I, p. 227.

15. Quoted in Henry Allen, 'Fall of the Falls', review of W. Irvin, *The New Niagara*, in *New York Review of Books* (9 January 1997), p. 46.

16. F. E. Trollope, *Frances Trollope*, I, pp. 130–31. Walter Stirling to George Harrison, 20 July 1832: Historical Society of Pennsylvania.

17. FT to JGP, 22 August 1831: Garnett–Pertz Papers.

18. ibid.

19. ibid.

20. FT to TAT, 12 October 1831: F. E. Trollope, *Frances Trollope*, I, pp. 136–7.

21. ibid., II, p. 64.

22. See C. G. Calloway, *The American Revolution in Indian Country: Crisis and Diversity in Native American Communities*, Cambridge, 1995.

23. FT to MRM, 29 May 1831: L'Estrange, *Friendships of M. R. Mitford*, I, p. 230.

24. F. E. Trollope, *Frances Trollope*, I, pp. 138–9. For the Reform Bill, see Wright, *Democracy and Reform 1815–1885*, and Evans, *Britain before the Reform Act*.

25. Quoted in Richard Mullen, *Birds of Passage: Five Englishwomen in Search of America*, London, 1994, p. 2. See also P. Neville-Sington, 'Introduction', *The Domestic Manners of the Americans*, Penguin Books, London, 1997.

26. *The Edinburgh Review*, 55 (July 1832), p. 496.

CHAPTER 8 *Fashionable Life*

1. F. E. Trollope, *Frances Trollope*, I, pp. 150–51. FT to JGP, 9 February 1832: Garnett–Pertz Papers.

2. Basil Hall to FT, 8 May 1832: Family Trollope Papers, Special Collections, UCLA Library. F. E. Trollope, *Frances Trollope*, I, pp. 158–9, 161.

3. ibid. Harriet Martineau, *An Autobiography*, 3rd edn, 2 vols., London, 1877, I, pp. 317–19; II, p. 94.

4. MRM to FT, 3 April 1832: Parrish Collection. FT to JPG, 27 June 1832; HG to JPG, 19 May 1832 and undated [end of 1833]: Garnett–Pertz Papers.

5. E. T. Coke, *A Subaltern's Furlough: Descriptive of Scenes in Various Parts of the United States . . . during the Summer and Autumn of 1832*, London, 1833, pp. 167–8.

6. The American review appears in *The Illinois Monthly Magazine*, 2 (1832), p. 505. Fanny repeats Irving's comment in a letter to JPG, 22 March 1832: Garnett–Pertz Papers. For the rest see Coke, *Subaltern's Furlough*, p. 174; T. L. Nichols, *Forty Years of American Life*, 2 vols., London, 1864, II, p. 22; Mullen, *Birds of Passage*, pp. 89, 125.

7. The reviews appear in *The Edinburgh Review*, 55 (July 1832), p. 485; *The Gentleman's Magazine* (April 1832), p. 346; Basil Hall to FT, 21 January 1833: Trollope Family Papers, Special Collections, UCLA Library.

8. *The Literary Gazette* (24 March 1832), p. 178.

9. Mark Twain, from suppressed passages in *Life on the Mississippi* (1883); quoted in Smalley, 'Introduction', *The Domestic Manners*, p. v. Richard

Mullen includes Twain's marginal notes in his edition of *The Domestic Manners*, p. 369.

10. FT to MRM, 16 September 1831 and 23 April 1832: L'Estrange, *Friendships of M. R. Mitford*, I, pp. 229, 233–4. F. E. Trollope, *Frances Trollope*, p. 166.

11. FT to JGP, 27 June 1832: Garnett–Pertz Papers. F. E. Trollope, *Frances Trollope*, I, p. 171. This and other such sketches, charades, etc., are among the Trollope Family Papers, University of Illinois Library, Urbana-Champaign. For Tom's recollections, see T. A. Trollope, *What I Remember*, I, chaps. 9–12.

12. FT to JGP, 20 May 1829 and 6 August 1824: Garnett–Pertz Papers.

13. HG to JPG, 12 January 1830 and 26 November 1831: Garnett–Pertz Papers.

14. FT to JGP, 22 August 1831: Garnett–Pertz Papers.

15. Three letters from Whately, who had by this time left Oxford to become Archbishop of Dublin, are among the Trollope Family Papers, Special Collections, UCLA Library.

16. F. E. Trollope, *Frances Trollope*, I, pp. 125–6, 144–5, 167.

17. FT to JGP, 25 November 1831 and 18 February 1833: Garnett–Pertz Papers. FT to TAT: F. E. Trollope, *Frances Trollope*, I, p. 148.

18. ibid., I, pp. 147–53.

19. ibid., I, p. 163. FT to 'Georgina' [?Georgina Bent Shute, Fanny Bent's half sister], undated [1832]: Taylor Collection.

20. F. E. Trollope, *Frances Trollope*, I, p. 163.

21. ibid, I., pp. 164, 180–83.

22. FT to JPG, 18 April 1831 and 12 March 1830: Garnett–Pertz Papers. FT to MRM, 23 April 1832: L'Estrange, *Friendships of M. R. Mitford*, I, p. 234.

23. Henry's letters to his parents while touring the West Country survive in the Taylor Collection. His admission form to the Geological Society survives in the Society's archives. For the popularity of geology, see John Wyatt, *Wordsworth and the Geologists*, Cambridge, 1996.

24. FT to Richard Bentley, 5 December 1835: Taylor Collection. FT to JGP, 18 April 1831: Garnett–Pertz Papers.

25. FT to Whittaker, 25 July 1832: Parrish Collection. Basil Hall to

FT, undated [1832]: Trollope Family Papers, Special Collections, UCLA Library. FT to TAT: F. E. Trollope, *Frances Trollope*, I, p. 159.

26. FT to TAT: ibid., I, pp. 169–70. FT to MRM, 23 April 1832: L'Estrange, *Friendships of M. R. Mitford*, I, p. 234; her reply to FT is quoted in T. A. Trollope, *What I Remember*, II, pp. 240–41.

27. FT to JGP, 16 February 1833: Garnett–Pertz Papers. George Bartley to FT, 29 January 1833: Trollope Family Papers, Special Collections, UCLA Library. *The Westminster Review*, 18 (1833), p. 213; *The Quarterly Review*, 48 (1832), p. 508.

28. F. E. Trollope, *Frances Trollope*, I, p. 179.

29. MRM to FT: T. A. Trollope, *What I Remember*, II, pp. 240–41.

30. *The Spectator*, 6 (1833), pp. 526–7.

31. FT to JGP, 22 March and 27 June 1832; see also FT to JGP, 25 November 1831: Garnett–Pertz Papers.

32. FT to JGP, 18 February 1833: Garnett–Pertz Papers. F. E. Trollope, *Frances Trollope*, I, pp. 179–80.

33. FT to JGP, 22 March 1832: Garnett–Pertz Papers.

34. FT to JGP, 24 September 1833: Garnett–Pertz Papers.

35. F. E. Trollope, *Frances Trollope*, I, p. 170. FT to JGP, [March 1834]: Garnett–Pertz Papers. FT to Mrs Bartley, 30 January 1834: Parrish Collection; see also FT to Murray, 6 March 1834: John Murray Archives.

36. FT to JGP, 13 July 1834: Garnett–Pertz Papers.

37. Trollope's correspondence with Northwick is in the Greater London Record Office, Acc. 76.

CHAPTER 9 *Travels and Travellers*

1. FT to JGP, [March 1834]: Garnett–Pertz Papers.

2. F. E. Trollope, *Frances Trollope*, I, pp. 204–5.

3. FT to Col. James Grant, 3 June [1834]: Parrish Collection.

4. For Tom's recollections of Bruges, teaching in London and Paris, see T. A. Trollope, *What I Remember*, I, chaps. 12–14.

5. F. E. Trollope, *Frances Trollope*, I, p. 199.

6. FT to JGP, 13 July 1834: Garnett–Pertz Papers. F. E. Trollope, *Frances Trollope*, I, p. 199.

7. The document, 'Rec'd and Recorded 15 July 1834', is in the Hamilton County Court House Deed Book, 49, no. 450, pp. 592–3: Cincinnati Historical Society. For the reputation and subsequent fate of the Bazaar, see especially Venable, *Beginnings of Literary Culture.*

8. For Henry's illness and the Trollopes in Bruges, told mainly through Fanny's letters to Tom, see F. E. Trollope, *Frances Trollope*, I, pp. 207–50.

9. Murray to FT, 16 July 1834; F. Marryat to Murray, undated: John Murray Archives.

10. FT to Dr Edwin Harrison, 17 October 1834: Parrish Collection.

11. FT to TAT: F. E. Trollope, *Frances Trollope*, I, pp. 223–4.

12. FT to Murray, 20 January 1835: John Murray Archives.

13. FT to William Drury, 31 October 1834: Taylor Collection.

14. FT to Murray, 22 July 1834: John Murray Archives.

15. The agreements with Bentley are dated 10 and 28 March (with a memorandum of 23 November 1835): British Library, Add MS 46612, ff. 150, 156–7. For the comment on coining money, see MG to JGP, 18 July 1835: Garnett–Pertz Papers.

16. Murray to FT, 16 July 1834: John Murray Archives.

17. For Fanny as the 'Lion of Paris', see MG to JGP, 18 July 1835: Garnett–Pertz Papers. For Madame Récamier and Mary Clarke, who later married the Orientalist Julius Mohl, see M. C. M. Simpson, *Letters and Recollections of Julius and Mary Mohl*, London, 1887; Kathleen O'Meara, *Madame Mohl*, London, 1885; Cynthia Gladwyn's essay in *Genius in the Drawing-Room: The Literary Salon in the Nineteenth and Twentieth Centuries*, P. Quennell, London, 1980.

18. See FT to Murray, 7 November 1835: John Murray Archives; FT to Bentley, 21 October 1835: Taylor Collection; MG to JGP, 22 November 1835: Garnett–Pertz Papers.

19. An extract from the Registry of the Prerogative Court of Canterbury, dated 29 June 1836, is in the Parrish Collection.

CHAPTER 10 *A Romance of Vienna*

1. F. E. Trollope, *Frances Trollope*, I, pp. 254–5.

2. AT to TAT: ibid., I, pp. 259–60.

3. See FT to Mrs Thackeray, 17 February 1836: Trollope Family Papers, Special Collections, UCLA Library. For Tom's recollections of Emily's death, Austria and Birmingham, see T. A. Trollope, *What I Remember*, chaps. 14–19.

4. See FT to John MacGregor, 23 March 1836: Historical Society of Pennsylvania; FT to Mrs Murray, 31 March 1836: John Murray Archives.

5. FT to TAT: F. E. Trollope, *Frances Trollope*, I, pp. 248–50.

6. FT to Bentley, 24 June 1835: Taylor Collection. *The Athenaeum* (14 September 1833), p. 618; ibid. (9 November 1833), pp. 752–3.

7. FT to Bentley, 5 December 1835: Taylor Collection.

8. See Clare Midgley, *Women Against Slavery: The British Campaigns, 1780–1870*, New York, 1993, and the review by Anne Summers in *The Times Literary Supplement* (25 June 1993), p. 12.

9. FT to Bentley, 28 March 1836: Taylor Collection. Agreement between FT and Bentley, 27 April 1836: British Library, Add MS 46612, ff. 240–11. For the ins and outs of publishing, see Robert L. Patten, *Charles Dickens and His Publishers*, Oxford, 1978, chap. 1.

10. Charles Buller to Bentley/FT, [30 October 1837]: Parrish Collection. The connection between *The Vicar of Wrexhill* and Henrietta Skerrett is made in T. H. S. Escott, *Anthony Trollope, His Work, Associates and Literary Origins*, London, 1913, p. 30.

11. FT to Bentley, [15 July 1836]: Parrish Collection.

12. MG to JGP, 14 August 1836: Garnett–Pertz Papers.

13. F. E. Trollope, *Frances Trollope*, I, pp. 266–7.

14. Cecilia Trollope to TAT: ibid., I, p. 274.

15. *The Spectator*, 11 (1838), pp. 209–10.

16. FT to JGP, 17 January 1837: Taylor Collection (not the Garnett–Pertz Papers).

17. FT to TAT: F. E. Trollope, *Frances Trollope*, I, pp. 275–6.

18. FT to Bentley, 27 February 1837: Taylor Collection.

19. Fanny's letter to Mr Latimer of Oxford, 24 February 1836 and Mr Mist of Soho Square, 3 October 1837, are both in the Parrish Collection. FT lists her Hadley guests in a letter to JGP, 26 January 1838: Garnett–Pertz Papers. For Kater, see F. E. Trollope, *Frances Trollope*, I, p. 234.

20. For Hugel's visit to Hadley, see ibid., I, pp. 290–1. MG to JGP, 18 July 1835: Garnett–Pertz Papers.

21. MG to JGP, 16 April 1839: Garnett–Pertz Papers. FT to TAT: F. E. Trollope, *Frances Trollope*, I, pp. 286–7.

22. *The Literary Gazette* (3 March 1838), pp. 131–3. FT to Bentley, 13 August and 15 December 1837: Taylor Collection.

23. FT to Mr Horness, 14 December 1837; FT to Bentley, 30 August 1835: Parrish Collection; FT to Bentley, 15 November [1835]: Taylor Collection. See also FT's letter to Whittaker on behalf of a 'gentleman from Paris', 7 January 1834: Trollope Family Papers, Special Collections, UCLA Library. MRM to FT, 18 September 1831: Reading Public Library; FT to MRM, 27 December 1832: L'Estrange, *Friendships of M. Mitford*, I, pp. 243–4.

24. FT to Murray, 20 January and 30 March 1835: John Murray Archives. AT to Bentley, 24 May 1835: A. Trollope, *Letters*, I, p. 1.

25. FT to Bentley, 13 August 1837: Taylor Collection. For the reaction to *The Vicar of Wrexhill*, see F. E. Trollope, *Frances Trollope*, I, pp. 257–8; II, 294–6.

26. *The Athenaeum*, no. 517 (1837), p. 708; *The Times* (25 October 1837); [W. M. Thackeray,] *Fraser's Magazine* (January 1838), p. 79.

27. FT to TAT, 12 September and 27 September 1837: Parrish Collection. FT to TAT: F. E. Trollope, *Frances Trollope*, I, pp. 285–6. See also FT to Bentley, 19 September 1837: Taylor Collection.

28. For Tom's plans, see FT to Bentley, 21 May 1838: Taylor Collection. FT to TAT, 17 May 1838: Parrish Collection. FT to TAT: F. E. Trollope, *Frances Trollope*, I, pp. 288–9.

29. FT to JGP, 26 January 1838: Garnett-Pertz Papers. For Green's verses, see F. E. Trollope, *Frances Trollope*, I, pp. 292–4. For records of Fanny renting the house, see the Monken Hadley church rate books from 1836 to 1838: Local Studies and Archives, Hendon Library, Barnet Council, London. The cottage is listed as 'empty' on 30 August 1838.

CHAPTER 11 *The Life and Adventures of a Clever Woman*

1. F. E. Trollope, *Frances Trollope*, II, p. 261.

2. FT to JGP, 26 September 1839: Garnett–Petz Papers. Haliburton to FT, 3 August 1843: F. E. Trollope, *Frances Trollope*, I, pp. 297–8. Grattan to FT, 13 May 1841: T. A. Trollope, *What I Remember*, II, pp. 350ff. For Tom's impressions of Grattan and Haliburton, see ibid., I, pp. 359–60.

3. Dickens to Bentley, 30 November 1836: Dickens, *Letters*, I, p. 202. For Fanny's meeting with Dickens, see F. E. Trollope, *Frances Trollope*, I, p. 295.

4. ibid., II, p. 260. Agreement between FT and Bentley, 8 August 1838: Taylor Collection. The review of *The Widow Barnaby* appears in *The Athenaeum*, no. 584 (1839), pp. 9–10. Fanny first mentioned the 'Widow' to Bentley in a letter dated 15 December 1837: Taylor Collection.

5. ibid.

6. *The Times* (24 January 1839).

7. FT to MRM, 2 August 1837: L'Estrange, *Friendships of M. R. Mitford*, II, p. 26.

8. From the opening of the third sequel, *The Barnabys in America* (1843).

9. FT to unknown correspondent, 23 December 1838: Parrish Collection.

10. For Tom's recollections of the wedding and the other events in this chapter, see T. A. Trollope, *What I Remember*, II, chaps. 1–3.

11. For a discussion of *Michael Armstrong* and *Jonathan Jefferson Whitlaw*, see Susan Kissel, *In Common Cause: The 'Conservative' Frances Trollope and the 'Radical' Frances Wright*, Bowling Green, OH, 1993.

12. Fanny describes the terms for the two books to her brother, Henry Milton, in a letter dated 9 March 1839: Parrish Collection. Dickens to S. Laman Blanchard, 9 February 1839: Dickens, *Letters*, I, pp. 506–8.

13. Dickens to Edward Fitzgerald, 29 December 1838 and S. Laman Blanchard, 9 February 1839: ibid., I, pp. 484, 507.

14. MRM to E. Barrett, 3 January 1840: L'Estrange, *Friendships of M. R. Mitford*, II, p. 217.

15. *The Athenaeum*, no. 165 (1839), pp. 587–90; *The Bolton Free Press* (22 February 1840); *The New Monthly Magazine* (March 1839), p. 565.

16. For Colburn's 'puffery', see W. E. Houghton, ed., *The Wellesley Index to Victorian Periodicals 1834–1900*, Toronto and Buffalo, 1979, pp. 161ff. F. E. Trollope, *Frances Trollope*, I, p. 301.

17. FT to Henry Milton, 9 March 1839: Parrish Collection. Cecilia Tilley to FT: quoted in Victoria Glendinning, *Trollope*, London, 1992, p. 96.

18. FT to [?Captain Thomas Hamilton, undated]: Parrish Collection.

19. FT to JGP, 26 September 1839: Garnett–Pertz Papers.

20. ibid.

21. HG to JGP, 4 December 1839: Garnett–Pertz Papers. The comment on her 'Austrian sins', in a letter to Cecilia Tilley, is in F. E. Trollope, *Frances Trollope*, I, p. 312. Fanny's letter to an unknown publisher or reviewer, dated 26 December 1838, is in the Berg Collection, New York Public Library.

22. MG to JGP, 8 March 1840; FT to JGP, 24 May 1840; HG to JGP, 10 January 1840: Garnett–Pertz Papers. FT to Cecilia Tilley, 23 March 1840: Taylor Collection. FT to Cecilia Tilley, 6 January 1840: F. E. Trollope, *Frances Trollope*, I, p. 314.

23. Dickens' comment on Colburn is quoted in Dickens, *Letters*, II, p. 249. For Tom on Lady Bulwer, see T. A. Trollope, *What I Remember*, II, pp. 82–8.

24. *Morning Post* (28, 30 March 1840): quoted in Louisa Devey, *Life of Rosina, Lady Lytton*, London, 1887, pp. 185, 190.

25. FT to Cecilia Tilley, 13 February 1840: F. E. Trollope, *Frances Trollope*, I, p. 308.

26. FT to Lady Bulwer, 3 July 1840: General Collection, Princeton University Library; Lady Bulwer to FT, 20 July 1840: Trollope Family Papers, Special Collections, UCLA Library.

27. FT to Lady Bulwer, undated and 9 July 1840: Devey, *Life of Rosina*, pp. 195–6, 201.

28. For animal magnetism, see Jonathan Miller, 'Going Unconscious', *The New York Review of Books* (20 April 1995), pp. 59–65.

29. For this episode, see T. A. Trollope, *What I Remember*, I, pp. 366–74. There are two letters from FT to Mrs Grant, 26 March 1840 and one undated: Parrish Collection. See also in this collection two letters to an unknown correspondent, dated 17 December 1840 and 18 December [1840]. E. Barrett to MRM, 26 July 1842: *Letters of E. B. Browning to M. R. Mitford*, II, p. 11.

30. FT to Cecilia Tilley, 23 March 1840: Taylor Collection.

31. *John Bull,* 20 (1840) p. 536. Agreement between FT and Bentley, 9 September 1840: British Library, Add MS 44163, f. 309.

32. E. Barrett to MRM, [23–25 December 1841]: *Letters of E. B. Barrett to M. R. Mitford,* I, p. 322.

33. Quoted in Escott, *Anthony Trollope,* pp. 31–2.

34. E. Barrett to MRM, [23–25 December 1841] and 11 January 1842; MRM to E. Barrett, 9 January 1842: *The Brownings' Correspondence,* X, pp. 193, 203–8.

35. FT to Lady Bulwer, 3 July 1840: General Collection, Princeton University Library. FT to Bentley, 21 August 1840: Taylor Collection. For the state of affairs in France, see F. E. Trollope, *Frances Trollope,* I, p. 315.

36. HG to JGP, 12 June 1840: Garnett–Pertz Papers.

37. AT to TAT, 25 May 1839: Parrish Collection; AT to unknown correspondent, 8 July 1866: A. Trollope, *Letters,* I, p. 344. For Hervieu, see Graves, *The Royal Academy of Arts.*

38. FT to MRM, undated: Parrish Collection.

39. FT to TAT: F. E. Trollope, *Frances Trollope,* I, p. 325.

CHAPTER 12 *A Visit to Italy*

1. R. P. Wunder, *Hiram Powers: Vermont Sculptor,* 1805–1873, 2 vols., Newark, DE, 1991.

2. For Tom's very full account of Italian life, see T. A. Trollope, *What I Remember,* vol. 2.

3. F. E. Trollope, *Frances Trollope,* I, p. 319.

4. British Library, Add MS 40490, ff. 65, 67–9.

5. *The Athenaeum,* nos. 781, 782 (1842), pp. 884–6, 906–9.

6. The correspondence between FT and Bentley, dated 21 May and 27 May 1838, is in the Taylor Collection.

7. F. E. Trollope, *Frances Trollope,* II, pp. 14–15.

8. John D. Sherwood, 'Visits to the Home of Authors', *Hours at Home* (July 1867); quoted in Dickens, *Letters,* II, p. 442n. Dickens to Andrew Bell, 12 October 1841: ibid., II, p. 402.

9. Dickens, 24 February, 15 March, 22 March, 1 April 1842: ibid., III, pp. 90, 135, 156, 175.

10. *New York Express* and *Morning Chronicle*; quoted ibid., III, p. 412n. Dickens to FT, 16 December 1842: ibid., III, pp. 395–6.

11. *John Bull*, 23 (1843), p. 732.

12. Dickens to FT, 19 January 1843: Dickens, *Letters*, III, pp. 427–8. For American publishers' dealings with Dickens and other British authors, see Patten, *Charles Dickens and His Publishers*, pp. 97–9.

13. FT to MRM, 18 December 1842: L'Estrange, ed., *Friendships of M. R. Mitford*, II, p. 79.

14. TAT to Harry Trollope, 26 June 1883: Trollope Family Papers, University of Illinois Library, Urbana-Champaign. EBB to Robert Browning, [30 June 1845]: P. Kelley and R. Hudson, eds., *The Brownings' Correspondence*, Winfield, KS, 1984 –, X, p. 283.

15. FT to MRM, undated: Parrish Collection. HG to JGP, 28 November 1840 and 5 April 1841: Garnett–Pertz Papers.

16. F. E. Trollope, *Frances Trollope*, II, p. 58.

17. *Galignani's Messenger* is quoted ibid., II, pp. 56–7.

18. EBB to MRM, 30 January [1849]: *Letters of E. B. Browning to M. R. Mitford*, III, p. 265.

19. Percy Fitzgerald, *Memories of Charles Dickens*, Bristol, 1913, p. 312.

20. F. E. Trollope, *Frances Trollope*, II, pp. 38–9.

21. FT to Rose Trollope, 7 August 1844: A. Trollope, *Letters*, p. 11.

22. TAT to John Murray, undated, and FT to John Murray, 28 August 1843: John Murray Archives.

23. *The Literary Gazette* (8 May 1841), pp. 292–3. FT to Cecilia Tilley, undated: quoted in Michael Sadleir, *Trollope: A Commentary*, London, 1927 (repr. ed., 1933), p. 141, and with slight variations in Glendinning, *Trollope*, p. 160 (without source). Both give the date of the letter as August 1846.

24. The review of *Father Eustace* is in *The Critic* (9 January 1847), pp. 26–7. For reviews of *The Macdermots of Ballycloran* and Anthony's other novels, see Donald Smalley, *Anthony Trollope: The Critical Heritage*, New York, 1969.

25. FT to unknown correspondent, 25 June 1847: Parrish Collection.

26. F. E. Trollope, *Frances Trollope*, II, chap. 5.

27. ibid., II, pp. 73–4.

28. ibid., II, p. 109.

29. FT to TAT, 26 January 1848: ibid., II, pp. 111–12. FT to TAT, 10 February 1848: Parrish Collection. HG to JGP, 12 December 1847: Garnett–Pertz Papers.

30. F. E. Trollope, *Frances Trollope*, II, pp. 117, 125. HG to JGP, 7 February 1848: Garnett–Pertz Papers. EBB to MRM, 28 May [1850]: *Letters of E. B. Browning to M. R. Mitford*, III, p. 241.

31. FT to TAT and Theodosia, [April 1848]: F. E. Trollope, *Frances Trollope*, II, pp. 127–8. HG to JGP, 30 May 1848: Garnett–Pertz Papers.

32. F. E. Trollope, *Frances Trollope*, II, p. 135.

33. For these events, see ibid., II, chap. 8.

34. FT to Rose Trollope, 20 April [1849]: Taylor Collection.

CHAPTER 13 *Charles Chesterfield; or the Adventures of a Youth of Genius*

1. F. E. Trollope, *Frances Trollope*, II, pp. 161–3. FT to AT and Rose, 15 August 1849: Taylor Collection.

2. F. E. Trollope, *Frances Trollope*, II, p. 140.

3. ibid., II, p. 99. HG to JGP, 26 September 1847: Garnett–Pertz Papers.

4. FT to TAT, 3 October 1849: F. E. Trollope, *Frances Trollope*, II, pp. 173–4.

5. FT to Theodosia Trollope, 11 April 1850: F. E. Trollope, *Frances Trollope*, II, p. 198.

6. FT to TAT and Theodosia, 26 May 1850: ibid., II, pp. 173–4. EBB to MRM, 15 June 1850: *Letters of E. B. Browning to M. R. Mitford*, III, p. 300.

7. Kate Field, 'English Authors in Florence', *The Atlantic Monthly* (December 1864). MRM to FT, 1 August 1852: Parrish Collection. AT to TAT, [August 1850]: F. E. Trollope, *Frances Trollope*, II, p. 213. EBB to MRM, 30 April 1850: *Letters of E. B. Browning to M. R. Mitford*, III, pp. 300–301.

8. EBB to Mrs Martin, 30 January 1851: F. G. Kenyon, ed., *The Letters of Elizabeth Barrett Browning*, 2 vols., London, 1897, I, p. 476. FT to TAT, [March 1850]: F. E. Trollope, *Frances Trollope*, II, p. 193. MRM to Mrs

Hoare, [autumn 1852]: L'Estrange, *Friendships of M. R. Mitford*, II, pp. 315–17.

9. F. E. Trollope, *Frances Trollope*, II, pp. 99–100. R. B. Martin, *Tennyson: The Unquiet Heart*, London, 1983, p. 361.

10. Bayard Taylor, *At Home and Abroad*, London, 1860, p. 40.

11. F. E. Trollope, *Frances Trollope*, II, pp. 54–5, 244, 261.

12. Dickens to FT, 20 September 1858: Dickens, *Letters*, VIII, p. 667. For the Ternans, see Claire Tomalin, *The Invisible Woman: The Story of Nelly Ternan and Charles Dickens*, London, 1990.

13. F. E. Trollope, *Frances Trollope*, II, pp. 235, 238, 252, 298.

14. ibid., II, pp. 211, 214. Escott, *Anthony Trollope*, pp. 54–5.

15. Lever is quoted in Giuliana Artom Treves, *The Golden Ring: The Anglo-Florentines 1847–1862*, translated by Sylvia Sprigge, London, 1956, p. 99. EBB to MRM, 19 October 1854: *Letters of E. B. Browning to M. R. Mitford*, III, p. 420. S. Baring-Gould, *Early Reminiscences*, Oxford, 1923, pp. 127–8.

16. 'Female Novelists, Part V, Mrs Trollope', *The New Monthly Magazine*, 96 (1852), p. 19. EBB to MRM, 6 June [1854]: *Letters of E. B. Browning to M. R. Mitford*, III, p. 411.

17. Henry Milton to FT: F. E. Trollope, *Frances Trollope*, II, p. 149.

18. Georg Pertz to FT, 2 November and FT to Georg Pertz, 14 November 1852: Garnett–Pertz Papers.

19. F. E. Trollope, *Frances Trollope*, II, p. 253.

20. For these séances, see ibid., chaps. 14 and 15; T. A. Trollope, *What I Remember*, I, pp. 374ff.

21. Dickens to FT, 19 June 1855: Dickens, *Letters*, VII, pp. 651–2. FT to James Jackson Jarvis, 21 and 31 December 1854: Beinecke Library, Yale University.

22. R. C. Terry, ed., *Trollope: Interviews and Recollections*, London, 1987, p. 23. EBB to Mrs Martin, 21 February [1856]: Kenyon, ed., *Letters of E. B. Browning*, II, p. 226.

23. Review of *Fashionable Life* in *The Critic* (1 September 1856), p. 420; review of *The Lottery of Marriage*, ibid. (15 May 1849), pp. 223–4; review of *The Abbess* in *The Spectator*, 6 (1833), pp. 526–7; review of *The Three Cousins* in *John Bull*, 27 (1847), p. 344. The comments from *The Morning*

Post are taken from the advertisement at the back of *Fashionable Life* (1856). The comparison with Thackeray is made in a review of *Gertrude* in *The Critic* (1 October 1855), p. 476.

24. Thackeray, review of *Jerome Paturot* in *Fraser's Magazine*, 18 (1843), p. 350. Fitzgerald, *Memories of Charles Dickens*, p. 312. EBB to Horne, 5–6 January 1844: *The Brownings' Correspondence*, VIII, p. 137. 'Memoir of Mrs Trollope', *The New Monthly Magazine* (1839).

25. Colburn to AT, 11 November 1848: A. Trollope, *Letters*, pp. 17–18.

26. Escott, *Anthony Trollope*, pp. 32–3. FT to AT, 8 July 1856: Trollope, *Letters*, I, pp. 44–5.

27. Review of *Second Love* in *The Critic* (15 April 1851), p. 566.

28. *The Literary Gazette*, no. 1193 (1840), pp. 754–5.

29. Review of *Young Love* in *The Critic* (15 November 1844), p. 183.

30. See N. J. Hall, *Trollope: A Biography*, Oxford, 1991, pp. 302–3.

31. FT to JGP, 2 August 1838: Garnett–Pertz Papers.

32. See A. Trollope, *Letters*, I, pp. 22, 34–5, 82. For Fanny's last few years, see F. E. Trollope, *Frances Trollope*, II, chaps. 15–17.

33. See Hall, *Salmagundi Aliena*.

34. *The Times* (23 May 1859).

35. Tom's comments are, of course, drawn from *What I Remember*. HG to JGP, 5 April 1841: Garnett–Pertz Papers. AT to Kate Field, 4 February 1862: A Trollope, *Letters*, pp. 174–5.

36. See T. A. Trollope, *What I Remember*, I, pp. 356–9; Alfred Austin, *An Autobiography*, 2 vols., London, 1911; also Escott, *Anthony Trollope*, pp. 153, 291, and Field, 'English Authors in Florence'.

37. Austin, *An Autobiography*. Browning to Isa Blagden, 19 October 1866: E. C. McAleer, *Dearest Isa: Robert Browning's Letters to Isabella Blagden*, Austin, TX, 1951, p. 249. Dickens's letter and Anthony's remark are quoted in T. A. Trollope, *What I Remember*, II, pp. 125–6; III, p. 41.

38. F. E. Trollope to an Italian friend, 23 November 1892: Bodleian Library, MS Eng. lett.d.493.

39. F. E. Trollope to George Bentley, 23 December 1894: Taylor Collection.

BIBLIOGRAPHY OF FANNY TROLLOPE'S WORKS

The Domestic Manners of the Americans, illustrated by A. Hervieu, 2 vols., London, Whittaker, Treacher & Co., 1832.

The Refugee in America; a Novel, 3 vols., London, Whittaker, Treacher & Co., 1832.

The Mother's Manual; or Illustrations of Matrimonial Economy. An Essay in Verse, illustrated by A. Hervieu, London, Treutel, Würtz and Richter, 1833.

The Abbess; a Romance, 3 vols., London, Whittaker, Treacher & Co., 1833.

Belgium and Western Germany in 1833; including Visits to Baden-Baden, Wiesbaden, Cassel, Hanover, the Harz Mountains, etc., 2 vols., London, John Murray, 1834.

Tremordyn Cliff, 3 vols., London, Richard Bentley, 1835.

Paris and the Parisians in 1835, illustrated by A. Hervieu, 2 vols., London, Richard Bentley, 1836.

The Life and Adventures of Jonathan Jefferson Whitlaw; or Scenes on the Mississippi, illustrated by A. Hervieu, 3 vols., London, Richard Bentley, 1836. Reissued as *Lynch Law* in 1857.

The Vicar of Wrexhill, illustrated by A. Hervieu, 3 vols., London, Richard Bentley, 1837.

Vienna and the Austrians, illustrated by A. Hervieu, 2 vols., London, Richard Bentley, 1838.

A Romance of Vienna, 3 vols., London, Richard Bentley, 1838.

The Widow Barnaby, 3 vols., London, Richard Bentley, 1839.

The Life and Adventures of Michael Armstrong, the Factory Boy, illustrated by A. Hervieu, R. W. Buss and T. Onwhyn. Published in twelve monthly numbers from March 1839 to February 1840 by Henry Colburn. First edition in 3 vols., London, Henry Colburn, 1839, and one-volume edition, 1840.

The Widow Married; a Sequel to the Widow Barnaby, illustrated by R. W. Buss. Published in *The New Monthly Magazine*, May 1839–June 1840. First edition in 3 vols., London, Henry Colburn, 1840.

One Fault; a Novel, 3 vols., London, Richard Bentley, 1840.

Charles Chesterfield; or the Adventures of a Youth of Genius, illustrated by 'Phiz' [H. K. Brown]. Published in *The New Monthly Magazine*, July 1840 – November 1841. First edition in 3 vols., London, Henry Colburn, 1841.

The Ward of Thorpe Combe, 3 vols., London, Richard Bentley, 1841. Reissued as *The Ward* in 1857.

The Blue Belles of England. Published in *The Metropolitan Magazine*, January 1841 – January 1842. First edition in 3 vols., London, Saunders & Otley, 1842.

A Visit to Italy, 2 vols., London, Richard Bentley, 1842.

The Barnabys in America: or Adventures of the Widow Wedded, illustrated by John Leech. Published in *The New Monthly Magazine*, April 1842 – September 1843. First edition in 3 vols., London, Henry Colburn, 1843.

Hargrave; or the Adventures of a Man of Fashion, 3 vols., London, Henry Colburn, 1843.

Jessie Phillips; a Tale of the Present Day, illustrated by John Leech. Published in eleven monthly parts from December 1842 to November 1843. First edition in 3 vols., London, Henry Colburn, 1843, and one-volume edition, 1844.

The Laurringtons; or Superior People, 3 vols., London, Longman, Brown, Green & Longmans, 1844.

Young Love; a Novel, 3 vols., London, Henry Colburn, 1844.

The Attractive Man, 3 vols., London, Henry Colburn, 1846.

The Robertses on their Travels. Published in *The New Monthly Magazine*, May 1844 – January 1846. First edition in 3 vols., London, Henry Colburn, 1846.

Travels and Travellers; a Series of Sketches, 2 vols., London, Henry Colburn, 1846. [A collection of eleven sketches, seven of which were first published in *The New Monthly Magazine* between October 1843 and June 1844.]

Father Eustace; a Tale of the Jesuits, 3 vols., London, Henry Colburn, 1847.

The Three Cousins, 3 vols., London, Henry Colburn, 1847.

Town and Country; a Novel, 3 vols., London, Henry Colburn, 1848. Reissued as *Days of the Regency* in 1857.

The Young Countess; or Love and Jealousy, 3 vols., London, Henry Colburn, 1848.

The Lottery of Marriage; a Novel, 3 vols., London, Henry Colburn, 1849.

The Old World and the New; a Novel, 3 vols., London, Henry Colburn, 1849.

Petticoat Government; a Novel, 3 vols., London, Henry Colburn, 1850.

Mrs Mathews; or Family Mysteries, 3 vols., London, Henry Colburn, 1851.

Second Love; or Beauty and Intellect, 3 vols., London, Henry Colburn, 1851.

Uncle Walter; a Novel, 3 vols., London, Henry Colburn, 1852.

The Young Heiress; a Novel, 3 vols., London, Hurst & Blackett, 1853.

The Life and Adventures of a Clever Woman. Illustrated with Occasional Extracts from her Diary, 3 vols., London, Hurst & Blackett, 1854.

Gertrude; or Family Pride, 3 vols., London, Hurst & Blackett, 1855.

Fashionable Life; or Paris and London, 3 vols., London, Hurst & Blackett, 1856.

INDEX

Other than in the entry under her name,
Fanny Trollope is referred to as FT.

399

B   Neville-Sington,
Trollope   Pamela.
N

           Fanny Trollope.

$26.95

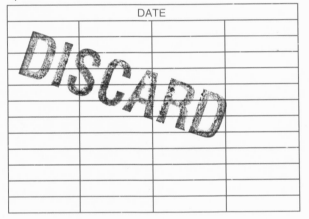
DATE			

12-16-98